Classics of Western Thought

Classics of Western Thought

UNDER THE GENERAL EDITORSHIP OF
Thomas H. Greer
MICHIGAN STATE UNIVERSITY

I. The Ancient World

EDITED BY Stebelton H. Nulle
MICHIGAN STATE UNIVERSITY

II. Middle Ages, Renaissance, and Reformation

EDITED BY Karl F. Thompson
MICHIGAN STATE UNIVERSITY

III. The Modern World

EDITED BY Charles Hirschfeld
MICHIGAN STATE UNIVERSITY

EDITED BY

Charles Hirschfeld

MICHIGAN STATE UNIVERSITY

CLASSICS OF

WESTERN THOUGHT

The

Modern

World

HARCOURT, BRACE & WORLD, INC.   NEW YORK AND BURLINGAME

General Introduction

The editors of this three-volume series strongly believe that the best means of introducing students to their humanistic heritage is through a selection of original writings by the great minds of the Western tradition. It is for this purpose that we have brought together what we regard as classics of the Western tradition—of Western *thought,* in the broad sense. This collection of primary documents is intended for use in college-level courses in humanities or in the history of civilization, normally in company with a brief narrative text.

The volume and range of documents in Western civilization are, of course, enormous, and good reasons can always be advanced for making one selection over another. We have decided to restrict our own choice to what is truly *classic,* that is to say, valuable both for its intrinsic merit and for having exerted a paramount influence on its own and later times. We have, therefore, selected writings that reveal judgment applied to observation and that display creative thought and literary skill. In deciding upon the length and quantity of selections, we have aimed to keep in balance two purposes: to make each document *long enough* to give a substantial view of the author's ideas and to offer, at the same time, a substantial *number* of the foremost writers. (In a few instances we have omitted a familiar classic because the full text is readily available in satisfactory and inexpensive paperback editions, as for example, Homer's *Iliad.*)

The documents appear for the most part in chronological order and are arranged in three manageable volumes: *The Ancient World* (Volume One); *Middle Ages, Renaissance, and Reformation* (Volume Two); and *The Modern World* (Volume Three). Each document is introduced by a brief account of the author's life, of his role in the shaping of the Western tradition, and of the significance of the particular work. As in the selection of the writings themselves, we have kept student and teacher continually in mind.

We believe that the chief merit of these volumes is that they are guided by our aggregate experience of many years in the classroom— teaching college and university courses in humanities and in the history of civilization.

THOMAS H. GREER

January, 1964

Preface

This volume, the third and last of *Classics of Western Thought,* offers classic and representative expressions of the main currents of Western thought of the last three hundred years. The selections reflect the modern mind in its variety and complexity—its history, literature, philosophy, science, and social and religious thought. The readings, arranged in the chronological order of their composition, fall into three broad groupings.

The origins of the modern world are to be found in the seventeenth and eighteenth centuries. Great advances in the natural sciences and mathematics effected an intellectual revolution that rejected medieval scholasticism and recast Western man's understanding of the universe and his place in it. The emergence of the modern European state system, composed of absolute, sovereign nation-states, further weakened the traditional political and economic order. Political absolutism was, in turn, challenged by the great liberal revolutions in England, America, and France. Liberalism in its many aspects found intellectual expression in the reforming gospel of the eighteenth-century Enlightenment or Age of Reason. Based on the findings and methods of science, it embodied a confident faith in the orderliness of nature and in the ability of man to be the master of his fate. Reason and order were also the shaping concepts of the neoclassical drama and poetry of the period.

In the nineteenth century, the development of the Industrial Revolution was accompanied by the triumph of political and economic liberalism and its extension in democratic thought and practice. Conservatism and socialism challenged this new order from the right and left respectively. Nationalism as a social and intellectual force came to dominate the European scene. The tenets of the Age of Reason gave way before the gospel of romanticism in the fields of intellectual and artistic endeavor. The biological theory of organic evolution gave a new direction to science, and its implications were worked out in social and philosophical thought as well.

Since 1880, the Western world has undergone catastrophic change and social and intellectual ferment and dislocation. World wars, economic crises, the rise and fall of empires, the appearance of collectivist and totalitarian societies and ideologies, the fantastic developments of science and technology, the emergence of a mass society— all have transformed the character of Western thought. The new age has wrought havoc with traditional modes of society and thought. Social and political thinkers, artists, and intellectuals have rebelled against all received tradition and sought through free experiment to give men a new sense of purpose and direction. Optimism and certainty have given way to growing doubts and pessimism. The rational tradition of centuries has been displaced by emphasis on the irrational and the indeterminate. The ensuing moral crisis has brought forth efforts to give men a new faith and a new reality by an active exercise of the will.

It has been impossible to represent all the diverse and conflicting aspects of the modern mind, particularly in the twentieth century, within the limits of one volume. The editors feel, however, that the selections included here provide a broad basis for understanding the social and intellectual problems and insights of contemporary civilization in the West, and they hope, above all, that the confrontation of the reader with these challenging statements of fundamental issues will in some measure stimulate his sense of involvement with the fate of man.

CHARLES HIRSCHFELD

January, 1964

Contents

General Introduction v

Preface vii

Classics of Western Thought

Francis Bacon

1

Novum Organum

Francis Bacon (1561–1626), a contemporary of Shakespeare and Queen Elizabeth, was a true "man of the Renaissance." Versatile, ambitious, and unscrupulous, he was a man of affairs as well as a man of letters and a philosopher. He attained the high office of Lord Chancellor under James I, but was impeached and found guilty of taking bribes, and died in disgrace. His *Essays* won him literary fame; however, his reputation rests largely on his work as the philosopher of scientific method who rejected the views of the Middle Ages and looked forward to the general acceptance of the new science, which would give men power over nature. A prophet of the scientific revolution of the seventeenth century, he thus helped to usher in a new age. In his philosophical works, Bacon attacked the deductive methods of scholasticism and formulated new principles of acquiring true and useful knowledge of the world through empiricism. He insisted on the necessity for direct observation of nature as the only way to know truth. The purpose of such knowledge was power, power to control nature and thereby advance the welfare of mankind. Bacon thus anticipated the eighteenth-century faith that man could be master of his destiny.

The *Novum Organum* (*New Organon,* or method of scientific inquiry, 1620) was intended to replace the old *Organon* of Aristotle. In this work, which consists of a series of aphorisms or short statements, Bacon analyzes the shortcomings of deductive, a priori methods of inquiry and proposes the inductive method, based on the direct observation of nature. While his formulation lacked precision and underrated the value of hypotheses, it was a significant attempt to free men's minds from barren prejudices, faulty thinking, loose use of language, and vain fictions, and to encourage them to go directly to nature to discover its secrets.

Francis Bacon, *Novum Organum,* in *The Works of Francis Bacon,* trans. J. Spedding (London: Longman, 1860), IV, 47–55, 79–82, 87–90, 93, 95–98, 110.

1

Man, being the servant and interpreter of Nature, can do and understand so much and so much only as he has observed in fact or in thought of the course of nature: beyond this he neither knows anything nor can do anything.

Neither the naked hand nor the understanding left to itself can effect much. It is by instruments and helps that the work is done, which are as much wanted for the understanding as for the hand. And as the instruments of the hand either give motion or guide it, so the instruments of the mind supply either suggestions for the understanding or cautions.

Human knowledge and human power meet in one; for where the cause is not known the effect cannot be produced. Nature to be commanded must be obeyed; and that which in contemplation is as the cause is in operation as the rule.

. . .

The cause and root of nearly all evils in the sciences is this that while we falsely admire and extol the powers of the human mind we neglect to seek for its true helps.

The subtlety of nature is greater many times over than the subtlety of the senses and understanding; so that all those specious meditations, speculations, and glosses in which men indulge are quite from the purpose, only there is no one by to observe it.

As the sciences which we now have do not help us in finding out new works, so neither does the logic which we now have help us in finding out new sciences.

The logic now in use serves rather to fix and give stability to the errors which have their foundation in commonly received notions than to help the search after truth. So it does more harm than good.

The syllogism is not applied to the first principles of sciences, and is applied in vain to intermediate axioms; being no match for the subtlety of nature. It commands assent therefore to the proposition, but does not take hold of the thing.

The syllogism consists of propositions, propositions consist of words, words are symbols of notions. Therefore if the notions themselves (which is the root of the matter) are confused and over-hastily abstracted from the facts, there can be no firmness in the superstructure. Our only hope therefore lies in a true induction.

. . .

The discoveries which have hitherto been made in the sciences are such as lie close to vulgar notions, scarcely beneath the surface. In order to penetrate into the inner and further recesses of nature, it is necessary that both notions and axioms be derived from things by a more sure and guarded way; and that a method of intellectual operation be introduced altogether better and more certain.

There are and can be only two ways of searching into and discovering truth. The one flies from the senses and particulars to the most general axioms, and from these principles, the truth of which it takes for settled and immoveable, proceeds to judgment and to the discovery of middle axioms. And this way is now in fashion. The other derives axioms from the senses and particulars, rising by a gradual and unbroken ascent, so that it arrives at the most general axioms last of all. This is the true way, but as yet untried.

The understanding left to itself takes the same course (namely, the former) which it takes in accordance with logical order. For the mind longs to spring up to positions of higher generality, that it may find rest there; and so after a little while wearies of experiment. But this evil is increased by logic, because of the order and solemnity of its disputations.

The understanding left to itself, in a sober, patient, and grave mind, especially if it be not hindered by received doctrines, tries a little that other way, which is the right one, but with little progress; since the understanding, unless directed and assisted, is a thing unequal, and quite unfit to contend with the obscurity of things.

Both ways set out from the senses and particulars, and rest in the highest generalities; but the difference between them is infinite. For the one just glances at experiment and particulars in passing, the other dwells duly and orderly among them. The one, again, begins at once by establishing certain abstract and useless generalities, the other rises by gradual steps to that which is prior and better known in the order of nature.

There is a great difference between the Idols of the human mind and the Ideas of the divine. That is to say, between certain empty dogmas, and the true signatures and marks set upon the works of creation as they are found in nature.

It cannot be that axioms established by argumentation should avail for the discovery of new works; since the subtlety of nature is greater many times over than the subtlety of argument. But axioms duly and orderly formed from particulars easily discover the way to new particulars, and thus render sciences active.

The axioms now in use, having been suggested by a scanty and manipular experience and a few particulars of most general occurrence, are made for the most part just large enough to fit and take these in: and therefore it is no wonder if they do not lead to new particulars. And if some opposite instance, not observed or not known before, chance to come in the way, the axiom is rescued and preserved by some frivolous distinction; whereas the truer course would be to correct the axiom itself.

The conclusions of human reason as ordinarily applied in matter of nature, I call for the sake of distinction *Anticipations of Nature* (as a thing rash or premature). That reason which is elicited from facts by a just and methodical process, I call *Interpretation of Nature*.

Anticipations are a ground sufficiently firm for consent; for even if men went mad all after the same fashion, they might agree one with another well enough.

For the winning of assent, indeed, anticipations are far more powerful than interpretations; because being collected from a few instances, and those for the most part of familiar occurrence, they straightway touch the understanding and fill the imagination; whereas interpretations on the other hand, being gathered here and there from very various and widely dispersed facts, cannot suddenly strike the understanding; and therefore they must needs, in respect of the opinions of the time, seem harsh and out of tune; much as the mysteries of faith do.

In sciences founded on opinions and dogmas, the use of anticipations and logic is good; for in them the object is to command assent to the proposition, not to master the thing.

Though all the wits of all the ages should meet together and combine and transmit their labours, yet will no great progress ever be made in science by means of anticipations; because radical errors in the first concoction of the mind are not to be cured by the excellence of functions and remedies subsequent.

It is idle to expect any great advancement in science from the superinducing and engrafting of new things upon old. We must begin anew from the very foundations, unless we would revolve for ever in a circle with mean and contemptible progress.

. . .

One method of delivery alone remains to us; which is simply this: we must lead men to the particulars themselves, and their series and order; while men on their side must force themselves for awhile to lay their notions by and begin to familiarise themselves with facts.

The doctrine of those who have denied that certainty could be attained at all, has some agreement with my way of proceeding at the first setting out; but they end in being infinitely separated and opposed. For the holders of that doctrine assert simply that nothing can be known; I also assert that not much can be known in nature by the way which is now in use. But then they go on to destroy the authority of the senses and understanding; whereas I proceed to devise and supply helps for the same.

The idols and false notions which are now in possession of the human understanding, and have taken deep root therein, not only so beset men's minds that truth can hardly find entrance, but even after entrance obtained, they will again in the very instauration of the sciences meet and trouble us, unless men being forewarned of the danger fortify themselves as far as may be against their assaults.

There are four classes of Idols which beset men's minds. To these for distinction's sake I have assigned names,—calling the first class *Idols of the Tribe;* the second, *Idols of the Cave;* the third, *Idols of the Market-place;* the fourth, *Idols of the Theatre.*

The formation of ideas and axioms by true induction is no doubt the proper remedy to be applied for the keeping off and clearing away of idols. To point them out, however, is of great use; for the doctrine of Idols is to the Interpretation of Nature what the doctrine of the refutation of Sophisms is to common Logic.

The Idols of the Tribe have their foundation in human nature itself, and in the tribe or race of men. For it is a false assertion that the sense of man is the measure of things. On the contrary, all perceptions as well of the sense as of the mind are according to the measure of the individual and not according to the measure of the universe. And the human understanding is like a false mirror, which, receiving rays irregularly, distorts and discolours the nature of things by mingling its own nature with it.

The Idols of the Cave are the idols of the individual man. For every one (besides the errors common to human nature in general) has a cave or den of his own, which refracts and discolours the light of nature; owing either to his own proper and peculiar nature; or to his education and conversation with others; or to the reading of books, and the authority of those whom he esteems and admires; or to the differences of impressions, accordingly as they take place in a mind preoccupied and predisposed or in a mind indifferent and settled; or the like. So that the spirit of man (according as it is meted out to different individuals) is in fact a thing variable and full of perturbation, and governed as it were by chance. Whence it was well observed by Heraclitus that men look for sciences in their own lesser worlds, and not in the greater or common world.

There are also Idols formed by the intercourse and association of men with each other, which I call Idols of the Market-place, on account of the commerce and consort of men there. For it is by discourse that men associate; and words are imposed according to the apprehension of the vulgar. And therefore the ill and unfit choice of words wonderfully obstructs the understanding. Nor do the definitions or explanations where with in some things learned men are wont to guard and defend themselves, by any means set the matter right. But words plainly force and overrule the understanding, and throw all into confusion, and lead men away into numberless empty controversies and idle fancies.

Lastly, there are Idols which have immigrated into men's minds from the various dogmas of philosophies, and also from wrong laws of demonstration. These I call Idols of the Theatre; because in my judgment all the received systems are but so many stage-plays, representing worlds of their own creation after an unreal and scenic fashion. Nor is it only of the systems now in vogue, or only of the ancient sects and philosophies, that I speak; for many more plays of the same kind may yet be composed and in like artificial manner set forth; seeing that errors the most widely different have nevertheless causes for the most part alike. Neither again do I mean this only of entire systems, but also of many principles and axioms in science, which by tradition, credulity, and negligence have come to be received.

. . .

Again there is another great and powerful cause why the sciences have made but little progress; which is this. It is not possible to run a course aright when the goal itself has not been rightly placed. Now the true and lawful goal of the sciences is none other than this: that human life be endowed with new discoveries and powers. But of this the great majority have no feeling, but are merely hireling and professorial; except when it occasionally happens that some workman of acuter wit and covetous of honour applies himself to a new invention; which he mostly does at the expense of his fortunes. But in general, so far are men from proposing to themselves to augment the mass of arts and sciences, that from the mass already at hand they neither take nor look for anything more than what they may turn to use in their lectures, or to gain, or to reputation, or to some similar advantage. And if any one out of all the multitude court science with honest affection and for her own sake, yet even with him the object will be found to be rather the variety of contemplations and doctrines than the severe and rigid search after truth. And if by chance there be one who seeks after truth in earnest, yet even he will propose to himself such a kind of truth as shall yield satisfaction to the mind and understanding in rendering causes for things long since discovered, and not the truth which shall lead to new assurance of works and new light of axioms. If then the end of the sciences has not as yet been well placed, it is not strange that men have erred as to the means.

And as men have misplaced the end and goal of the sciences; so again, even if they had placed it right, yet they have chosen a way to it which is altogether erroneous and impassible. And an astonishing thing it is to one who rightly considers the matter, that no mortal should have seriously applied himself to the opening and laying out of a road for the human understanding direct from the sense, by a course of experiment orderly conducted and well built up; but that all has been left either to the mist of tradition, or the whirl and eddy of argument, or the fluctuations and mazes of chance and of vague and ill-digested experience. Now let any man soberly and diligently consider what the way is by which men have been accustomed to proceed in the investigation and discovery of things; and in the first place he will no doubt remark a method of discovery very simple and inartificial; which is the most ordinary method, and is no more than this. When a man addresses himself to discover something, he first seeks out and sets before him all that has been said about it by others; then he begins to meditate for himself; and so by much agitation and working of the wit solicits and as it were evokes his own spirit to give him oracles: which method has no foundation at all, but rests only upon opinions and is carried about with them.

Another may perhaps call in logic to discover it for him; but that has no relation to the matter except in name. For logical invention does not discover principles and chief axioms, of which arts are composed, but only such things as appear to be consistent with them. For if you grow more curious and importunate and busy, and question her of probations and invention of principles or primary axioms, her answer is well known: she refers you to the faith you are bound to give to the principles of each separate art.

There remains simple experience; which, if taken as it comes, is called accident; if sought for, experiment. But this kind of experience is no better than a broom without its band, as the saying is;— a mere groping, as of men in the dark, that feel all round them for the chance of finding their way; when they had much better wait for daylight, or light a candle, and then go. But the true method of experience on the contrary first lights the candle, and then by means of the candle shows the way; commencing as it does with experience duly ordered and digested, not bungling or erratic, and from it educing axioms, and from established axioms again new experiments; even as it was not without order and method that the divine word operated on the created mass. Let men therefore cease to wonder that the course of science is not yet wholly run, seeing that they have gone altogether astray; either leaving and abandoning experience entirely, or losing their way in it and wandering round and round as in a labyrinth; whereas a method rightly ordered leads by an unbroken route through the woods of experience to the open ground of axioms.

This evil however has been strangely increased by an opinion or conceit, which though of long standing is vain and hurtful; namely, that the dignity of the human mind is impaired by long and close intercourse with experiments and particulars, subject to sense and bound in matter; especially as they are laborious to search, ignoble to meditate, harsh to deliver, illiberal to practise, infinite in number, and minute in subtlety. So that it has come at length to this, that the true way is not merely deserted, but shut out and stopped up; experience being, I do not say abandoned or badly managed, but rejected with disdain.

Again, men have been kept back as by a kind of enchantment from progress in the sciences by reverence for antiquity, by the authority of men accounted great in philosophy, and then by general consent.

. . .

Neither is it to be forgotten that in every age Natural Philosophy has had a troublesome adversary and hard to deal with; namely, superstition, and the blind and immoderate zeal of religion. For we see among the Greeks that those who first proposed to men's then uninitiated ears the natural causes for thunder and for storms, were thereupon found guilty of impiety. Nor was much more forbearance shown by some of the ancient fathers of the Christian church to those who on most convincing grounds (such as no one in his senses would now think of contradicting) maintained that the earth was round, and of consequence asserted the existence of the antipodes.

Moreover, as things now are, to discourse of nature is made harder and more perilous by the summaries and systems of the schoolmen; who having reduced theology into regular order as well as they were able, and fashioned it into the shape of an art, ended in incorporating the contentious and thorny philosophy of Aristotle, more than was fit, with the body of religion.

To the same result, though in a different way, tend the speculations of those who have taken upon them to deduce the truth of
the Christian religion from the principles of philosophers, and to
confirm it by their authority; pompously solemnising this union of
the sense and faith as a lawful marriage, and entertaining men's
minds with a pleasing variety of matter, but all the while disparaging things divine by mingling them with things human. Now in
such mixtures of theology with philosophy only the received doctrines of philosophy are included; while new ones, albeit changes for
the better, are all but expelled and exterminated.

Lastly, you will find that by the simpleness of certain divines, access to any philosophy, however pure, is well nigh closed. Some are
weakly afraid lest a deeper search into nature should transgress the
permitted limits of sobermindedness; wrongfully wresting and transferring what is said in holy writ against those who pry into sacred
mysteries, to the hidden things of nature, which are barred by no
prohibition. Others with more subtlety surmise and reflect that if
second causes are unknown everything can more readily be referred
to the divine hand and rod; a point in which they think religion
greatly concerned; which is in fact nothing else but to seek to gratify
God with a lie. Others fear from past example that movements and
changes in philosophy will end in assaults on religion. And others
again appear apprehensive that in the investigation of nature something may be found to subvert or at least shake the authority of
religion, especially with the unlearned. But these two last fears seem
to me to savour utterly of carnal wisdom; as if men in the recesses
and secret thoughts of their hearts doubted and distrusted the
strength of religion and the empire of faith over the sense, and
therefore feared that the investigation of truth in nature might be
dangerous to them. But if the matter be truly considered, natural
philosophy is after the word of God at once the surest medicine
against superstition, and the most approved nourishment for faith,
and therefore she is rightly given to religion as her most faithful
handmaid, since the one displays the will of God, the other his
power. For he did not err who said "Ye err in that ye know not the
Scriptures and the power of God," thus coupling and blending in
an indissoluble bond information concerning his will and meditation concerning his power. Meanwhile it is not surprising if the
growth of Natural Phlosophy is checked, when religion, the thing
which has most power over men's minds, has by the simpleness and

incautious zeal of certain persons been drawn to take part against
her.

. . .

But by far the greatest obstacle to the progress of science and to
the undertaking of new tasks and provinces therein, is found in this
—that men despair and think things impossible. For wise and serious
men are wont in these matters to be altogether distrustful; considering with themselves the obscurity of nature, the shortness of life, the
deceitfulness of the senses, the weakness of the judgment, the difficulty of experiment and the like; and so supposing that in the
revolution of time and of the ages of the world the sciences have
their ebbs and flows; that at one season they grow and flourish, at
another wither and decay, yet in such sort that when they have
reached a certain point and condition they can advance no further.
If therefore any one believes or promises more, they think this comes
of an ungoverned and unripened mind, and that such attempts have
prosperous beginnings, become difficult as they go on, and end in
confusion.

. . .

No one has yet been found so firm of mind and purpose as reso-
lutely to compel himself to sweep away all theories and common
notions, and to apply the understanding, thus made fair and even,
to a fresh examination of particulars. Thus it happens that human
knowledge, as we have it, is a mere medley and ill-digested mass,
made up of much credulity and much accident, and also of the
childish notions which we at first imbibed.

. . .

But not only is a greater abundance of experiments to be sought
for and procured, and that too of a different kind from those hitherto tried; an entirely different method, order, and process for carrying on and advancing experience must also be introduced. For experience, when it wanders in its own track, is, as I have already
remarked, mere groping in the dark, and confounds men rather than
instructs them. But when it shall proceed in accordance with a fixed
law, in regular order, and without interruption, then may better
things be hoped of knowledge.

. . .

But after this store of particulars has been set out duly and in order before our eyes, we are not to pass at once to the investigation and discovery of new particulars or works; or at any rate if we do so we must not stop there. For although I do not deny that when all the experiments of all the arts shall have been collected and digested, and brought within one man's knowledge and judgment, the mere transferring of the experiments of one art to others may lead, by means of that experience which I term *literate,* to the discovery of many new things of service to the life and state of man, yet it is no great matter that can be hoped from that; but from the new light of axioms, which having been educed from those particulars by a certain method and rule, shall in their turn point out the way again to new particulars, greater things may be looked for. For our road does not lie on a level, but ascends and descends; first ascending to axioms, then descending to works.

The understanding must not however be allowed to jump and fly from particulars to remote axioms and of almost the highest generality (such as the first principles, as they are called, of arts and things), and taking stand upon them as truths that cannot be shaken, proceed to prove and frame the middle axioms by reference to them; which has been the practice hitherto; the understanding being not only carried that way by a natural impulse, but also by the use of syllogistic demonstration trained and inured to it. But then, and then only, may we hope well of the sciences, when in a just scale of ascent, and by successive steps not interrupted or broken, we rise from particulars to lesser axioms; and then to middle axioms, one above the other; and last of all to the most general. For the lowest axioms differ but slightly from bare experience, while the highest and most general (which we now have) are notional and abstract and without solidity. But the middle are the true and solid and living axioms, on which depend the affairs and fortunes of men; and above them again, last of all, those which are indeed the most general; such I mean as are not abstract, but of which those intermediate axioms are really limitations.

The understanding must not therefore be supplied with wings, but rather hung with weights, to keep it from leaping and flying. Now this has never yet been done; when it is done, we may entertain better hopes of the sciences.

.   .   .

But in establishing axioms by this kind of induction, we must also examine and try whether the axiom so established be framed to the measure of those particulars only from which it is derived, or whether it be larger and wider. And if it be larger and wider, we must observe whether by indicating to us new particulars it confirm that wideness and largeness as by a collateral security; that we may not either stick fast in things already known, or loosely grasp at shadows and abstract forms; not at things solid and realised in matter. And when this process shall have come into use, then at last shall we see the dawn of a solid hope.

. . .

Again, it will be thought, no doubt, that the goal and mark of knowledge which I myself set up (the very point which I object to in others) is not the true or the best; for that the contemplation of truth is a thing worthier and loftier than all utility and magnitude of works; and that this long and anxious dwelling with experience and matter and the fluctuations of individual things, drags down the mind to earth, or rather sinks it to a very Tartarus of turmoil and confusion; removing and withdrawing it from the serene tranquillity of abstract wisdom, a condition far more heavenly. Now to this I readily assent; and indeed this which they point at as so much to be preferred, is the very thing of all others which I am about. For I am building in the human understanding a true model of the world, such as it is in fact, not such as a man's own reason would have it to be; a thing which cannot be done without a very diligent dissection and anatomy of the world. But I say that those foolish and apish images of worlds which the fancies of men have created in philosophical systems, must be utterly scattered to the winds. Be it known then how vast a difference there is (as I said above) between the Idols of the human mind and the Ideas of the divine. The former are nothing more than arbitrary abstractions; the latter are the creator's own stamp upon creation, impressed and defined in matter by true and exquisite lines. Truth therefore and utility are here the very same things: and works themselves are of greater value as pledges of truth than as contributing to the comforts of life.

René Descartes

2

Discourse on Method

If Bacon stressed the empirical element in scientific inquiry, René Descartes (1596–1650) established the necessity for a rigorous, rational analysis and explanation of natural phenomena. A more profound and precise thinker than Bacon, Descartes was also an important scientist in his own right. He was a mathematical genius who worked out the new discipline of analytic geometry. Descartes' philosophical work ranged, with typical French clarity, over the fields of metaphysics, ethics, and psychology, and he is generally considered the founder of modern philosophy. His emphasis on mathematical methods of reasoning gave contemporary scientists a means of guaranteeing the certainty of their knowledge of the physical universe. Descartes himself never lost the impress of his early training in the methods of scholasticism or in the orthodox Catholic faith. In fact, he thought he was establishing a rational basis for religious belief. But the Church thought otherwise and condemned his work. What brought ecclesiastical condemnation was Descartes' dualism—his belief that mind and matter were essentially different substances subject to different laws. It was this philosophical dualism that enabled him to separate scientific inquiry from religious thought and to treat the world of nature as a mechanical one, operating strictly according to mathematical law. Belief in the universe as an orderly system whose parts derive from the whole and where all forces emanate from a single center eventually led to the world view of the eighteenth-century Enlightenment.

The following selection from the *Discourse on Method* (1637), the most important of Descartes' philosophical writings, is an expression of his radical skepticism of all knowledge and philosophical premises based on authority or unclear thinking, and of his insistence on the acceptance as indubitably true of only those things that are perceived clearly and distinctly in the light of reason. It also shows how Descartes proceeds, from clearly estab-

René Descartes, *Discourse on Method*, in *The Method, Meditations and Philosophy of Descartes*, trans. John Veitch (New York: Tudor, 1901), 159–64, 170–77.

lished premises, to prove by deductive reasoning the existence of God, the world, and man.

———————————————— ▪ ————————————————

For my own part, I should doubtless have belonged to the latter class of those who accept the opinions of others, had I received instruction from but one master, or had I never known the diversities of opinion that from time immemorial have prevailed among men of the greatest learning. But I had become aware, even so early as during my college life, that no opinion, however absurd and incredible, can be imagined, which has not been maintained by some one of the philosophers; and afterward in the course of my travels I remarked that all those whose opinions are decidedly repugnant to ours are not on that account barbarians and savages, but on the contrary that many of these nations make an equally good, if not a better, use of their Reason than we do. I took into account also the very different character which a person brought up from infancy in France or Germany exhibits, from that which, with the same mind originally, this individual would have possessed had he lived always among the Chinese or with savages, and the circumstance that in dress itself the fashion which pleased us ten years ago, and which may again, perhaps, be received into favor before ten years have gone, appears to us at this moment extravagant and ridiculous. I was thus led to infer that the ground of our opinions is far more custom and example than any certain knowledge. And, finally, although such be the ground of our opinions, I remarked that a plurality of suffrages is no guarantee of truth where it is at all of difficult discovery, as in such cases it is much more likely that it will be found by one than by many. I could, however, select from the crowd no one whose opinions seemed worthy of preference and thus I found myself constrained, as it were, to use my own Reason in the conduct of my life.

But like one walking alone and in the dark, I resolved to proceed so slowly and with such circumspection, that if I did not advance far, I would at least guard against falling. I did not even choose to dismiss summarily any of the opinions that had crept into my belief without having been introduced by Reason, but first of all took sufficient time carefully to satisfy myself of the general nature of the task I was setting myself, and ascertain the true Method by which to arrive at the knowledge of whatever lay within the compass of my powers.

Among the branches of Philosophy, I had, at an earlier period, given some attention to Logic, and among those of the Mathematics to Geometrical Analysis and Algebra,—three Arts or Sciences which ought, as I conceived, to contribute something to my design. But, on examination, I found that, as for Logic, its syllogisms and the majority of its other precepts are of avail rather in the communication of what we already know, or even as the Art of Lully, in speaking without judgment of things of which we are ignorant, than in the investigation of the unknown; and although this Science contains indeed a number of correct and very excellent precepts, there are, nevertheless, so many others, and these either injurious or superfluous, mingled with the former, that it is almost quite as difficult to effect a severance of the true from the false as it is to extract a Diana or a Minerva from a rough block of marble. Then as to the Analysis of the ancients and the Algebra of the moderns, besides that they embrace only matters highly abstract, and, to appearance, of no use, the former is so exclusively restricted to the consideration of figures, that it can exercise the Understanding only on condition of greatly fatiguing the Imagination; and, in the latter, there is so complete a subjection to certain rules and formulas, that there results an art full of confusion and obscurity calculated to embarrass, instead of a science fitted to cultivate the mind. By these considerations I was induced to seek some other Method which would comprise the advantages of the three and be exempt from their defects. And as a multitude of laws often only hampers justice, so that a state is best governed when, with few laws, these are rigidly administered; in like manner, instead of the great number of precepts of which Logic is composed, I believed that the four following would prove perfectly sufficient for me, provided I took the firm and unwavering resolution never in a single instance to fail in observing them.

The first was never to accept anything for true which I did not clearly know to be such; that is to say, carefully to avoid precipitancy and prejudice, and to comprise nothing more in my judgment than what was presented to my mind so clearly and distinctly as to exclude all ground of doubt.

The second, to divide each of the difficulties under examination

I had hitherto taken for demonstrations; and finally, when I considered that the very same thoughts (presentations) which we experience when awake may also be experienced when we are asleep, while there is at that time not one of them true, I supposed that all the objects (presentations) that had ever entered into my mind when awake, had in them no more truth than the illusions of my dreams. But immediately upon this I observed that, whilst I thus wished to think that all was false, it was absolutely necessary that I, who thus thought, should be somewhat; and as I observed that this truth, I THINK, HENCE I AM, was so certain and of such evidence, that no ground of doubt, however extravagant, could be alleged by the Sceptics capable of shaking it, I concluded that I might, without scruple, accept it as the first principle of the Philosophy of which I was in search.

In the next place, I attentively examined what I was, and as I observed that I could suppose that I had no body, and that there was no world nor any place in which I might be; but that I could not therefore suppose that I was not; and that, on the contrary, from the very circumstance that I thought to doubt of the truth of all things, it most clearly and certainly followed that I was; while, on the other hand, if I had only ceased to think, although all the other objects which I had ever imagined had been in reality existent, I would have had no reason to believe that I existed; I thence concluded that I was a substance whose whole essence or nature consists only in thinking, and which, that it may exist, has need of no place, nor is dependent on any material thing; so that "I," that is to say, the mind by which I am what I am, is wholly distinct from the body, and is even more easily known than the latter, and is such, that although the latter were not, it would still continue to be all that it is.

After this I inquired in general into what is essential to the truth and certainty of a proposition; for since I had discovered one which I knew to be true, I thought that I must likewise be able to discover the ground of this certitude. And as I observed that in the words I THINK, HENCE I AM, there is nothing at all which gives me assurance of their truth beyond this, that I see very clearly that in order to think it is necessary to exist, I concluded that I might take, as a general rule, the principle, that all the things which we very clearly and distinctly conceive are true, only observing, however,

into as many parts as possible, and as might be necessary for its adequate solution.

The third, to conduct my thoughts in such order that, by commencing with objects the simplest and easiest to know, I might ascend by little and little, and, as it were, step by step, to the knowledge of the more complex; assigning in thought a certain order even to those objects which in their own nature do not stand in a relation of antecedence and sequence.

At the last, in every case to make enumerations so complete, and reviews so general, that I might be assured that nothing was omitted.

The long chains of simple and easy reasonings by means of which geometers are accustomed to reach the conclusions of their most difficult demonstrations, had led me to imagine that all things, to the knowledge of which man is competent, are mutually connected in the same way, and that there is nothing so far removed from us as to be beyond our reach, or so hidden that we cannot discover it, provided only we abstain from accepting the false for the true, and always preserve in our thoughts the order necessary for the deduction of one truth from another. And I had little difficulty in determining the objects with which it was necessary to commence, for I was already persuaded that it must be with the simplest and easiest to know, and considering that of all those who have hitherto sought truth in the Sciences, the mathematicians alone have been able to find any demonstrations, that is, any certain and evident reasons, I did not doubt but that such must have been the rule of their investigations. I resolved to commence, therefore, with the examination of the simplest objects, not anticipating, however, from this any other advantage than that to be found in accustoming my mind to the love and nourishment of truth, and to a distaste for all such reasonings as were unsound. But I had no intention on that account of attempting to master all the particular Sciences commonly denominated Mathematics: but observing that, however different their objects, they all agree in considering only the various relations or proportions subsisting among those objects, I thought it best for my purpose to consider these proportions in the most general form possible, without referring them to any objects in particular, except such as would most facilitate the knowledge of them, and without by any means restricting them to these, that afterward I might thus be the better able to apply them to every other class of objects to

which they are legitimately applicable. Perceiving further, that in
order to understand these relations I should sometimes have to
consider them one by one, and sometimes only to bear them in
mind, or embrace them in the aggregate, I thought that, in order the
better to consider them individually, I should view them as subsisting between straight lines, than which I could find no objects more
simple, or capable of being more distinctly represented to my imagination and senses; and on the other hand, that in order to retain
them in the memory, or embrace an aggregate of many, I should
express them by certain characters the briefest possible. In this way
I believed that I could borrow all that was best both in Geometrical
Analysis and in Algebra, and correct all the defects of the one by
help of the other.

And, in point of fact, the accurate observance of these few precepts gave me, I take the liberty of saying, such ease in unraveling
all the questions embraced in these two sciences, that in the two
or three months I devoted to their examination, not only did I
reach solutions of questions I had formerly deemed exceedingly difficult, but even as regards questions of the solution of which I continued ignorant, I was enabled, as it appeared to me, to determine
the means whereby, and the extent to which, a solution was possible;
results attributable to the circumstance that I commenced with the
simplest and most general truths, and that thus each truth discovered was a rule available in the discovery of subsequent ones. Nor
in this perhaps shall I appear too vain, if it be considered that, as the
truth on any particular point is one, whoever apprehends the truth,
knows all that on that point can be known. The child, for example,
who has been instructed in the elements of Arithmetic, and has made
a particular addition, according to rule, may be assured that he has
found, with respect to the sum of the numbers before him, all that
in this instance is within the reach of human genius. Now, in conclusion, the Method which teaches adherence to the true order, and
an exact enumeration of all the conditions of the thing sought includes all that gives certitude to the rules of Arithmetic.

But the chief ground of my satisfaction with this Method was the
assurance I had of thereby exercising my reason in all matters, if
not with absolute perfection, at least with the greatest attainable by
me: besides, I was conscious that by its use my mind was becoming
gradually habituated to clearer and more distinct conceptions of its
objects; and I hoped also, from not having restricted this Method

to any particular matter, to apply it to the difficulties of the other
Sciences, with not less success than to those of Algebra. I should not,
however, on this account have ventured at once on the examination of all the difficulties of the Sciences which presented themselves to me, for this would have been contrary to the order prescribed in the Method, but observing that the knowledge of such is
dependent on principles borrowed from Philosophy, in which I
found nothing certain, I thought it necessary, first of all to endeavor
to establish its principles. And because I observed, besides, that an
inquiry of this kind was of all others of the greatest moment, and
one in which precipitancy and anticipation in judgment were most
to be dreaded, I thought that I ought not to approach it till I had
reached a more mature age (being at that time but twenty-three),
and had first of all employed much of my time in preparation for
the work, as well by eradicating from my mind all the erroneous
opinions I had up to that moment accepted, as by amassing variety
of experience to afford materials for my reasonings, and by continually exercising myself in my chosen Method with a view to increased skill in its application.

. . .

I am in doubt as to the propriety of making my first meditations,
in the place above mentioned, matter of discourse; for these are so
metaphysical, and so uncommon, as not, perhaps, to be acceptable to
everyone. And yet, that it may be determined whether the foundations that I have laid are sufficiently secure, I find myself in a
measure constrained to advert to them. I had long before remarked
that, in relation to practice, it is sometimes necessary to adopt, as
if above doubt, opinions which we discern to be highly uncertain, as
has been already said; but as I then desired to give my attention
solely to the search after truth, I thought that a procedure exactly
the opposite was called for, and that I ought to reject as absolutely
false all opinions in regard to which I could suppose the least
ground for doubt, in order to ascertain whether after that there remained aught in my belief that was wholly indubitable. Accordingly, seeing that our senses sometimes deceive us, I was willing to
suppose that there existed nothing really such as they presented to
us; and because some men err in reasoning, and fall into paralo-
gisms, even on the simplest matters of Geometry, I, convinced that I
was as open to error as any other, rejected as false all the reasonings

that there is some difficulty in rightly determining the objects which we distinctly conceive.

In the next place, from reflecting on the circumstance that I doubted, and that consequently my being was not wholly perfect (for I clearly saw that it was a greater perfection to know than to doubt), I was led to inquire whence I had learned to think of something more perfect than myself; and I clearly recognized that I must hold this notion from some Nature which in reality was more perfect. As for the thoughts of many other objects external to me, as of the sky, the earth, light, heat, and a thousand more, I was less at a loss to know whence these came; for since I remarked in them nothing which seemed to render them superior to myself, I could believe that, if these were true, they were dependencies on my own nature, in so far as it possessed a certain perfection, and, if they were false, that I held them from nothing, that is to say, that they were in me because of a certain imperfection of my nature. But this could not be the case with the idea of a Nature more perfect than myself; for to receive it from nothing was a thing manifestly impossible; and, because it is not less repugnant that the more perfect should be an effect of, and dependence on the less perfect, than that something should proceed from nothing, it was equally impossible that I could hold it from myself: accordingly, it but remained that it had been placed in me by a Nature which was in reality more perfect than mine, and which even possessed within itself all the perfections of which I could form any idea: that is to say, in a single word, which was God. And to this I added that, since I knew some perfections which I did not possess, I was not the only being in existence, (I will here, with your permission, freely use the terms of the Schools); but on the contrary, that there was of necessity some other more perfect Being upon whom I was dependent, and from whom I had received all that I possessed; for if I had existed alone, and independently of every other being, so as to have had from myself all the perfection, however little, which I actually possessed, I should have been able, for the same reason, to have had from myself the whole remainder of perfection, of the want of which I was conscious, and thus could of myself have become infinite, eternal, immutable, omniscient, all-powerful, and, in fine, have possessed all the perfections which I could recognize in God. For in order to know the nature of God (whose existence has been established by the preceding reasonings), as far as my own nature permitted, I had only to consider in reference to all the properties of which I found in my mind some idea, whether their possession was a mark of perfection; and I was assured that no one which indicated any imperfection was in him, and that none of the rest was awanting. Thus I perceived that doubt, inconstancy, sadness, and such like, could not be found in God, since I myself would have been happy to be free from them. Besides, I had ideas of many sensible and corporeal things; for although I might suppose that I was dreaming, and that all which I saw or imagined was false, I could not, nevertheless, deny that the ideas were in reality in my thoughts. But because I had already very clearly recognized in myself that the intelligent nature is distinct from the corporeal, and as I observed that all composition is an evidence of dependency, and that a state of dependency is manifestly a state of imperfection, I therefore determined that it could not be a perfection in God to be compounded of these two natures, and that consequently he was not so compounded; but that if there were any bodies in the world, or even any intelligences, or other natures that were not wholly perfect, their existence depended on his power in such a way that they could not subsist without him for a single moment.

I was disposed straightway to search for other truths; and when I had represented to myself the object of the geometers, which I conceived to be a continuous body, or a space indefinitely extended in length, breadth, and height or depth, divisible into divers parts which admit of different figures and sizes, and of being moved or transposed in all manner of ways (for all this the geometers suppose to be in the object they contemplate), I went over some of their simplest demonstrations. And, in the first place, I observed, that the great certitude which by common consent is accorded to these demonstrations, is founded solely upon this, that they are clearly conceived in accordance with the rules I have already laid down. In the next place, I perceived that there was nothing at all in these demonstrations which could assure me of the existence of their object; thus, for example, supposing a triangle to be given, I distinctly perceived that its three angles were necessarily equal to two right angles, but I did not on that account perceive anything which could assure me that any triangle existed; while, on the contrary, recurring to the examination of the idea of a Perfect Being, I found that the existence of the Being was comprised in the idea in the same way that the equality of its three angles to two right angles is comprised in the idea of a triangle, or as in the idea of a sphere, the equidistance of all points on its surface from the center or even still more clearly; and that consequently it is at least as certain that God, who is this Perfect Being, is, or exists, as any demonstration of Geometry can be.

But the reason which leads many to persuade themselves that there is a difficulty in knowing this truth, and even also in knowing what their mind really is, is that they never raise their thoughts above sensible objects, and are so accustomed to consider nothing except by way of imagination, which is a mode of thinking limited to material objects, that all that is not imaginable seems to them not intelligible. The truth of this is sufficiently manifest from the single circumstance, that the philosophers of the Schools accept as a maxim that there is nothing in the Understanding which was not previously in the Senses, in which however it is certain that the ideas of God and of the soul have never been; and it appears to me that they who make use of their imagination to comprehend these ideas do exactly the same thing as if, in order to hear sounds or smell odors, they strove to avail themselves of their eyes; unless indeed that there is this difference, that the sense of sight does not afford us an inferior assurance to those of smell or hearing; in place of which, neither our imagination nor our senses can give us assurance of anything unless our Understanding intervene.

Finally, if there be still persons who are not sufficiently persuaded of the existence of God and of the soul, by the reasons I have adduced, I am desirous that they should know that all the other propositions, of the truth of which they deem themselves perhaps more assured, as that we have a body, and that there exist stars and an earth, and such like, are less certain; for, although we have a moral assurance of these things, which is so strong that there is an appearance of extravagance in doubting of their existence, yet at the same time no one, unless his intellect is impaired, can deny, when the question relates to a metaphysical certitude, that there is sufficient reason to exclude entire assurance, in the observation that when asleep we can in the same way imagine ourselves possessed of another body and that we see other stars and another earth, when there is nothing of the kind. For how do we know that the thoughts which occur in dreaming are false rather than those others which we experience when awake, since the former are

often not less vivid and distinct than the latter? And though men of
the highest genius study this question as long as they please, I do
not believe that they will be able to give any reason which can be
sufficient to remove this doubt, unless they presuppose the existence
of God. For, in the first place, even the principle which I have already taken as a rule, viz., that all the things which we clearly and
distinctly conceive are true, is certain only because God is or exists,
and because he is a Perfect Being, and because all that we possess
is derived from him: whence it follows that our ideas or notions,
which to the extent of their clearness and distinctness are real, and
proceed from God, must to that extent be true. Accordingly,
whereas we not unfrequently have ideas or notions in which some
falsity is contained, this can only be the case with such as are to
some extent confused and obscure, and in this proceed from nothing (participate of negation), that is, exist in us thus confused because we are not wholly perfect. And it is evident that it is not less
repugnant that falsity or imperfection, in so far as it is imperfection,
should proceed from God, than that truth or perfection should
proceed from nothing. But if we did not know that all which
we possess of real and true proceeds from a Perfect and Infinite
Being, however clear and distinct our ideas might be, we should
have no ground on that account for the assurance that they possessed
the perfection of being true.

But after the knowledge of God and of the soul has rendered
us certain of this rule, we can easily understand that the truth of
the thoughts we experience when awake, ought not in the slightest
degree to be called in question on account of the illusions of our
dreams. For if it happened that an individual, even when asleep,
had some very distinct idea, as, for example, if a geometer should
discover some new demonstration, the circumstance of his being
asleep would not militate against its truth; and as for the most ordinary error of our dreams, which consists in their representing to
us various objects in the same way as our external senses, this is
not prejudicial, since it leads us very properly to suspect the truth
of the ideas of sense; for we are not unfrequently deceived in the
same manner when awake; as when persons in the jaundice see all
objects yellow, or when the stars or bodies at a great distance appear
to us much smaller than they are. For, in fine, whether awake or
asleep, we ought never to allow ourselves to be persuaded of the
truth of anything unless on the evidence of our Reason. And it

must be noted that I say of our REASON, and not of our imagination
or of our senses: thus, for example, although we very clearly see
the sun, we ought not therefore to determine that it is only of the
size which our sense of sight presents; and we may very distinctly
imagine the head of a lion joined to the body of a goat, without
being therefore shut up to the conclusion that a chimera exists;
for it is not a dictate of Reason that what we thus see or imagine
is in reality existent; but it plainly tells us that all our ideas or
notions contain in them some truth; for otherwise it could not be
that God, who is wholly perfect and veracious, should have placed
them in us. And because our reasonings are never so clear or so
complete during sleep as when we are awake, although sometimes
the acts of our imagination are then as lively and distinct, if not
more so than in our waking moments, Reason further dictates that,
since all our thoughts cannot be true because of our partial imperfection, those possessing truth must infallibly be found in the
experience of our waking moments rather than in that of our
dreams.

Thomas Hobbes

— *3* —

Leviathan

The new seventeenth-century science found philosophical expression in the work of Thomas Hobbes (1588–1679). The patronage of the Cavendishes, a powerful, noble English family, to whom he owed his social position and his livelihood, enabled Hobbes to carry on his scientific and philosophical studies and to travel and meet the leading intellectual figures of his day. He knew the work of Bacon, Descartes, Galileo, and other scientists and incorporated their methods and findings into his own philosophy. He completely rejected medieval scholasticism and evolved a system that was materialist and determinist. For Hobbes, man and his ideas were simply forms of matter in motion. Such unorthodox views brought down on his head charges of impiety and atheism and earned him such epithets as the "Bugbear of the Nation" and the "Monster of Malmesbury."

Hobbes's political views, expressed systematically in his masterpiece, *Leviathan* (1651), were shaped as much by his own assumptions of philosophical materialism as by the personal and political circumstances of his troubled times. Living through the bloody conflicts of the English civil wars, Hobbes was stirred by "grief for the present calamities of my country," and his primary concern was the restoration of peace and order to England. His association with aristocratic circles inclined him to accept a strong monarchy as the instrument of such peace.

The *Leviathan* is a vigorous and realistic exposition of the case for political absolutism. Absolute sovereignty, Hobbes argues, is indispensable for the maintenance of order. His theories, however, pleased neither his royalist friends nor his Puritan enemies. For, though he favored an absolute monarchy, he was ready to accept any government powerful enough to maintain civil peace. Hobbes also rejected the traditional concepts of the divine rights of kings and the organic community. In his view, the origins of society were wholly secular and atomistic: society resulted from

Thomas Hobbes, *Leviathan*, in *The English Works of Thomas Hobbes* (London: John Bohn, 1839), III, 85–86, 110–18, 153–54, 157–66, 168–70, 322–23.

a social contract among selfish, warring individuals moved by necessity and fear. Sovereignty, once delegated, was irrevocable and indivisible. Since the seventeenth century, Hobbes's influence and reputation as a realistic political scientist have steadily grown. His ideas have increasingly served as a rationale for the exercise of absolute power and the glorification of the state.

OF THE DIFFERENCE OF MANNERS

By manners, I mean not here, decency of behaviour; as how one should salute another, or how a man should wash his mouth, or pick his teeth before company, and such other points of the *small morals;* but those qualities of mankind, that concern their living together in peace, and unity. To which end we are to consider, that the felicity of this life, consisteth not in the repose of a mind satisfied. For there is no such *finis ultimus,* utmost aim, nor *summum bonum,* greatest good, as is spoken of in the books of the old moral philosophers. Nor can a man any more live, whose desires are at an end, than he, whose senses and imaginations are at a stand. Felicity is a continual progress of the desire, from one object to another; the attaining of the former, being still but the way to the latter. The cause whereof is, that the object of man's desire, is not to enjoy once only, and for one instant of time; but to assure for ever, the way of his future desire. And therefore the voluntary actions, and inclinations of all men, tend, not only to the procuring, but also to the assuring of a contented life; and differ only in the way: which ariseth partly from the diversity of passions, in divers men; and partly from the difference of the knowledge, or opinion each one has of the causes, which produce the effect desired.

So that in the first place, I put for a general inclination of all mankind, a perpetual and restless desire of power after power, that ceaseth only in death. And the cause of this, is not always that a man hopes for a more intensive delight, than he has already attained to; or that he cannot be content with a moderate power: but because he cannot assure the power and means to live well, which he hath present, without the acquisition of more. And from hence it is, that kings, whose power is greatest, turn their endeavours to the assuring it at home by laws, or abroad by wars: and when that is done, there succeedeth a new desire; in some, of fame from new conquest; in others, of ease and sensual pleasure; in others, of admiration, or being flattered for excellence in some art, or other ability of the mind.

. . .

OF THE NATURAL CONDITION OF MANKIND AS CONCERNING THEIR FELICITY, AND MISERY

Nature hath made men so equal, in the faculties of the body, and mind; as that though there be found one man sometimes manifestly stronger in body, or of quicker mind than another; yet when all is reckoned together, the difference between man, and man, is not so considerable, as that one man can thereupon claim to himself any benefit, to which another may not pretend, as well as he. For as to the strength of body, the weakest has strength enough to kill the strongest, either by secret machination, or by confederacy with others, that are in the same danger with himself.

And as to the faculties of the mind, setting aside the arts grounded upon words, and especially that skill of proceeding upon general, and infallible rules, called science; which very few have, and but in few things; as being not a native faculty, born with us; nor attained, as prudence, while we look after somewhat else, I find yet a greater equality amongst men, than that of strength. For prudence, is but experience; which equal time, equally bestows on all men, in those things they equally apply themselves unto. That which may perhaps make such equality incredible, is but a vain conceit of one's own wisdom, which almost all men think they have in a greater degree, than the vulgar; that is, than all men but themselves, and a few others, whom by fame, or for concurring with themselves, they approve. For such is the nature of men, that howsoever they may acknowledge many others to be more witty, or more eloquent, or more learned; yet they will hardly believe there be many so wise as themselves; for they see their own wit at hand, and other men's at a distance. But this proveth rather that men are in that point equal, than unequal. For there is not ordinarily a greater sign of the equal distribution of any thing, than that every man is contented with his share.

From this equality of ability, ariseth equality of hope in the attaining of our ends. And therefore if any two men desire the same thing, which nevertheless they cannot both enjoy, they become enemies; and in the way to their end, which is principally their own conservation, and sometimes their delectation only, endeavour to destroy, or subdue one another. And from hence it comes to pass, that where an invader hath no more to fear, than another man's single power; if one plant, sow, build, or possess a convenient seat, others may probably be expected to come prepared with forces united, to dispossess, and deprive him, not only of the fruit of his labour, but also of his life, or liberty. And the invader again is in the like danger of another.

And from this diffidence of one another, there is no way for any man to secure himself, so reasonable, as anticipation; that is, by force, or wiles, to master the persons of all men he can, so long, till he see no other power great enough to endanger him: and this is no more than his own conservation requireth, and is generally allowed. Also because there be some, that taking pleasure in contemplating their own power in the acts of conquest, which they pursue farther than their security requires; if others, that otherwise would be glad to be at ease within modest bounds, should not by invasion increase their power, they would not be able, long time, by standing only on their defence, to subsist. And by consequence, such augmentation of dominion over men being necessary to a man's conservation, it ought to be allowed him.

Again, men have no pleasure, but on the contrary a great deal of grief, in keeping company, where there is no power able to over-awe them all. For every man looketh that his companion should value him, at the same rate he sets upon himself: and upon all signs of contempt, or undervaluing, naturally endeavours, as far as he dares, (which amongst them that have no common power to keep them in quiet, is far enough to make them destroy each other), to extort a greater value from his contemners, by damage; and from others, by the example.

So that in the nature of man, we find three principal causes of quarrel. First, competition; secondly, diffidence; thirdly, glory. The first, maketh men invade for gain; the second, for safety; and the third, for reputation. The first use violence, to make themselves masters of other men's persons, wives, children, and cattle; the second, to defend them; the third, for trifles, as a word, a smile, a different opinion, and any other sign of undervalue, either direct in their persons, or by reflection in their kindred, their friends, their nation, their profession, or their name.

Hereby it is manifest, that during the time men live without a common power to keep them all in awe, they are in that condition which is called war; and such a war, as is of every man, against every man. For War, consisteth not in battle only, or the act of fighting; but in a tract of time, wherein the will to contend by battle is sufficiently known: and therefore the notion of time, is to be considered in the nature of war; as it is in the nature of weather. For as the nature of foul weather, lieth not in a shower or two of rain; but in an inclination thereto of many days together: so the nature of war, consisteth not in actual fighting; but in the known disposition thereto, during all the time there is no assurance to the contrary. All other time is Peace.

Whatsoever therefore is consequent to a time of war, where every man is enemy to every man; the same is consequent to the time, wherein men live without other security, than what their own strength, and their own invention shall furnish them withal. In such condition, there is no place for industry; because the fruit thereof is uncertain: and consequently no culture of the earth; no navigation, nor use of the commodities that may be imported by sea; no commodious building; no instruments of moving, and removing, such things as require much force; no knowledge of the face of the earth; no account of time; no arts; no letters; no society; and which is worst of all, continual fear, and danger of violent death; and the life of man, solitary, poor, nasty, brutish, and short.

It may seem strange to some man, that has not well weighed these things; that nature should thus dissociate, and render men apt to invade, and destroy one another: and he may therefore, not trusting to this inference, made from the passions, desire perhaps to have the same confirmed by experience. Let him therefore consider with himself, when taking a journey, he arms himself, and seeks to go well accompanied; when going to sleep, he locks his doors; when even in his house he locks his chests; and this when he knows there be laws, and public officers, armed, to revenge all injuries shall be done him; what opinion he has of his fellow-subjects, when he rides armed; of his fellow citizens, when he locks his doors; and of his children, and servants, when he locks his chests. Does he not there as much accuse mankind by his actions, as I do by my words? But neither of us accuse man's nature in it. The desires, and other passions of man, are in themselves no sin. No more are the actions, that proceed from those passions, till they know a law that forbids them: which till laws be made they cannot know: nor can any law be made, till they have agreed upon the person that shall make it.

It may peradventure be thought, there was never such a time, nor condition of war as this; and I believe it was never generally so, over all the world: but there are many places, where they live so now. For the savage people in many places of America, except the government of small families, the concord whereof dependeth on natural lust, have no government at all; and live at this day in that brutish manner, as I said before. Howsoever, it may be perceived what manner of life there would be, where there were no common power to fear, by the manner of life, which men that have formerly lived under a peaceful government, use to degenerate into, in a civil war.

But though there had never been any time, wherein particular men were in a condition of war one against another; yet in all times, kings, and persons of sovereign authority, because of their independency, are in continual jealousies, and in the state and posture of gladiators; having their weapons pointing, and their eyes fixed on one another; that is, their forts, garrisons, and guns upon the frontiers of their kingdoms; and continual spies upon their neighbours; which is a posture of war. But because they uphold thereby, the industry of their subjects; there does not follow from it, that misery, which accompanies the liberty of particular men.

To this war of every man, against every man, this also is consequent; that nothing can be unjust. The notions of right and wrong, justice and injustice have there no place. Where there is no common power, there is no law: where no law, no injustice. Force, and fraud, are in war the two cardinal virtues. Justice, and injustice are none of the faculties neither of the body, nor mind. If they were, they might be in a man that were alone in the world, as well as his senses, and passions. They are qualities, that relate to men in society, not in solitude. It is consequent also to the same condition, that there be no propriety, no dominion, no *mine* and *thine* distinct; but only that to be every man's, that he can get: and for so long, as he can keep it. And thus much for the ill condition, which man by mere nature is actually placed in; though with a possibility to come out of it, consisting partly in the passions, partly in his reason.

The passions that incline men to peace, are fear of death; desire of such things as are necessary to commodious living; and a hope by their industry to obtain them. And reason suggesteth convenient articles of peace, upon which men may be drawn to agreement. These articles, are they, which otherwise are called the Laws of Nature: whereof I shall speak more particularly. . . .

OF THE FIRST AND SECOND NATURAL LAWS . . .

The Right of Nature, which writers commonly call *jus naturale,* is the liberty each man hath, to use his own power, as he will himself, for the preservation of his own nature; that is to say, of his own life; and consequently, of doing any thing, which in his own judgment, and reason, he shall conceive to be the aptest means thereunto.

By Liberty, is understood, according to the proper signification of the word, the absence of external impediments: which impediments, may oft take away part of a man's power to do what he would; but cannot hinder him from using the power left him, according as his judgment, and reason shall dictate to him.

A Law of Nature, *lex naturalis,* is a precept or general rule, found out by reason, by which a man is forbidden to do that, which is destructive of his life, or taketh away the means of preserving the same; and to omit that, by which he thinketh it may be best preserved. For though they that speak of this subject, use to confound *jus,* and *lex, right* and *law:* yet they ought to be distinguished; because Right, consisteth in liberty to do, or to forbear: whereas Law, determineth, and bindeth to one of them: so that law, and right, differ as much, as obligation, and liberty; which in one and the same matter are inconsistent.

And because the condition of man, as hath been declared in the precedent chapter, is a condition of war of every one against every one; in which case every one is governed by his own reason; and there is nothing he can make use of, that may not be a help unto him, in preserving his life against his enemies; it followeth, that in such a condition, every man has a right to every thing; even to one another's body. And therefore, as long as this natural right of every man to every thing endureth, there can be no security to any man, how strong or wise soever he be, of living out the time, which nature ordinarily alloweth men to live. And consequently it is a precept, or general rule of reason, *that every man, ought to endeavour peace, as far as he has hope of obtaining it; and when he cannot obtain it, that he may seek, and use, all helps, and advantages of war.* The first branch of which rule, containeth the first, and fundamental law of nature; which is, *to seek peace, and follow it.* The second, the sum of the right of nature; which is, *by all means we can, to defend ourselves.*

From this fundamental law of nature, by which men are commanded to endeavour peace, is derived this second law; *that a man be willing, when others are so too, as far-forth, as for peace, and defence of himself he shall think it necessary, to lay down this right to all things; and be contented with so much liberty against other men, as he would allow other men against himself.* For as long as every man holdeth this right, of doing any thing he liketh; so long are all men in the condition of war. But if other men will not lay down their right, as well as he; then there is no reason for any one, to divest himself of his: for that were to expose himself to prey, which no man is bound to, rather than to dispose himself to peace. This is that law of the Gospel; *whatsoever you require that others should do to you, that do ye to them.* And that law of all men, *quod tibi fieri non vis, alteri ne feceris.*

. . .

OF THE CAUSES, GENERATION, AND DEFINITION
OF A COMMONWEALTH

The final cause, end, or design of men, who naturally love liberty, and dominion over others, in the introduction of that restraint upon themselves, in which we see them live in commonwealths, is the foresight of their own preservation, and of a more contented life thereby; that is to say, of getting themselves out from that miserable condition of war, which is necessarily consequent, as hath been shown, to the natural passions of men, when there is no visible power to keep them in awe, and tie them by fear of punishment to the performance of their covenants, and observation of those laws of nature set down. . . .

For the laws of nature, as *justice, equity, modesty, mercy,* and, in sum, *doing to others, as we would be done to,* of themselves, without the terror of some power, to cause them to be observed, are contrary to our natural passions, that carry us to partiality, pride, revenge, and the like. And covenants, without the sword, are but words, and of no strength to secure a man at all. Therefore notwithstanding the laws of nature (which every one hath then kept, when he has the will to keep them, when he can do it safely) if there be no power erected, or not great enough for our security; every man will, and may lawfully rely on his own strength and art, for caution against all other men. And in all places, where men have lived by small families, to rob and spoil one another, has been a trade, and so far from being reputed against the law of nature, that the greater spoils they gained, the greater was their honour; and men observed no other laws therein, but the laws of honour; that is, to abstain from cruelty, leaving to men their lives, and instruments of husbandry. And as small families did then; so now do cities and kingdoms which are but greater families, for their own security, enlarge their dominions, upon all pretences of danger, and fear of invasion, or assistance that may be given to invaders, and endeavour as much as they can, to subdue, or weaken their neighbours, by open force, and secret arts, for want of other caution, justly; and are remembered for it in after ages with honour.

❧   · · ·

The only way to erect such a common power, as may be able to defend them from the invasion of foreigners, and the injuries of one another, and thereby to secure them in such sort, as that by their own industry, and by the fruits of the earth, they may nourish themselves and live contentedly; is, to confer all their power and strength upon one man, or upon one assembly of men, that may reduce all their wills, by plurality of voices, unto one will: which is as much as to say, to appoint one man, or assembly of men, to bear their person; and every one to own, and acknowledge himself to be author of whatsoever he that so beareth their person, shall act, or cause to be acted, in those things which concern the common peace and safety; and therein to submit their wills, everyone to his will, and their judgments, to his judgment. This is more than consent, or concord; it is a real unity of them all, in one and the same person, made by covenant of every man with every man, in such manner, as if every man should say to every man, *I authorize and give up my right of governing myself, to this man, or to this assembly of men, on this condition, that thou give up thy right to him, and authorize all his actions in like manner.* This done, the multitude so united in one person, is called a Commonwealth, in Latin *civitas.* This is the generation of that great Leviathan, or rather, to speak more reverently, of that *mortal god,* to which we owe under the *immortal God,* our peace and defence. For by this authority, given him by every particular man in the commonwealth, he hath the use of so much power and strength conferred on him, that by terror thereof, he is enabled to form the wills of them all, to peace at home, and mutual aid against their enemies abroad. And in him consisteth the essence of the commonwealth; which, to define it, is one *person, of whose acts a great multitude, by mutual covenants one with another, have made themselves every one the author, to the end he may use the strength and means of them all, as he shall think expedient, for their peace and common defence.*

And he that carrieth this person, is called Sovereign, and said to have *sovereign power;* and every one besides, his Subject.

The attaining to this sovereign power, is by two ways. One, by natural force; as when a man maketh his children, to submit themselves, and their children to his government, as being able to destroy them if they refuse; or by war subdueth his enemies to his will, giving them their lives on that condition. The other, is when men agree amongst themselves, to submit to some man, or assembly of men, voluntarily, on confidence to be protected by him against all others. This latter, may be called a political commonwealth, or commonwealth by *institution;* and the former, a commonwealth by *acquisition.* And first, I shall speak of a commonwealth by institution.

OF THE RIGHTS OF SOVEREIGNS BY INSTITUTION

A *commonwealth* is said to be *instituted,* when a *multitude* of men do agree, and *covenant, every one, with every one,* that to whatsoever *man,* or *assembly of men,* shall be given by the major part, the *right to present* the person of them all, that is to say, to be their *representative;* every one, as well he that voted for it, as he that *voted against it,* shall *authorize* all the actions and judgments, of that man, or assembly of men, in the same manner, as if they were his own, to the end, to live peaceably amongst themselves, and be protected against other men.

From this institution of a commonwealth are derived all the *rights,* and *faculties* of him, or them, on whom the sovereign power is conferred by the consent of the people assembled.

First, because they covenant, it is to be understood, they are not obliged by former covenant to any thing repugnant hereunto. And consequently they that have already instituted a commonwealth, being thereby bound by covenant, to own the actions, and judgments of one, cannot lawfully make a new covenant, amongst themselves, to be obedient to any other, in any thing whatsoever, without his permission. And therefore, they that are subjects to a monarch, cannot without his leave cast off monarchy, and return to the confusion of a disunited multitude; nor transfer their person from him that beareth it, to another man, or other assembly of men: for they are bound every man to every man, to own, and be reputed author of all, that he that already is their sovereign, shall do, and judge fit to be done: so that any one man dissenting, all the rest should break their covenant made to that man, which is injustice: and they have also every man given the sovereignty to him that beareth their person; and therefore if they depose him, they take from him that which is his own, and so again it is injustice. Besides, if he that attempteth to depose his sovereign, be killed, or punished by him for such attempt, he is author of his own punishment, as being by the institution, author of all his sovereign shall do: and because it is injustice for a man to do any thing, for which he may be punished by his own authority, he is also upon that title, unjust. And whereas some men have pretended for their disobedience to their sovereign, a new covenant, made, not with men, but with God; this also is unjust: for there is no covenant with God, but by mediation of somebody that representeth God's person; which none doth but God's lieutenant, who hath the sovereignty under God. But this pretence of cove-nant with God, is so evident a lie, even in the pretenders' own consciences, that it is not only an act of an unjust, but also of a vile, and unmanly disposition.

Secondly, because the right of bearing the person of them all, is given to him they make sovereign, by covenant only of one to another, and not of him to any of them; there can happen no breach of covenant on the part of the sovereign; and consequently none of his subjects, by any pretence of forfeiture, can be freed from his subjection. That he which is made sovereign maketh no covenant with his subjects beforehand, is manifest; because either he must make it with the whole multitude, as one party to the covenant; or he must make a several covenant with every man. With the whole, as one party, it is impossible; because as yet they are not one person: and if he make so many several covenants as there be men, those covenants after he hath the sovereignty are void; because what act soever can be pretended by any one of them for breach thereof, is the act both of himself, and of all the rest, because done in the person, and by the right of every one of them in particular. Besides, if any one, or more of them, pretend a breach of the covenant made by the sovereign at his institution; and others, or one other of his subjects, or himself alone, pretend there was no such breach, there is in this case, no judge to decide the controversy; it returns therefore to the sword again; and every man recovereth the right of protecting himself by his own strength, contrary to the design they had in the institution. It is therefore in vain to grant sovereignty by way of precedent covenant. The opinion that any monarch receiveth his power by covenant, that is to say, on condition, proceedeth from want of understanding this easy truth, that covenants being but words and breath, have no force to oblige, contain, constrain, or protect any man, but what it has from the public sword; that is, from the united hands of that man, or assembly of men that hath the sovereignty, and whose actions are avouched by them all, and performed by the strength of them all, in him united. But when an assembly of men is made sovereign; then no man imagineth any such covenant to have passed in the institution; for no man is so dull as to say, for example, the people of Rome made a covenant with the Romans, to hold the sovereignty on such or such conditions; which not performed, the Romans might lawfully depose the Roman people. That men see not the reason to be alike in a monarchy, and in a popular government, proceedeth from the ambition of some, that are kinder to the government of an assembly, whereof they may hope to participate, than of monarchy, which they despair to enjoy.

Thirdly, because the major part hath by consenting voices declared a sovereign; he that disented must now consent with the rest; that is, be contented to avow all the actions he shall do, or else justly be destroyed by the rest. For if he voluntarily entered into the congregation of them that were assembled, he sufficiently declared thereby his will, and therefore tacitly covenanted, to stand to what the major part should ordain: and therefore if he refuse to stand thereto, or make protestation against any of their decrees, he does contrary to his convenant, and therefore unjustly. And whether he be of the congregation, or not; and whether his consent be asked, or not, he must either submit to their decrees, or be left in the condition of war he was in before; wherein he might without injustice be destroyed by any man whatsoever.

Fourthly, because every subject is by this institution author of all the actions, and judgments of the sovereign instituted; it follows, that whatsoever he doth, it can be no injury to any of his subjects; nor ought he to be by any of them accused of injustice. For he that doth anything by authority from another, doth therein no injury to him by whose authority he acteth: but by this institution of a commonweath, every particular man is author of all the sovereign doth: and consequently he that complaineth of injury from his sovereign, complaineth of that whereof he himself is author; and therefore ought not to accuse any man but himself; no nor himself of injury; because to do injury to one's self, is impossible. It is true that they that have sovereign power may commit iniquity; but not injustice, or injury in the proper signification.

Fifthly, and consequently to that which was said last, no man that hath sovereign power can justly be put to death, or otherwise in any manner by his subjects punished. For seeing every subject is author of the actions of his sovereign; he punisheth another for the actions committed by himself.

And because the end of this institution, is the peace and defence of them all; and whosoever has right to the end, has right to the means; it belongeth of right, to whatsoever man, or assembly that hath the sovereignty, to be judge both of the means of peace and defence, and also of the hindrances, and disturbances of the same; and to do whatsoever he shall think necessary to be done, both beforehand, for the preserving of peace and security, by prevention of discord at home, and hostility from abroad; and, when peace and security are lost, for the recovery of the same. And therefore,

Sixthly, it is annexed to the sovereignty, to be judge of what opinions and doctrines are averse, and what conducing to peace; and consequently, on what occasions, how far, and what men are to be trusted withal, in speaking to multitudes of people; and who shall examine the doctrines of all books before they be published. For the actions of men proceed from their opinions; and in the well-governing of opinions, consisteth the well-governing of men's actions, in order to their peace, and concord. And though in matter of doctrine, nothing ought to be regarded but the truth; yet this is not repugnant to regulating the same by peace. For doctrine repugnant to peace, can no more be true, than peace and concord can be against the law of nature. It is true, that in a commonwealth, where by the negligence, or unskilfulness of governors, and teachers, false doctrines are by time generally received; the contrary truths may be generally offensive. Yet the most sudden, and rough busling in of a new truth, that can be, does never break the peace, but only sometimes awake the war. For those men that are so remissly governed, that they dare take up arms to defend, or introduce an opinion, are still in war; and their condition not peace, but only a cessation of arms for fear of one another; and they live, as it were, in the precincts of battle continually. It belongeth therefore to him that hath the sovereign power, to be judge, or constitute all judges of opinions and doctrines, as a thing necessary to peace; thereby to prevent discord and civil war.

Seventhly, is annexed to the sovereignty, the whole power of prescribing the rules, whereby every man may know, what goods he may enjoy, and what actions he may do, without being molested by any of his fellow-subjects; and this is it men call *propriety*. For before constitution of sovereign power, as hath already been shown, all men had right to all things; which necessarily causeth war: and therefore this propriety, being necessary to peace, and depending on sovereign power, is the act of that power, in order to the public peace. These rules of propriety, or *meum* and *tuum*, and of *good, evil, lawful,* and *unlawful* in the actions of subjects, are the civil laws; that is to say, the laws of each commonwealth in particular; though the name of civil law be now restrained to the ancient civil laws of the city of Rome; which being the head of a great part of the world, her laws at that time were in these parts the civil law.

Eighthly, is annexed to the sovereignty, the right of judicature; that is to say, of hearing and deciding all controversies, which may arise concerning law, either civil, or natural; or concerning fact. For without the decision of controversies, there is no protection of one subject, against the injuries of another; the laws concerning *meum* and *tuum* are in vain; and to every man remaineth, from the natural and necessary appetite of his own conservation, the right of protecting himself by his private strength, which is the condition of war, and contrary to the end for which every commonwealth is instituted.

Ninthly, is annexed to the sovereignty, the right of making war and peace with other nations, and commonwealths; that is to say, of judging when it is for the public good, and how great forces are to be assembled, armed, and paid for that end; and to levy money upon the subjects, to defray the expenses thereof. For the power by which the people are to be defended, consisteth in their armies; and the strength of an army, in the union of their strength under one command; which command the sovereign instituted, therefore hath; because the command of the *militia,* without other institution, maketh him that hath it sovereign. And therefore whosoever is made general of an army, he that hath the sovereign power is always generalissimo.

* * *

This great authority being indivisible, and inseparably annexed to the sovereignty, there is little ground for the opinion of them, that say of sovereign kings, though they be *singulis majores,* of greater power than every one of their subjects, yet they be *universis minores,* of less power than them all together. For if by *all together,* they mean not the collective body as one person, then *all together,* and *every one,* signify the same; and the speech is absurd. But if by *all together,* they understand them as one person, which person the sovereign bears, then the power of all together, is the same with the sovereign's power; and so again the speech is absurd: which absurdity they see well enough, when the sovereignty is in an assembly of the people; but in a monarch they see it not; and yet the power of sovereignty is the same in whomsoever it be placed.

And as the power, so also the honour of the sovereign, ought to be greater, than that of any, or all the subjects. For in the sovereignty is the fountain of honour. The dignities of lord, earl, duke, and prince are his creatures. As in the presence of the master, the servants are equal, and without any honour at all; so are the subjects, in the presence of the sovereign. And though they shine some more, some less, when they are out of his sight; yet in his presence, they shine no more than the stars in the presence of the sun.

But a man may here object, that the condition of subjects is very miserable; as being obnoxious to the lusts, and other irregular passions of him, or them that have so unlimited a power in their hands. And commonly they that live under a monarch, think it the fault of monarchy; and they that live under the government of democracy, or other sovereign assembly, attribute all the inconvenience to that form of commonwealth; whereas the power in all forms, if they be perfect enough to protect them, is the same: not considering that the state of man can never be without some incommodity or other; and that the greatest, that in any form of government can possibly happen to the people in general, is scarce sensible in respect of the miseries, and horrible calamities, that accompany a civil war, or that dissolute condition of masterless men, without subjection to laws, and a coercive power to tie their hands from rapine and revenge: nor considering that the greatest pressure of sovereign governors, proceedeth not from any delight, or profit they can expect in the damage or weakening of their subjects, in whose vigour, consisteth their own strength and glory; but in the restiveness of themselves, that unwillingly contributing to their own defence, make it necessary for their governors to draw from them what they can in time of peace, that they may have means on any emergent occasion, or sudden need, to resist, or take advantage on their enemies. For all men are by nature provided of notable multiplying glasses, that is their passions and self-love, through which, every little payment appeareth a great grievance; but are destitute of those prospective glasses, namely moral and civil science, to see afar off the miseries that hang over them, and cannot without such payments be avoided.

•   •   •

OF THE OFFICE OF THE SOVEREIGN REPRESENTATIVE

The office of the sovereign, be it a monarch or an assembly, consisteth in the end, for which he was trusted with the sovereign power, namely the procuration of *the safety of the people;* to which he is obliged by the law of nature, and to render an account thereof to God, the author of that law, and to none but him. But by safety here, is not meant a bare preservation, but also all other contentments of life, which every man by lawful industry, without danger, or hurt to the commonwealth, shall acquire to himself.

And this is intended should be done, not by care applied to individuals, further than their protection from injuries, when they shall complain; but by a general providence, contained in public instruction, both of doctrine, and example; and in the making and executing of good laws, to which individual persons may apply their own cases.

And because, if the essential rights of sovereignty, specified before . . . be taken away, the commonwealth is thereby dissolved, and every man returneth into the condition, and calamity of a war with every other man, which is the greatest evil that can happen in this life; it is the office of the sovereign, to maintain those rights entire; and consequently against his duty, first, to transfer to another, or to lay from himself any of them. For he that deserteth the means, deserteth the ends; and he deserteth the means, that being the sovereign, acknowledgeth himself subject to the civil laws; and renounceth the power of supreme judicature; or of making war, or peace by his own authority; or of judging of the necessities of the commonwealth; or of levying money and soldiers, when, and as much as in his own conscience he shall judge necessary; or of making officers, and ministers both of war and peace; or of appointing teachers, and examining what doctrines are conformable, or contrary to the defence, peace, and good of the people. Secondly, it is against his duty, to let the people be ignorant, or misinformed of the grounds, and reasons of those his essential rights; because thereby men are easy to be seduced, and drawn to resist him, when the commonwealth shall require their use and exercise.

Blaise Pascal

4

Thoughts

Blaise Pascal (1623–1662) is famous both as a scientist-mathematician and as a Christian thinker and apologist. In his youth he was a mathematical prodigy who wrote a book on conic sections at the age of sixteen. Later, he went on to become a colleague of Descartes and other French scientists, to formulate "Pascal's principle" in physics, to invent one of the first computers, and to make important contributions to probability theory. At the age of twenty-three, he underwent a mystical experience which converted him to Jansenism, that austere, almost Calvinist version of Roman Catholicism. Some years later, after the death of his father, a worsening of his own physical condition, and another conversion experience in 1654, he gave up his scientific work, rejected the world in order to participate in the life of the Jansenist Community at Port Royal, and spent the rest of his life elaborating and defending his religious views. In recent years Pascal's reputation has rested more on his role as a precursor of modern religious existentialism than on his role as a scientist. After his final conversion, Pascal was torn between his first love for science and his new religious faith; his *Thoughts (Pensées)* are essentially an attempt to reconcile the method of science with the content of religion. He accepts Descartes' method of reaching certainty through total doubt, but rejects Descartes' conclusions. Reason is indeed the key to understanding nature, but is useless as a means of understanding and satisfying man's spiritual needs or of resolving the bewildering paradoxes of life. Reason cannot know God or prove his existence. The real test for such religious truths, according to Pascal, is not their rational consistency but their moral value. Moral certainty—the faith that life has some purpose and value—can come only from an act of will. Only such self-conscious choice distinguishes man from

Blaise Pascal, *Thoughts and Minor Works*, trans. W. F. Trotter *et al.*, in *Harvard Classics* (New York: Collier, 1910), XLVIII, 25–31, 42–43, 45, 62–64, 71–72, 77–79, 82, 98–99, 120, 124, 131–35, 137, 145–47, 150, 175. Reprinted with permission.

nature and raises him above the predicament of a miserable, blundering animal.

The *Thoughts* are the fragmentary notes for a defense of Christianity that Pascal wrote in his last years. They were first published, in imperfect and incomplete form, in 1670 (eight years after his death); a complete, scholarly edition appeared in 1844. Full of brilliant paradoxes and acute insights into human behavior, the *Thoughts* embody Pascal's anguished struggle to find certainty and his alternation between despair, mystical hope, and pious resignation. The selections given here have been rearranged in order to provide greater clarity and continuity.

When I consider the short duration of my life, swallowed up in the eternity before and after, the little space which I fill and even can see, engulfed in the infinite immensity of spaces of which I am ignorant and which know me not, I am frightened and am astonished at being here rather than there; for there is no reason why here rather than there, why now rather than then. Who has put me here? By whose order and direction have this place and time been allotted to me?

The eternal silence of these infinite spaces frightens me.

How many kingdoms know us not!

Why is my knowledge limited? Why my stature? Why my life to one hundred years rather than to a thousand? What reason has nature had for giving me such, and for choosing this number rather than another in the infinity of those from which there is no more reason to choose one than another, trying nothing else?

The last act is tragic, however happy all the rest of the play is; at the last a little earth is thrown upon our head, and that is the end for ever.

We are fools to depend upon the society of our fellow-men. Wretched as we are, powerless as we are, they will not aid us; we shall die alone. We should therefore act as if we were alone, and in that case should we build fine houses, etc. We should seek the truth without hesitation; and, if we refuse it, we show that we value the esteem of men more than the search for truth.

Between us and heaven or hell there is only life, which is the frailest thing in the world.

Let us imagine a number of men in chains and all condemned to death, where some are killed each day in the sight of the others, and those who remain see their own fate in that of their fellows and wait their turn, looking at each other sorrowfully and without hope. It is an image of the condition of men.

Let man then contemplate the whole of nature in her full and grand majesty, and turn his vision from the low objects which surround him. Let him gaze on that brilliant light, set like an eternal lamp to illumine the universe; let the earth appear to him a point in comparison with the vast circle described by the sun; and let him wonder at the fact that this vast circle is itself but a very fine point in comparison with that described by the stars in their revolution round the firmament. But if our view be arrested there, let our imagination pass beyond; it will sooner exhaust the power of conception than nature that of supplying material for conception. The whole visible world is only an imperceptible atom in the ample bosom of nature. No idea approaches it. We may enlarge our conceptions beyond all imaginable space; we only produce atoms in comparison with the reality of things. It is an infinite sphere, the centre of which is everywhere, the circumference nowhere. In short, it is the greatest sensible mark of the almighty power of God that imagination loses itself in that thought.

Returning to himself, let man consider what he is in comparison with all existence; let him regard himself as lost in this remote corner of nature; and from the little cell in which he finds himself lodged, I mean the universe, let him estimate at their true value the earth, kingdoms, cities, and himself. What is a man in the Infinite?

But to show him another prodigy equally astonishing, let him examine the most delicate things he knows. Let a mite be given him, with its minute body and parts incomparably more minute, limbs with their joints, veins in the limbs, blood in the veins, humours in the blood, drops in the humours, vapours in the drops. Dividing these last things again, let him exhaust his powers of conception, and let the last object at which he can arrive be now that of our discourse. Perhaps he will think that here is the smallest point in nature. I will let him see therein a new abyss. I will paint for him not only the visible universe, but all that he can conceive of nature's immensity in the womb of this abridged atom. Let him see therein an infinity of universes, each of which has its firmament, its planets, its earth, in the same proportion as in the visible world; in each earth animals, and in the last mites, in which he will find again all that the first had, finding still in these others the same thing without end and without cessation. Let him lose himself in wonders as amazing in their littleness as the others in their vastness. For who will not be astounded at the fact that our body, which a little while ago was imperceptible in the universe, itself imperceptible in the bosom of the whole, is now a colossus, a world, or rather a whole, in respect of the nothingness which we cannot reach? He who regards himself in this light will be afraid of himself, and observing himself sustained in the body given by nature between those two abysses of the Infinite and Nothing, will tremble at the sight of these marvels; and I think that, as his curiosity changes into admiration, he will be more disposed to contemplate them in silence than to examine them with presumption.

For, in fact, what is man in nature? A Nothing in comparison with the Infinite, an All in comparison with the Nothing, a mean between nothing and everything. Since he is infinitely removed from comprehending the extremes, the end of things and their beginning are hopelessly hidden from him in an impenetrable secret; he is equally incapable of seeing the Nothing from which he was made, and the Infinite in which he is swallowed up.

What will he do then, but perceive the appearance of the middle of things, in an eternal despair of knowing either their beginning or their end. All things proceed from the Nothing, and are borne towards the Infinite. Who will follow these marvellous processes? The Author of these wonders understands them. None other can do so.

Through failure to contemplate these Infinites, men have rashly rushed into the examination of nature, as though they bore some proportion to her. It is strange that they have wished to understand the beginnings of things, and thence to arrive at the knowledge of the whole, with a presumption as infinite as their object. For surely this design cannot be formed without presumption or without a capacity infinite like nature. . . . We naturally believe ourselves far more capable of reaching the centre of things than of embracing their circumference. The visible extent of the world visibly exceeds us; but as we exceed little things, we think ourselves more capable of knowing them. And yet we need no less capacity for attaining the Nothing than the All. Infinite capacity is required for both, and it seems to me that whoever shall have understood the ultimate principles of being might also attain to the knowledge of the Infinite. The one depends on the other, and one leads to the other. These extremes meet and reunite by force of distance and find each other in God, and in God alone.

Let us, then, take our compass; we are something, and we are not everything. The nature of our existence hides from us the knowledge of first beginnings which are born of the Nothing; and the littleness of our being conceals from us the sight of the Infinite.

Our intellect holds the same position in the world of thought as our body occupies in the expanse of nature.

Limited as we are in every way, this state which holds the mean between two extremes is present in all our impotence. Our senses perceive no extreme. Too much sound deafens us; too much light dazzles us; too great distance or proximity hinders our view. Too great length and too great brevity of discourse tend to obscurity; too much truth is paralysing (I know some who cannot understand that to take four from nothing leaves nothing). First principles are too self-evident for us; too much pleasure disagrees with us. Too many concords are annoying in music; too many benefits irritate us; we wish to have the wherewithal to overpay our debts. . . . We feel neither extreme heat nor extreme cold. Excessive qualities are prejudicial to us and not perceptible by the senses; we do not feel but suffer them. Extreme youth and extreme age hinder the mind, as also too much and too little education. In short, extremes are for us as though they were not, and we are not within their notice. They escape us, or we them.

This is our true state; this is what makes us incapable of certain knowledge and of absolute ignorance. We sail within a vast sphere, ever drifting in uncertainty, driven from end to end. When we think to attach ourselves to any point and to fasten to it, it wavers and leaves us; and if we follow it, it eludes our grasp, slips past us, and vanishes for ever. Nothing stays for us. This is our natural condition and yet most contrary to our inclination; we burn with desire to find solid ground and an ultimate sure foundation whereon to build a tower reaching to the Infinite. But our whole groundwork cracks, and the earth opens to abysses.

Let us, therefore, not look for certainty and stability. Our reason is always deceived by fickle shadows; nothing can fix the finite between the two Infinites, which both enclose and fly from it.

If this be well understood, I think that we shall remain at rest, each in the state wherein nature has placed him. As this sphere which has fallen to us as our lot is always distant from either extreme, what matters it that man should have a little more knowledge of the universe? If he has it, he but gets a little higher. Is he not always infinitely removed from the end, and is not the duration of our life equally removed from eternity, even if it lasts ten years longer?

In comparison with these Infinites, all finites are equal, and I see no reason for fixing our imagination on one more than on another. The only comparison which we make of ourselves to the finite is painful to us.

If man made himself the first object of study, he would see how incapable he is of going further. How can a part know the whole? But he may perhaps aspire to know at least the parts to which he bears some proportion. But the parts of the world are all so related and linked to one another that I believe it impossible to know one without the other and without the whole.

Man, for instance, is related to all he knows. He needs a place wherein to abide, time through which to live, motion in order to live, elements to compose him, warmth and food to nourish him, air to breathe. He sees light; he feels bodies; in short, he is in a dependent alliance with everything. To know man, then, it is necessary to know how it happens that he needs air to live, and, to know the air, we must know how it is thus related to the life of man, etc. Flame cannot exist without air; therefore, to understand the one, we must understand the other.

Since everything, then, is cause and effect, dependent and supporting, mediate and immediate, and all is held together by a natural though imperceptible chain which binds together things most distant and most different, I hold it equally impossible to know the parts without knowing the whole and to know the whole without knowing the parts in detail.

And what completes our incapability of knowing things is the fact that they are simple and that we are composed of two opposite natures, different in kind, soul and body. For it is impossible that our rational part should be other than spiritual; and if any one maintain that we are simply corporeal, this would far more exclude us from the knowledge of things, there being nothing so inconceivable as to say that matter knows itself. It is impossible to imagine how it should know itself.

So, if we are simply material, we can know nothing at all; and if we are composed of mind and matter, we cannot know perfectly things which are simple, whether spiritual or corporeal. Hence it comes that almost all philosophers have confused ideas of things, and speak of material things in spiritual terms, and of spiritual things in material terms. For they say boldly that bodies have a tendency to fall, that they seek after their centre, that they fly from destruction, that they fear the void, that they have inclinations, sympathies, antipathies, all of which attributes pertain only to mind. And in speaking of minds, they consider them as in a place, and attribute to them movement from one place or another; and these are qualities which belong only to bodies.

Instead of receiving the ideas of these things in their purity, we colour them with our own qualities, and stamp with our composite being all the simple things which we contemplate.

Who would not think, seeing us compose all things of mind and body, but that this mixture would be quite intelligible to us? Yet it is the very thing we least understand. Man is to himself the most wonderful object in nature; for he cannot conceive what the body is, still less what the mind is, and least of all how a body should be united to a mind. This is the consummation of his difficulties, and yet it is his very being. . . .

We do not require great education of the mind to understand that here is no real and lasting satisfaction; that our pleasures are only vanity; that our evils are infinite; and, lastly, that death, which threatens us every moment, must infallibly place us within a few years under the dreadful necessity of being for ever either annihilated or unhappy.

There is nothing more real than this, nothing more terrible. Be we as heroic as we like, that is the end which awaits the noblest life in the world. Let us reflect on this and then say whether it is not beyond doubt that there is no good in this life but in the hope of another; that we are happy only in proportion as we draw near it; and that, as there are no more woes for those who have complete assurance of eternity, so there is no more happiness for those who have no insight into it.

Surely then it is a great evil thus to be in doubt, but it is at least an indispensable duty to seek when we are in such doubt; and thus the doubter who does not seek is altogether completely unhappy and completely wrong. And if besides this he is easy and content, professes to be so, and indeed boasts of it; if it is this state itself which is the subject of his joy and vanity, I have no words to describe so silly a creature.

How can people hold these opinions? What joy can we find in the expectation of nothing but hopeless misery? What reason for boasting that we are in impenetrable darkness? . . .

This is what I see and what troubles me. I look on all sides, and I see only darkness everywhere. Nature presents to me nothing which is not matter of doubt and concern. If I saw nothing there which revealed a Divinity, I would come to a negative conclusion; if I saw everywhere the signs of a Creator, I would remain peacefully in faith. But, seeing too much to deny and too little to be sure, I am in a state to be pitied; wherefore I have a hundred times wished that if a God maintains Nature, she should testify to Him unequivocally, and that, if the signs she gives are deceptive, she should suppress them altogether; that she should say everything or nothing, that I might see which cause I ought to follow. Whereas in my present state, ignorant of what I am or of what I ought to do, I know neither my condition nor my duty. My heart inclines wholly to know where is the true good, in order to follow it; nothing would be too dear to me for eternity.

I envy those whom I see living in the faith with such carelessness and who make such a bad use of a gift of which it seems to me I would make such a different use.

Self-love.—The nature of self-love and of this human Ego is to love self only and consider self only. But what will man do? He cannot prevent this object that he loves from being full of faults and wants. He wants to be great, and he sees himself small. He wants to be happy, and he sees himself miserable. He wants to be perfect, and he sees himself full of imperfections. He wants to be the object of love and esteem among men, and he sees that his faults merit only their hatred and contempt. This embarrassment in which he finds himself produces in him the most unrighteous and criminal passion that can be imagined; for he conceives a mortal enmity against that truth which reproves him and which convinces him of his faults. He would annihilate it, but, unable to destroy it in its essence, he destroys it as far as possible in his own knowledge and in that of others; that is to say, he devotes all his attention to hiding his faults both from others and from himself, and he cannot endure either that others should point them out to him, or that they should see them.

Truly it is an evil to be full of faults; but it is a still greater evil to be full of them and to be unwilling to recognise them, since that is to add the further fault of a voluntary illusion. We do not like others to deceive us; we do not think it fair that they should be held in higher esteem by us than they deserve; it is not, then, fair that we should deceive them and should wish them to esteem us more highly than we deserve.

Thus, when they discover only the imperfections and vices which we really have, it is plain they do us no wrong, since it is not they who cause them; they rather do us good, since they help us to free ourselves from an evil, namely, the ignorance of these imperfections. We ought not to be angry at their knowing our faults and despising us; it is but right that they should know us for what we are and should despise us, if we are contemptible. . . . Man is, then, only disguise, falsehood, and hypocrisy, both in himself and in regard to others. He does not wish any one to tell him the truth; he avoids telling it to others, and all these dispositions, so removed from justice and reason, have a natural root in his heart.

Misery.—The only thing which consoles us for our miseries is diversion, and yet this is the greatest of our miseries. For it is this which principally hinders us from reflecting upon ourselves and which makes us insensibly ruin ourselves. Without this we should be in a state of weariness, and this weariness would spur us to seek a more solid means of escaping from it. But diversion amuses us, and leads us unconsciously to death.

He who will know fully the vanity of man has only to consider the causes and effects of love. The cause is a *je ne sais quoi* (Corneille), and the effects are dreadful. This *je ne sais quoi*, so small an object that we cannot recognise it, agitates a whole country, princes, armies, the entire world.

Cleopatra's nose: had it been shorter, the whole aspect of the world would have been altered.

The greatness of man.—The greatness of man is so evident that it is even proved by his wretchedness. For what in animals is *nature,* we call in man *wretchedness;* by which we recognise that, his nature being now like that of animals, he has fallen from a better nature which once was his. . . .

The greatness of man is great in that he knows himself to be miserable. A tree does not know itself to be miserable. It is then being miserable to know oneself to be miserable; but it is also being great to know that one is miserable.

All these same miseries prove man's greatness. They are the miseries of a great lord, of a deposed king.

Notwithstanding the sight of all our miseries, which press upon us and take us by the throat, we have an instinct which we cannot repress and which lifts us up.

Greatness and wretchedness.—Wretchedness being deduced from greatness, and greatness from wretchedness, some have inferred man's wretchedness all the more because they have taken his greatness as a proof of it, and others have inferred his greatness with all the more force, because they have inferred it from his very wretchedness. All that the one party has been able to say in proof of his greatness has only served as an argument of his wretchedness to the others, because the greater our fall, the more wretched we are, and *vice versa.* The one party is brought back to the other in an endless circle, it being certain that, in proportion as men possess light, they discover both the greatness and the wretchedness of man. In a word, man knows that he is wretched. He is therefore wretched, because he is so; but he is really great because he knows it.

Thought.—All the dignity of man consists in thought. Thought is, therefore, by its nature a wonderful and incomparable thing. It must have strange defects to be contemptible. But it has such, so that nothing is more ridiculous. How great it is in its nature! How vile it is in its defects!

But what is this thought? How foolish it is!

Thought constitutes the greatness of man.

Man is but a reed, the most feeble thing in nature; but he is a thinking reed. The entire universe need not arm itself to crush him. A vapour, a drop of water suffices to kill him. But, if the universe were to crush him, man would still be more noble than that which killed him, because he knows that he dies and the advantage which the universe has over him; the universe knows nothing of this.

All our dignity consists, then, in thought. By it we must elevate ourselves, and not by space and time which we cannot fill. Let us endeavour, then, to think well; this is the principle of morality.

A thinking reed.—It is not from space that I must seek my dignity, but from the government of my thought. I shall have no more if I possess worlds. By space the universe encompasses and swallows me up like an atom; by thought I comprehend the world.

There is internal war in man between reason and the passions.
If he had only reason without passions . . .
If he had only passions without reason . . .
But having both, he cannot be without strife, being unable to be at peace with the one without being at war with the other. Thus he is always divided against and opposed to himself.

There is nothing so conformable to reason as this disavowal of reason.

If we submit everything to reason, our religion will have no mysterious and supernatural element. If we offend the principles of reason, our religion will be absurd and ridiculous.

All our reasoning reduces itself to yielding to feeling.
But fancy is like, though contrary to, feeling, so that we cannot distinguish between these contraries. One person says that my feeling is fancy, another that his fancy is feeling. We should have a rule. Reason offers itself; but it is pliable in every sense; and thus there is no rule.

The heart has its reasons, which reason does not know. We feel it in a thousand things. I say that the heart naturally loves the Universal Being, and also itself naturally, according as it gives itself to them; and it hardens itself against one or the other at its will. You have rejected the one and kept the other. Is it by reason that you love yourself?

It is the heart which experiences God, and not the reason. This, then, is faith: God felt by the heart, not by the reason.

Instinct, reason.—We have an incapacity of proof, insurmountable by all dogmatism. We have an idea of truth, invincible to all scepticism.

We desire truth, and find within ourselves only uncertainty.
We seek happiness, and find only misery and death.
We cannot but desire truth and happiness, and are incapable of certainty or happiness. This desire is left to us, partly to punish us, partly to make us perceive wherefrom we are fallen.

There is an universal and essential difference between the actions of the will and all other actions.
The will is one of the chief factors in belief, not that it creates belief, but because things are true or false according to the aspect in which we look at them. The will, which prefers one aspect to another, turns away the mind from considering the qualities of all that it does not like to see; and thus the mind, moving in accord with the will, stops to consider the aspect which it likes and so judges by what it sees.

After having shown the vileness and the greatness of man.—Let man now know his value. Let him love himself, for there is in him a nature capable of good; let him not for this reason love the vileness which is in him. Let him despise himself, for this capacity is barren; but let him not therefore despise this natural capacity. Let him hate himself, let him love himself; he has within him the capacity of knowing the truth and of being happy, but he possesses no truth, either constant or satisfactory.

I would then lead man to the desire of finding truth; to be free from passions, and ready to follow it where he may find it, knowing how much his knowledge is obscured by the passions. I would, indeed, that he should hate in himself the lust which determined his will by itself so that it may not blind him in making his choice, and may not hinder him when he has chosen.

All these contradictions, which seem most to keep me from the knowledge of religion, have led me most quickly to the true one.

The chief arguments of the sceptics—I pass over the lesser ones —are that we have no certainty of the truth of these principles apart from faith and revelation, except in so far as we naturally perceive them in ourselves. Now this natural intuition is not a convincing proof of their truth; since, having no certainty, apart from faith, whether man was created by a good God, or by a wicked demon, or by chance, it is doubtful whether these principles given to us are true, or false, or uncertain, according to our origin. Again, no person is certain, apart from faith, whether he is awake or sleeps, seeing that during sleep we believe that we are awake as firmly as we do when we *are* awake; we believe that we see space, figure, and motion; we are aware of the passage of time, we measure it; and in fact we act as if we were awake. So that half of our life being passed in sleep, we have on our own admission no idea of truth, whatever we may imagine. As all our intuitions are, then, illusions, who knows whether the other half of our life, in which we think we are awake, is not another sleep a little different from the former, from which we awake when we suppose ourselves asleep?

These are the chief arguments on one side and the other.

I omit minor ones, such as the sceptical talk against the impressions of custom, education, manners, country and the like. Though these influence the majority of common folk, who dogmatise only on shallow foundations, they are upset by the least breath of the sceptics. We have only to see their books if we are not sufficiently convinced of this, and we shall very quickly become so, perhaps too much.

I notice the only strong point of the dogmatists, namely, that, speaking in good faith and sincerely, we cannot doubt natural principles. Against this the sceptics set up in one word the uncertainty of our origin, which includes that of our nature. The dogmatists have been trying to answer this objection ever since the world began.

So there is open war among men, in which each must take a part and side either with dogmatism or scepticism. For he who thinks to remain neutral is above all a sceptic. This neutrality is the essence of the sect; he who is not against them is essentially for them. [In this appears their advantage.] They are not for themselves; they are neutral, indifferent, in suspense as to all things, even themselves being no exception.

What, then, shall man do in this state? Shall he doubt everything? Shall he doubt whether he is awake, whether he is being pinched, or whether he is being burned? Shall he doubt whether he doubts?

Shall he doubt whether he exists? We cannot go so far as that; and I lay it down as a fact that there never has been a real complete sceptic. Nature sustains our feeble reason and prevents it raving to this extent.

Shall he, then, say, on the contrary, that he certainly possesses truth—he who, when pressed ever so little, can show no title to it and is forced to let go his hold?

What a chimera, then, is man! What a novelty! What a monster, what a chaos, what a contradiction, what a prodigy! Judge of all things, imbecile worm of the earth; depositary of truth, a sink of uncertainty and error; the pride and refuse of the universe!

Who will unravel this tangle? Nature confutes the sceptics, and reason confutes the dogmatists. What, then, will you become, O men! who try to find out by your natural reason what is your true condition? You cannot avoid one of these sects, nor adhere to one of them.

Know then, proud man, what a paradox you are to yourself. Humble yourself, weak reason; be silent, foolish nature; learn that man infinitely transcends man, and learn from your Master your true condition, of which you are ignorant. Hear God.

For in fact, if man had never been corrupt, he would enjoy in his innocence both truth and happiness with assurance; and if man had always been corrupt, he would have no idea of truth or bliss. But, wretched as we are, and more so than if there were no greatness in our condition, we have an idea of happiness and cannot reach it. We perceive an image of truth and possess only a lie. Incapable of absolute ignorance and of certain knowledge, we have thus been manifestly in a degree of perfection from which we have unhappily fallen.

Christianity is strange. It bids man recognise that he is vile, even abominable, and bids him desire to be like God. Without such a counterpoise, this dignity would make him horribly vain, or this humiliation would make him terribly abject.

With how little pride does a Christian believe himself united to God! With how little humiliation does he place himself on a level with the worms of earth!

A glorious manner to welcome life and death, good and evil!

Jean Racine

5

Phaedra

Jean Racine (1639–1699) was the greatest tragic dramatist of the French
neoclassical theater and, in the opinion of many, the greatest dramatist
in the modern world after Shakespeare. He was trained for a career in
the Church, and his work always retained the impress of the austere
Jansenism to which he had given his allegiance. When Racine turned to
literature, he achieved quick success and became a member of the company of literary lights that adorned the court of Louis XIV. His tragedies
were written in a manner that conformed admirably to the highly stylized,
cultivated court life of the Sun King. Then, at the height of his success,
Racine retired from the theater and its easy morals to a life of quiet,
domestic piety.

Racine's tragedies were modeled on those of the Greeks; in them, he
merged the Greek sense of fate with the Jansenist emphasis on original
sin. In contrast to the precious and complex subtleties of the baroque
manner, Racine's plays embodied the neoclassical ideals of order, symmetry,
and clarity. They may be seen as expressions of Cartesian rationalism in
drama, portraying in disciplined form and elevated language the universal, tragic aspects of the conflict of human passion with rational duty.
The controlled form served to accentuate the violence of the passions
portrayed. Dramatically, the characters determined the action: the pro-
tagonists were all persons of strong emotions who became the victims
of their feelings.

Phaedra (1677) is based on the *Hippolytus* of Euripides but differs
from its model in making the queen the heroine. The play shuns the
framework of workaday reality and physical details and concentrates on
the timeless and the universal. Despite this abstract quality, it is rooted
in the real truths of human feelings. It is the story of the overwhelming
passion of Phaedra for Hippolytus, her stepson. The queen is torn be-

Jean Racine, *Phaedra*, trans. Robert B. Boswell, in *Plays by Greek, Spanish,
French, German, and English Dramatists* (New York: Colonial, 1900), I, 326–75.

tween her desire and her sense of sin and, after suffering remorse and
horror over the consequences of her guilty passion, is driven to her tragic
doom.

DRAMATIS PERSONAE

THESEUS, *Son of Aegeus and King of Athens*
PHAEDRA, *Wife of Theseus and Daughter of Minos and Pasiphaë*
HIPPOLYTUS, *Son of Theseus and Antiope, Queen of the Amazons*
ARICIA, *Princess of the Blood Royal of Athens*
OENONE, *Nurse of Phaedra*
THERAMENES, *Tutor of Hippolytus*
ISMENE, *bosom friend of Aricia*
PANOPE, *Waiting-woman of Phaedra*
GUARDS

The scene is laid at Troezen, a town of the Peloponnesus

ACT ONE

SCENE I

Hippolytus, Theramenes

HIPPOLYTUS   My mind is settled, dear Theramenes,
And I can stay no more in lovely Troezen.
In doubt that racks my soul with mortal anguish,
I grow ashamed of such long idleness.
Six months and more my father has been gone,
And what may have befallen one so dear
I know not, nor what corner of the earth
Hides him.
    THERAMENES   And where, prince, will you look for him?
Already, to content your just alarm,
Have I not cross'd the seas on either side
Of Corinth, ask'd if aught were known of Theseus
Where Acheron is lost among the Shades,
Visited Elis, doubled Toenarus,
And sail'd into the sea that saw the fall

Of Icarus? Inspired with what new hope,
Under what favor'd skies think you to trace
His footsteps? Who knows if the King, your father,
Wishes the secret of his absence known?
Perchance, while we are trembling for his life,
The hero calmly plots some fresh intrigue,
And only waits till the deluded fair—

    HIPPOLYTUS   Cease, dear Theramenes, respect the name
Of Theseus. Youthful errors have been left
Behind, and no unworthy obstacle
Detains him. Phaedra long has fix'd a heart
Inconstant once, nor need she fear a rival.
In seeking him I shall but do my duty,
And leave a place I dare no longer see.

    THERAMENES   Indeed! When, prince, did you begin to dread
These peaceful haunts, so dear to happy childhood,
Where I have seen you oft prefer to stay,
Rather than meet the tumult and the pomp
Of Athens and the court? What danger shun you,
Or shall I say what grief?

    HIPPOLYTUS   That happy time
Is gone, and all is changed, since to these shores
The gods sent Phaedra.

    THERAMENES   I perceive the cause
Of your distress. It is the queen whose sight
Offends you. With a step-dame's spite she schemed
Your exile soon as she set eyes on you.
But if her hatred is not wholly vanish'd,
It has at least taken a milder aspect.
Besides, what danger can a dying woman,
One too who longs for death, bring on your head?
Can Phaedra, sick'ning of a dire disease
Of which she will not speak, weary of life
And of herself, form any plots against you?

    HIPPOLYTUS   It is not her vain enmity I fear:
Another foe alarms Hippolytus.
I fly, it must be own'd, from young Aricia,
The sole survivor of an impious race.

    THERAMENES   What! You become her persecutor too!

The gentle sister of the cruel sons
Of Pallas shared not in their perfidy;
Why should you hate such charming innocence?

HIPPOLYTUS   I should not need to fly, if it were hatred.

THERAMENES   May I then learn the meaning of your flight?
Is this the proud Hippolytus I see,
Than whom there breathed no fiercer foe to love
And to that yoke which Theseus has so oft
Endured? And can it be that Venus, scorn'd
So long, will justify your sire at last?
Has she, then, setting you with other mortals,
Forced e'en Hippolytus to offer incense
Before her? Can you love?

HIPPOLYTUS   Friend, ask me not.
You, who have known my heart from infancy
And all its feelings of disdainful pride,
Spare me the shame of disavowing all
That I profess'd. Born of an Amazon,
The wildness that you wonder at I suck'd
With mother's milk. When come to riper age,
Reason approved what Nature had implanted.
Sincerely bound to me by zealous service,
You told me then the story of my sire,
And know how oft, attentive to your voice,
I kindled when I heard his noble acts,
As you described him bringing consolation
To mortals for the absence of Alcides,
The highways clear'd of monsters and of robbers,
Procrustes, Cercyon, Sciro, Sinnis slain,
The Epidaurian giant's bones dispersed,
Crete reeking with the blood of Minotaur.
But when you told me of less glorious deeds,
Troth plighted here and there and everywhere,
Young Helen stolen from her home at Sparta,
And Periboea's tears in Salamis,
With many another trusting heart deceived
Whose very names have 'scaped his memory,
Forsaken Ariadne to the rocks
Complaining last, this Phaedra, bound to him
By better ties—you know with what regret

I heard and urged you to cut short the tale,
Happy had I been able to erase
From my remembrance that unworthy part
Of such a splendid record. I, in turn,
Am I too made the slave of love, and brought
To stoop so low? The more contemptible
That no renown is mine such as exalts
The name of Theseus, that no monsters quell'd
Have given me a right to share his weakness.
And if my pride of heart must needs be humbled,
Aricia should have been the last to tame it.
Was I beside myself to have forgotten
Eternal barriers of separation
Between us? By my father's stern command
Her brethren's blood must ne'er be reinforced
By sons of hers; he dreads a single shoot
From stock so guilty, and would fain with her
Bury their name, that, even to the tomb
Content to be his ward, for her no torch
Of Hymen may be lit. Shall I espouse
Her rights against my sire, rashly provoke   •
His wrath, and launch upon a mad career—
    THERAMENES   The gods, dear prince, if once your hour is
    come,
Care little for the reasons that should guide us.
Wishing to shut your eyes, Theseus unseals them;
His hatred, stirring a rebellious flame
Within you, lends his enemy new charms.
And, after all, why should a guiltless passion
Alarm you? Dare you not essay its sweetness,
But follow rather a fastidious scruple?
Fear you to stray where Hercules has wander'd?
What heart so stout that Venus has not vanquish'd?
Where would you be yourself, so long her foe,
Had your own mother, constant in her scorn
Of love, ne'er glowed with tenderness for Theseus?
What boots it to affect a pride you feel not?
Confess it, all is changed; for some time past
You have been seldom seen with wild delight
Urging the rapid car along the strand,

Or, skilful in the art that Neptune taught,
Making th' unbroken steed obey the bit;
Less often have the woods return'd your shouts;
A secret burden on your spirits cast
Has dimm'd your eye. How can I doubt you love?
Vainly would you conceal the fatal wound.
Has not the fair Aricia touch'd your heart?

    HIPPOLYTUS   Theramenes, I go to find my father.

    THERAMENES   Will you not see the queen before you start,
My prince?

    HIPPOLYTUS   That is my purpose: you can tell her.
Yes, I will see her; duty bids me do it.
But what new ill vexes her dear Oenone?

SCENE II

Hippolytus, Oenone, Theramenes

    OENONE   Alas, my lord, what grief was e'er like mine?
The queen has almost touch'd the gates of death.
Vainly close watch I keep by day and night,
E'en in my arms a secret malady
Slays her, and all her senses are disorder'd.
Weary yet restless from her couch she rises,
Pants for the outer air, but bids me see
That no one on her misery intrudes.
She comes.

    HIPPOLYTUS   Enough. She shall not be disturb'd,
Nor be confronted with a face she hates.

SCENE III

Phaedra, Oenone

    PHAEDRA   We have gone far enough. Stay, dear Oenone;
Strength fails me, and I needs must rest awhile.
My eyes are dazzled with this glaring light
So long unseen, my trembling knees refuse
Support. Ah me!

    OENONE   Would Heaven that our tears
Might bring relief!

    PHAEDRA   Ah, how these cumbrous gauds,
These veils oppress me! What officious hand

Has tied these knots, and gather'd o'er my brow
These clustering coils? How all conspires to add
To my distress!

OENONE   What is one moment wish'd,
The next, is irksome. Did you not just now,
Sick of inaction, bid us deck you out,
And, with your former energy recall'd,
Desire to go abroad, and see the light
Of day once more? You see it, and would fain
Be hidden from the sunshine that you sought.

PHAEDRA   Thou glorious author of a hapless race,
Whose daughter 'twas my mother's boast to be,
Who well may'st blush to see me in such plight,
For the last time I come to look on thee,
O Sun!

OENONE   What! Still are you in love with death?
Shall I ne'er see you, reconciled to life,
Forego these cruel accents of despair?

PHAEDRA   Would I were seated in the forest's shade!
When may I follow with delighted eye,
Thro' glorious dust flying in full career,
A chariot—

OENONE   Madam?

PHAEDRA   Have I lost my senses?
What said I? and where am I? Whither stray
Vain wishes? Ah! The gods have made me mad.
I blush, Oenone, and confusion covers
My face, for I have let you see too clearly
The shame and grief that, in my own despite,
O'erflow these eyes of mine.

OENONE   If you must blush,
Blush at a silence that inflames your woes.
Resisting all my care, deaf to my voice,
Will you have no compassion on yourself,
But let your life be ended in mid course?
What evil spell has drain'd its fountain dry?
Thrice have the shades of night obscured the heav'ns
Since sleep has enter'd thro' your eyes, and thrice
The dawn has chased the darkness thence, since food
Pass'd your wan lips, and you are faint and languid.

To what dread purpose is your heart inclined?
How dare you make attempts upon your life,
And so offend the gods who gave it you,
Prove false to Theseus and your marriage vows,
Ay, and betray your most unhappy children,
Bending their necks yourself beneath the yoke?
That day, be sure, which robs them of their mother,
Will give high hopes back to the stranger's son,
To that proud enemy of you and yours,
To whom an Amazon gave birth, I mean
Hippolytus—

PHAEDRA   Ye gods!

OENONE   Ah, this reproach
Moves you!

PHAEDRA   Unhappy woman, to what name
Gave your mouth utterance?

OENONE   Your wrath is just.
'Tis well that that ill-omen'd name can rouse
Such rage. Then live. Let love and duty urge
Their claims. Live, suffer not this son of Scythia,
Crushing your children 'neath his odious sway,
To rule the noble offspring of the gods,
The purest blood of Greece. Make no delay;
Each moment threatens death; quickly restore
Your shatter'd strength, while yet the torch of life
Holds out, and can be fann'd into a flame.

PHAEDRA   Too long have I endured its guilt and shame!

OENONE   Why? What remorse gnaws at your heart? What
  crime
Can have disturb'd you thus? Your hands are not
Polluted with the blood of innocence?

PHAEDRA   Thanks be to Heav'n, my hands are free from
  stain.
Would that my soul were innocent as they!

OENONE   What awful project have you then conceived,
Whereat your conscience should be still alarm'd?

PHAEDRA   Have I not said enough? Spare me the rest.
I die to save myself a full confession.

OENONE   Die then, and keep a silence so inhuman;
But seek some other hand to close your eyes.

Tho' but a spark of life remains within you,
My soul shall go before you to the Shades.
A thousand roads are always open thither;
Pain'd at your want of confidence, I'll choose
The shortest. Cruel one, when has my faith
Deceived you? Think how in my arms you lay
New born. For you, my country and my children
I have forsaken. Do you thus repay
My faithful service?

    PHAEDRA   What do you expect
From words so bitter? Were I to break silence,
Horror would freeze your blood.

    OENONE   What can you say
To horrify me more than to behold
You die before my eyes?

    PHAEDRA   When you shall know
My crime, my death will follow none the less,
But with the added stain of guilt.

    OENONE   Dear Madam,
By all the tears that I have shed for you,
By these weak knees I clasp, relieve my mind
From torturing doubt.

    PHAEDRA   It is your wish. Then rise.

    OENONE   I hear you. Speak.

    PHAEDRA   Heav'ns! How shall I begin?

    OENONE   Dismiss vain fears, you wound me with distrust.

    PHAEDRA   O fatal animosity of Venus!
Into what wild distractions did she cast
My mother!

    OENONE   Be they blotted from remembrance,
And for all time to come buried in silence.

    PHAEDRA   My sister Ariadne, by what love
Were you betray'd to death, on lonely shores
Forsaken!

    OENONE   Madam, what deep-seated pain
Prompts these reproaches against all your kin?

    PHAEDRA   It is the will of Venus, and I perish,
Last, most unhappy of a family
Where all were wretched.

    OENONE   Do you love?

PHAEDRA   I feel
All its mad fever.

OENONE   Ah! For whom?

PHAEDRA   Hear now
The crowning horror. Yes, I love—my lips
Tremble to say his name.

OENONE   Whom?

PHAEDRA   Know you him,
Son of the Amazon, whom I've oppress'd
So long?

OENONE   Hippolytus? Great gods!

PHAEDRA   'Tis you
Have named him.

OENONE   All my blood within my veins
Seems frozen. O despair; O cursèd race!
Ill-omen'd journey! Land of misery!
Why did we ever reach thy dangerous shores?

PHAEDRA   My wound is not so recent. Scarcely had I
Been bound to Theseus by the marriage yoke,
And happiness and peace seem'd well secured,
When Athens show'd me my proud enemy.
I look'd, alternately turn'd pale and blush'd
To see him, and my soul grew all distraught;
A mist obscured my vision, and my voice
Falter'd, my blood ran cold, then burn'd like fire;
Venus I felt in all my fever'd frame,
Whose fury had so many of my race
Pursued. With fervent vows I sought to shun
Her torments, built and deck'd for her a shrine,
And there, 'mid countless victims did I seek
The reason I had lost; but all for nought,
No remedy could cure the wounds of love!
In vain I offer'd incense on her altars;
When I invoked her name, my heart adored
Hippolytus, before me constantly;
And when I made her altars smoke with victims,
'Twas for a god whose name I dared not utter.
I fled his presence everywhere, but found him—
O crowning horror!—in his father's features.
Against myself, at last, I raised revolt,

And stirr'd my courage up to persecute
The enemy I loved. To banish him
I wore a step-dame's harsh and jealous carriage,
With ceaseless cries I clamor'd for his exile,
Till I had torn him from his father's arms.
I breathed once more, Oenone; in his absence
My days flow'd on less troubled than before,
And innocent. Submissive to my husband,
I hid my grief, and of our fatal marriage
Cherish'd the fruits. Vain caution! Cruel Fate!
Brought hither by my spouse himself, I saw
Again the enemy whom I had banish'd,
And the old wound too quickly bled afresh.
No longer is it love hid in my heart,
But Venus in her might seizing her prey.
I have conceived just terror for my crime;
I hate my life, and hold my love in horror.
Dying I wish'd to keep my fame unsullied,
And bury in the grave a guilty passion;
But I have been unable to withstand
Tears and entreaties, I have told you all;
Content, if only, as my end draws near,
You do not vex me with unjust reproaches,
Nor with vain efforts seek to snatch from death
The last faint lingering sparks of vital breath.

SCENE IV

Phaedra, Oenone, Panope

PANOPE   Fain would I hide from you tidings so sad,
But 'tis my duty, Madam, to reveal them.
The hand of death has seized your peerless husband,
And you are last to hear of this disaster.
  OENONE   What say you, Panope?
  PANOPE   The queen, deceived
By a vain trust in Heav'n, begs safe return
For Theseus, while Hippolytus his son
Learns of his death from vessels that are now
In port.
  PHAEDRA   Ye gods!

PANOPE   Divided counsels sway
The choice of Athens; some would have the prince,
Your child, for master; others, disregarding
The laws, dare to support the stranger's son.
'Tis even said that a presumptuous faction
Would crown Aricia and the house of Pallas.
I deem'd it right to warn you of this danger.
Hippolytus already is prepared
To start, and should he show himself at Athens,
'Tis to be fear'd the fickle crowd will all
Follow his lead.

OENONE   Enough. The queen, who hears you,
By no means will neglect this timely warning.

SCENE V

Phaedra, Oenone

OENONE   Dear lady, I had almost ceased to urge
The wish that you should live, thinking to follow
My mistress to the tomb, from which my voice
Had fail'd to turn you; but this new misfortune
Alters the aspect of affairs, and prompts
Fresh measures. Madam, Theseus is no more,
You must supply his place. He leaves a son,
A slave, if you should die, but, if you live,
A King. On whom has he to lean but you?
No hand but yours will dry his tears. Then live
For him, or else the tears of innocence
Will move the gods, his ancestors, to wrath
Against his mother. Live, your guilt is gone,
No blame attaches to your passion now.
The King's decease has freed you from the bonds
That made the crime and horror of your love.
Hippolytus no longer need be dreaded,
Him you may see henceforth without reproach.
It may be, that, convinced of your aversion,
He means to head the rebels. Undeceive him,
Soften his callous heart, and bend his pride.
King of this fertile land, in Troezen here
His portion lies; but as he knows, the laws

Give to your son the ramparts that Minerva
Built and protects. A common enemy
Threatens you both, unite then to oppose
Aricia.

    PHAEDRA To your counsel I consent.
Yes, I will live, if life can be restored,
If my affection for a son has pow'r
To rouse my sinking heart at such a dangerous hour.

ACT TWO

SCENE I

Aricia, Ismene

    ARICIA Hippolytus request to see me here!
Hippolytus desire to bid farewell!
Is 't true, Ismene? Are you not deceived?

    ISMENE This is the first result of Theseus' death.
Prepare yourself to see from every side
Hearts turn toward you that were kept away
By Theseus. Mistress of her lot at last,
Aricia soon shall find all Greece fall low,
To do her homage.

    ARICIA   'Tis not then, Ismene,
An idle tale? Am I no more a slave?
Have I no enemies?

    ISMENE   The gods oppose
Your peace no longer, and the soul of Theseus
Is with your brothers.

    ARICIA   Does the voice of fame
Tell how he died?

    ISMENE   Rumors incredible
Are spread. Some say that, seizing a new bride,
The faithless husband by the waves was swallow'd.
Others affirm, and this report prevails,
That with Pirithoüs to the world below
He went, and saw the shores of dark Cocytus,
Showing himself alive to the pale ghosts;
But that he could not leave those gloomy realms,
Which whoso enters there abides forever.

    ARICIA Shall I believe that ere his destined hour

A mortal may descend into the gulf
Of Hades? What attraction could o'ercome
Its terrors?

ISMENE   He is dead, and you alone
Doubt it. The men of Athens mourn his loss.
Troezen already hails Hippolytus
As King. And Phaedra, fearing for her son,
Asks counsel of the friends who share her trouble,
Here in this palace.

ARICIA   Will Hippolytus,
Think you, prove kinder than his sire, make light
My chains, and pity my misfortunes?

ISMENE   Yes,
I think so, Madam.

ARICIA   Ah, you know him not
Or you would never deem so hard a heart
Can pity feel, or me alone except
From the contempt in which he holds our sex.
Has he not long avoided every spot
Where we resort?

ISMENE   I know what tales are told
Of proud Hippolytus, but I have seen
Him near you, and have watch'd with curious eye
How one esteem'd so cold would bear himself.
Little did his behavior correspond
With what I look'd for; in his face confusion
Appear'd at your first glance, he could not turn
His languid eyes away, but gazed on you.
Love is a word that may offend his pride,
But what the tongue disowns, looks can betray.

ARICIA   How eagerly my heart hears what you say,
Tho' it may be delusion, dear Ismene!
Did it seem possible to you, who know me,
That I, sad sport of a relentless Fate,
Fed upon bitter tears by night and day,
Could ever taste the maddening draught of love?
The last frail offspring of a royal race,
Children of Earth, I only have survived
War's fury. Cut off in the flow'r of youth,
Mown by the sword, six brothers have I lost,

The hope of an illustrious house, whose blood
Earth drank with sorrow, near akin to his
Whom she herself produced. Since then, you know
How thro' all Greece no heart has been allow'd
To sigh for me, lest by a sister's flame
The brothers' ashes be perchance rekindled.
You know, besides, with what disdain I view'd
My conqueror's suspicions and precautions,
And how, opposed as I have ever been
To love, I often thank'd the King's injustice
Which happily confirm'd my inclination.
But then I never had beheld his son.
Not that, attracted merely by the eye,
I love him for his beauty and his grace,
Endowments which he owes to Nature's bounty,
Charms which he seems to know not or to scorn.
I love and prize in him riches more rare,
The virtues of his sire, without his faults.
I love, as I must own, that generous pride
Which ne'er has stoop'd beneath the amorous yoke.
Phaedra reaps little glory from a lover
So lavish of his sighs; I am too proud
To share devotion with a thousand others,
Or enter where the door is always open.
But to make one who ne'er has stoop'd before
Bend his proud neck, to pierce a heart of stone,
To bind a captive whom his chains astonish,
Who vainly 'gainst a pleasing yoke rebels—
That piques my ardor, and I long for that.
'Twas easier to disarm the god of strength
Than this Hippolytus, for Hercules
Yielded so often to the eyes of beauty,
As to make triumph cheap. But, dear Ismene,
I take too little heed of opposition
Beyond my pow'r to quell, and you may hear me,
Humbled by sore defeat, upbraid the pride
I now admire. What! Can he love? and I
Have had the happiness to bend—

ISMENE   He comes.
Yourself shall hear him.

SCENE II

Hippolytus, Aricia, Ismene

HIPPOLYTUS   Lady, ere I go
My duty bids me tell you of your change
Of fortune. My worst fears are realized;
My sire is dead. Yes, his protracted absence
Was caused as I foreboded. Death alone,
Ending his toils, could keep him from the world
Conceal'd so long. The gods at last have doom'd
Alcides' friend, companion, and successor.
I think your hatred, tender to his virtues,
Can hear such terms of praise without resentment,
Knowing them due. One hope have I that soothes
My sorrow: I can free you from restraint.
Lo, I revoke the laws whose rigor moved
My pity; you are at your own disposal,
Both heart and hand; here, in my heritage,
In Troezen, where my grandsire Pittheus reign'd
Of yore and I am now acknowledged King,
I leave you free, free as myself—and more.

ARICIA   Your kindness is too great, 'tis overwhelming.
Such generosity, that pays disgrace
With honor, lends more force than you can think
To those harsh laws from which you would release me.

HIPPOLYTUS   Athens, uncertain how to fill the throne
Of Theseus, speaks of you, anon of me,
And then of Phaedra's son.

ARICIA   Of me, my lord?

HIPPOLYTUS   I know myself excluded by strict law:
Greece turns to my reproach a foreign mother.
But if my brother were my only rival,
My rights prevail o'er his clearly enough
To make me careless of the law's caprice.
My forwardness is check'd by juster claims:
To you I yield my place, or, rather, own
That it is yours by right, and yours the sceptre,
As handed down from Earth's great son, Erechtheus.
Adoption placed it in the hands of Aegeus:

Athens, by him protected and increased,
Welcomed a king so generous as my sire,
And left your hapless brothers in oblivion.
Now she invites you back within her walls;
Protracted strife has cost her groans enough,
Her fields are glutted with your kinsmen's blood
Fatt'ning the furrows out of which it sprung
At first. I rule this Troezen; while the son
Of Phaedra has in Crete a rich domain.
Athens is yours. I will do all I can
To join for you the votes divided now
Between us.

    ARICIA   Stunn'd at all I hear, my lord,
I fear, I almost fear a dream deceives me.
Am I indeed awake? Can I believe
Such generosity? What god has put it
Into your heart? Well is the fame deserved
That you enjoy! That fame falls short of truth!
Would you for me prove traitor to yourself?
Was it not boon enough never to hate me,
So long to have abstain'd from harboring
The enmity—

    HIPPOLYTUS   To hate you? I, to hate you?
However darkly my fierce pride was painted,
Do you suppose a monster gave me birth?
What savage temper, what envenom'd hatred
Would not be mollified at sight of you?
Could I resist the soul-bewitching charm—

    ARICIA Why, what is this, Sir?

    HIPPOLYTUS   I have said too much
Not to say more. Prudence in vain resists
The violence of passion. I have broken
Silence at last, and I must tell you now
The secret that my heart can hold no longer.

    You see before you an unhappy instance
Of hasty pride, a prince who claims compassion.
I, who, so long the enemy of Love,
Mock'd at his fetters and despised his captives,
Who, pitying poor mortals that were shipwreck'd,
In seeming safety view'd the storms from land,

Now find myself to the same fate exposed,
Toss'd to and fro upon a sea of troubles!
My boldness has been vanquish'd in a moment,
And humbled is the pride wherein I boasted.
For nearly six months past, ashamed, despairing,
Bearing where'er I go the shaft that rends
My heart, I struggle vainly to be free
From you and from myself; I shun you, present;
Absent, I find you near; I see your form
In the dark forest depths; the shades of night,
Nor less broad daylight, bring back to my view
The charms that I avoid; all things conspire
To make Hippolytus your slave. For fruit
Of all my bootless sighs, I fail to find
My former self. My bow and javelins
Please me no more, my chariot is forgotten,
With all the Sea-God's lessons; and the woods
Echo my groans instead of joyous shouts
Urging my fiery steeds.
                            Hearing this tale
Of passion so uncouth, you blush perchance
At your own handiwork. With what wild words
I offer you my heart, strange captive held
By silken jess! But dearer in your eyes
Should be the offering, that this language comes
Strange to my lips; reject not vows express'd
So ill, which but for you had ne'er been form'd.

SCENE III

Hippolytus, Aricia, Theramenes, Ismene

THERAMENES Prince, the Queen comes. I herald her approach.
'Tis you she seeks.
      HIPPOLYTUS   Me?
      THERAMENES   What her thought may be
I know not. But I speak on her behalf.
She would converse with you ere you go hence.
      HIPPOLYTUS What shall I say to her? Can she expect—

ARICIA   You cannot, noble Prince, refuse to hear her,
Howe'er convinced she is your enemy,
Some shade of pity to her tears is due.

HIPPOLYTUS   Shall we part thus? and will you let me go,
Not knowing if my boldness has offended
The goddess I adore? Whether this heart,
Left in your hands—

ARICIA   Go, Prince, pursue the schemes
Your generous soul dictates, make Athens own
My sceptre. All the gifts you offer me
Will I accept, but this high throne of empire
Is not the one most precious in my sight.

SCENE IV

Hippolytus, Theramenes

HIPPOLYTUS   Friend, is all ready? But the Queen approaches.
Go, see the vessel in fit trim to sail.
Haste, bid the crew aboard, and hoist the signal;
Then soon return, and so deliver me
From interview most irksome.

SCENE V

Phaedra, Hippolytus, Oenone

PHAEDRA [*to Oenone*]   There I see him!
My blood forgets to flow, my tongue to speak
What I am come to say.

OENONE   Think of your son,
How all his hopes depend on you.

PHAEDRA   I hear
You leave us, and in haste. I come to add
My tears to your distress, and for a son
Plead my alarm. No more has he a father,
And at no distant day my son must witness
My death. Already do a thousand foes
Threaten his youth. You only can defend him.
But in my secret heart remorse awakes,
And fear lest I have shut your ears against

His cries. I tremble lest your righteous anger
Visit on him ere long the hatred earn'd
By me, his mother.

HIPPOLYTUS   No such base resentment,
Madam, is mine.

PHAEDRA   I could not blame you, Prince,
If you should hate me. I have injured you:
So much you know, but could not read my heart.
T' incur your enmity has been mine aim:
The self-same borders could not hold us both;
In public and in private I declared
Myself your foe, and found no peace till seas
Parted us from each other. I forbade
Your very name to be pronounced before me.
And yet if punishment should be proportion'd
To the offence, if only hatred draws
Your hatred, never woman merited
More pity, less deserved your enmity.

HIPPOLYTUS   A mother jealous of her children's rights
Seldom forgives the offspring of a wife
Who reign'd before her. Harassing suspicions
Are common sequels of a second marriage.
Of me would any other have been jealous
No less than you, perhaps more violent?

PHAEDRA   Ah, Prince, how Heav'n has from the general
    law
Made me exempt, be that same Heav'n my witness!
Far different is the trouble that devours me!

HIPPOLYTUS   This is no time for self-reproaches, Madam.
It may be that your husband still beholds
The light, and Heav'n may grant him safe return,
In answer to our prayers. His guardian god
Is Neptune, ne'er by him invoked in vain.

PHAEDRA   He who has seen the mansions of the dead
Returns not thence. Since to those gloomy shores
Theseus is gone, 'tis vain to hope that Heav'n
May send him back. Prince, there is no release
From Acheron's greedy maw. And yet, methinks,
He lives, and breathes in you. I see him still
Before me, and to him I seem to speak;

My heart—
       Oh! I am mad; do what I will,
I cannot hide my passion.

HIPPOLYTUS   Yes, I see
The strange effects of love. Theseus, tho' dead,
Seems present to your eyes, for in your soul
There burns a constant flame.

PHAEDRA   Ah, yes, for Theseus
I languish and I long, not as the Shades
Have seen him, of a thousand different forms
The fickle lover, and of Pluto's bride
The would-be ravisher, but faithful, proud
E'en to a slight disdain, with youthful charms
Attracting every heart, as gods are painted,
Or like yourself. He had your mien, your eyes,
Spoke and could blush like you, when to the isle
Of Crete, my childhood's home, he cross'd the waves,
Worthy to win the love of Minos' daughters.
What were you doing then? Why did he gather
The flow'r of Greece, and leave Hippolytus?
Oh, why were you too young to have embark'd
On board the ship that brought thy sire to Crete?
At your hands would the monster then have perish'd,
Despite the windings of his vast retreat.
To guide your doubtful steps within the maze
My sister would have arm'd you with the clue.
But no, therein would Phaedra have forestall'd her,
Love would have first inspired me with the thought;
And I it would have been whose timely aid
Had taught you all the labyrinth's crooked ways.
What anxious care a life so dear had cost me!
No thread had satisfied your lover's fears:
I would myself have wish'd to lead the way,
And share the peril you were bound to face;
Phaedra with you would have explored the maze,
With you emerged in safety, or have perish'd.

HIPPOLYTUS   Gods! What is this I hear? Have you **forgotten**
That Theseus is my father and your husband?

PHAEDRA   Why should you fancy I have lost remembrance
Thereof, and am regardless of mine honor?

HIPPOLYTUS   Forgive me, Madam. With a blush I own
That I misconstrued words of innocence.
For very shame I cannot bear your sight
Longer. I go—
    PHAEDRA   Ah! cruel Prince, too well
You understood me. I have said enough
To save you from mistake. I love. But think not
That at the moment when I love you most
I do not feel my guilt; no weak compliance
Has fed the poison that infects my brain.
The ill-starr'd object of celestial vengeance,
I am not so detestable to you
As to myself. The gods will bear me witness,
Who have within my veins kindled this fire,
The gods, who take a barbarous delight
In leading a poor mortal's heart astray.
Do you yourself recall to mind the past:
'Twas not enough for me to fly, I chased you
Out of the country, wishing to appear
Inhuman, odious; to resist you better,
I sought to make you hate me. All in vain!
Hating me more I loved you none the less:
New charms were lent to you by your misfortunes.
I have been drown'd in tears, and scorch'd by fire;
Your own eyes might convince you of the truth,
If for one moment you could look at me.
What is 't I say? Think you this vile confession
That I have made is what I meant to utter?
Not daring to betray a son for whom
I trembled, 'twas to beg you not to hate him
I came. Weak purpose of a heart too full
Of love for you to speak of aught besides!
Take your revenge, punish my odious passion;
Prove yourself worthy of your valiant sire,
And rid the world of an offensive monster!
Does Theseus' widow dare to love his son?
The frightful monster! Let her not escape you!
Here is my heart. This is the place to strike.
Already prompt to expiate its guilt,

I feel it leap impatiently to meet
Your arm. Strike home. Or, if it would disgrace you
To steep your hand in such polluted blood,
If that were punishment too mild to slake
Your hatred, lend me then your sword, if not
Your arm. Quick, give 't.

  OENONE   What, Madam, will you do?
Just gods! But someone comes. Go, fly from shame,
You cannot 'scape if seen by any thus.

SCENE VI

Hippolytus, Theramenes

  THERAMENES   Is that the form of Phaedra that I see
Hurried away? What mean these signs of sorrow?
Where is your sword? Why are you pale, confused?

  HIPPOLYTUS   Friend, let us fly. I am, indeed, confounded
With horror and astonishment extreme.
Phaedra—but no; gods, let this dreadful secret
Remain forever buried in oblivion.

  THERAMENES   The ship is ready if you wish to sail.
But Athens has already giv'n her vote;
Their leaders have consulted all her tribes;
Your brother is elected, Phaedra wins.

  HIPPOLYTUS   Phaedra?

  THERAMENES   A herald, charged with a commission
From Athens, has arrived to place the reins
Of power in her hands. Her son is King.

  HIPPOLYTUS   Ye gods, who know her, do ye thus reward
Her virtue?

  THERAMENES   A faint rumor meanwhile whispers
That Theseus is not dead, but in Epirus
Has shown himself. But, after all my search,
I know too well—

  HIPPOLYTUS   Let nothing be neglected.
This rumor must be traced back to its source.
If it be found unworthy of belief,
Let us set sail, and cost whate'er it may,
To hands deserving trust the sceptre's sway.

ACT THREE

SCENE I

Phaedra, Oenone

PHAEDRA   Ah! Let them take elsewhere the worthless hon-
ors
They bring me. Why so urgent I should see them?
What flattering balm can soothe my wounded heart?
Far rather hide me: I have said too much.
My madness has burst forth like streams in flood,
And I have utter'd what should ne'er have reach'd
His ear. Gods! How he heard me! How reluctant
To catch my meaning, dull and cold as marble,
And eager only for a quick retreat!
How oft his blushes made my shame the deeper!
Why did you turn me from the death I sought?
Ah! When his sword was pointed to my bosom,
Did he grow pale, or try to snatch it from me?
That I had touch'd it was enough for him
To render it forever horrible,
Leaving defilement on the hand that holds it.
   OENONE   Thus brooding on your bitter disappointment,
You only fan a fire that must be stifled.
Would it not be more worthy of the blood
Of Minos to find peace in nobler cares,
And, in defiance of a wretch who flies
From what he hates, reign, mount the proffer'd throne?
   PHAEDRA   I reign! Shall I the rod of empire sway,
When reason reigns no longer o'er myself?
When I have lost control of all my senses?
When 'neath a shameful yoke I scarce can breathe?
When I am dying?
   OENONE   Fly.
   PHAEDRA   I cannot leave him.
   OENONE   Dare you not fly from him you dared to banish?
   PHAEDRA   The time for that is past. He knows my frenzy.
I have o'erstepp'd the bounds of modesty,
And blazon'd forth my shame before his eyes.
Hope stole into my heart against my will.

Did you not rally my declining pow'rs?
Was it not you yourself recall'd my soul
When fluttering on my lips, and with your counsel,
Lent me fresh life, and told me I might love him?

OENONE   Blame me or blame me not for your misfortunes,
Of what was I incapable, to save you?
But if your indignation e'er was roused
By insult, can you pardon his contempt?
How cruelly his eyes, severely fix'd,
Survey'd you almost prostrate at his feet!
How hateful then appear'd his savage pride!
Why did not Phaedra see him then as I
Beheld him?

PHAEDRA   This proud mood that you resent
May yield to time. The rudeness of the forests
Where he was bred, inured to rigorous laws,
Clings to him still; love is a word he ne'er
Had heard before. It may be his surprise
Stunn'd him, and too much vehemence was shown
In all I said.

OENONE   Remember that his mother
Was a barbarian.

PHAEDRA   Scythian tho' she was,
She learnt to love.

OENONE   He has for all the sex
Hatred intense.

PHAEDRA   Then in his heart no rival
Shall ever reign. Your counsel comes too late.
Oenone, serve my madness, not my reason.
His heart is inaccessible to love:
Let us attack him where he has more feeling.
The charms of sovereignty appear'd to touch him;
He could not hide that he was drawn to Athens;
His vessels' prows were thither turn'd already,
All sail was set to scud before the breeze.
Go you on my behalf, to his ambition
Appeal, and let the prospect of the crown
Dazzle his eyes. The sacred diadem
Shall deck his brow, no higher honor mine
Than there to bind it. His shall be the pow'r

I cannot keep; and he shall teach my son
How to rule men. It may be he will deign
To be to him a father. Son and mother
He shall control. Try ev'ry means to move him;
Your words will find more favor than can mine.
Urge him with groans and tears; show Phaedra dying,
Nor blush to use the voice of supplication.
In you is my last hope; I'll sanction all
You say; and on the issue hangs my fate.

scene II

PHAEDRA [*alone*]   Venus implacable, who seest me shamed
And, sore confounded, have I not enough
Been humbled? How can cruelty be stretch'd
Farther? Thy shafts have all gone home, and thou
Hast triumph'd. Would'st thou win a new renown?
Attack an enemy more contumacious:
Hippolytus neglects thee, braves thy wrath,
Nor ever at thine altars bow'd the knee.
Thy name offends his proud, disdainful ears.
Our interests are alike: avenge thyself,
Force him to love—
                            But what is this? Oenone
Return'd already? He detests me then,
And will not hear you.

scene III

Phaedra, Oenone

OENONE   Madam, you must stifle
A fruitless love. Recall your former virtue:
The king who was thought dead will soon appear
Before your eyes, Theseus has just arrived,
Theseus is here. The people flock to see him
With eager haste. I went by your command
To find the prince, when with a thousand shouts
The air was rent—
      PHAEDRA   My husband is alive,
That is enough, Oenone. I have own'd

A passion that dishonors him. He lives:
I ask to know no more.

OENONE   What?

PHAEDRA   I foretold it,
But you refused to hear. Your tears prevail'd
Over my just remorse. Dying this morn,
I had deserved compassion; your advice
I took, and die dishonor'd.

OENONE   Die?

PHAEDRA   Just Heav'ns!
What have I done to-day? My husband comes,
With him his son: and I shall see the witness
Of my adulterous flame watch with what face
I greet his father, while my heart is big
With sighs he scorn'd, and tears that could not move him
Moisten mine eyes. Think you that his respect
For Theseus will induce him to conceal
My madness, nor disgrace his sire and king?
Will he be able to keep back the horror
He has for me? His silence would be vain.
I know my treason, and I lack the boldness
Of those abandon'd women who can taste
Tranquillity in crime, and show a forehead
All unabash'd. I recognize my madness,
Recall it all. These vaulted roofs, methinks,
These walls can speak, and, ready to accuse me,
Wait but my husband's presence to reveal
My perfidy. Death only can remove
This weight of horror. Is it such misfortune
To cease to live? Death causes no alarm
To misery. I only fear the name
That I shall leave behind me. For my sons
How sad a heritage! The blood of Jove
Might justly swell the pride that boasts descent
From Heav'n, but heavy weighs a mother's guilt
Upon her offspring. Yes, I dread the scorn
That will be cast on them with too much truth,
For my disgrace. I tremble when I think
That, crush'd beneath that curse, they'll never dare
To raise their eyes.

OENONE   Doubt not I pity both;
Never was fear more just than yours. Why then
Expose them to this ignominy? Why
Will you accuse yourself? You thus destroy
The only hope that's left; it will be said
That Phaedra, conscious of her perfidy,
Fled from her husband's sight. Hippolytus
Will be rejoiced that, dying, you should lend
His charge support. What can I answer him?
He'll find it easy to confute my tale,
And I shall hear him with an air of triumph
To every open ear repeat your shame.
Sooner than that may fire from heav'n consume me!
Deceive me not. Say, do you love him still?
How look you now on this contemptuous prince?

PHAEDRA   As on a monster frightful to mine eyes.

OENONE   Why yield him then an easy victory?
You fear him. Venture to accuse him first,
As guilty of the charge which he may bring
This day against you. Who can say 'tis false?
All tells against him: in your hands his sword
Happily left behind, your present trouble,
Your past distress, your warnings to his father,
His exile which your earnest pray'rs obtain'd.

PHAEDRA   What! Would you have me slander innocence?

OENONE   My zeal has need of nought from you but silence.
Like you I tremble, and am loath to do it;
More willingly I'd face a thousand deaths.
But since without this bitter remedy
I lose you, and to me your life outweighs
All else, I'll speak. Theseus, howe'er enraged,
Will do no worse than banish him again.
A father, when he punishes, remains
A father, and his ire is satisfied
With a light sentence. But if guiltless blood
Should flow, is not your honor of more moment?
A treasure far too precious to be risk'd?
You must submit, whatever it dictates;
For, when our reputation is at stake,

All must be sacrificed, conscience itself.
But someone comes. 'Tis Theseus.
PHAEDRA   And I see
Hippolytus, my ruin plainly written
In his stern eyes. Do what you will; I trust
My fate to you. I cannot help myself.

SCENE IV

Theseus, Hippolytus, Phaedra, Oenone, Theramenes

THESEUS   Fortune no longer fights against my wishes,
Madam, and to your arms restores—
PHAEDRA   Stay, Theseus!
Do not profane endearments that were once
So sweet, but which I am unworthy now
To taste. You have been wrong'd. Fortune has proved
Spiteful, nor in your absence spared your wife.
I am unfit to meet your fond caress,
How I may bear my shame my only care
Henceforth.

SCENE V

Theseus, Hippolytus, Theramenes

THESEUS   Strange welcome for your father, this!
What does it mean, my son?
HIPPOLYTUS   Phaedra alone
Can solve this mystery. But if my wish
Can move you, let me never see her more;
Suffer Hippolytus to disappear
Forever from the home that holds your wife.
THESEUS   You, my son! Leave me?
HIPPOLYTUS   'Twas not I who sought her:
'Twas you who led her footsteps to these shores.
At your departure you thought meet, my lord,
To trust Aricia and the Queen to this
Troezenian land, and I myself was charged
With their protection. But what cares henceforth
Need keep me here? My youth of idleness

Has shown its skill enough o'er paltry foes
That range the woods. May I not quit a life
Of such inglorious ease, and dip my spear
In nobler blood? Ere you had reach'd my age
More than one tyrant, monster more than one
Had felt the weight of your stout arm. Already,
Successful in attacking insolence,
You had removed all dangers that infested
Our coasts to east and west. The traveller fear'd
Outrage no longer. Hearing of your deeds,
Already Hercules relied on you,
And rested from his toils. While I, unknown
Son of so brave a sire, am far behind
Even my mother's footsteps. Let my courage
Have scope to act, and if some monster yet
Has 'scaped you, let me lay the glorious spoils
Down at your feet; or let the memory
Of death faced nobly keep my name alive,
And prove to all the world I was your son.

    THESEUS   Why, what is this? What terror has possess'd
My family to make them fly before me?
If I return to find myself so fear'd,
So little welcome, why did Heav'n release me
From prison? My sole friend, misled by passion,
Was bent on robbing of his wife the tyrant
Who ruled Epirus. With regret I lent
The lover aid, but Fate had made us blind,
Myself as well as him. The tyrant seized me
Defenceless and unarm'd. Pirithoüs
I saw with tears cast forth to be devour'd
By savage beasts that lapp'd the blood of men.
Myself in gloomy caverns he enclosed,
Deep in the bowels of the earth, and nigh
To Pluto's realms. Six months I lay ere Heav'n
Had pity, and I 'scaped the watchful eyes
That guarded me. Then did I purge the world
Of a foul foe, and he himself has fed
His monsters. But, when with expectant joy
To all that is most precious I draw near
Of what the gods have left me, when my soul

Looks for full satisfaction in a sight
So dear, my only welcome is a shudder,
Embrace rejected, and a hasty flight.
Inspiring, as I clearly do, such terror,
Would I were still a prisoner in Epirus!
Phaedra complains that I have suffer'd outrage.
Who has betray'd me? Speak. Why was I not
Avenged? Has Greece, to whom mine arm so oft
Brought useful aid, shelter'd the criminal?
You make no answer. Is my son, mine own
Dear son, confederate with mine enemies?
I'll enter. This suspense is overwhelming.
I'll learn at once the culprit and the crime,
And Phaedra must explain her troubled state.

SCENE VI

Hippolytus, Theramenes

HIPPOLYTUS What do these words portend, which seem'd
to freeze
My very blood? Will Phaedra, in her frenzy,
Accuse herself, and seal her own destruction?
What will the King say? Gods! What fatal poison
Has love spread over all his house! Myself,
Full of a fire his hatred disapproves,
How changed he finds me from the son he knew!
With dark forebodings is my mind alarm'd,
But innocence has surely nought to fear.
Come, let us go, and in some other place
Consider how I best may move my sire
To tenderness, and tell him of a flame
Vex'd but not vanquish'd by a father's blame.

ACT FOUR

SCENE I

Theseus, Oenone

THESEUS Ah! What is this I hear? Presumptuous traitor!
And would he have disgraced his father's honor?
With what relentless footsteps Fate pursues me!

Whither I go I know not, nor where now
I am. O kind affection ill repaid!
Audacious scheme! Abominable thought!
To reach the object of his foul desire
The wretch disdain'd not to use violence.
I know this sword that served him in his fury,
The sword I gave him for a nobler use.
Could not the sacred ties of blood restrain him?
And Phaedra—was she loath to have him punish'd?
She held her tongue. Was that to spare the culprit?

    OENONE   Nay, but to spare a most unhappy father.
O'erwhelm'd with shame that her eyes should have kindled
So infamous a flame and prompted him
To crime so heinous, Phaedra would have died.
I saw her raise her arm, and ran to save her.
To me alone you owe it that she lives;
And, in my pity both for her and you,
Have I against my will interpreted
Her tears.

    THESEUS   The traitor! He might well turn pale.
'Twas fear that made him tremble when he saw me.
I was astonish'd that he show'd no pleasure;
His frigid greeting chill'd my tenderness.
But was this guilty passion that devours him
Declared already ere I banish'd him
From Athens?

    OENONE   Sire, remember how the Queen
Urged you. Illicit love caused all her hatred.

    THESEUS   And then this fire broke out again at Troezen?

    OENONE   Sire, I have told you all. Too long the Queen
Has been allow'd to bear her grief alone.
Let me now leave you and attend to her.

SCENE II

Theseus, Hippolytus

    THESEUS   Ah! There he is. Great gods! That noble mien
Might well deceive an eye less fond than mine!
Why should the sacred stamp of virtue gleam

Upon the forehead of an impious wretch?
Ought not the blackness of a traitor's heart
To show itself by sure and certain signs?
    HIPPOLYTUS My father, may I ask what fatal cloud
Has troubled your majestic countenance?
Dare you not trust this secret to your son?
    THESEUS Traitor, how dare you show yourself before me?
Monster, whom Heaven's bolts have spared too long!
Survivor of that robber crew whereof
I cleansed the earth. After your brutal lust
Scorn'd even to respect my marriage bed,
You venture—you, my hated foe—to come
Into my presence, here, where all is full
Of your foul infamy, instead of seeking
Some unknown land that never heard my name.
Fly, traitor, fly! Stay not to tempt the wrath
That I can scarce restrain, nor brave my hatred.
Disgrace enough have I incurr'd forever
In being father of so vile a son,
Without your death staining indelibly
The glorious record of my noble deeds.
Fly, and unless you wish quick punishment
To add you to the criminals cut off
By me, take heed this sun that lights us now
Ne'er see you more set foot upon this soil.
I tell you once again—fly, haste, return not,
Rid all my realms of your atrocious presence.
    To thee, to thee, great Neptune, I appeal;
If erst I clear'd thy shores of foul assassins,
Recall thy promise to reward those efforts,
Crown'd with success, by granting my first pray'r.
Confined for long in close captivity,
I have not yet call'd on thy pow'rful aid,
Sparing to use the valued privilege
Till at mine utmost need. The time is come,
I ask thee now. Avenge a wretched father!
I leave this traitor to thy wrath; in blood
Quench his outrageous fires, and by thy fury
Theseus will estimate thy favor tow'rds him.

HIPPOLYTUS   Phaedra accuses me of lawless passion!
This crowning horror all my soul confounds;
Such unexpected blows, falling at once,
O'erwhelm me, choke my utterance, strike me dumb.
THESEUS   Traitor, you reckon'd that in timid silence
Phaedra would bury your brutality.
You should not have abandon'd in your flight
The sword that in her hands helps to condemn you
Or rather, to complete your perfidy,
You should have robb'd her both of speech and life.
HIPPOLYTUS   Justly indignant at a lie so black
I might be pardon'd if I told the truth;
But it concerns your honor to conceal it.
Approve the reverence that shuts my mouth;
And, without wishing to increase your woes,
Examine closely what my life has been.
Great crimes are never single, they are link'd
To former faults. He who has once transgress'd
May violate at last all that men hold
Most sacred; vice, like virtue, has degrees
Of progress; innocence was never seen
To sink at once into the lowest depths
Of guilt. No virtuous man can in a day
Turn traitor, murderer, an incestuous wretch.
The nursling of a chaste, heroic mother,
I have not proved unworthy of my birth.
Pittheus, whose wisdom is by all esteem'd,
Deign'd to instruct me when I left her hands.
It is no wish of mine to vaunt my merits,
But, if I may lay claim to any virtue,
I think beyond all else I have display'd
Abhorrence of those sins with which I'm charged.
For this Hippolytus is known in Greece,
So continent that he is deem'd austere.
All know my abstinence inflexible:
The daylight is not purer than my heart.
How then could I, burning with fire profane—
THESEUS   Yes, dastard, 'tis that very pride condemns you.
I see the odious reason of your coldness:
Phaedra alone bewitch'd your shameless eyes;

Your soul, to others' charms indifferent,
Disdain'd the blameless fires of lawful love.

HIPPOLYTUS No, father, I have hidden it too long,
This heart has not disdain'd a sacred flame.
Here at your feet I own my real offence:
I love, and love in truth where you forbid me;
Bound to Aricia by my heart's devotion,
The child of Pallas has subdued your son.
A rebel to your laws, her I adore,
And breathe forth ardent sighs for her alone.

THESEUS You love her? Heav'ns!
                                        But no, I see the trick.
You feign a crime to justify yourself.

HIPPOLYTUS Sir, I have shunn'd her for six months, and
    still
Love her. To you yourself I came to tell it,
Trembling the while. Can nothing clear your mind
Of your mistake? What oath can reassure you?
By heav'n and earth and all the pow'rs of nature—

THESEUS The wicked never shrink from perjury.
Cease, cease, and spare me irksome protestations,
If your false virtue has no other aid.

HIPPOLYTUS Tho' it to you seem false and insincere,
Phaedra has secret cause to know it true.

THESEUS Ah! how your shamelessness excites my wrath!

HIPPOLYTUS What is my term and place of banishment?

THESEUS Were you beyond the Pillars of Alcides,
Your perjured presence were too near me yet.

HIPPOLYTUS What friends will pity me, when you forsake
And think me guilty of a crime so vile?

THESEUS Go, look you out for friends who hold in honor
Adultery and clap their hands at incest,
Low, lawless traitors, steep'd in infamy,
The fit protectors of a knave like you.

HIPPOLYTUS Are incest and adultery the words
You cast at me? I hold my tongue. Yet think
What mother Phaedra had; too well you know
Her blood, not mine, is tainted with those horrors.

THESEUS What! Does your rage before my eyes lose all
Restraint? For the last time—out of my sight!

Hence, traitor! Wait not till a father's wrath
Force thee away 'mid general execration.

SCENE III

THESEUS [*alone*]   Wretch! Thou must meet inevitable ruin.
Neptune has sworn by Styx—to gods themselves
A dreadful oath—and he will execute
His promise. Thou canst not escape his vengeance.
I loved thee; and, in spite of thine offence,
My heart is troubled by anticipation
For thee. But thou hast earn'd thy doom too well.
Had father ever greater cause for rage?
Just gods, who see the grief that overwhelms me,
Why was I cursed with such a wicked son?

SCENE IV

Phaedra, Theseus

PHAEDRA   My lord, I come to you, fill'd with just dread.
Your voice raised high in anger reach'd mine ears,
And much I fear that deeds have follow'd threats.
Oh, if there yet is time, spare your own offspring,
Respect your race and blood, I do beseech you.
Let me not hear that blood cry from the ground;
Save me the horror and perpetual pain
Of having caused his father's hand to shed it.

THESEUS   No, Madam, from that stain my hand is free
But, for all that, the wretch has not escaped me.
The hand of an Immortal now is charged
With his destruction. 'Tis a debt that Neptune
Owes me, and you shall be avenged.

PHAEDRA   A debt
Owed you? Pray'rs made in anger—

THESEUS   Never fear
That they will fail. Rather join yours to mine.
In all their blackness paint for me his crimes,
And fan my tardy passion to white heat.
But yet you know not all his infamy;
His rage against you overflows in slanders;

Your mouth, he says, is full of all deceit,
He says Aricia has his heart and soul,
That her alone he loves.

PHAEDRA   Aricia?

THESEUS   Ay,

He said it to my face: an idle pretext!
A trick that gulls me not! Let us hope Neptune
Will do him speedy justice. To his altars
I go, to urge performance of his oaths.

SCENE V

PHAEDRA [*alone*] Ah, he is gone! What tidings struck mine
ears?
What fire, half smother'd, in my heart revives?
What fatal stroke falls like a thunderbolt?
Stung by remorse that would not let me rest,
I tore myself out of Oenone's arms,
And flew to help Hippolytus with all
My soul and strength. Who knows if that repentance
Might not have moved me to accuse myself?
And, if my voice had not been choked with shame,
Perhaps I had confess'd the frightful truth.
Hippolytus can feel, but not for me!
Aricia has his heart, his plighted troth.
Ye gods, when, deaf to all my sighs and tears,
He arm'd his eye with scorn, his brow with threats,
I deem'd his heart, impregnable to love,
Was fortified 'gainst all my sex alike.
And yet another has prevail'd to tame
His pride, another has secured his favor.
Perhaps he has a heart easily melted;
I am the only one he cannot bear!
And shall I charge myself with his defence?

SCENE VI

Phaedra, Oenone

PHAEDRA Know you, dear Nurse, what I have learn'd just
now?

OENONE No; but I come in truth with trembling limbs.

I dreaded with what purpose you went forth,
The fear of fatal madness made me pale.

    PHAEDRA Who would have thought it, Nurse? I had a rival.

    OENONE A rival?

    PHAEDRA   Yes, he loves. I cannot doubt it.
This wild untamable Hippolytus,
Who scorn'd to be admired, whom lovers' sighs
Wearied, this tiger, whom I fear'd to rouse,
Fawns on a hand that has subdued his pride:
Aricia has found entrance to his heart.

    OENONE Aricia?

    PHAEDRA   Ah! anguish as yet untried!
For what new tortures am I still reserved?
All I have undergone, transports of passion,
Longings and fears, the horrors of remorse,
The shame of being spurn'd with contumely,
Were feeble foretastes of my present torments.
They love each other! By what secret charm
Have they deceived me? Where, and when, and how
Met they? You knew it all. Why was I cozen'd?
You never told me of those stolen hours
Of amorous converse. Have they oft been seen
Talking together? Did they seek the shades
Of thickest woods? Alas! full freedom had they
To see each other. Heav'n approved their sighs;
They loved without the consciousness of guilt;
And every morning's sun for them shone clear,
While I, an outcast from the face of Nature,
Shunn'd the bright day, and sought to hide myself.
Death was the only god whose aid I dared
To ask: I waited for the grave's release.
Water'd with tears, nourish'd with gall, my woe
Was all too closely watch'd; I did not dare
To weep without restraint. In mortal dread
Tasting this dangerous solace, I disguised
My terror 'neath a tranquil countenance,
And oft had I to check my tears, and smile.

    OENONE What fruit will they enjoy of their vain love?
They will not see each other more.

That love
ik,
orn the madness
xile
thousand oaths
ffer
me?
oy'd.
ul stock
hment
brothers'.
e.
senses?
lore
and yet
his I claim
ir
orth has pass'd
athe
nds are ready
ence.
l dare
spring?
: was , of an ods;
My ancestors fill all the univers.
Where can I hide? In the dark realms of Pluto?
But there my father holds the fatal urn;
His hand awards th' irrevocable doom:
Minos is judge of all the ghosts in hell.
Ah! how his awful shade will start and shudder
When he shall see his daughter brought before him,
Forced to confess sins of such varied dye,
Crimes it may be unknown to hell itself!
What wilt thou say, my father, at a sight
So dire? I think I see thee drop the urn,
And, seeking some unheard-of punishment,
Thyself become my executioner.
Spare me! A cruel goddess has destroy'd
Thy race; and in my madness recognize

Her wrath. Alas! My aching heart has reap'd
No fruit of pleasure from the frightful crime
The shame of which pursues me to the grave,
And ends in torment life-long misery.

    OENONE   Ah, Madam, pray dismiss a groundless dread:
Look less severely on a venial error.
You love. We cannot conquer destiny.
You were drawn on as by a fatal charm.
Is that a marvel without precedent
Among us? Has love triumph'd over you,
And o'er none else? Weakness is natural
To man. A mortal, to a mortal's lot
Submit. You chafe against a yoke that others
Have long since borne. The dwellers in Olympus,
The gods themselves, who terrify with threats
The sins of men, have burn'd with lawless fires.

    PHAEDRA   What words are these I hear? What counsel this
You dare to give me? Will you to the end
Pour poison in mine ears? You have destroy'd me.
You brought me back when I should else have quitted
The light of day, made me forget my duty
And see Hippolytus, till then avoided.
What hast thou done? Why did your wicked mouth
With blackest lies slander his blameless life?
Perhaps you've slain him, and the impious pray'r
Of an unfeeling father has been answer'd.
No, not another word! Go, hateful monster;
Away, and leave me to my piteous fate.
May Heav'n with justice pay you your deserts!
And may your punishment forever be
A terror to all those who would, like you,
Nourish with artful wiles the weaknesses
Of princes, push them to the brink of ruin
To which their heart inclines, and smooth the path
Of guilt. Such flatterers doth the wrath of Heav'n
Bestow on kings as its most fatal gift.

    OENONE [alone]   O gods! to serve her what have I not done?
This is the due reward that I have won.

Her wrath. Alas! My aching heart has reap'd
No fruit of pleasure from the frightful crime
The shame of which pursues me to the grave,
And ends in torment life-long misery.

OENONE   Ah, Madam, pray dismiss a groundless dread:
Look less severely on a venial error.
You love. We cannot conquer destiny.
You were drawn on as by a fatal charm.
Is that a marvel without precedent
Among us? Has love triumph'd over you,
And o'er none else? Weakness is natural
To man. A mortal, to a mortal's lot
Submit. You chafe against a yoke that others
Have long since borne. The dwellers in Olympus,
The gods themselves, who terrify with threats
The sins of men, have burn'd with lawless fires.

PHAEDRA   What words are these I hear? What counsel this
You dare to give me? Will you to the end
Pour poison in mine ears? You have destroy'd me.
You brought me back when I should else have quitted
The light of day, made me forget my duty
And see Hippolytus, till then avoided.
What hast thou done? Why did your wicked mouth
With blackest lies slander his blameless life?
Perhaps you've slain him, and the impious pray'r
Of an unfeeling father has been answer'd.
No, not another word! Go, hateful monster;
Away, and leave me to my piteous fate.
May Heav'n with justice pay you your deserts!
And may your punishment forever be
A terror to all those who would, like you,
Nourish with artful wiles the weaknesses
Of princes, push them to the brink of ruin
To which their heart inclines, and smooth the path
Of guilt. Such flatterers doth the wrath of Heav'n
Bestow on kings as its most fatal gift.

OENONE [alone]   O gods! to serve her what have I not done?
This is the due reward that I have won.

PHAEDRA   That love
Will last forever. Even while I speak,
Ah, fatal thought, they laugh to scorn the madness
Of my distracted heart. In spite of exile
That soon must part them, with a thousand oaths
They seal yet closer union. Can I suffer
A happiness, Oenone, which insults me?
I crave your pity. She must be destroy'd.
My husband's wrath against a hateful stock
Shall be revived, nor must the punishment
Be light: the sister's guilt passes the brothers'.
I will entreat him in my jealous rage.
    What am I saying? Have I lost my senses?
Is Phaedra jealous, and will she implore
Theseus for help? My husband lives, and yet
I burn. For whom? Whose heart is this I claim
As mine? At every word I say, my hair
Stands up with horror. Guilt henceforth has pass'd
All bounds. Hypocrisy and incest breathe
At once thro' all. My murderous hands are ready
To spill the blood of guileless innocence.
Do I yet live, wretch that I am, and dare
To face this holy Sun from whom I spring?
My father's sire was king of all the gods;
My ancestors fill all the universe.
Where can I hide? In the dark realms of Pluto?
But there my father holds the fatal urn;
His hand awards th' irrevocable doom:
Minos is judge of all the ghosts in hell.
Ah! how his awful shade will start and shudder
When he shall see his daughter brought before him,
Forced to confess sins of such varied dye,
Crimes it may be unknown to hell itself!
What wilt thou say, my father, at a sight
So dire? I think I see thee drop the urn,
And, seeking some unheard-of punishment,
Thyself become my executioner.
Spare me! A cruel goddess has destroy'd
Thy race; and in my madness recognize

ACT FIVE

SCENE I

Hippolytus, Aricia

ARICIA Can you keep silent in this mortal peril?
Your father loves you. Will you leave him thus
Deceived? If in your cruel heart you scorn
My tears, content to see me nevermore,
Go, part from poor Aricia; but at least,
Going, secure the safety of your life.
Defend your honor from a shameful stain,
And force your father to recall his pray'rs.
There yet is time. Why out of mere caprice
Leave the field free to Phaedra's calumnies?
Let Theseus know the truth.

HIPPOLYTUS   Could I say more,
Without exposing him to dire disgrace?
How should I venture, by revealing all,
To make a father's brow grow red with shame?
The odious mystery to you alone
Is known. My heart has been outpour'd to none
Save you and Heav'n. I could not hide from you
(Judge if I love you), all I fain would hide
E'en from myself. But think under what seal
I spoke. Forget my words, if that may be;
And never let so pure a mouth disclose
This dreadful secret. Let us trust to Heav'n
My vindication, for the gods are just;
For their own honor will they clear the guiltless;
Sooner or later punish'd for her crime,
Phaedra will not escape the shame she merits.
I ask no other favor than your silence;
In all besides I give my wrath free scope.
Make your escape from this captivity,
Be bold to bear me company in flight;
Linger not here on this accursèd soil,
Where virtue breathes a pestilential air.
To cover your departure take advantage
Of this confusion, caused by my disgrace.

The means of flight are ready, be assured;
You have as yet no other guards than mine.
Pow'rful defenders will maintain our quarrel;
Argos spreads open arms, and Sparta calls us.
Let us appeal for justice to our friends,
Nor suffer Phaedra, in a common ruin
Joining us both, to hunt us from the throne,
And aggrandize her son by robbing us.
Embrace this happy opportunity:
What fear restrains? You seem to hesitate.
Your interest alone prompts me to urge
Boldness. When I am all on fire, how comes it
That you are ice? Fear you to follow then
A banish'd man?

    ARICIA   Ah, dear to me would be
Such exile! With what joy, my fate to yours
United, could I live, by all the world
Forgotten! But not yet has that sweet tie
Bound us together. How then can I steal
Away with you? I know the strictest honor
Forbids me not out of your father's hands
To free myself; this is no parent's home,
And flight is lawful when one flies from tyrants.
But you, Sir, love me; and my virtue shrinks—

    HIPPOLYTUS   No, no, your reputation is to me
As dear as to yourself. A nobler purpose
Brings me to you. Fly from your foes, and follow
A husband. Heav'n, that sends us these misfortunes,
Sets free from human instruments the pledge
Between us. Torches do not always light
The face of Hymen.

                 At the gates of Troezen,
'Mid ancient tombs where princes of my race
Lie buried, stands a temple ne'er approach'd
By perjurers, where mortals dare not make
False oaths, for instant punishment befalls
The guilty. Falsehood knows no stronger check
Than what is present there—the fear of death
That cannot be avoided. Thither then
We'll go, if you consent, and swear to love

Forever, take the guardian god to witness
Our solemn vows, and his paternal care
Entreat. I will invoke the name of all
The holiest Pow'rs; chaste Dian, and the Queen
Of Heav'n, yea all the gods who know my heart
Will guarantee my sacred promises.

ARICIA   The King draws near. Depart—make no delay.
To mask my flight, I linger yet one moment.
Go you; and leave with me some trusty guide,
To lead my timid footsteps to your side.

SCENE II

Theseus, Aricia, Ismene

THESEUS   Ye gods, throw light upon my troubled mind,
Show me the truth which I am seeking here.

ARICIA [*aside to Ismene*]   Get ready, dear Ismene, for our
flight.

SCENE III

Theseus, Aricia

THESEUS   Your color comes and goes, you seem confused,
Madam! What business had my son with you?

ARICIA   Sire, he was bidding me farewell forever.

THESEUS   Your eyes, it seems, can tame that stubborn
pride;
And the first sighs he breathes are paid to you.

ARICIA   I can't deny the truth; he has not, Sire,
Inherited your hatred and injustice;
He did not treat me like a criminal.

THESEUS   That is to say, he swore eternal love.
Do not rely on that inconstant heart;
To others has he sworn as much before.

ARICIA   He, Sire?

THESEUS   You ought to check his roving taste.
How could you bear a partnership so vile?

ARICIA   And how can you endure that vilest slanders
Should make a life so pure as black as pitch?
Have you so little knowledge of his heart?
Do you so ill distinguish between guilt
And innocence? What mist before your eyes

Blinds them to virtue so conspicuous?
Ah! 'tis too much to let false tongues defame him.
Repent; call back your murderous wishes, Sire;
Fear, fear lest Heav'n in its severity
Hate you enough to hear and grant your pray'rs.
Oft in their wrath the gods accept our victims,
And oftentimes chastise us with their gifts.

    THESEUS No, vainly would you cover up his guilt
Your love is blind to his depravity.
But I have witness irreproachable:
Tears have I seen, true tears, that may be trusted.

    ARICIA Take heed, my lord. Your hands invincible
Have rid the world of monsters numberless;
But all are not destroy'd, one you have left
Alive—your son forbids me to say more.
Knowing with what respect he still regards you,
I should too much distress him if I dared
Complete my sentence. I will imitate
His reverence, and, to keep silence, leave you.

SCENE IV

    THESEUS [*alone*] What is there in her mind? What mean-
      ing lurks
In speech begun but to be broken short?
Would both deceive me with a vain pretence?
Have they conspired to put me to the torture?
And yet, despite my stern severity,
What plaintive voice cries deep within my heart?
A secret pity troubles and alarms me.
Oenone shall be questioned once again,
I must have clearer light upon this crime.
Guards, bid Oenone come, and come alone.

SCENE V

Theseus, Panope

    PANOPE I know not what the Queen intends to do,
But from her agitation dread the worst.
Fatal despair is painted on her features;

Death's pallor is already in her face.
Oenone, shamed and driven from her sight,
Has cast herself into the ocean depths.
None knows what prompted her to deed so rash;
And now the waves hide her from us forever.

THESEUS What say you?

PANOPE Her sad fate seems to have added
Fresh trouble to the Queen's tempestuous soul.
Sometimes, to soothe her secret pain, she clasps
Her children close, and bathes them with her tears;
Then suddenly, the mother's love forgotten,
She thrusts them from her with a look of horror.
She wanders to and fro with doubtful steps;
Her vacant eye no longer knows us. Thrice
She wrote, and thrice did she, changing her mind,
Destroy the letter ere 'twas well begun.
Vouchsafe to see her, Sire: vouchsafe to help her.

THESEUS Heav'ns! Is Oenone dead, and Phaedra bent
On dying too? Oh, call me back my son!
Let him defend himself, and I am ready
To hear him. Be not hasty to bestow
Thy fatal bounty, Neptune; let my pray'rs
Rather remain ever unheard. Too soon
I lifted cruel hands, believing lips
That may have lied! Ah! What despair may follow!

SCENE VI

Theseus, Theramenes

THESEUS Theramenes, is 't thou? Where is my son?
I gave him to thy charge from tenderest childhood.
But whence these tears that overflow thine eyes?
How is it with my son?

THERAMENES Concern too late!
Affection vain! Hippolytus is dead.

THESEUS Gods!

THERAMENES I have seen the flow'r of all mankind
Cut off, and I am bold to say that none
Deserved it less.

THESEUS What! My son dead! When I

Was stretching out my arms to him, has Heav'n
Hasten'd his end? What was this sudden stroke?
    THERAMENES Scarce had we pass'd out of the gates of
      Troezen,
He silent in his chariot, and his guards,
Downcast and silent too, around him ranged;
To the Mycenian road he turn'd his steeds,
Then, lost in thought allow'd the reins to lie
Loose on their backs. His noble chargers, erst
So full of ardor to obey his voice,
With head depress'd and melancholy eye
Seem'd now to mark his sadness and to share it.
A frightful cry, that issues from the deep,
With sudden discord rends the troubled air;
And from the bosom of the earth a groan
Is heard in answer to that voice of terror.
Our blood is frozen at our very hearts;
With bristling manes the list'ning steeds stand still.
Meanwhile upon the watery plain there rises
A mountain billow with a mighty crest
Of foam, that shoreward rolls, and, as it breaks,
Before our eyes vomits a furious monster.
With formidable horns its brow is arm'd,
And all its body clothed with yellow scales,
In front a savage bull, behind a dragon
Turning and twisting in impatient rage.
Its long continued bellowings make the shore
Tremble; the sky seems horror-struck to see it;
The earth with terror quakes; its poisonous breath
Infects the air. The wave that brought it ebbs
In fear. All fly, forgetful of the courage
That cannot aid, and in a neighboring temple
Take refuge—all save bold Hippolytus.
A hero's worthy son, he stays his steeds,
Seizes his darts, and, rushing forward, hurls
A missile with sure aim that wounds the monster
Deep in the flank. With rage and pain it springs
E'en to the horses' feet, and, roaring, falls,
Writhes in the dust, and shows a fiery throat
That covers them with flames, and blood, and smoke.

Fear lends them wings; deaf to his voice for once,
And heedless of the curb, they onward fly.
Their master wastes his strength in efforts vain;
With foam and blood each courser's bit is red.
Some say a god, amid this wild disorder,
Is seen with goads pricking their dusty flanks.
O'er jaggèd rocks they rush urged on by terror;
Crash! goes the axle-tree. Th' intrepid youth
Sees his car broken up, flying to pieces;
He falls himself, entangled in the reins.
Pardon my grief. That cruel spectacle
Will be for me a source of endless tears.
I saw thy hapless son, I saw him, Sire,
Dragg'd by the horses that his hands had fed,
Pow'rless to check their fierce career, his voice
But adding to their fright, his body soon
One mass of wounds. Our cries of anguish fill
The plain. At last they slacken their swift pace,
Then stop, not far from those old tombs that mark
Where lie the ashes of his royal sires.
Panting I thither run, and after me
His guard, along the track stain'd with fresh blood
That reddens all the rocks; caught in the briers
Locks of his hair hang dripping, gory spoils!
I come, I call him. Stretching forth his hand,
He opes his dying eyes, soon closed again.
"The gods have robb'd me of a guiltless life,"
I hear him say: "Take care of sad Aricia
When I am dead. Dear friend, if e'er my father
Mourn, undeceived, his son's unhappy fate
Falsely accused; to give my spirit peace,
Tell him to treat his captive tenderly,
And to restore—" With that the hero's breath
Fails, and a mangled corpse lies in my arms,
A piteous object, trophy of the wrath
Of Heav'n—so changed, his father would not know him.

    THESEUS   Alas, my son! Dear hope forever lost!
The ruthless gods have served me but too well.
For what a life of anguish and remorse
Am I reserved!

THERAMENES   Aricia at that instant,
Flying from you, comes timidly, to take him
For husband, there, in presence of the gods.
Thus drawing nigh, she sees the grass all red
And reeking, sees (sad sight for lover's eyes!)
Hippolytus stretch'd there, pale and disfigured.
But, for a time doubtful of her misfortune,
Unrecognized the hero she adores,
She looks, and asks—"Where is Hippolytus?"
Only too sure at last that he lies there
Before her, with sad eyes that silently
Reproach the gods, she shudders, groans, and falls,
Swooning and all but lifeless, at his feet.
Ismene, all in tears, kneels down beside her,
And calls her back to life—life that is nought
But sense of pain. And I, to whom this light
Is darkness now, come to discharge the duty
The hero has imposed on me, to tell thee
His last request—a melancholy task.
But hither comes his mortal enemy.

SCENE VII

Theseus, Phaedra, Theramenes, Panope, Guards

THESEUS   Madam, you've triumph'd, and my son is kill'd!
Ah, but what room have I for fear! How justly
Suspicion racks me that in blaming him
I err'd! But he is dead; accept your victim;
Rightly or wrongly slain, let your heart leap
For joy. My eyes shall be forever blind:
Since you accuse him, I'll believe him guilty.
His death affords me cause enough for tears,
Without a foolish search for further light
Which, pow'rless to restore him to my grief,
Might only serve to make me more unhappy.
Far from this shore and far from you I'll fly,
For here the image of my mangled son
Would haunt my memory and drive me mad.
From the whole world I fain would banish me,

For all the world seems to rise up in judgment
Against me; and my very glory weights
My punishment; for, were my name less known,
'Twere easier to hide me. All the favors
The gods have granted me I mourn and hate,
Nor will I importune them with vain pray'rs
Henceforth forever. Give me what they may,
What they have taken will all else outweigh.

  PHAEDRA Theseus, I cannot hear you and keep silence:
I must repair the wrong that he has suffer'd—
Your son was innocent.

  THESEUS   Unhappy father!
And it was on your word that I condemn'd him!
Think you such cruelty can be excused—

  PHAEDRA Moments to me are precious; hear me, Theseus.
'Twas I who cast an eye of lawless passion
On chaste and dutiful Hippolytus.
Heav'n in my bosom kindled baleful fire,
And vile Oenone's cunning did the rest;
She fear'd Hippolytus, knowing my madness,
Would make that passion known which he regarded
With horror; so advantage of my weakness
She took, and hastened to accuse him first.
For that she has been punish'd, tho' too mildly;
Seeking to shun my wrath she cast herself
Beneath the waves. The sword ere now had cut
My thread of life, but slander'd innocence
Made its cry heard, and I resolved to die
In a more lingering way, confessing first
My penitence to you. A poison, brought
To Athens by Medea, runs thro' my veins.
Already in my heart the venom works,
Infusing there a strange and fatal chill;
Already as thro' thickening mists I see
The spouse to whom my presence is an outrage;
Death, from mine eyes veiling the light of heav'n,
Restores its purity that they defiled.

  PANOPE She dies, my lord!

  THESEUS   Would that the memory

Of her disgraceful deed could perish with her!
Ah, disabused too late! Come, let us go,
And with the blood of mine unhappy son
Mingle our tears, clasping his dear remains,
In deep repentance for a pray'r detested.
Let him be honor'd as he well deserves;
And, to appease his sore offended ghost,
Be her near kinsmen's guilt whate'er it may,
Aricia shall be held my daughter from to-day.

John Locke

John Locke

—————— 6 ——————

*An Essay Concerning
Human Understanding*

John Locke (1632–1704) carried on the empirical tradition in philosophy
that was so important for the development of scientific method. A contemporary of Newton, Locke did for human nature what Newton did for
the cosmos and became the official philosopher of his age. He was, however,
no "closet thinker." Living through the English revolutions of the seventeenth century, Locke had strong political preferences and acted on them.
He opposed royal absolutism and supported the Whigs in their bid for
parliamentary supremacy; for these activities, Locke suffered exile and loss
of his fortune. He was also a student of science, a practicing physician, a
friend of leading scientists, and one of the founders of the Royal Society.
Philosophically, Locke was an empiricist, although he was not thoroughly
consistent in his views. He said he was driven to study the process of
knowing because of the fruitlessness of metaphysical discussions of absolute
truth and reality. For Locke, there were no absolute principles of knowledge. All knowledge was partial and tentative, formed progressively by the
use of what was given in sense perception. By his common-sense arguments, Locke freed the psychological process of knowing from the incubus
of innate ideas and brought it down to earth. He thus discredited abstract
rationalism, which hampered scientific investigation, and banished original
sin and heredity as the chief sources of human behavior. This environ-
mental psychology gave men an instrument with which to refashion the
world, for, if men were the products of their environment, then by changing the environment they could remake mankind—a basic article of faith
of the Enlightenment.

In *An Essay Concerning Human Understanding* (1690), Locke explores
introspectively the operations of the mind and tells us what knowledge is,

John Locke, *An Essay Concerning Human Understanding,* in *The Philosophical
Works of John Locke,* ed. J. A. St. John (London: George Bell and Sons, 1892),
I, 134–37, 142–47, 205–08, 210–11, 221–27, 279–80.

how it is acquired, and how valid it is. He denies the existence of innate logical or moral principles, picturing the mind at birth as a blank tablet (*tabula rasa*) on which experience and reasoning write the script. His theory, which may seem commonplace and incomplete today, was quite revolutionary in its time.

NO INNATE PRINCIPLES IN THE MIND

The way shown how we come by any Knowledge, sufficient to prove it not innate.—It is an established opinion amongst some men that there are in the understanding certain innate principles; some primary notions, characters, as it were, stamped upon the mind of man, which the soul receives in its very first being, and brings into the world with it. It would be sufficient to convince unprejudiced readers of the falseness of this supposition, if I should only show (as I hope I shall in the following parts of this discourse) how men, barely by the use of their natural faculties, may attain to all the knowledge they have, without the help of any innate impressions, and may arrive at certainty, without any such original notions or principles. For I imagine any one will easily grant that it would be impertinent to suppose the ideas of colours innate in a creature to whom God hath given sight, and a power to receive them by the eyes from external objects: and no less unreasonable would it be to attribute several truths to the impressions of nature and innate characters, when we may observe in ourselves faculties fit to attain as easy and certain knowledge of them, as if they were originally imprinted on the mind.

But because a man is not permitted without censure to follow his own thoughts in the search of truth, when they lead him ever so little out of the common road, I shall set down the reasons that made me doubt of the truth of that opinion, as an excuse for my mistake, if I be in one; which I leave to be considered by those who, with me, dispose themselves to embrace truth wherever they find it.

General Assent the great Argument.—There is nothing more commonly taken for granted than that there are certain principles, both speculative and practical, (for they speak of both,) universally agreed upon by all mankind, which therefore, they argue, must needs be constant impressions, which the souls of men receive in their first beings, and which they bring into the world with them, as necessarily and really as they do any of their inherent faculties.

Universal Consent proves nothing innate.—This argument, drawn from universal consent, has this misfortune in it, that if it were true in matter of fact, that there were certain truths wherein all mankind agreed, it would not prove them innate, if there can be any other way shown how men may come to that universal agreement in the things they do consent in, which I presume may be done.

"What is, is," and *"it is impossible for the same Thing to be and not to be,"* not universally assented to.—But, which is worse, this argument of universal consent, which is made use of to prove innate principles, seems to me a demonstration that there are none such; because there are none to which all mankind give an universal assent. I shall begin with the speculative, and instance in those magnified principles of demonstration, "whatsoever is, is," and "it is impossible for the same thing to be and not to be;" which, of all others, I think have the most allowed title to innate. These have so settled a reputation of maxims universally received, that it will no doubt be thought strange if any one should seem to question it. But yet I take liberty to say, that these propositions are so far from having an universal assent, that there are a great part of mankind to whom they are not so much as known.

Not on the Mind naturally imprinted, because not known to Children, Idiots, &c.—For, first, it is evident that all children and idiots have not the least apprehension or thought of them; and the want of that is enough to destroy that universal assent which must needs be the necessary concomitant of all innate truths: it seeming to me near a contradiction to say that there are truths imprinted on the soul which it perceives or understands not; imprinting, if it signify anything, being nothing else but the making certain truths to be perceived. For to imprint anything on the mind without the mind's perceiving it, seems to me hardly intelligible. If therefore children and idiots have souls, have minds, with those impressions upon them, they must unavoidably perceive them, and necessarily know and assent to these truths; which since they do not, it is evident that there are no such impressions. For if they are not notions naturally imprinted, how can they be innate? and if they are notions imprinted, how can they be unknown? To say a notion is imprinted on the mind, and yet at the same time to say that the mind is ignorant of it, and never yet took notice of it, is to make this impression nothing. No proposition can be said to be in the mind which it never yet knew, which it was never yet conscious of.

• • •

The Steps by which the Mind attains several Truths.—The senses at first let in particular ideas, and furnish the yet empty cabinet; and the mind by degrees growing familiar with some of them, they are lodged in the memory, and names got to them. Afterwards, the mind proceeeding further, abstracts them, and by degrees learns the use of general names. In this manner the mind comes to be furnished with ideas and language, the materials about which to exercise its discursive faculty; and the use of reason becomes daily more visible, as these materials that give it employment increase. But though the having of general ideas and the use of general words and reason usually grow together, yet I see not how this any way proves them innate. The knowledge of some truths, I confess, is very early in the mind; but in a way that shows them not to be innate. For if we will observe, we shall find it still to be about ideas not innate but acquired; it being about those first which are imprinted by external things, with which infants have earliest to do, which make the most frequent impressions on their senses. In ideas thus got the mind discovers that some agree and others differ, probably as soon as it has any use of memory, as soon as it is able to retain and perceive distinct ideas. But whether it be then or no, this is certain, it does so long before it has the use of words, or comes to that which we commonly call "the use of reason." For a child knows as certainly before it can speak the difference between the ideas of sweet and bitter (i.e., that sweet is not bitter), as it knows afterwards (when it comes to speak) that wormwood and sugarplums are not the same thing.

A child knows not that three and four are equal to seven, till he comes to be able to count seven, and has got the name and idea of equality; and then, upon explaining those words, he presently assents to, or rather perceives the truth of that proposition. But neither does he then readily assent because it is an innate truth, nor was his assent wanting till then because he wanted the use of reason; but the truth of it appears to him as soon as he has settled in his mind the clear and distinct ideas that these names stand for; and then he knows the truth of that proposition upon the same grounds and by the same means that he knew before that a rod and cherry are not the same thing; and upon the same ground also that he may come to know afterwards "that it is impossible for the same thing to be and not to be," as shall be more fully shown hereafter. So that the later it is before any one comes to have those general ideas about which those maxims are, or to know the signification of those general terms that stand for them, or to put together in his mind the ideas they stand for, the later also will it be before he comes to assent to those maxims, whose terms, with the ideas they stand for, being no more innate than those of a cat or a weasel, he must stay till time and observation have acquainted him with them; and then he will be in a capacity to know the truth of these maxims, upon the first occasion that shall make him put together those ideas in his mind, and observe whether they agree or disagree, according as is expressed in those propositions. And therefore it is that a man knows that eighteen and nineteen are equal to thirty-seven, by the same self-evidence that he knows one and two to be equal to three: yet a child knows this not so soon as the other; not for want of the use of reason, but because the ideas the words eighteen, nineteen, and thirty-seven stand for, are not so soon got as those which are signified by one, two, and three.

Assenting as soon as proposed and understood, proves them not innate.—This evasion therefore of general assent when men come to the use of reason, failing as it does, and leaving no difference between those supposed innate and other truths that are afterwards acquired and learnt, men have endeavoured to secure an universal assent to those they call maxims, by saying they are generally assented to as soon as proposed, and the terms they are proposed in understood: seeing all men, even children, as soon as they hear and understand the terms assent to these propositions, they think it is sufficient to prove them innate. For since men never fail after they have once understood the words, to acknowledge them for undoubted truths, they would infer that certainly these propositions were first lodged in the understanding which, without any teaching, the mind, at the very first proposal, immediately closes with and assents to, and after that never doubts again.

If such an Assent be a Mark of Innate, then "that one and two are equal to three, that Sweetness is not Bitterness," and a thousand the like, must be innate.—In answer to this, I demand "whether ready assent given to a proposition, upon first hearing and under-

standing the terms, be a certain mark of an innate principle?"
If it be not, such a general assent is in vain urged as a proof of them:
if it be said that it is a mark of innate, they must then allow all
such propositions to be innate which are generally assented to as
soon as heard, whereby they will find themselves plentifully stored
with innate principles. For upon the same ground, viz., of assent
at first hearing and understanding the terms, that men would have
those maxims pass for innate, they must also admit several propositions about numbers to be innate; and thus, that one and two are
equal to three, that two and two are equal to four, and a multitude
of other the like propositions in numbers, that everybody assents
to at first hearing and understanding the terms, must have a place
amongst these innate axioms. Nor is this the prerogative of numbers alone, and propositions made about several of them; but even
natural philosophy, and all the other sciences, afford propositions
which are sure to meet with assent as soon as they are understood.
That two bodies cannot be in the same place, is a truth that nobody
any more sticks at than at these maxims, "that it is impossible for
the same thing to be and not to be, that white is not black, that a
square is not a circle, that bitterness is not sweetness:" these and a
million of such other propositions, as many at least as we have distinct ideas of, every man in his wits, at first hearing and knowing
what the names stand for, must necessarily assent to. If these men will
be true to their own rule, and have assent at first hearing and understanding the terms to be a mark of innate, they must allow not only
as many innate propositions as men have distinct ideas, but as
many as men can make propositions wherein different ideas are
denied one of another. Since every proposition, wherein one different idea is denied of another, will as certainly find assent at first
hearing and understanding the terms as this general one, "it is impossible for the same thing to be and not to be," or that which is
the foundation of it, and is the easier understood of the two, "the
same is not different;" by which account they will have legions of
innate propositions of this one sort, without mentioning any other.
But since no proposition can be innate unless the ideas about which
it is be innate, this will be to suppose all our ideas of colours,
sounds, tastes, figure, &c. innate, than which there cannot be anything more opposite to reason and experience. Universal and ready
assent upon hearing and understanding the terms is, I grant, a mark
of self-evidence; but self-evidence, depending not on innate impres-

sions, but on something else, (as we shall show hereafter,) belongs to several propositions which nobody was yet so extravagant as to pretend to be innate.

. . . .

OF IDEAS IN GENERAL, AND THEIR ORIGINAL

Idea is the Object of Thinking.—Every man being conscious to himself that he thinks, and that which his mind is applied about whilst thinking, being the ideas that are there, it is past doubt that men have in their minds several ideas, such as are those expressed by the words whiteness, hardness, sweetness, thinking, motion, man, elephant, army, drunkenness, and others. It is in the first place then to be inquired how he comes by them. I know it is a received doctrine that men have native ideas and original characters stamped upon their minds in their very first being. This opinion I have at large examined already; and I suppose what I have [already] said . . . will be much more easily admitted when I have shown whence the understanding may get all the ideas it has, and by what ways and degrees they may come into the mind; for which I shall appeal to every one's own observation and experience.

All Ideas come from Sensation or Reflection.—Let us then suppose the mind to be, as we say, white paper, void of all characters, without any ideas; how comes it to be furnished? Whence comes it by that vast store which the busy and boundless fancy of man has painted on it with an almost endless variety? Whence has it all the materials of reason and knowledge? To this I answer in one word, from experience; in that all our knowledge is founded, and from that it ultimately derives itself. Our observation employed either about external sensible objects, or about the internal operations of our minds, perceived and reflected on by ourselves, is that which supplies our understandings with all the materials of thinking. These two are the fountains of knowledge from whence all the ideas we have or can naturally have do spring.

The Objects of Sensation one Source of Ideas.—First, our senses, conversant about particular sensible objects, do convey into the mind several distinct perceptions of things, according to those various ways wherein those objects do affect them: and thus we come by those ideas we have, of yellow, white, heat, cold, soft, hard, bitter, sweet, and all those which we call sensible qualities; which when I say the senses convey into the mind, I mean, they from external objects convey into the mind what produces there those perceptions. This great source of most of the ideas we have, depending wholly upon our senses, and derived by them to the understanding, I call Sensation.

The Operations of our Minds, the other Source of them.—Secondly, the other fountain, from which experience furnisheth the understanding with ideas, is the perception of the operations of our own mind within us, as it is employed about the ideas it has got; which operations, when the soul comes to reflect on and consider, do furnish the understanding with another set of ideas, which could not be had from things without; and such are perception, thinking, doubting, believing, reasoning, knowing, willing, and all the different actings of our own minds; which we being conscious of, and observing in ourselves, do from these receive into our understandings as distinct ideas, as we do from bodies affecting our senses. This source of ideas every man has wholly in himself; and though it be not sense, as having nothing to do with external objects, yet it is very like it, and might properly enough be called internal sense. But as I call the other Sensation, so I call this Reflection, the ideas it affords being such only as the mind gets by reflecting on its own operations within itself. By reflection then, in the following part of this discourse, I would be understood to mean that notice which the mind takes of its own operations, and the manner of them; by reason whereof there come to be ideas of these operations in the understanding. These two, I say, viz., external material things, as the objects of sensation; and the operations of our own minds within, as the objects of reflection; are to me the only originals from whence all our ideas take their beginnings. The term operations here I use in a large sense, as comprehending not barely the actions of the mind about its ideas, but some sort of passions arising sometimes from them, such as is the satisfaction or uneasiness arising from any thought.

All our Ideas are of the one or the other of these.—The understanding seems to me not to have the least glimmering of any ideas which it doth not receive from one of these two. External objects furnish the mind with the ideas of sensible qualities, which are all those different perceptions they produce in us; and the mind furnishes the understanding with ideas of its own operations.

These, when we have taken a full survey of them, and their sev-

eral modes, combinations, and relations, we shall find to contain all
our whole stock of ideas; and that we have nothing in our minds,
which did not come in one of these two ways. Let any one examine
his own thoughts, and thoroughly search into his understanding;
and then let him tell me, whether all the original ideas he has there,
are any other than of the objects of his senses, or of the operations of
his mind, considered as objects of his reflection: and how great a
mass of knowledge soever he imagines to be lodged there, he will,
upon taking a strict view, see that he has not any idea in his mind,
but what one of these two have imprinted; though, perhaps, with
infinite variety compounded and enlarged by the understanding, as
we shall see hereafter.

.   .   .

The Soul begins to have Ideas when it begins to perceive.—To
ask at what time a man has first any ideas, is to ask when he begins
to perceive; having ideas, and perception, being the same thing. I
know it is an opinion, that the soul always thinks, and that it has
the actual perception of ideas in itself constantly, as long as it
exists, and that actual thinking is as inseparable from the soul as
actual extension is from the body; which if true, to inquire after
the beginning of a man's ideas, is the same as to inquire after the
beginning of his soul: for by this account, soul and its ideas, as
body and its extension, will begin to exist both at the same time.

.   .   .

*No Ideas but from Sensation and Reflection, evident, if we observe
Children.*—I see no reason, therefore, to believe that the soul thinks
before the senses have furnished it with ideas to think on; and as
those are increased and retained, so it comes, by exercise, to improve its faculty of thinking in the several parts of it, as well as,
afterwards, by compounding those ideas and reflecting on its own
operations; it increases its stock, as well as facility, in remembering,
imagining, reasoning, and other modes of thinking.

He that will suffer himself to be informed by observation and
experience, and not make his own hypothesis the rule of nature,
will find few signs of a soul accustomed to much thinking in a new-
born child, and much fewer of any reasoning at all; and yet it is
hard to imagine that the rational soul should think so much, and
not reason at all. And he that will consider that infants newly

come into the world spend the greatest part of their time in sleep, and are seldom awake but when either hunger calls for the teat, or some pain (the most importunate of all sensations) or some other violent impression on the body forces the mind to perceive and attend to it; he, I say, who considers this, will perhaps find reason to imagine that a foetus in the mother's womb differs not much from the state of a vegetable, but passes the greatest part of its time without perception or thought, doing very little in a place where it needs not seek for food, and is surrounded with liquor, always equally soft, and near of the same temper; where the eyes have no light, and the ears so shut up, are not very susceptible of sounds; and where there is little or no variety, or change of objects to move the senses.

Follow a child from its birth, and observe the alterations that time makes, and you shall find, as the mind by the senses comes more and more to be furnished with ideas, it comes to be more and more awake; thinks more, the more it has matter to think on. After some time it begins to know the objects which, being most familiar with it, have made lasting impressions: thus it comes by degrees to know the persons it daily converses with and distinguishes them from strangers, which are instances and effects of its coming to re- tain and distinguish the ideas the senses convey to it. And so we may observe how the mind, by degrees, improves in these, and advances to the exercise of those other faculties of enlarging, compounding, and abstracting its ideas, and of reasoning about them, and reflect- ing upon all these; of which I shall have occasion to speak more hereafter.

If it shall be demanded, then, when a man begins to have any ideas, I think the true answer is, when he first has any sensation; for, since there appear not to be any ideas in the mind before the senses have conveyed any in, I conceive that ideas in the understand- ing are coeval with sensation, which is such an impression or motion made in some part of the body, as produces some perception in the understanding. It is about these impressions made on our senses by outward objects, that the mind seems first to employ itself in such operations as we call perception, remembering, consideration, rea- soning, &c.

The Original of all our Knowledge.—In time the mind comes to reflect on its own operations about the ideas got by sensation, and thereby stores itself with a new set of ideas which I call ideas of reflection. These are the impressions that are made on our senses by outward objects that are extrinsical to the mind, and its own operations, proceeding from powers intrinsical and proper to itself; which, when reflected on by itself, becoming also objects of its contemplation, are, as I have said, the original of all knowledge. Thus the first capacity of human intellect is, that the mind is fitted to receive the impressions made on it, either through the senses by outward objects, or by its own operations when it reflects on them. This is the first step a man makes towards the discovery of anything, and the groundwork whereon to build all those notions which ever he shall have naturally in this world. All those sublime thoughts which tower above the clouds, and reach as high as heaven itself, take their rise and footing here: in all that good extent wherein the mind wanders, in those remote speculations it may seem to be elevated with, it stirs not one jot beyond those ideas which sense or reflection has offered for its contemplation.

In the Reception of simple Ideas, the Understanding is for the most part passive.—In this part the understanding is merely passive; and whether or not it will have these beginnings, and, as it were, materials of knowledge, is not in its own power: for the objects of our senses do, many of them, obtrude their particular ideas upon our minds whether we will or not; and the operations of our minds will not let us be without, at least, some obscure notions of them. No man can be wholly ignorant of what he does when he thinks. These simple ideas, when offered to the mind, the understanding can no more refuse to have, nor alter, when they are imprinted, nor blot them out, and make new ones itself, than a mirror can refuse, alter, or obliterate the images or ideas which the objects set before it do therein produce. As the bodies that surround us do diversely affect our organs, the mind is forced to receive the impressions, and cannot avoid the perception of those ideas that are annexed to them.

OF SIMPLE IDEAS

Uncompounded Appearances.—The better to understand the nature, manner, and extent of our knowledge, one thing is carefully to be observed concerning the ideas we have; and that is, that some of them are simple and some complex.

Though the qualities that affect our senses are, in the things themselves, so united and blended, that there is no separation, no distance between them; yet it is plain, the ideas they produce in the mind enter by the senses simple and unmixed. For though the sight and touch often take in from the same object, at the same time, different ideas; as a man sees at once motion and colour; the hand feels softness and warmth in the same piece of wax; yet the simple ideas thus united in the same subject, are as perfectly distinct as those that come in by different senses: the coldness and hardness which a man feels in a piece of ice being as distinct ideas in the mind, as the smell and whiteness of a lily, or as the taste of sugar, and smell of a rose. And there is nothing can be plainer to a man, than the clear and distinct perception he has of those simple ideas; which being each in itself uncompounded, contains in it nothing but one uniform appearance or conception in the mind, and is not distinguishable into different ideas.

The Mind can neither make nor destroy them.—These simple ideas, the materials of all our knowledge, are suggested and furnished to the mind only by those two ways above mentioned, viz., sensation and reflection. When the understanding is once stored with these simple ideas, it has the power to repeat, compare, and unite them, even to an almost infinite variety, and so can make at pleasure new complex ideas. But it is not in the power of the most exalted wit, or enlarged understanding, by any quickness or variety of thought, to invent or frame one new simple idea in the mind, not taken in by the ways before mentioned: nor can any force of the understanding destroy those that are there. The dominion of man, in this little world of his own understanding, being muchwhat the same as it is in the great world of visible things; wherein his power, however managed by art and skill, reaches no farther than to compound and divide the materials that are made to his hand; but can do nothing towards the making the least particle of new matter, or destroying one atom of what is already in being. The same inability will every one find in himself, who shall go about to fashion in his understanding one simple idea, not received in by his senses from external objects, or by reflection from the operations of his own mind about them. I would have any one try to fancy any taste which had never affected his palate, or frame the idea of a scent he had never smelt; and when he can do this, I will also conclude that a blind man hath ideas of colours, and a deaf man true distinct notions of sounds.

This is the reason why, though we cannot believe it impossible to God to make a creature with other organs, and more ways to convey into the understanding the notice of corporeal things than those five, as they are usually counted, which he has given to man; yet I think it is not possible for any one to imagine any other qualities in bodies, howsoever constituted, whereby they can be taken notice of, besides sounds, tastes, smells, visible and tangible qualities. And had mankind been made but with four senses, the qualities then which are the object of the fifth sense, had been as far from our notice, imagination, and conception, as now any belonging to a sixth, seventh, or eighth sense can possibly be; which, whether yet some other creatures, in some other parts of this vast and stupendous universe, may not have, will be a great presumption to deny. He that will not set himself proudly at the top of all things, but will consider the immensity of this fabric, and the great variety that is to be found in this little and inconsiderable part of it which he has to do with, may be apt to think, that in other mansions of it there may be other and different intelligent beings, of whose faculties he has as little knowledge or apprehension, as a worm shut up in one drawer of a cabinet hath of the senses or understanding of a man: such variety and excellency being suitable to the wisdom and power of the Maker. I have here followed the common opinion of man's having but five senses, though, perhaps, there may be justly counted more; but either supposition serves equally to my present purpose.

OF IDEAS OF ONE SENSE

Division of simple Ideas.—The better to conceive the ideas we receive from sensation, it may not be amiss for us to consider them in reference to the different ways whereby they make their approaches to our minds, and make themselves perceivable by us.

First, then, There are some which come into our minds by one sense only.

Secondly, There are others that convey themselves into the mind by more senses than one.

Thirdly, Others that are had from reflection only.

Fourthly, There are some that make themselves way, and are suggested to the mind by all the ways of sensation and reflection.

We shall consider them apart under their several heads.

Ideas of one Sense, as Colours, of Seeing; Sound, of Hearing, &c.—
There are some ideas which have admittance only through one sense,
which is peculiarly adapted to receive them. Thus light and colours,
as white, red, yellow, blue, with their several degrees or shades and
mixtures, as green, scarlet, purple, sea-green, and the rest, come in
only by the eyes; all kinds of noises, sounds, and tones, only by
the ears; the several tastes and smells, by the nose and palate.
And if these organs, or the nerves, which are the conduits to convey
them from without to their audience in the brain,—the mind's
presence-room, as I may so call it,—are any of them so disordered as
not to perform their functions, they have no postern to be admitted
by, no other way to bring themselves into view, and be perceived by
the understanding.

The most considerable of those belonging to the touch, are heat
and cold, and solidity: all the rest, consisting almost wholly in the
sensible configuration, as smooth and rough; or else more or less
firm adhesion of the parts, as hard and soft, tough and brittle, are
obvious enough.

· · ·

OF COMPLEX IDEAS

Made by the Mind out of simple Ones.—We have hitherto considered those ideas, in the reception whereof the mind is only passive,
which are those simple ones received from sensation and reflection
before mentioned, whereof the mind cannot make one to itself,
nor have any idea which does not wholly consist of them. But as
the mind is wholly passive in the reception of all its simple ideas,
so it exerts several acts of its own, whereby out of its simple ideas,
as the materials and foundations of the rest, the others are framed.
The acts of the mind, wherein it exerts its power over its simple
ideas, are chiefly these three: 1. Combining several simple ideas
into one compound one, and thus all complex ideas are made.
2. The second is bringing two ideas, whether simple or complex,
together, and setting them by one another so as to take a view of
them at once, without uniting them into one, by which way it gets
all its ideas of relations. 3. The third is separating them from all
other ideas that accompany them in their real existence: this is
called abstraction, and thus all its general ideas are made. This

shows man's power, and its ways of operation, to be much the same in the material and intellectual world. For the materials in both being such as he has no power over, either to make or destroy, all that man can do is either to unite them together, or to set them by one another, or wholly separate them. I shall here begin with the first of these in the consideration of complex ideas, and come to the other two in their due places. As simple ideas are observed to exist in several combinations united together, so the mind has a power to consider several of them united together as one idea; and that not only as they are united in external objects, but as itself has joined them together. Ideas thus made up of several simple ones put together, I call complex; such as are beauty, gratitude, a man, an army, the universe, which, though complicated of various simple ideas, or complex ideas made up of simple ones, yet are, when the mind pleases, considered each by itself as one entire thing, and signified by one name.

Made voluntarily.—In this faculty of repeating and joining together its ideas, the mind has great power in varying and multiplying the objects of its thoughts, infinitely beyond what sensation or reflection furnished it with; but all this still confined to those simple ideas which it received from those two sources, and which are the ultimate materials of all its compositions: for simple ideas are all from things themselves, and of these the mind can have no more, nor other than what are suggested to it. It can have no other ideas of sensible qualities than what come from without by the senses, nor any ideas of other kind of operations of a thinking substance, than what it finds in itself; but when it has once got these simple ideas, it is not confined barely to observation, and what offers itself from without; it can, by its own power, put together those ideas it has, and make new complex ones, which it never received so united.

John Locke

7

Of Civil Government

Locke opposed dogmatism not only in philosophy but also in religion and politics. He favored a greater degree of freedom in religion and education. In political thought, he provided the philosophical basis of classical liberalism—the theory and practice of limited, representative government. He wished to liberate society from the unnatural restrictions imposed by royal absolutism and to free the individual for maximum development according to the laws of nature. Locke's political ideas, set down in *Two Treatises of Government* (1690), served as a justification of the English "Glorious Revolution" of 1688 and strongly influenced the American and French Revolutions and, subsequently, the development of constitutional democracy. The First Treatise attacked the theory of absolute monarchy. The purpose of the Second Treatise, *Of Civil Government,* from which this selection is taken, was, as Locke said in the preface, "to establish the throne of our great restorer, our present King William; to make good his title in the consent of the people . . . , and to justify to the world the people of England whose love of their just and natural rights, with their resolution to preserve them, saved the nation. . . ." Although the Second Treatise sounds like a response to the events of 1688–1689, it was actually written some years before, probably in 1681. In this work, Locke based all government on the natural rights of man and on the social contract. Specifically, this meant that government should rest on the consent of the governed and be limited in its powers. It is important to note the secular origin of government in Locke's theory as well as its fundamental individualism, which held that individual men were free moral agents who existed prior to the establishment of government and were the very basis of it. Locke thus denied the intrinsic authority of the state; he lodged sovereignty

John Locke, *Two Treatises of Government,* in *The Works of John Locke* (London: Thomas Tegg, 1823), V, 339–42, 352–54, 394–96, 411–15, 457, 459–60, 469–73, 483–85.

in the individuals who make up the state and held that no government might intrude into their private affairs.

OF THE STATE OF NATURE

To understand political power right, and derive it from its original, we must consider what state all men are naturally in, and that is, a state of perfect freedom to order their actions and dispose of their possessions and persons, as they think fit, within the bounds of the law of nature; without asking leave, or depending upon the will of any other man.

A state also of equality, wherein all the power and jurisdiction is reciprocal, no one having more than another; there being nothing more evident than that creatures of the same species and rank, promiscuously born to all the same advantages of nature, and the use of the same faculties, should also be equal one amongst another without subordination or subjection; unless the Lord and Master of them all should, by any manifest declaration of his will, set one above another, and confer on him, by an evident and clear appointment, an undoubted right to dominion and sovereignty.

· · ·

But though this be a state of liberty, yet it is not a state of licence: though man in that state have an uncontrollable liberty to dispose of his person or possessions, yet he has not liberty to destroy himself, or so much as any creature in his possession, but where some nobler use than its bare preservation calls for it. The state of nature has a law of nature to govern it, which obliges every one: and reason, which is that law, teaches all mankind, who will but consult it, that being all equal and independent, no one ought to harm another in his life, health, liberty, or possessions: for men being all the workmanship of one omnipotent and infinitely wise Maker; all the servants of one sovereign Master, sent into the world by his order, and about his business; they are his property, whose workmanship they are, made to last during his, not another's pleasure: and being furnished with like faculties, sharing all in one community of nature, there cannot be supposed any such subordination among us that may authorize us to destroy another, as if we were made for one another's uses, as the inferior ranks of creatures are for ours. Every one, as he is bound to preserve himself, and not to quit his station wilfully, so by the like reason, when his own preservation comes not in competition, ought he, as much as he can, to preserve the rest of mankind, and may not, unless it be to do justice to an offender, take away or impair the life, or what tends to the preservation of life, the liberty, health, limb, or goods of another.

And that all men may be restrained from invading others' rights, and from doing hurt to one another, and the law of nature be observed, which willeth the peace and preservation of all mankind, the execution of the law of nature is, in that state, put into every man's hands, whereby every one has a right to punish the transgressors of that law to such a degree as may hinder its violation: for the law of nature would, as all other laws that concern men in this world, be in vain, if there were nobody that in the state of nature had a power to execute that law, and thereby preserve the innocent, and restrain offenders. And if any one in the state of nature may punish another for any evil he has done, every one may do so: for in that state of perfect equality, where naturally there is no superiority or jurisdiction of one over another, what any may do in prosecution of that law every one must needs have a right to do.

.   .   .

OF PROPERTY

Whether we consider natural reason, which tells us, that men, being once born, have a right to their preservation, and consequently to meat and drink, and such other things as nature affords for their subsistence; or revelation, which gives us an account of those grants God made of the world to Adam, and to Noah, and his sons; it is very clear, that God, as king David says, Psal. cxv. 16, "has given the earth to the children of men;" given it to mankind in common. But this being supposed, it seems to some a very great difficulty how any one should ever come to have a property in any thing: I will not content myself to answer, that if it be difficult to make out property, upon a supposition that God gave the world to Adam and his posterity in common, it is impossible that any man, but one universal monarch, should have any property, upon a supposition that God gave the world to Adam, and his heirs in succession, exclusive of all the rest of his posterity. But I shall endeavour to show how men might come to have a property in several parts of that which God gave to mankind in common, and that without any express compact of all the commoners.

God, who hath given the world to men in common, hath also given them reason to make use of it to the best advantage of life and convenience. The earth, and all that is therein, is given to men for the support and comfort of their being. And though all the fruits it naturally produces, and beasts it feeds, belong to mankind in common, as they are produced by the spontaneous hand of nature; and nobody has originally a private dominion, exclusive of the rest of mankind, in any of them, as they are thus in their natural state: yet being given for the use of men, there must of necessity be a means to appropriate them some way or other before they can be of any use, or at all beneficial to any particular man. The fruit, or venison, which nourishes the wild Indian, who knows no enclosure, and is still a tenant in common, must be his, and so his, *i.e.*, a part of him, that another can no longer have any right to it, before it can do him any good for the support of his life.

Though the earth, and all inferior creatures, be common to all men, yet every man has a property in his own person: this nobody has any right to but himself. The labour of his body, and the work of his hands, we may say, are properly his. Whatsoever then he removes out of the state that nature hath provided, and left it in, he hath mixed his labour with, and joined to it something that is his own, and thereby makes it his property. It being by him removed from the common state nature hath placed it in, it hath by this labour something annexed to it that excludes the common right of other men. For this labour being the unquestionable property of the labourer, no man but he can have a right to what that is once joined to, at least where there is enough, and as good, left in common for others.

.   .   .

OF THE BEGINNING OF POLITICAL SOCIETIES

Men being, as has been said, by nature all free, equal, and independent, no one can be put out of this estate, and subjected to the political power of another, without his own consent. The only way

whereby any one divests himself of his natural liberty, and puts
on the bonds of civil society, is by agreeing with other men to
join and unite into a community, for their comfortable, safe, and
peaceable living one amongst another, in a secure enjoyment of
their properties, and a greater security against any that are not of
it. This any number of men may do, because it injures not the
freedom of the rest; they are left as they were in the liberty of the
state of nature. When any number of men have so consented to
make one community or government, they are thereby presently
incorporated, and make one body politic, wherein the majority
have a right to act and conclude the rest.

For when any number of men have, by the consent of every
individual, made a community, they have thereby made that community one body, with a power to act as one body, which is only
by the will and determination of the majority; for that which acts
any community being only the consent of the individuals of it,
and it being necessary to that which is one body to move one way;
it is necessary the body should move that way whither the greater
force carries it, which is the consent of the majority: or else it is
impossible it should act or continue one body, one community,
which the consent of every individual that united into it agreed
that it should; and so every one is bound by that consent to be
concluded by the majority. And therefore we see that in assemblies,
empowered to act by positive laws, where no number is set by that
positive law which empowers them, the act of the majority passes
for the act of the whole, and of course determines; as having, by
the law of nature and reason, the power of the whole.

And thus every man, by consenting with others to make one
body politic under one government, puts himself under an obligation to every one of that society to submit to the determination of
the majority, and to be concluded by it; or else this original compact, whereby he with others incorporate into one society, would
signify nothing, and be no compact, if he be left free, and under
no other ties than he was in before in the state of nature. For
what appearance would there be of any compact? what new engagement, if he were no farther tied by any decrees of the society than
he himself thought fit, and did actually consent to? This would be
still as great a liberty as he himself had before his compact, or
any one else in the state of nature hath, who may submit himself
and consent to any acts of it if he thinks fit.

For if the consent of the majority shall not, in reason, be received as the act of the whole, and conclude every individual, nothing but the consent of every individual can make any thing to be the act of the whole: but such a consent is next to impossible ever to be had, if we consider the infirmities of health, and avocations of business, which in a number, though much less than that of a commonwealth, will necessarily keep many away from the public assembly. To which if we add the variety of opinions, and contrariety of interests which unavoidably happen in all collections of men, the coming into society upon such terms would be only like Cato's coming into the theatre, only to go out again. Such a constitution as this would make the mighty leviathan of a shorter duration than the feeblest creatures, and not let it outlast the day it was born in: which cannot be supposed, till we can think that rational creatures should desire and constitute societies only to be dissolved: for where the majority cannot conclude the rest, there they cannot act as one body, and consequently will be immediately dissolved again.

Whosoever therefore out of a state of nature unite into a community, must be understood to give up all the power necessary to the ends for which they unite into society, to the majority of the community, unless they expressly agreed in any number greater than the majority. And this is done by barely agreeing to unite into one political society, which is all the compact that is, or needs be, between the individuals that enter into, or make up a commonwealth. And thus that which begins and actually constitutes any political society, is nothing but the consent of any number of freemen capable of a majority, to unite and incorporate into such a society. And this is that, and that only, which did or could give beginning to any lawful government in the world.

. . .

OF THE ENDS OF POLITICAL SOCIETY AND GOVERNMENT

If man in the state of nature be so free as has been said; if he be absolute lord of his own person and possessions, equal to the greatest, and subject to nobody, why will he part with his freedom, why will he give up this empire, and subject himself to the dominion and control of any other power? To which it is obvious to answer, that though in the state of nature he hath such a right, yet the enjoyment of it is very uncertain, and constantly exposed to the invasion of others; for all being kings as much as he, every man his equal, and the greater part no strict observers of equity and justice, the enjoyment of the property he has in this state is very unsafe, very unsecure. This makes him willing to quit a condition, which, however free, is full of fears and continual dangers: and it is not without reason that he seeks out, and is willing to join in society with others, who are already united, or have a mind to unite, for the mutual preservation of their lives, liberties, and estates, which I call by the general name property.

The great and chief end, therefore, of men's uniting into commonwealths, and putting themselves under government, is the preservation of their property. To which in the state of nature there are many things wanting.

First, There wants an established, settled, known law, received and allowed by common consent to be the standard of right and wrong, and the common measure to decide all controversies between them: for though the law of nature be plain and intelligible to all rational creatures; yet men being biased by their interest, as well as ignorant for want of studying it, are not apt to allow of it as a law binding to them in the application of it to their particular cases.

Secondly, In the state of nature there wants a known and indifferent judge, with authority to determine all differences according to the established law: for every one in that state being both judge and executioner of the law of nature, men being partial to themselves, passion and revenge is very apt to carry them too far, and with too much heat, in their own cases; as well as negligence and unconcernedness, to make them too remiss in other men's.

Thirdly, In the state of nature there often wants power to back and support the sentence when right, and to give it due execution. They who by any injustice offend, will seldom fail, where they are able, by force to make good their injustice; such resistance many times makes the punishment dangerous, and frequently destructive to those who attempt it.

Thus mankind, notwithstanding all the privileges of the state of nature, being but in an ill condition, while they remain in it, are quickly driven into society. Hence it comes to pass, that we seldom find any number of men live any time together in this state. The inconveniencies that they are therein exposed to, by the irregular and uncertain exercise of the power every man has of punishing the transgressions of others, make them take sanctuary under the established laws of government, and therein seek the preservation of their property. It is this makes them so willingly give up every one his single power of punishing, to be exercised by such alone as shall be appointed to it amongst them; and by such rules as the community, or those authorized by them to that purpose, shall agree on. And in this we have the original right of both the legislative and executive power, as well as of the governments and societies themselves.

For in the state of nature, to omit the liberty he has of innocent delights, a man has two powers.

The first is to do whatsoever he thinks fit for the preservation of himself and others within the permission of the law of nature: by which law, common to them all, he and all the rest of mankind are one community, make up one society, distinct from all other creatures. And, were it not for the corruption and viciousness of degenerate men, there would be no need of any other; no necessity that men should separate from this great and natural community, and by positive agreements combine into smaller and divided associations.

The other power a man has in the state of nature, is the power to punish the crimes committed against that law. Both these he gives up when he joins in a private, if I may so call it, or particular politic society, and incorporates into any commonwealth, separate from the rest of mankind.

The first power, viz. "of doing whatsoever he thought fit for the preservation of himself" and the rest of mankind, he gives up to be regulated by laws made by the society, so far forth as the preservation of himself and the rest of that society shall require; which laws of the society in many things confine the liberty he had by the law of nature.

Secondly, The power of punishing he wholly gives up, and engages his natural force (which he might before employ in the execution of the law of nature, by his own single authority, as he thought fit), to assist the executive power of the society, as the law thereof shall require: for being now in a new state, wherein he is to enjoy many conveniencies, from the labour, assistance, and society of others in the same community, as well as protection from its whole strength; he is to part also with as much of his natural liberty, in providing for himself, as the good, prosperity, and safety of the society shall require; which is not only necessary, but just, since the other members of the society do the like.

But though men, when they enter into society, give up the equality, liberty, and executive power they had in the state of nature, into the hands of the society, to be so far disposed of by the legislative as the good of the society shall require; yet it being only with an intention in every one the better to preserve himself, his liberty and property (for no rational creature can be supposed to change his condition with an intention to be worse); the power of the society, or legislative constituted by them, can never be supposed to extend farther than the common good; but is obliged to secure every one's property, by providing against those three defects abovementioned, that made the state of nature so unsafe and uneasy. And so whoever has the legislative or supreme power of any commonwealth, is bound to govern by established standing laws, promulgated and known to the people, and not by extemporary decrees; by indifferent and upright judges, who are to decide controversies by those laws; and to employ the force of the community at home, only in the execution of such laws; or abroad to prevent or redress foreign injuries, and secure the community from inroads and invasion. And all this to be directed to no other end but the peace, safety, and public good of the people.

*   *   *

OF TYRANNY

As usurpation is the exercise of power, which another hath a right to, so tyranny is the exercise of power beyond right, which nobody can have a right to. And this is making use of the power any one has in his hands, not for the good of those who are under it, but for his own private, separate advantage.—When the governor, however entitled, makes not the law, but his will, the rule; and his commands and actions are not directed to the preservation of the properties of his people, but the satisfaction of his own ambition, revenge, covetousness, or any other irregular passion.

*   *   *

Wherever law ends, tyranny begins, if the law be transgressed to another's harm; and whosoever in authority exceeds the power given him by the law, and makes use of the force he has under his command, to compass that upon the subject which the law allows not, ceases in that to be a magistrate; and, acting without authority, may be opposed as any other man who by force invades the right of another. This is acknowledged in subordinate magistrates. He that hath authority to seize my person in the street, may be opposed as a thief and a robber if he endeavours to break into my house to execute a writ, notwithstanding that I know he has such a warrant, and such a legal authority as will impower him to arrest me abroad. And why this should not hold in the highest, as well as in the most inferior magistrate, I would gladly be informed. Is it reasonable that the eldest brother, because he has the greatest part of his father's estate, should thereby have a right to take away any of his younger brother's portions? or that a rich man, who possessed a whole country, should from thence have a right to seize, when he pleased, the cottage and garden of his poor neighbour? The being rightfully possessed of great power and riches, exceedingly beyond the greatest part of the sons of Adam, is so far from being an excuse, much less a reason, for rapine and oppression, which the endamaging another without authority is, that it is a great aggravation of it: for the exceeding the bounds of authority is no more a right in a great, than in a petty officer; no more justifiable in a king than a constable; but is so much the worse in him, in that he has more trust put in him, has already a much greater share than the rest of his brethren, and is supposed, from the advantages of his education, employment, and counsellors, to be more knowing in the measures of right and wrong.

"May the commands then of a prince be opposed? may he be resisted as often as any one shall find himself aggrieved, and but imagine he has not right done him? This will unhinge and overturn all politics, and, instead of government and order, leave nothing but anarchy and confusion."

To this I answer, that force is to be opposed to nothing but to unjust and unlawful force; whoever makes any opposition in any other case, draws on himself a just condemnation both from God and man; and so no such danger or confusion will follow, as is often suggested.

• • •

The reason why men enter into society is the preservation of their property; and the end why they choose and authorize a legislative is, that there may be laws made, and rules set, as guards and fences to the properties of all the members of the society: to limit the power, and moderate the dominion, of every part and member of the society: for since it can never be supposed to be the will of the society that the legislative should have a power to destroy that which every one designs to secure by entering into society, and for which the people submitted themselves to legislators of their own making; whenever the legislators endeavour to take away and destroy the property of the people, or to reduce them to slavery under arbitrary power, they put themselves into a state of war with the people, who are thereupon absolved from any farther obedience, and are left to the common refuge, which God hath provided for all men, against force and violence. Whensoever therefore the legislative shall transgress this fundamental rule of society; and either by ambition, fear, folly, or corruption, endeavour to grasp themselves, or put into the hands of any other, an absolute power over the lives, liberties, and estates of the people; by this breach of trust they forfeit the power the people had put into their hands for quite contrary ends, and it devolves to the people, who have a right to resume their original liberty, and, by the establishment of a new legislative, (such as they shall think fit) provide for their own safety and security, which is the end for which they are in society. What I have said here, concerning the legislative in general, holds true also concerning the supreme executor, who having a double trust put in him, both to have a part in the legislative, and the supreme execution of the law, acts against both, when he goes about to set up his own arbitrary will as the law of the society. He acts also contrary to his trust, when he either employs the force, treasure, and offices of the society to corrupt the representatives, and gain them to his purposes; or openly pre-engages the electors, and prescribes to their choice, such, whom he has, by solicitations, threats, promises, or otherwise, won to his designs; and employs them to bring in such, who have promised beforehand what to vote, and what to enact. Thus to regulate candidates and electors, and new-model the ways of election, what is it but to cut up the government by the roots, and poison the very fountain of public security? for the people having reserved to themselves the choice of their representatives, as the fence to their properties,

could do it for no other end, but that they might always be freely
chosen, and so chosen, freely act, and advise, as the necessity of the
commonwealth and the public good should, upon examination
and mature debate, be judged to require. This, those who give their
votes before they hear the debate, and have weighed the reasons
on all sides, are not capable of doing. To prepare such an assembly
as this, and endeavour to set up the declared abettors of his own
will, for the true representatives of the people, and the law-makers
of the society, is certainly as great a breach of trust, and as perfect
a declaration of a design to subvert the government, as is possible
to be met with. To which if one shall add rewards and punishments visibly employed to the same end, and all the arts of per-
verted law made use of, to take off and destroy all that stand in
the way of such a design, and will not comply and consent to
betray the liberties of their country, it will be past doubt what
is doing. What power they ought to have in the society, who thus
employ it contrary to the trust that went along with it in its first
institution, is easy to determine; and one cannot but see, that he,
who has once attempted any such thing as this, cannot any longer
be trusted.

To this perhaps it will be said, that the people being ignorant,
and always discontented, to lay the foundation of government in
the unsteady opinion and uncertain humour of the people, is to
expose it to certain ruin; and no government will be able long
to subsist, if the people may set up a new legislative, whenever
they take offence at the old one. To this I answer, quite the contrary. People are not so easily got out of their old forms, as some
are apt to suggest. They are hardly to be prevailed with to amend
the acknowledged faults in the frame they have been accustomed
to. And if there be any original defects, or adventitious ones introduced by time, or corruption; it is not an easy thing to get
them changed, even when all the world sees there is an opportunity
for it. This slowness and aversion in the people to quit their old
constitutions, has in the many revolutions, which have been seen
in this kingdom, in this and former ages, still kept us to, or, after
some interval of fruitless attempts, still brought us back again to,
our old legislative of king, lords, and commons: and whatever
provocations have made the crown be taken from some of our
princes' heads, they never carried the people so far as to place it in
another line.

But it will be said, this hypothesis lays a ferment for frequent rebellion. To which I answer,

First, No more than any other hypothesis: for when the people are made miserable, and find themselves exposed to the ill usage of arbitrary power, cry up their governors as much as you will, for sons of Jupiter; let them be sacred and divine, descended, or authorized from heaven; give them out for whom or what you please, the same will happen. The people generally ill-treated, and contrary to right, will be ready upon any occasion to ease themselves of a burden that sits heavy upon them. They will wish, and seek for the opportunity, which in the change, weakness, and accidents of human affairs, seldom delays long to offer itself. He must have lived but a little while in the world, who has not seen examples of this in his time; and he must have read very little, who cannot produce examples of it in all sorts of governments in the world.

Secondly, I answer, such revolutions happen not upon every little mismanagement in public affairs. Great mistakes in the ruling part, many wrong and inconvenient laws, and all the slips of human frailty, will be born by the people without mutiny or murmur. But if a long train of abuses, prevarications, and artifices, all tending the same way, make the design visible to the people, and they cannot but feel what they lie under, and see whither they are going; it is not to be wondered, that they should then rouse themselves, and endeavour to put the rule into such hands which may secure to them the ends for which government was at first erected; and without which, ancient names, and specious forms, are so far from being better, that they are much worse, than the state of nature, or pure anarchy; the inconveniencies, being all as great and as near, but the remedy farther off and more difficult.

Thirdly, I answer, that this doctrine of a power in the people of providing for their safety anew, by a new legislative, when their legislators have acted contrary to their trust, by invading their property, is the best fence against rebellion, and the probablest means to hinder it: for rebellion being an opposition, not to persons, but authority, which is founded only in the constitutions and laws of the government; those, whoever they be, who by force break through, and by force justify their violation of them, are truly and properly rebels: for when men, by entering into society and civil government, have excluded force, and introduced laws for the preservation of property, peace, and unity amongst themselves; those who set up force again in opposition to the laws, do *rebellare*, that is, bring back again the state of war, and are properly rebels: which they who are in power (by the pretence they have to authority; the temptation of force they have in their hands, and the flattery of those about them), being likeliest to do; the properest way to prevent the evil is to show them the danger and injustice of it, who are under the greatest temptation to run into it.

. . .

Here, it is like, the common question will be made, "Who shall be judge, whether the prince or legislative act contrary to their trust?" This, perhaps, ill-affected and factious men may spread amongst the people, when the prince only makes use of his due prerogative. To this I reply, "The people shall be judge;" for who shall be judge whether his trustee or deputy acts well, and according to the trust reposed in him, but he who deputes him, and must, by having deputed him, have still a power to discard him, when he fails in his trust? If this be reasonable in particular cases of private men, why should it be otherwise in that of the greatest moment, where the welfare of millions is concerned, and also where the evil, if not prevented, is greater, and the redress very difficult, dear, and dangerous?

But farther, this question, ("Who shall be judge?") cannot mean, that there is no judge at all: for where there is no judicature on earth, to decide controversies amongst men, God in heaven is judge. He alone, it is true, is judge of the right. But every man is judge for himself, as in all other cases, so in this, whether another hath put himself into a state of war with him, and whether he should appeal to the supreme Judge, as Jephthah did.

If a controversy arise betwixt a prince and some of the people, in a matter where the law is silent or doubtful, and the thing be of great consequence, I should think the proper umpire, in such a case, should be the body of the people: for in cases where the prince hath a trust reposed in him, and is dispensed from the common ordinary rules of the law; there, if any men find themselves aggrieved, and think the prince acts contrary to, or beyond that trust, who so proper to judge as the body of the people (who, at first, lodged that trust in him), how far they meant it should extend? But if the prince, or whoever they be in the administration, decline that way of determination, the appeal then lies nowhere but to Heaven; force between either persons, who have no known superior on earth, or which permits no appeal to a judge on earth, being properly a state of war, wherein the appeal lies only to Heaven; and in that state the injured party must judge for himself, when he will think fit to make use of that appeal, and put himself upon it.

To conclude, The power that every individual gave the society, when he entered into it, can never revert to the individuals again, as long as the society lasts, but will always remain in the community; because without this there can be no community, no commonwealth, which is contrary to the original agreement: so also when the society hath placed the legislative in any assembly of men, to continue in them and their successors, with direction and authority for providing such successors, the legislative can never revert to the people whilst that government lasts; because, having provided a legislative with power to continue for ever, they have given up their political power to the legislative, and cannot resume it. But if they have set limits to the duration of their legislative, and made this supreme power in any person, or assembly, only temporary; or else, when by the miscarriages of those in authority it is forfeited; upon the forfeiture, or at the determination of the time set, it reverts to the society, and the people have a right to act as supreme, and continue the legislative in themselves; or erect a new form, or under the old form place it in new hands, as they think good.

Alexander Pope

— 8 —

Essay on Man

The European Enlightenment, or Age of Reason, was characterized by views about God, the world, and man that were rooted in the scientific outlook of the seventeenth century. The leading thinkers and artists of the Age of Reason accepted the view of a rational, benevolent, natural order, which had been created by God and whose meaning and mode of operation could be divined by rational man as a guide to the good life. They stated this ideal in a moderate way, inspired by ancient, classical models; thus they expressed, they felt, the old, timeless truths in a manner appropriate to their own times. One of the best representatives of this rationalistic, neoclassical tendency in literature was Alexander Pope, the English poet (1688–1744). He may, indeed, be called the spokesman in verse of the Age of Reason. For, despite an unpleasant personality, a physical disability, and a religious handicap (he was a professing Roman Catholic in a country that still legally discriminated against that faith), Pope achieved great popular success, and the income from the sale of his works enabled him to devote his life to literature.

Above all, Pope was a poet, a great English poet. Rarely lyrical or personal, his verse was mainly a vehicle for the expression of profound moral truths and common sense about nature and man. Following the accepted neoclassical rules of the craft, his verse exhibited a polished elegance, yet transcended social conformity and poetic commonplaces. The carefully wrought poetic lines and balanced rhythms contain paradox, wit, satire, and even deep feeling, which raised them to the level of great, imaginative art.

The *Essay on Man* (1734) was written in the form of four epistles addressed to the English rationalist-deist, Henry St. John, Lord Bolingbroke. The poem is written in heroic couplets of clear, short lines—often balancing

Alexander Pope, *Essay on Man*, in *Poetical Works of Alexander Pope* (Boston: Little, Brown, 1854), II, 36–48.

contrasting ideas—that have the effect of epigrams. It deals with the problem of evil in the world and man's moral duty. Pope affirms that the universe, though rational, is not wholly intelligible, and that man can find fulfillment in the cosmic order only if he avoids the faulty reasoning that leads to false pride and discontent. Voicing not only his own creed but the philosophical beliefs of his time, Pope presents a good statement of natural religion, or deism.

EPISTLE I

Awake, my St. John! leave all meaner things
To low ambition, and the pride of Kings.
Let us (since Life can little more supply
Than just to look about us and to die)
Expatiate free o'er all this scene of Man;
A mighty maze! but not without a plan;
A Wild, where weeds and flow'rs promiscuous shoot;
Or Garden, tempting with forbidden fruit.
Together let us beat this ample field,
Try what the open, what the covert yield;
The latent tracts, the giddy heights, explore
Of all who blindly creep, or sightless soar;
Eye Nature's walks, shoot Folly as it flies,
And catch the Manners living as they rise;
Laugh where we must, be candid where we can;
But vindicate the ways of God to Man.

I. Say first, of God above, or Man below,
What can we reason, but from what we know?
Of Man, what see we but his station here,
From which to reason, or to which refer?
Thro' worlds unnumber'd tho' the God be known,
'T is ours to trace him only in our own.
He, who thro' vast immensity can pierce,
See worlds on worlds compose one universe,
Observe how system into system runs,
What other planets circle other suns,

What vary'd Being peoples ev'ry star,
May tell why Heav'n has made us as we are.
But of this frame the bearings, and the ties,
The strong connexions, nice dependencies,
Gradations just, has thy pervading soul
Look'd thro'? or can a part contain the whole?
Is the great chain, that draws all to agree,
And drawn supports, upheld by God, or thee?

II. Presumptuous Man! the reason wouldst thou find,
Why form'd so weak, so little, and so blind?
First, if thou canst, the harder reason guess,
Why form'd no weaker, blinder, and no less?
Ask of thy mother earth, why oaks are made
Taller or stronger than the weeds they shade?
Or ask of yonder argent fields above,
Why Jove's satellites are less than Jove?
Of Systems possible, if 't is confest
That Wisdom infinite must form the best,
Where all must full or not coherent be,
And all that rises, rise in due degree;
Then, in the scale of reas'ning life, 't is plain,
There must be, somewhere, such a rank as Man:
And all the question (wrangle e'er so long)
Is only this, if God has plac'd him wrong?
Respecting Man, whatever wrong we call,
May, must be right, as relative to all.
In human works, tho' labour'd on with pain,
A thousand movements scarce one purpose gain;
In God's, one single can its end produce;
Yet serves to second too some other use.
So Man, who here seems principal alone,
Perhaps acts second to some sphere unknown,
Touches some wheel, or verges to some goal;
'T is but a part we see, and not a whole.
When the proud steed shall know why Man restrains
His fiery course, or drives him o'er the plains:
When the dull Ox, why now he breaks the clod,
Is now a victim, and now Egypt's God:

Then shall Man's pride and dulness comprehend
His actions', passions', being's, use and end;
Why doing, suff'ring, check'd, impell'd; and why
This hour a slave, the next a deity.

Then say not Man's imperfect, Heav'n in fault;
Say rather, Man's as perfect as he ought:
His knowledge measur'd to his state and place;
His time a moment, and a point his space.
If to be perfect in a certain sphere,
What matter, soon or late, or here or there?
The blest to-day is as completely so,
As who began a thousand years ago.

III. Heav'n from all creatures hides the book of Fate,
All but the page prescrib'd, their present state:
From brutes what men, from men what spirits know:
Or who could suffer Being here below?
The lamb thy riot dooms to bleed to-day,
Had he thy Reason, would he skip and play?
Pleas'd to the last, he crops the flow'ry food,
And licks the hand just rais'd to shed his blood.
Oh blindness to the future! kindly giv'n,
That each may fill the circle mark'd by Heav'n:
Who sees with equal eye, as God of all,
A hero perish, or a sparrow fall,
Atoms or systems into ruin hurl'd,
And now a bubble burst, and now a world.

Hope humbly then; with trembling pinions soar;
Wait the great teacher Death; and God adore.
What future bliss, he gives not thee to know,
But gives that Hope to be thy blessing now.
Hope springs eternal in the human breast:
Man never Is, but always To be blest:
The soul, uneasy and confin'd from home,
Rests and expatiates in a life to come.

Lo, the poor Indian! whose untutor'd mind
Sees God in clouds, or hears him in the wind:
His soul, proud Science never taught to stray
Far as the solar walk, or milky way;

Yet simple Nature to his hope has giv'n,
Behind the cloud-topt hill, an humbler heav'n;
Some safer world in depth of woods embrac'd,
Some happier island in the wat'ry waste,
Where slaves once more their native land behold,
No fiends torment, no Christians thirst for gold.
To Be, contents his natural desire,
He asks no Angel's wing, no Seraph's fire;
But thinks, admitted to that equal sky,
His faithful dog shall bear him company.

    IV. Go, wiser thou! and, in thy scale of sense,
Weigh thy Opinion against Providence;
Call imperfection what thou fancy'st such,
Say, here he gives too little, there too much:
Destroy all Creatures for thy sport or gust,
Yet cry, If Man's unhappy, God's unjust;
If Man alone engross not Heav'n's high care,
Alone made perfect here, immortal there:
Snatch from his hand the balance and the rod,
Re-judge his justice, be the God of God.
In Pride, in reas'ning Pride, our error lies;
All quit their sphere, and rush into the skies.
Pride still is aiming at the blest abodes,
Men would be Angels, Angels would be Gods.
Aspiring to be Gods, if Angels fell,
Aspiring to be Angels, Men rebel:
And who but wishes to invert the laws
Of Order, sins against th' Eternal Cause.

    V. Ask for what end the heav'nly bodies shine,
Earth for whose use? Pride answers, " 'T is for mine:
For me kind Nature wakes her genial Pow'r,
Suckles each herb, and spreads out ev'ry flow'r;
Annual for me, the grape, the rose renew
The juice nectareous, and the balmy dew;
For me, the mine a thousand treasures brings;
For me, health gushes from a thousand springs;
Seas roll to waft me, suns to light me rise;
My foot-stool earth, my canopy the skies."

But errs not Nature from this gracious end,
From burning suns when livid deaths descend,
When earthquakes swallow, or when tempests sweep
Towns to one grave, whole nations to the deep?
"No, ('t is reply'd) the first Almighty Cause
Acts not by partial, but by gen'ral laws;
Th' exceptions few; some change since all began:
And what created perfect?"—Why then Man?
If the great end be human Happiness,
Then Nature deviates; and can Man do less?
As much that end a constant course requires
Of show'rs and sun-shine, as of Man's desires;
As much eternal springs and cloudless skies,
As Men for ever temp'rate, calm, and wise.
If plagues or earthquakes break not Heav'n's design,
Why then a Borgia, or a Catiline?
Who knows but he, whose hand the lightning forms,
Who heaves old Ocean, and who wings the storms;
Pours fierce Ambition in a Caesar's mind,
Or turns young Ammon loose to scourge mankind?
From pride, from pride, our very reas'ning springs;
Account for moral, as for nat'ral things:
Why charge we Heav'n in those, in these acquit?
In both, to reason right is to submit.
  Better for Us, perhaps, it might appear,
Were there all harmony, all virtue here;
That never air or ocean felt the wind;
That never passion discompos'd the mind.
But all subsists by elemental strife;
And Passions are the elements of Life.
The gen'ral Order, since the whole began,
Is kept in Nature, and is kept in Man.

VI. What would this Man? Now upward will he soar.
And little less than Angel, would be more;
Now looking downwards, just as griev'd appears
To want the strength of bulls, the fur of bears.
Made for his use all creatures if he call,
Say what their use, had he the pow'rs of all?

Nature to these, without profusion, kind,
The proper organs, proper pow'rs assign'd;
Each seeming want compensated of course,
Here with degrees of swiftness, there of force;
All in exact proportion to the state;
Nothing to add, and nothing to abate.
Each beast, each insect, happy in its own:
Is Heav'n unkind to Man, and Man alone?
Shall he alone, whom rational we call,
Be pleas'd with nothing, if not bless'd with all?
  The bliss of Man (could Pride that blessing find)
Is not to act or think beyond mankind;
No pow'rs of body or of soul to share,
But what his nature and his state can bear.
Why has not Man a microscopic eye?
For this plain reason, Man is not a Fly.
Say what the use, were finer optics giv'n,
T' inspect a mite, not comprehend the heav'n?
Or touch, if tremblingly alive all o'er,
To smart and agonize at every pore?
Or quick effluvia darting thro' the brain,
Die of a rose in aromatic pain?
If nature thunder'd in his op'ning ears,
And stunn'd him with the music of the spheres,
How would he wish that Heav'n had left him still
The whisp'ring Zephyr, and the purling rill?
Who finds not Providence all good and wise,
Alike in what it gives, and what it denies?

  VII. Far as Creation's ample range extends,
The scale of sensual, mental pow'rs ascends:
Mark how it mounts, to Man's imperial race,
From the green myriads in the peopled grass:
What modes of sight betwixt each wide extreme,
The mole's dim curtain, and the lynx's beam:
Of smell, the headlong lioness between,
And hound sagacious on the tainted green:
Of hearing, from the life that fills the Flood,
To that which warbles thro' the vernal wood:

The spider's touch, how exquisitely fine!
Feels at each thread, and lives along the line:
In the nice bee, what sense so subtly true
From pois'nous herbs extracts the healing dew?
How Instinct varies in the grov'ling swine,
Compar'd, half-reas'ning elephant, with thine!
'Twixt that, and Reason, what a nice barrier,
For ever sep'rate, yet for ever near!
Remembrance and Reflection how ally'd;
What thin partitions Sense from Thought divide:
And Middle natures, how they long to join,
Yet never pass th' insuperable line!
Without this just gradation, could they be
Subjected, these to those, or all to thee?
The pow'rs of all subdu'd by thee alone,
Is not thy Reason all these pow'rs in one?

    VIII. See, thro' this air, this ocean, and this earth,
All matter quick, and bursting into birth.
Above, how high, progressive life may go!
Around, how wide! how deep extend below!
Vast chain of Being! which from God began,
Natures ethereal, human, angel, man,
Beast, bird, fish, insect, what no eye can see,
No glass can reach; from Infinite to thee,
From thee to Nothing.—On superior pow'rs
Were we to press, inferior might on ours:
Or in the full creation leave a void,
Where, one step broken, the great scale's destroy'd:
From Nature's chain whatever link you strike,
Tenth or ten thousandth, breaks the chain alike.
    And, if each system in gradation roll
Alike essential to th' amazing Whole,
The least confusion but in one, not all
That system only, but the Whole must fall.
Let Earth unbalanc'd from her orbit fly,
Planets and Suns run lawless thro' the sky;
Let ruling angels from their spheres be hurl'd,
Being on Being wreck'd, and world on world;

Heav'n's whole foundations to their centre nod,
And Nature tremble to the throne of God.
All this dread Order break—for whom? for thee?
Vile worm!—Oh Madness! Pride! Impiety!

IX. What if the foot, ordain'd the dust to tread,
Or hand, to toil, aspir'd to be the head?
What if the head, the eye, or ear repin'd
To serve mere engines to the ruling Mind?
Just as absurd for any part to claim
To be another, in this gen'ral frame:
Just as absurd, to mourn the tasks or pains,
The great directing Mind of All ordains.

All are but parts of one stupendous whole,
Whose body Nature is, and God the soul;
That, chang'd thro' all, and yet in all the same;
Great in the earth, as in th' ethereal frame;
Warms in the sun, refreshes in the breeze,
Glows in the stars, and blossoms in the trees,
Lives thro' all life, extends thro' all extent,
Spreads undivided, operates unspent;
Breathes in our soul, informs our mortal part,
As full, as perfect, in a hair as heart:
As full, as perfect, in vile Man that mourns,
As the rapt Seraph that adores and burns:
To him no high, no low, no great, no small;
He fills, he bounds, connects, and equals all.

X. Cease then, nor Order Imperfection name:
Our proper bliss depends on what we blame.
Know thy own point: This kind, this due degree
Of blindness, weakness, Heav'n bestows on thee.
Submit.—In this, or any other sphere,
Secure to be as blest as thou canst bear:
Safe in the hand of one disposing Pow'r,
Or in the natal, or the mortal hour.
All Nature is but Art, unknown to thee;
All Chance, Direction, which thou canst not see;
All Discord, Harmony not understood;
All partial Evil, universal Good:

And, spite of Pride, in erring Reason's spite,
One truth is clear, WHATEVER IS, IS RIGHT.

EPISTLE II

I. Know then thyself, presume not God to scan;
The proper study of Mankind is Man.
Plac'd on this isthmus of a middle state,
A Being darkly wise, and rudely great:
With too much knowledge for the Sceptic side,
With too much weakness for the Stoic's pride,
He hangs between; in doubt to act, or rest;
In doubt to deem himself a God, or Beast;
In doubt his Mind or Body to prefer;
Born but to die, and reas'ning but to err;
Alike in ignorance, his reason such,
Whether he thinks too little, or too much:
Chaos of Thought and Passion, all confus'd;
Still by himself abus'd, or disabus'd;
Created half to rise, and half to fall;
Great lord of all things, yet a prey to all;
Sole judge of Truth, in endless Error hurl'd:
The glory, jest, and riddle of the world!

Voltaire

9

Candide

François Marie Arouet (1694–1778), better known by his pen name, Voltaire, was perhaps the most characteristic and famous figure of the European Enlightenment. Born the son of a middle-class Parisian lawyer, he was a greatly gifted and prolific writer, pouring forth during his long life a flood of works on history, philosophy, drama, poetry, fiction, and biography. All Voltaire's works, in one way or another, reflected his belief in science, reason, and freedom; they also reflected his hatred of superstition, intolerance, and privilege, as the main sources of evil in the world. Voltaire eventually won fame and fortune in his lifetime, but not until after he had suffered for his views; because of them, he was thrown into the Bastille and exiled from France. Voltaire then devoted his life to trying to clear away what he thought was accumulated rubbish filling men's minds. He popularized the faith of the Enlightenment and became the leader and the symbol of the intellectual rebellion against traditional ideas and institutions. At the end of his life Voltaire was finally acclaimed in Paris; he may be considered one of the intellectual fathers of the French Revolution, whose leaders enshrined his ashes in the Pantheon in 1791. At once liberal and conservative, deist and agnostic, fighter and coward, shrewd, generous, miserly, and vindictive, Voltaire was, above all, a humanist who wished to better the world by turning nature to the uses of man through reason.

Candide, or Optimism (1759) was written when Voltaire was sixty-five years old and is now the most widely read of all his works. Written with wit and irony, and in a clear, lively style, Candide is a classic story of the young innocent learning about the wickedness of the world. The hero's rollicking adventures move along, showing him to be a man of common sense. The characters and events are symbols of ideas and institutions, which are subjected to a withering and delightful satire. Voltaire's conclusion is that the world is mad and that sane men should concern themselves with tasks that are within their power to accomplish.

Voltaire, *Candide* (New York: Illustrated Editions, 1930), 13–57.

CHAPTER I

In the castle of Baron Thunder-ten-tronckh in Westphalia there lived a youth, endowed by Nature with the most gentle character. His face was the expression of his soul. His judgment was quite honest and he was extremely simple-minded; and this was the reason, I think, that he was named Candide. Old servants in the house suspected that he was the son of the Baron's sister and a decent honest gentleman of the neighbourhood, whom this young lady would never marry because he could only prove seventy-two quarterings, and the rest of his genealogical tree was lost, owing to the injuries of time.

The Baron was one of the most powerful lords in Westphalia, for his castle possessed a door and windows. His Great Hall was even decorated with a piece of tapestry. The dogs in his stable-yards formed a pack of hounds when necessary; his grooms were his huntsmen; the village curate was his Grand Almoner. They all called him "My Lord," and laughed heartily at his stories.

The Baroness weighed about three hundred and fifty pounds, was therefore greatly respected, and did the honours of the house with a dignity which rendered her still more respectable. Her daughter Cunegonde, aged seventeen, was rosy-cheeked, fresh, plump and tempting. The Baron's son appeared in every respect worthy of his father. The tutor Pangloss was the oracle of the house, and little Candide followed his lessons with all the candour of his age and character.

Pangloss taught metaphysico-theologo-cosmolo-nigology. He proved admirably that there is no effect without a cause and that, in this best of all possible worlds, My Lord the Baron's castle was the best of castles and his wife the best of all possible Baronesses.

" 'Tis demonstrated," said he, "that things cannot be otherwise; for, since everything is made for an end, everything is necessarily for the best end. Observe that noses were made to wear spectacles; and so we have spectacles. Legs were visibly instituted to be breeched, and we have breeches. Stones were formed to be quarried and to build castles; and My Lord has a very noble castle; the greatest Baron in the province should have the best house; and as pigs were made to be eaten, we eat pork all the year round; consequently, those who have asserted that all is well, talk nonsense; they ought to have said that all is for the best."

Candide listened attentively and believed innocently; for he thought Miss Cunegonde extremely beautiful, although he was never bold enough to tell her so. He decided that after the happiness of being born Baron of Thunder-ten-tronckh, the second degree of happiness was to be Miss Cunegonde; the third, to see her every day; and the fourth to listen to Dr. Pangloss, the greatest philosopher of the province and therefore of the whole world.

One day when Cunegonde was walking near the castle, in a little wood which was called The Park, she observed Dr. Pangloss in the bushes, giving a lesson in experimental physics to her mother's waiting-maid, a very pretty and docile brunette. Miss Cunegonde had a great inclination for science and watched breathlessly the reiterated experiments she witnessed; she observed clearly the Doctor's sufficient reason, the effects and the causes, and returned home very much excited, pensive, filled with the desire of learning, reflecting that she might be the sufficient reason of young Candide and that he might be hers.

On her way back to the castle she met Candide and blushed; Candide also blushed. She bade him good-morning in a hesitating voice; Candide replied without knowing what he was saying. Next day, when they left the table after dinner, Cunegonde and Candide found themselves behind a screen; Cunegonde dropped her handkerchief, Candide picked it up; she innocently held his hand; the young man innocently kissed the young lady's hand with remarkable vivacity, tenderness and grace; their lips met, their eyes sparkled, their knees trembled, their hands wandered. Baron Thunder-ten-tronckh passed near the screen, and, observing this cause and effect, expelled Candide from the castle by kicking him in the backside frequently and hard. Cunegonde swooned; when she recovered her senses, the Baroness slapped her in the face; and all was in consternation in the noblest and most agreeable of all possible castles.

CHAPTER II

Candide, expelled from the earthly paradise, wandered for a long time without knowing where he was going, turning up his eyes to Heaven, gazing back frequently at the noblest of castles which held the most beautiful of young Baronesses; he lay down to sleep supperless between two furrows in the open fields; it snowed heavily in large flakes. The next morning the shivering Candide, penniless, dying of cold and exhaustion, dragged himself towards the neighbouring town, which was called Waldberghoff-trarbkdik-dorff. He halted sadly at the door of an inn. Two men dressed in blue noticed him.

"Comrade," said one, "there's a well-built young man of the right height."

They went up to Candide and very civilly invited him to dinner.

"Gentlemen," said Candide with charming modesty, "you do me a great honour, but I have no money to pay my share."

"Ah, sir," said one of the men in blue, "persons of your figure and merit never pay anything; are you not five feet five tall?"

"Yes, gentlemen," said he, bowing, "that is my height."

"Ah, sir, come to table; we will not only pay your expenses, we will never allow a man like you to be short of money; men were only made to help each other."

"You are in the right," said Candide, "that is what Dr. Pangloss was always telling me, and I see that everything is for the best."

They begged him to accept a few crowns, he took them and wished to give them an IOU; they refused to take it and all sat down to table.

"Do you not love tenderly . . ."

"Oh, yes," said he. "I love Miss Cunegonde tenderly."

"No," said one of the gentlemen. "We were asking if you do not tenderly love the King of the Bulgarians."

"Not a bit," said he, "for I have never seen him."

"What! He is the most charming of kings, and you must drink his health."

"Oh, gladly, gentlemen."

And he drank.

"That is sufficient," he was told. "You are now the support, the aid, the defender, the hero of the Bulgarians; your fortune is made and your glory assured."

They immediately put irons on his legs and took him to a regiment. He was made to turn to the right and left, to raise the ramrod and return the ramrod, to take aim, to fire, to double up, and he was given thirty strokes with a stick; the next day he drilled not quite so badly, and received only twenty strokes; the day after, he only had ten and was looked on as a prodigy by his comrades.

Candide was completely mystified and could not make out how he was a hero. One fine spring day he thought he would take a walk, going straight ahead, in the belief that to use his legs as he pleased was a privilege of the human species as well as of animals. He had not gone two leagues when four other heroes, each six feet tall, fell upon him, bound him and dragged him back to a cell. He was asked by his judges whether he would rather be thrashed thirty-six times by the whole regiment or receive a dozen lead bullets at once in his brain. Although he protested that men's wills are free and that he wanted neither one nor the other, he had to make a choice; by virtue of that gift of God which is called *liberty,* he determined to run the gauntlet thirty-six times and actually did so twice. There were two thousand men in the regiment. That made four thousand strokes which laid bare the muscles and nerves from his neck to his backside. As they were about to proceed to a third turn, Candide, utterly exhausted, begged as a favour that they would be so kind as to smash his head; he obtained this favour; they bound his eyes and he was made to kneel down. At that moment the King of the Bulgarians came by and inquired the victim's crime; and as this King was possessed of a vast genius, he perceived from what he learned about Candide that he was a young metaphysician very ignorant in worldly matters, and therefore pardoned him with a clemency which will be praised in all newspapers and all ages. An honest surgeon healed Candide in three weeks with the ointments recommended by Dioscorides. He had already regained a little skin and could walk when the King of the Bulgarians went to war with the King of the Abares.

CHAPTER III

Nothing could be smarter, more splendid, more brilliant, better drawn up than the two armies. Trumpets, fifes, hautboys, drums, cannons formed a harmony such as has never been heard even in hell. The cannons first of all laid flat about six thousand men on each side; then the musketry removed from the best of worlds some nine or ten thousand blackguards who infested its surface. The bayonet also was the sufficient reason for the death of some thousands of men. The whole might amount to thirty thousand souls. Candide, who trembled like a philosopher, hid himself as well as he could during this heroic butchery.

At last, while the two kings each commanded a Te Deum in his camp, Candide decided to go elsewhere to reason about effects and causes. He clambered over heaps of dead and dying men and reached a neighbouring village, which was in ashes; it was an Abare village which the Bulgarians had burned in accordance with international law. Here, old men dazed with blows watched the dying agonies of their murdered wives who clutched their children to their bleeding breasts; there, disembowelled girls who had been made to satisfy the natural appetites of heroes gasped their last sighs; others, half-burned, begged to be put to death. Brains were scattered on the ground among dismembered arms and legs.

Candide fled to another village as fast as he could; it belonged to the Bulgarians, and Abarian heroes had treated it in the same way. Candide, stumbling over quivering limbs or across ruins, at last escaped from the theatre of war, carrying a little food in his knapsack, and never forgetting Miss Cunegonde. His provisions were all gone when he reached Holland; but, having heard that everyone in that country was rich and a Christian, he had no doubt at all but that he would be as well treated as he had been in the Baron's castle before he had been expelled on account of Miss Cunegonde's pretty eyes.

He asked an alms of several grave persons, who all replied that if he continued in that way he would be shut up in a house of correction to teach him how to live.

He then addressed himself to a man who had been discoursing on charity in a large assembly for an hour on end. This orator, glancing at him askance, said:

"What are you doing here? Are you for the good cause?"

"There is no effect without a cause," said Candide modestly. "Everything is necessarily linked up and arranged for the best. It was necessary that I should be expelled from the company of Miss Cunegonde, that I ran the gauntlet, and that I beg my bread until I can earn it; all this could not have happened differently."

"My friend," said the orator, "do you believe that the Pope is Anti-Christ?"

"I had never heard so before," said Candide, "but whether he is or isn't, I am starving."

"You don't deserve to eat," said the other. "Hence, rascal; hence, you wretch; and never come near me again."

The orator's wife thrust her head out of the window and seeing a man who did not believe that the Pope was Anti-Christ, she poured on his head a full . . . O Heavens! To what excess religious zeal is carried by ladies!

A man who had not been baptised, an honest Anabaptist named Jacques, saw the cruel and ignominious treatment of one of his brothers, a featherless two-legged creature with a soul; he took him home, cleaned him up, gave him bread and beer, presented him with two florins, and even offered to teach him to work at the manufacture of Persian stuffs which are made in Holland. Candide threw himself at the man's feet, exclaiming:

"Dr. Pangloss was right in telling me that all is for the best in this world, for I am vastly more touched by your extreme generosity than by the harshness of the gentleman in the black cloak and his good lady."

The next day when he walked out he met a beggar covered with sores, dull-eyed, with the end of his nose fallen away, his mouth awry, his teeth black, who talked huskily, was tormented with a violent cough and spat out a tooth at every cough.

CHAPTER IV

Candide, moved even more by compassion than by horror, gave this horrible beggar the two crowns he had received from the honest Anabaptist, Jacques. The phantom gazed fixedly at him, shed tears and threw its arms round his neck. Candide recoiled in terror.

"Alas!" said the wretch to the other wretch, "don't you recognise your dear Pangloss?"

"What do I hear? You, my dear master! You, in this horrible state! What misfortune has happened to you? Why are you no longer in the noblest of castles? What has become of Miss Cunegonde, the pearl of young ladies, the masterpiece of Nature?"

"I am exhausted," said Pangloss. Candide immediately took him to the Anabaptist's stable, where he gave him a little bread to eat; and when Pangloss had recovered:

"Well!" said he, "Cunegonde?"

"Dead," replied the other.

At this word Candide swooned; his friend restored him to his senses with a little bad vinegar which happened to be in the stable. Candide opened his eyes.

"Cunegonde dead! Ah! best of worlds, where are you? But what illness did she die of? Was it because she saw me kicked out of her father's noble castle?"

"No," said Pangloss. "She was disembowelled by Bulgarian soldiers, after having been raped to the limit of possibility; they broke the Baron's head when he tried to defend her; the Baroness was cut to pieces; my poor pupil was treated exactly like his sister; and as to the castle, there is not one stone standing on another, not a barn, not a sheep, not a duck, not a tree; but we were well avenged, for the Abares did exactly the same to a neighbouring barony which belonged to a Bulgarian Lord."

At this, Candide swooned again; but, having recovered and having said all that he ought to say, he inquired the cause and effect, the sufficient reason which had reduced Pangloss to so piteous a state.

"Alas!" said Pangloss, " 'tis love; love, the consoler of the human race, the preserver of the universe, the soul of all tender creatures, gentle love."

"Alas!" said Candide, "I am acquainted with this love, this sovereign of hearts, this soul of our soul; it has never brought me anything but one kiss and twenty kicks in the backside. How could this beautiful cause produce in you so abominable an effect?"

Pangloss replied as follows:

"My dear Candide! You remember Paquette, the maid-servant of our august Baroness; in her arms I enjoyed the delights of Paradise which have produced the tortures of Hell by which you see I am devoured; she was infected and perhaps is dead. Paquette received this present from a most learned monk, who had it from the source; for he received it from an old countess, who had it from a cavalry captain, who owed it to a marchioness, who derived it from a page, who had received it from a Jesuit, who, when a novice, had it in a direct line from one of the companions of Christopher Columbus. For my part, I shall not give it to anyone, for I am dying."

"O Pangloss!" exclaimed Candide, "this is a strange genealogy! Wasn't the devil at the root of it?"

"Not at all," replied that great man. "It was something indispensable in this best of worlds, a necessary ingredient; for, if Columbus in an island of America had not caught this disease, which

poisons the source of generation, and often indeed prevents generation, we should not have chocolate and cochineal; it must also be
noticed that hitherto in our continent this disease is peculiar to
us, like theological disputes. The Turks, the Indians, the Persians,
the Chinese, the Siamese and the Japanese are not yet familiar
with it; but there is a sufficient reason why they in their turn
should become familiar with it in a few centuries. Meanwhile, it
has made marvellous progress among us, and especially in those
large armies composed of honest, well-bred stipendiaries who decide the destiny of States; it may be asserted that when thirty
thousand men fight a pitched battle against an equal number of
troops, there are about twenty thousand with the pox on either
side."

"Admirable!" said Candide. "But you must get cured."

"How can I?" said Pangloss. "I haven't a sou, my friend, and in
the whole extent of this globe, you cannot be bled or receive an
enema without paying or without someone paying for you."

This last speech determined Candide; he went and threw himself at the feet of his charitable Anabaptist, Jacques, and drew so
touching a picture of the state to which his friend was reduced
that the good easy man did not hesitate to succour Pangloss; he
had him cured at his own expense. In this cure Pangloss only lost
one eye and one ear. He could write well and knew arithmetic
perfectly. The Anabaptist made him his bookkeeper. At the end
of two months he was compelled to go to Lisbon on business and
took his two philosophers on the boat with him. Pangloss explained
to him how everything was for the best. Jacques was not of this
opinion.

"Men," said he, "must have corrupted nature a little, for they
were not born wolves, and they have become wolves. God did not
give them twenty-four-pounder cannons or bayonets, and they have
made bayonets and cannons to destroy each other. I might bring
bankruptcies into the account and Justice which seizes the goods
of bankrupts in order to deprive the creditors of them."

"It was all indispensable," replied the one-eyed doctor, "and
private misfortunes make the public good, so that the more private
misfortunes there are, the more everything is well."

While he was reasoning, the air grew dark, the winds blew from
the four quarters of the globe and the ship was attacked by the most
horrible tempest in sight of the port of Lisbon.

CHAPTER V

Half the enfeebled passengers, suffering from that inconceivable anguish which the rolling of a ship causes in the nerves and in all the humours of bodies shaken in contrary directions, did not retain strength enough even to trouble about the danger. The other half screamed and prayed; the sails were torn, the masts broken, the vessel was leaking. Those worked who could, no one co-operated, no one commanded. The Anabaptist tried to help the crew a little; he was on the main-deck; a furious sailor struck him violently and stretched him on the deck; but the blow he delivered gave him so violent a shock that he fell head-first out of the ship. He remained hanging and clinging to part of the broken mast. The good Jacques ran to his aid, helped him to climb back, and from the effort he made was flung into the sea in full view of the sailor, who allowed him to drown without condescending even to look at him. Candide came up, saw his benefactor reappear for a moment and then be engulfed for ever. He tried to throw himself after him into the sea; he was prevented by the philosopher Pangloss, who proved to him that the Lisbon roads had been expressly created for the Anabaptist to be drowned in them. While he was proving this *a priori*, the vessel sank, and everyone perished except Pangloss, Candide and the brutal sailor who had drowned the virtuous Anabaptist; the blackguard swam successfully to the shore and Pangloss and Candide were carried there on a plank.

When they had recovered a little, they walked toward Lisbon; they had a little money by the help of which they hoped to be saved from hunger after having escaped the storm.

Weeping the death of their benefactor, they had scarcely set foot in the town when they felt the earth tremble under their feet; the sea rose in foaming masses in the port and smashed the ships which rode at anchor. Whirlwinds of flame and ashes covered the streets and squares; the houses collapsed, the roofs were thrown upon the foundations, and the foundations were scattered; thirty thousand inhabitants of every age and both sexes were crushed under the ruins. Whistling and swearing, the sailor said:

"There'll be something to pick up here."

"What can be the sufficient reason for this phenomenon?" said Pangloss.

"It is the last day!" cried Candide.

The sailor immediately ran among the debris, dared death to find money, found it, seized it, got drunk, and having slept off his wine, purchased the favours of the first woman of good-will he met on the ruins of the houses and among the dead and dying. Pangloss, however, pulled him by the sleeve.

"My friend," said he, "this is not well, you are disregarding universal reason, you choose the wrong time."

"Blood and 'ounds!" he retorted, "I am a sailor and I was born in Batavia; four times have I stamped on the crucifix during four voyages to Japan; you have found the right man for your universal reason!"

Candide had been hurt by some falling stones; he lay in the street covered with debris. He said to Pangloss:

"Alas! Get me a little wine and oil; I am dying."

"This earthquake is not a new thing," replied Pangloss. "The town of Lima felt the same shocks in America last year; similar causes produce similar effects; there must certainly be a train of sulphur underground from Lima to Lisbon."

"Nothing is more probable," replied Candide; "but, for God's sake, a little oil and wine."

"What do you mean, probable?" replied the philosopher; "I maintain that it is proved."

Candide lost consciousness, and Pangloss brought him a little water from a neighbouring fountain.

Next day they found a little food as they wandered among the ruins and regained a little strength. Afterwards they worked like others to help the inhabitants who had escaped death. Some citizens they had assisted gave them as good a dinner as could be expected in such a disaster; true, it was a dreary meal; the hosts watered their bread with their tears, but Pangloss consoled them by assuring them that things could not be otherwise.

"For," said he, "all this is for the best; for, if there is a volcano at Lisbon, it cannot be anywhere else; for it is impossible that things should not be where they are; for all is well."

A little, dark man, a familiar of the Inquisition, who sat beside him, politely took up the conversation, and said:

"Apparently you do not believe in original sin; for, if everything is for the best, there was neither fall nor punishment."

"I most humbly beg your excellency's pardon," replied Pangloss still more politely, "for the fall of man and the curse necessarily entered into the best of all possible worlds."

"Then you do not believe in free-will?" said the familiar.

"Your excellency will pardon me," said Pangloss; "free-will can exist with absolute necessity; for it was necesary that we should be free; for in short, limited will . . ."

Pangloss was in the middle of his phrase when the familiar nodded to his armed attendant who was pouring out port or Oporto wine for him.

CHAPTER VI

After the earthquake which destroyed three-quarters of Lisbon, the wise men of that country could discover no more efficacious way of preventing a total ruin than by giving the people a splendid *auto-da-fé*. It was decided by the university of Coimbre that the sight of several persons being slowly burned in great ceremony is an infallible secret for preventing earthquakes.

Consequently they had arrested a Biscayan convicted of having married his fellow-godmother, and two Portuguese who, when eating a chicken had thrown away the bacon; after dinner they came and bound Dr. Pangloss and his disciple Candide, one because he had spoken and the other because he had listened with an air of approbation; they were both carried separately to extremely cool apartments, where there was never any discomfort from the sun; a week afterwards each was dressed in a sanbenito and their heads were ornamented with paper mitres; Candide's mitre and sanbenito were painted with flames upside down and with devils who had neither tails nor claws; but Pangloss's devils had claws and tails, and his flames were upright.

Dressed in this manner they marched in procession and listened to a most pathetic sermon, followed by lovely plain-song music. Candide was flogged in time to the music, while the singing went on; the Biscayan and the two men who had not wanted to eat bacon were burned, and Pangloss was hanged, although this is not the custom. The very same day, the earth shook again with a terrible clamour.

Candide, terrified, dumbfounded, bewildered, covered with blood, quivering from head to foot, said to himself:

"If this is the best of all possible worlds, what are the others? Let it pass that I was flogged, for I was flogged by the Bulgarians, but, O my dear Pangloss! The greatest of philosophers! Must I see you hanged without knowing why! O my dear Anabaptist! The best of men! Was it necessary that you should be drowned in port! O Miss Cunegonde! The pearl of women! Was it necessary that your belly should be slit!"

He was returning, scarcely able to support himself, preached at, flogged, absolved and blessed, when an old woman accosted him and said:

"Courage, my son, follow me."

CHAPTER VII

Candide did not take courage, but he followed the old woman to a hovel; she gave him a pot of ointment to rub on, and left him food and drink; she pointed out a fairly clean bed; near the bed there was a suit of clothes.

"Eat, drink, sleep," said she, "and may our Lady of Atocha, my Lord Saint Anthony of Padua and my Lord Saint James of Compostella take care of you; I shall come back to-morrow."

Candide, still amazed by all he had seen, by all he had suffered, and still more by the old woman's charity, tried to kiss her hand.

"'Tis not my hand you should kiss," said the old woman, "I shall come back to-morrow. Rub on the ointment, eat and sleep."

In spite of all his misfortune, Candide ate and went to sleep. Next day the old woman brought him breakfast, examined his back and smeared him with another ointment; later she brought him dinner, and returned in the evening with supper. The next day she went through the same ceremony.

"Who are you?" Candide kept asking her. "Who has inspired you with so much kindness? How can I thank you?"

The good woman never made any reply; she returned in the evening without any supper.

"Come with me," said she, "and do not speak a word."

She took him by the arm and walked into the country with him for about a quarter of a mile; they came to an isolated house, surrounded with gardens and canals. The old woman knocked at a little door. It was opened; she led Candide up a back stairway into a gilded apartment, left him on a brocaded sofa, shut the door and went away. Candide thought he was dreaming, and felt that his whole life was a bad dream and the present moment an agreeable dream.

The old woman soon reappeared; she was supporting with some difficulty a trembling woman of majestic stature, glittering with precious stones and covered with a veil.

"Remove the veil," said the old woman to Candide. The young man advanced and lifted the veil with a timid hand. What a moment! What a surprise! He thought he saw Miss Cunegonde, in fact he was looking at her, it was she herself. His strength failed him, he could not utter a word and fell at her feet. Cunegonde fell on the sofa. The old woman dosed them with distilled waters; they recovered their senses and began to speak: at first they uttered only broken words, questions and answers at cross purposes, sighs, tears, exclamations. The old woman advised them to make less noise and left them alone.

"What! Is it you?" said Candide. "You are alive, and I find you here in Portugal! Then you were not raped? Your belly was not slit, as the philosopher Pangloss assured me?"

"Yes, indeed," said the fair Cunegonde; "but those two accidents are not always fatal."

"But your father and mother were killed?"

" 'Tis only too true," said Cunegonde, weeping.

"And your brother?"

"My brother was killed too."

"And why are you in Portugal? And how did you know I was here? And by what strange adventure have you brought me to this house?"

"I will tell you everything," replied the lady, "but first of all you must tell me everything that has happened to you since the innocent kiss you gave me and the kicks you received."

Candide obeyed with profound respect; and, although he was bewildered, although his voice was weak and trembling, although his back was still a little painful, he related in the most natural manner all he had endured since the moment of their separation. Cunegonde raised her eyes to Heaven; she shed tears at the death of the good Anabaptist and Pangloss, after which she spoke as follows to Candide, who did not miss a word and devoured her with his eyes.

CHAPTER VIII

"I was fast asleep in bed when it pleased Heaven to send the Bulgarians to our noble castle of Thunder-ten-tronckh; they murdered my father and brother and cut my mother to pieces. A large Bulgarian six feet tall, seeing that I had swooned at the spectacle, began to rape me; this brought me to, I recovered my senses, I screamed, I struggled, I bit, I scratched, I tried to tear out the big Bulgarian's eyes, not knowing that what was happening in my father's castle was a matter of custom; the brute stabbed me with a knife in the left side where I still have the scar."

"Alas! I hope I shall see it," said the naïf Candide.

"You shall see it," said Cunegonde, "but let me go on."

"Go on," said Candide.

She took up the thread of her story as follows:

"A Bulgarian captain came in, saw me covered with blood, and the soldier did not disturb himself. The captain was angry at the brute's lack of respect to him, and killed him on my body. Afterwards, he had me bandaged and took me to his billet as a prisoner of war. I washed the few shirts he had and did the cooking; I must admit he thought me very pretty; and I will not deny that he was very well built and that his skin was white and soft; otherwise he had little wit and little philosophy; it was plain that he had not been brought up by Dr. Pangloss. At the end of three months he lost all his money and got tired of me; he sold me to a Jew named Don Issachar, who traded in Holland and Portugal and had a passion for women. This Jew devoted himself to my person but he could not triumph over it; I resisted him better than the Bulgarian soldier; a lady of honour may be raped once, but it strengthens her virtue. In order to subdue me, the Jew brought me to this country house. Up till then I believed that there was nothing on earth so splendid as the castle of Thunder-ten-tronckh; I was undeceived.

"One day the Grand Inquisitor noticed me at Mass; he ogled me continually and sent a message that he wished to speak to me on secret affairs. I was taken to his palace; I informed him of my birth; he pointed out how much it was beneath my rank to belong to an Israelite. A proposition was made on his behalf to Don Issachar to give me up to His Lordship. Don Issachar, who is the court banker and a man of influence, would not agree. The Inquisitor threatened him with an *auto-da-fé*. At last the Jew was frightened and made a bargain whereby the house and I belong to both in common. The Jew has Mondays, Wednesdays and the Sabbath day, and the Inquisitor has the other days of the week. This arrangement has lasted for six months. It has not been without quarrels; for it has often been debated whether the night between Saturday and Sunday belonged to the old law or the new. For my part, I have hitherto resisted them both; and I think that is the reason why they still love me.

"At last My Lord the Inquisitor was pleased to arrange an *auto-da-fé* to remove the scourge of earthquakes and to intimidate Don Issachar. He honoured me with an invitation. I had an excellent seat; and refreshments were served to the ladies between the Mass and the execution. I was indeed horror-stricken when I saw the burning of the two Jews and the honest Biscayan who had married his fellow-godmother; but what was my surprise, my terror, my anguish, when I saw in a sanbenito and under a mitre a face which resembled Pangloss's! I rubbed my eyes, I looked carefully, I saw him hanged; and I fainted. I had scarcely recovered my senses when I saw you stripped naked; that was the height of horror, of consternation, of grief and despair. I will frankly tell you that your skin is even whiter and of a more perfect tint than that of my Bulgarian captain. This spectacle redoubled all the feelings which crushed and devoured me. I exclaimed, I tried to say: 'Stop, barbarians!' but my voice failed and my cries would have been useless. When you had been well flogged, I said to myself: 'How does it happen that the charming Candide and the wise Pangloss are in Lisbon, the one to receive a hundred lashes, and the other to be hanged, by order of My Lord the Inquisitor, whose darling I am? Pangloss deceived me cruelly when he said that all is for the best in the world.'

"I was agitated, distracted, sometimes beside myself and sometimes ready to die of faintness, and my head was filled with the massacre of my father, of my mother, of my brother, the insolence of my horrid Bulgarian soldier, the gash he gave me, my slavery, my life as a kitchen-wench, my Bulgarian captain, my horrid Don Issachar, my abominable Inquisitor, the hanging of Dr. Pangloss, that long plain-song *miséréré* during which you were flogged, and above all the kiss I gave you behind the screen that day when I saw you for the last time. I praised God for bringing you back to me through so many trials, I ordered my old woman to take care of you and to bring you here as soon as she could. She has carried out my commission very well; I have enjoyed the inexpressible pleasure of seeing you again, of listening to you, and of speaking to you. You must be very hungry; I have a good appetite; let us begin by having supper."

Both sat down to supper; and after supper they returned to the handsome sofa we have already mentioned; they were still there when Signor Don Issachar, one of the masters of the house, arrived. It was the day of the Sabbath. He came to enjoy his rights and to express his tender love.

CHAPTER IX

This Issachar was the most choleric Hebrew who had been seen in Israel since the Babylonian captivity.

"What!" said he. "Bitch of a Galilean, isn't it enough to have the Inquisitor? Must this scoundrel share with me too?"

So saying, he drew a long dagger which he always carried and, thinking that his adversary was unarmed, threw himself upon Candide; but our good Westphalian had received an excellent sword from the old woman along with his suit of clothes. He drew his sword, and although he had a most gentle character, laid the Israelite stone-dead on the floor at the feet of the fair Cunegonde.

"Holy Virgin!" she exclaimed, "what will become of us? A man killed in my house! If the police come we are lost."

"If Pangloss had not been hanged," said Candide, "he would have given us good advice in this extremity, for he was a great philosopher. In default of him, let us consult the old woman."

She was extremely prudent and was beginning to give her advice when another little door opened. It was an hour after midnight, and Sunday was beginning.

This day belonged to My Lord the Inquisitor. He came in and saw the flogged Candide sword in hand, a corpse lying on the ground, Cunegonde in terror, and the old woman giving advice.

At this moment, here is what happened in Candide's soul and the manner of his reasoning:

"If this holy man calls for help, he will infallibly have me burned; he might do as much to Cunegonde; he had me pitilessly lashed;

he is my rival; I am in the mood to kill, there is no room for hesitation."

His reasoning was clear and swift; and, without giving the Inquisitor time to recover from his surprise, he pierced him through and through and cast him beside the Jew.

"Here's another," said Cunegonde, "there is no chance of mercy; we are excommunicated, our last hour has come. How does it happen that you, who were born so mild, should kill a Jew and a prelate in two minutes?"

"My dear young lady," replied Candide, "when a man is in love, jealous, and has been flogged by the Inquisition, he is beside himself."

The old woman then spoke up and said:

"In the stable are three Andalusian horses, with their saddles and bridles; let the brave Candide prepare them; madam has moidores and diamonds; let us mount quickly, although I can only sit on one buttock, and go to Cadiz; the weather is beautifully fine, and it is most pleasant to travel in the coolness of the night."

Candide immediately saddled the three horses. Cunegonde, the old woman and he rode thirty miles without stopping.

While they were riding away, the Holy Hermandad arrived at the house; My Lord was buried in a splendid church and Issachar was thrown into a sewer.

Candide, Cunegonde and the old woman had already reached the little town of Avacena in the midst of the mountains of the Sierra Morena; and they talked in their inn as follows.

CHAPTER X

"Who can have stolen my pistoles and my diamonds?" said Cunegonde, weeping. "How shall we live? What shall we do? Where shall we find Inquisitors and Jews to give me others?"

"Alas!" said the old woman, "I strongly suspect a reverend Franciscan father who slept in the same inn at Badajoz with us; Heaven forbid that I should judge rashly! But he twice came into our room and left long before we did."

"Alas!" said Candide, "the good Pangloss often proved to me that this world's goods are common to all men and that everyone has an equal right to them. According to these principles the monk should have left us enough to continue our journey. Have you nothing left then, my fair Cunegonde?"

"Not a maravedi," said she.

"What are we to do?" said Candide.

"Sell one of the horses," said the old woman. "I will ride postillion behind Miss Cunegonde, although I can only sit on one buttock, and we will get to Cadiz."

In the same hotel there was a Benedictine friar. He bought the horse very cheap. Candide, Cunegonde and the old woman passed through Lucena, Chillas, Lebrixa, and at last reached Cadiz. A fleet was there being equipped and troops were being raised to bring to reason the reverend Jesuit fathers of Paraguay, who were accused of causing the revolt of one of their tribes against the kings of Spain and Portugal near the town of Sacramento. Candide, having served with the Bulgarians, went through the Bulgarian drill before the general of the little army with so much grace, celerity, skill, pride and agility, that he was given the command of an infantry company. He was now a captain; he embarked with Miss Cunegonde, the old woman, two servants, and the two Andalusian horses which had belonged to the Grand Inquisitor of Portugal.

During the voyage they had many discussions about the philosophy of poor Pangloss.

"We are going to a new world," said Candide, "and no doubt it is there that everything is for the best; for it must be admitted that one might lament a little over the physical and moral happenings in our own world."

"I love you with all my heart," said Cunegonde, "but my soul is still shocked by what I have seen and undergone."

"All will be well," replied Candide; "the sea in this new world already is better than the seas of our Europe; it is calmer and the winds are more constant. It is certainly the new world which is the best of all possible worlds."

"God grant it!" said Cunegonde, "but I have been so horribly unhappy in mine that my heart is nearly closed to hope."

"You complain," said the old woman to them. "Alas! you have not endured such misfortunes as mine."

Cunegonde almost laughed and thought it most amusing of the old woman to assert that she was more unfortunate.

"Alas! my dear," said she, "unless you have been raped by two

Bulgarians, stabbed twice in the belly, have had two castles destroyed, two fathers and mothers murdered before your eyes, and have seen two of your lovers flogged in an *auto-de-fé,* I do not see how you can surpass me; moreover, I was born a Baroness with seventy-two quarterings and I have been a kitchen-wench."

"You do not know my birth," said the old woman, "and if I showed you my backside you would not talk as you do and you would suspend your judgment."

This speech aroused intense curiosity in the minds of Cunegonde and Candide. And the old woman spoke as follows.

CHAPTER XI

"My eyes were not always bloodshot and red-rimmed; my nose did not always touch my chin and I was not always a servant. I am the daughter of Pope Urban X and the Princess of Palestrina. Until I was fourteen I was brought up in a palace to which all the castles of your German Barons would not have served as stables; and one of my dresses cost more than all the magnificence of Westphalia. I increased in beauty, in grace, in talents, among pleasures, respect and hopes; already I inspired love, my breasts were forming; and what breasts! White, firm, carved like those of the Venus de' Medici. And what eyes! What eyelids! What black eyebrows! What fire shone from my two eyeballs, and dimmed the glitter of the stars, as the local poets pointed out to me. The women who dressed and undressed me fell into ecstasy when they beheld me in front and behind; and all the men would have liked to be in their place.

"I was betrothed to a ruling prince of Massa-Carrara. What a prince! As beautiful as I was, formed of gentleness and charms, brilliantly witty and burning with love; I loved him with a first love, idolatrously and extravagantly. The marriage ceremonies were arranged with unheard-of pomp and magnificence; there were continual fêtes, revels and comic operas; all Italy wrote sonnets for me, and not a good one among them.

"I touched the moment of my happiness when an old marchioness who had been my prince's mistress invited him to take chocolate with her; less than two hours afterwards he died in horrible convulsions; but that is only a trifle. My mother was in despair, though less distressed than I, and wished to absent herself for a time from a place so disastrous. She had a most beautiful estate near Gaeta; we embarked on a galley, gilded like the altar of St. Peter's at Rome. A Salle pirate swooped down and boarded us; our soldiers defended us like soldiers of the Pope; they threw down their arms, fell on their knees and asked the pirates for absolution *in articulo mortis.*

"They were immediately stripped as naked as monkeys and my mother, our ladies of honour and myself as well. The diligence with which these gentlemen strip people is truly admirable; but I was still more surprised by their inserting a finger in a place belonging to all of us where we women usually only allow the end of a syringe. This appeared to me a very strange ceremony; but that is how we judge everything when we leave our own country. I soon learned that it was to find out if we had hidden any diamonds there; 'tis a custom established from time immemorial among the civilised nations who roam the seas. I have learned that the religious Knights of Malta never fail in it when they capture Turks and Turkish women; this is an international law which has never been broken.

"I will not tell you how hard it is for a young princess to be taken with her mother as a slave to Morocco; you will also guess all we had to endure in the pirates' ship. My mother was still very beautiful; our ladies of honour, even our waiting-maids possessed more charms than could be found in all Africa; and I was ravishing, I was beauty, grace itself, and I was a virgin; I did not remain so long; the flower which had been reserved for the handsome prince of Massa-Carrara was ravished from me by a pirate captain; he was an abominable negro who thought he was doing me a great honour. The Princess of Palestrina and I must indeed have been strong to bear up against all we endured before our arrival in Morocco! But let that pass; these things are so common that they are not worth mentioning.

"Morocco was swimming in blood when we arrived. The fifty sons of the Emperor Muley Ismael had each a faction; and this produced fifty civil wars, of blacks against blacks, browns against browns, mulattoes against mulattoes. There was continual carnage throughout the whole extent of the empire.

"Scarcely had we landed when the blacks of a party hostile to that of my pirate arrived with the purpose of depriving him of his booty. After the diamonds and the gold, we were the most valuable possessions. I witnessed a fight such as is never seen in your European climates. The blood of the northern peoples is not sufficiently ardent; their madness for women does not reach the point which is common in Africa. The Europeans seem to have milk in their veins; but vitriol and fire flow in the veins of the inhabitants of Mount Atlas and the neighbouring countries. They fought with the fury of the lions, tigers and serpents of the country to determine who should have us. A Moor grasped my mother by the right arm, my captain's lieutenant held her by the left arm; a Moorish soldier held one leg and one of our pirates seized the other. In a moment nearly all our women were seized in the same way by four soldiers. My captain kept me hidden behind him; he had a scimitar in his hand and killed everybody who opposed his fury. I saw my mother and all our Italian women torn in pieces, gashed, massacred by the monsters who disputed them. The prisoners, my companions, those who had captured them, soldiers, sailors, blacks, browns, whites, mulattoes and finally my captain were all killed and I remained expiring on a heap of corpses. As everyone knows, such scenes go on in an area of more than three hundred square leagues and yet no one ever fails to recite the five daily prayers ordered by Mahomet.

"With great difficulty I extricated myself from the bloody heaps of corpses and dragged myself to the foot of a large orange-tree on the bank of a stream; there I fell down with terror, weariness, horror, despair and hunger. Soon afterwards, my exhausted senses fell into a sleep which was more like a swoon than repose. I was in this state of weakness and insensibility between life and death when I felt myself oppressed by something which moved on my body. I opened my eyes and saw a white man of good appearance who was sighing and muttering between his teeth: *O che sciagura d'essere senza coglioni!*

CHAPTER XII

"Amazed and delighted to hear my native language, and not less surprised at the words spoken by this man, I replied that there were greater misfortunes than that of which he complained. In a few words I informed him of the horrors I had undergone and then swooned again. He carried me to a neighbouring house, had me put to bed, gave me food, waited on me, consoled me, flattered me, told me he had never seen anyone so beautiful as I, and that he had never so much regretted that which no one could give back to him.

" 'I was born at Naples,' he said, 'and every year they make two or three thousand children there into capons; some die of it, others acquire voices more beautiful than women's, and others become the governors of States. This operation was performed upon me with very great success and I was a musician in the chapel of the Princess of Palestrina.'

" 'Of my mother,' I exclaimed.

" 'Of your mother!' cried he, weeping. 'What! Are you that young princess I brought up to the age of six and who even then gave promise of being as beautiful as you are?'

" 'I am! my mother is four hundred yards from here, cut into quarters under a heap of corpses. . . .'

"I related all that had happened to me; he also told me his adventures and informed me how he had been sent to the King of Morocco by a Christian power to make a treaty with that monarch whereby he was supplied with powder, cannons and ships to help to exterminate the commerce of other Christians.

" 'My mission is accomplished,' said this honest eunuch, 'I am about to embark at Ceuta and I will take you back to Italy. *Ma che sciagura d'essere senza coglioni!*'

"I thanked him with tears of gratitude; and instead of taking me back to Italy he conducted me to Algiers and sold me to the Dey. I had scarcely been sold when the plague which had gone through Africa, Asia and Europe broke out furiously in Algiers. You have seen earthquakes; but have you ever seen the plague?"

"Never," replied the Baroness.

"If you had," replied the old woman, "you would admit that it is much worse than an earthquake. It is very common in Africa; I caught it. Imagine the situation of a Pope's daughter aged fifteen, who in three months had undergone poverty and slavery, had been raped nearly every day, had seen her mother cut into four pieces, had undergone hunger and war, and was now dying of the plague in Algiers. However, I did not die; but my eunuch and the Dey and almost all the seraglio of Algiers perished.

"When the first ravages of this frightful plague were over, the

Dey's slaves were sold. A merchant bought me and carried me to Tunis; he sold me to another merchant who re-sold me at Tripoli; from Tripoli I was re-sold to Alexandria, from Alexandria re-sold to Smyrna, from Smyrna to Constantinople. I was finally bought by an Aga of the Janizaries, who was soon ordered to defend Azov against the Russians who were besieging it.

"The Aga, who was a man of great gallantry, took his whole seraglio with him, and lodged us in a little fort on the islands of Palus-Maeotis, guarded by two black eunuchs and twenty soldiers. He killed a prodigious number of Russians, but they returned the compliment as well. Azov was given up to fire and blood, neither sex nor age was pardoned; only our little fort remained; and the enemy tried to reduce it by starving us. The twenty Janizaries had sworn never to surrender us. The extremities of hunger to which they were reduced forced them to eat our two eunuchs for fear of breaking their oath. Some days later they resolved to eat the women.

"We had with us a most pious and compassionate Imam who delivered a fine sermon to them by which he persuaded them not to kill us altogether.

" 'Cut,' said he, 'only one buttock from each of these ladies and you will make very good cheer; if you have to return, there will still be as much left in a few days; Heaven will be pleased at so charitable an action and you will be saved.'

"He was very eloquent and persuaded them. This horrible operation was performed upon us; the Imam anointed us with the same balm that is used for children who have just been circumcised; we were all at the point of death.

"Scarcely had the Janizaries finished the meal we had supplied when the Russians arrived in flat-bottomed boats; not a Janizary escaped. The Russians paid no attention to the state we were in. There are French doctors everywhere; one of them who was very skilful, took care of us; he healed us, and I shall remember all my life that, when my wounds were cured, he made propositions to me. For the rest, he told us all to cheer up; he told us that the same thing had happened in several sieges and that it was a law of war.

"As soon as my companions could walk they were sent to Moscow. I fell to the lot of a Boyar who made me his gardener and gave me twenty lashes a day. But at the end of two years this lord was broken

on the wheel with thirty other Boyars owing to some court disturbance, and I profited by this adventure; I fled; I crossed all
Russia; for a long time I was servant in an inn at Riga, then at
Rostock, at Wismar, at Leipzig, at Cassel, at Utrecht, at Leyden,
at the Hague, at Rotterdam; I have grown old in misery and in
shame, with only half a backside, always remembering that I was the
daughter of a Pope; a hundred times I wanted to kill myself, but
I still loved life. This ridiculous weakness is perhaps the most
disastrous of our inclinations; for is there anything sillier than to
desire to bear continually a burden one always wishes to throw on
the ground; to look upon oneself with horror and yet to cling to
oneself; in short, to caress the serpent which devours us until he has
eaten our heart?

"In the countries it has been my fate to traverse and in the inns
where I have served I have seen a prodigious number of people
who hated their lives; but I have only seen twelve who voluntarily
put an end to their misery: three negroes, four Englishmen, four
Genevans and a German professor named Robeck. I ended up as
servant to the Jew, Don Issachar; he placed me in your service,
my fair young lady; I attached myself to your fate and have been
more occupied with your adventures than with my own. I should
never even have spoken of my misfortunes, if you had not piqued
me a little and if it had not been the custom on board ship to tell
stories to pass the time. In short, Miss, I have had experience, I
know the world; provide yourself with an entertainment, make each
passenger tell you his story; and if there is one who has not often
cursed his life, who has not often said to himself that he was the
most unfortunate of men, throw me head-first into the sea."

[In the New World, Candide meets with further adventures that
show the stupidity, cruelty, and greed of men. Only in El Dorado,
a paradise in the interior of South America, does he find a society
in which people are naturally kind, courteous, generous, and reasonable. Having lost his beloved Cunegonde to a Spanish colonial
grandee, he makes plans to win her back by bribery and decides to
return to Europe. En route he falls in with Martin, a disillusioned
pessimist, and under the latter's tutelage begins to doubt Pangloss's optimism, "the mania of maintaining that everything is well
when we are wretched." Martin argues that their misadventures

prove that the world is evil and was created only to infuriate us. Back in Europe, Candide meets with evidence for this view in the behavior of intellectuals, prostitutes, monks, and deposed kings. Nowhere can he find a truly happy man. In the end, Candide is reunited in marriage with Cunegonde, now ugly and shrewish, and settles down on a small farm near Constantinople to a life of unending boredom. Taking his cue from a simple Turkish farmer, he concludes that the only prescription for sanity is that "we must cultivate our gardens." *Ed.*]

Jean Jacques Rousseau

10

The Social Contract

In the midst of the middle-class liberalism of eighteenth-century France, Jean Jacques Rousseau (1712–1778) was a startling and important exception. Though sharing some of the ideas of the Enlightenment, he was violently opposed to others. Born into a Swiss Protestant family of lowly origin, Rousseau remained an outsider and a rebel, a rootless vagabond who rejected any place in French society. He was an unhappy, impractical man, with an unstable personality, whose life ended in madness. He was, nonetheless, an emotional democrat who spoke up sincerely for the common man; his ideas were probably the greatest influence on the course of the French Revolution, especially in its radical stage. Subsequently, Rousseau was hailed as the prophet of democracy and nationalism; totalitarian movements have even found inspiration in his ideas of the sovereignty of collective authority. Rousseau was, in addition, one of the first exponents of that combination of ideas and attitudes toward life typical of the philosophical and literary movement called romanticism.

Rousseau shared the Enlightenment belief in progress and in the goodness of man and his infinite perfectibility. He violently attacked the social order of his day as artificial, corrupt, and corrupting. But he refused to accept the simple equivalence of reason and nature. Nature was good, but, since reason was part of civilization, it was evil: reason was not the guide to truth. To achieve truth and justice, Rousseau advocated that man return to nature and trust his untaught feelings. The primitive and unsophisticated elements in man were the sources of strength to remake the individual and society.

The Social Contract (1762) was, in substance, Rousseau's prescription for the just society. In a powerful and closely reasoned exposition, he reconciled the freedom of the individual and the authority of the state in an organic community which embodied "the general will," directed to the

Jean Jacques Rousseau, *The Social Contract*, trans. Henry J. Tozer (New York: Scribner, 1898), 100, 103–05, 109–14, 119–20, 123–28, 131–33, 197–201.

common welfare. Such a community, originating in a "contract" among free and equal individuals, was one of democratic equality, based on the sovereignty of the people, and gave all men a real sense of belonging.

Man is born free, and everywhere he is in chains. Many a one believes himself the master of others, and yet he is a greater slave than they. How has this change come about? I do not know. What can render it legitimate? I believe that I can settle this question.

If I considered only force and the results that proceed from it, I should say that so long as a people is compelled to obey and does obey, it does well; but that, so soon as it can shake off the yoke and does shake it off, it does better; for, if men recover their freedom by virtue of the same right by which it was taken away, either they are justified in resuming it, or there was no justification for depriving them of it. But the social order is a sacred right which serves as a foundation for all others. This right however, does not come from nature. It is therefore based on conventions. The question is to know what these conventions are. Before coming to that, I must establish what I have just laid down.

THE RIGHT OF THE STRONGEST

The strongest man is never strong enough to be always master, unless he transforms his power into right, and obedience into duty. Hence the right of the strongest—a right apparently assumed in irony, and really established in principle. But will this phrase never be explained to us? Force is a physical power; I do not see what morality can result from its effects. To yield to force is an act of necessity, not of will; it is at most an act of prudence. In what sense can it be a duty?

Let us assume for a moment this pretended right. I say that nothing results from it but inexplicable nonsense; for if force constitutes right, the effect changes with the cause, and any force which overcomes the first succeeds to its rights. As soon as men can disobey with impunity, they may do so legitimately; and since the strongest is always in the right, the only thing is to act in such a way that one may be the strongest. But what sort of a right is it that perishes when force ceases? If it is necessary to obey by compulsion, there is no need to obey from duty; and if men are no longer forced to obey, obligation is at an end. We see, then, that this word *right* adds nothing to force; it here means nothing at all.

Obey the powers that be. If that means, Yield to force, the precept is good but superfluous; I reply that it will never be violated. All power comes from God, I admit; but every disease comes from him too; does it follow that we are prohibited from calling in a physician? If a brigand should surprise me in the recesses of a wood, am I bound not only to give up my purse when forced, but am I also morally bound to do so when I might conceal it? For, in effect, the pistol which he holds is a superior force.

Let us agree, then, that might does not make right, and that we are bound to obey none but lawful authorities. Thus my original question ever recurs.

SLAVERY

Since no man has any natural authority over his fellow-men, and since force is not the source of right, conventions remain as the basis of all lawful authority among men.

If an individual, says Grotius, can alienate his liberty and become the slave of a master, why should not a whole people be able to alienate theirs, and become subject to a king? In this there are many equivocal terms requiring explanation; but let us confine ourselves to the word *alienate*. To alienate is to give or sell. Now, a man who becomes another's slave does not give himself; he sells himself at the very least for his subsistence. But why does a nation sell itself? So far from a king supplying his subjects with their subsistence, he draws his from them; and, according to Rabelais, a king does not live on a little. Do subjects, then, give up their persons on condition that their property also shall be taken? I do not see what is left for them to keep.

It will be said that the despot secures to his subjects civil peace. Be it so; but what do they gain by that, if the wars which his ambition brings upon them, together with his insatiable greed and the vexations of his administration, harass them more than their own dissensions would? What do they gain by it if this tranquillity is itself one of their miseries? Men live tranquilly also in dungeons;

is that enough to make them contented there? The Greeks confined in the cave of the Cyclops lived peacefully until their turn came to be devoured.

To say that a man gives himself for nothing is to say what is absurd and inconceivable; such an act is illegitimate and invalid, for the simple reason that he who performs it is not in his right mind. To say the same thing of a whole nation is to suppose a nation of fools; and madness does not confer rights.

Even if each person could alienate himself, he could not alienate his children; they are born free men; their liberty belongs to them, and no one has a right to dispose of it except themselves. Before they have come to years of discretion, the father can, in their name, stipulate conditions for their preservation and welfare, but not surrender them irrevocably and unconditionally; for such a gift is contrary to the ends of nature, and exceeds the rights of paternity. In order, then, that an arbitrary government might be legitimate, it would be necessary that the people in each generation should have the option of accepting or rejecting it; but in that case such a government would no longer be arbitrary.

To renounce one's liberty is to renounce one's quality as a man, the rights and also the duties of humanity. For him who renounces everything there is no possible compensation. Such a renunciation is incompatible with man's nature, for to take away all freedom from his will is to take away all morality from his actions. In short, a convention which stipulates absolute authority on the one side and unlimited obedience on the other is vain and contradictory. Is it not clear that we are under no obligations whatsoever towards a man from whom we have a right to demand everything? And does not this single condition, without equivalent, without exchange, involve the nullity of the act? For what right would my slave have against me, since all that he has belongs to me? His rights being mine, this right of me against myself is a meaningless phrase.

· · ·

THE SOCIAL PACT

I assume that men have reached a point at which the obstacles that endanger their preservation in the state of nature overcome by their resistance the forces which each individual can exert with a view to maintaining himself in that state. Then this primitive condition can no longer subsist, and the human race would perish unless it changed its mode of existence.

Now, as men cannot create any new forces, but only combine and direct those that exist, they have no other means of self-preservation than to form by aggregation a sum of forces which may overcome the resistance, to put them in action by a single motive power, and to make them work in concert.

This sum of forces can be produced only by the combination of many; but the strength and freedom of each man being the chief instruments of his preservation, how can he pledge them without injuring himself, and without neglecting the cares which he owes to himself? This difficulty, applied to my subject, may be expressed in these terms:—

"To find a form of association which may defend and protect with the whole force of the community the person and property of every associate, and by means of which each, coalescing with all, may nevertheless obey only himself, and remain as free as before." Such is the fundamental problem of which the social contract furnishes the solution.

The clauses of this contract are so determined by the nature of the act that the slightest modification would render them vain and ineffectual; so that, although they have never perhaps been formally enunciated, they are everywhere the same, everywhere tacitly admitted and recognised, until, the social pact being violated, each man regains his original rights and recovers his natural liberty, whilst losing the conventional liberty for which he renounced it.

These clauses, rightly understood, are reducible to one only, viz. the total alienation to the whole community of each associate with all his rights; for, in the first place, since each gives himself up entirely, the conditions are equal for all; and, the conditions being equal for all, no one has any interest in making them burdensome to others.

Further, the alienation being made without reserve, the union is as perfect as it can be, and an individual associate can no longer claim anything; for, if any rights were left to individuals, since there would be no common superior who could judge between them and the public, each, being on some point his own judge, would soon claim to be so on all; the state of nature would still subsist, and the association would necessarily become tyrannical or useless.

In short, each giving himself to all, gives himself to nobody; and as there is not one associate over whom we do not acquire the same rights which we concede to him over ourselves, we gain the equivalent of all that we lose, and more power to preserve what we have.

If, then, we set aside what is not of the essence of the social contract, we shall find that it is reducible to the following terms: "Each of us puts in common his person and his whole power under the supreme direction of the general will; and in return we receive every member as an indivisible part of the whole."

Forthwith, instead of the individual personalities of all the contracting parties, this act of association produces a moral and collective body, which is composed of as many members as the assembly has voices, and which receives from this same act its unity, its common self (*moi*), its life, and its will. This public person, which is thus formed by the union of all the individual members, formerly took the name of *city,* and now takes that of *republic* or *body politic,* which is called by its members *State* when it is passive, *sovereign* when it is active, *power* when it is compared to similar bodies. With regard to the associates, they take collectively the name of *people,* and are called individually *citizens,* as participating in the sovereign power, and *subjects,* as subjected to the laws of the State. But these terms are often confused and are mistaken one for another; it is sufficient to know how to distinguish them when they are used with complete precision.

THE SOVEREIGN

We see from this formula that the act of association contains a reciprocal engagement between the public and individuals, and that every individual, contracting so to speak with himself, is engaged in a double relation, viz. as a member of the sovereign towards individuals, and as a member of the State towards the sovereign. But we cannot apply here the maxim of civil law that no one is bound by engagements made with himself; for there is a great difference between being bound to oneself and to a whole of which one forms part.

We must further observe that the public resolution which can bind all subjects to the sovereign in consequence of the two different relations under which each of them is regarded cannot, for a contrary reason, bind the sovereign to itself; and that accordingly it is contrary to the nature of the body politic for the sovereign to impose on itself a law which it cannot transgress. As it can only be considered under one and the same relation, it is in the position of an individual contracting with himself; whence we see that there is not, nor can be, any kind of fundamental law binding upon the body of the people, not even the social contract. This does not imply that such a body cannot perfectly well enter into engagements with others in what does not derogate from this contract; for, with regard to foreigners, it becomes a simple being, an individual.

But the body politic or sovereign, deriving its existence only from the sanctity of the contract, can never bind itself, even to others, in anything that derogates from the original act, such as alienation of some portion of itself, or submission to another sovereign. To violate the act by which it exists would be to annihilate itself; and what is nothing produces nothing.

So soon as the multitude is thus united in one body, it is impossible to injure one of the members without attacking the body, still less to injure the body without the members feeling the effects. Thus duty and interest alike oblige the two contracting parties to give mutual assistance; and the men themselves should seek to combine in this twofold relationship all the advantages which are attendant on it.

Now, the sovereign, being formed only of the individuals that compose it, neither has nor can have any interest contrary to theirs; consequently the sovereign power needs no guarantee towards its subjects, because it is impossible that the body should wish to injure all its members; and we shall see hereafter that it can injure no one as an individual. The sovereign, for the simple reason that it is so, is always everything that it ought to be.

But this is not the case as regards the relation of subjects to the sovereign, which, notwithstanding the common interest, would have no security for the performance of their engagements, unless it found means to ensure their fidelity.

Indeed, every individual may, as a man, have a particular will contrary to, or divergent from, the general will which he has as a citizen; his private interest may prompt him quite differently from the common interest; his absolute and naturally independent existence may make him regard what he owes to the common cause as a gratuitous contribution, the loss of which will be less harmful to others than the payment of it will be burdensome to him; and, regarding the moral person that constitutes the State as an imaginary being because it is not a man, he would be willing to enjoy the rights of a citizen without being willing to fulfil the duties of a subject. The progress of such injustice would bring about the ruin of the body politic.

In order, then, that the social pact may not be a vain formulary, it tacitly includes this engagement, which can alone give force to the others,—that whoever refuses to obey the general will shall be constrained to do so by the whole body; which means nothing else than that he shall be forced to be free; for such is the condition which, uniting every citizen to his native land, guarantees him from all personal dependence, a condition that ensures the control and working of the political machine, and alone renders legitimate civil engagements, which, without it, would be absurd and tyrannical, and subject to the most enormous abuses.

THE CIVIL STATE

The passage from the state of nature to the civil state produces in man a very remarkable change, by substituting in his conduct justice for instinct, and by giving his actions the moral quality that they previously lacked. It is only when the voice of duty succeeds physical impulse, and law succeeds appetite, that man, who till then had regarded only himself, sees that he is obliged to act on other principles, and to consult his reason before listening to his inclinations. Although, in this state, he is deprived of many advantages that he derives from nature, he acquires equally great ones in return; his faculties are exercised and developed; his ideas are expanded; his feelings are ennobled; his whole soul is exalted to such a degree that, if the abuses of this new condition did not often degrade him below that from which he has emerged, he ought to bless without ceasing the happy moment that released him from it for ever, and transformed him from a stupid and ignorant animal into an intelligent being and a man.

Let us reduce this whole balance to terms easy to compare. What man loses by the social contract is his natural liberty and an unlimited right to anything which tempts him and which he is able to attain; what he gains is civil liberty and property in all that he possesses. In order that we may not be mistaken about these compensations, we must clearly distinguish natural liberty, which is limited only by the powers of the individual, from civil liberty, which is limited by the general will; and possession, which is nothing but the result of force or the right of first occupancy, from property, which can be based only on a positive title.

Besides the preceding, we might add to the acquisitions of the civil state moral freedom, which alone renders man truly master of himself; for the impulse of mere appetite is slavery, while obedience to a self-prescribed law is liberty. But I have already said too much on this head, and the philosophical meaning of the term *liberty* does not belong to my present subject.

. . .

THAT SOVEREIGNTY IS INALIENABLE

The first and most important consequence of the principles above established is that the general will alone can direct the forces of the State according to the object of its institution, which is the common good; for if the opposition of private interests has rendered necessary the establishment of societies, the agreement of these same interests has rendered it possible. That which is common to these different interests forms the social bond; and unless there were some point in which all interests agree, no society could exist. Now, it is solely with regard to this common interest that the society should be governed.

I say, then, that sovereignty, being nothing but the exercise of the general will, can never be alienated, and that the sovereign power, which is only a collective being, can be represented by itself alone; power indeed can be transmitted, but not will.

In fact, if it is not impossible that a particular will should agree on some point with the general will, it is at least impossible that this agreement should be lasting and constant; for the particular will naturally tends to preferences, and the general will to equality. It is still more impossible to have a security for this agreement; even though it should always exist, it would not be a result of art, but of chance. The sovereign may indeed say: "I will now what a certain man wills, or at least what he says that he wills"; but he cannot say: "What that man wills to-morrow, I shall also will," since it is absurd that the will should bind itself as regards the future, and since it is not incumbent on any will to consent to anything contrary to the welfare of the being that wills. If, then, the nation simply promises to obey, it dissolves itself by that act and loses its character as a people; the moment there is a master, there is no longer a sovereign, and forthwith the body politic is destroyed.

This does not imply that the orders of the chiefs cannot pass for decisions of the general will, so long as the sovereign, free to oppose them, refrains from doing so. In such a case the consent of the people should be inferred from the universal silence.

.   .   .

WHETHER THE GENERAL WILL CAN ERR

It follows from what precedes that the general will is always right and always tends to the public advantage; but it does not follow that the resolutions of the people have always the same rectitude. Men always desire their own good, but do not always discern it; the people are never corrupted, though often deceived, and it is only then that they seem to will what is evil.

There is often a great deal of difference between the will of all and the general will; the latter regards only the common interest, while the former has regard to private interests, and is merely a sum of particular wills; but take away from these same wills the pluses and minuses which cancel one another, and the general will remains as the sum of the differences.

If the people came to a resolution when adequately informed and without any communication among the citizens, the general will would always result from the great number of slight differences, and the resolution would always be good. But when factions, partial associations, are formed to the detriment of the whole society, the will of each of these associations becomes general with reference to its members, and particular with reference to the State; it may then be said that there are no longer as many voters as there are men, but only as many voters as there are associations. The differences become less numerous and yield a less general result. Lastly, when one of these associations becomes so great that it predominates over all the rest, you no longer have as the result a sum of small differences, but a single difference; there is then no longer a general will, and the opinion which prevails is only a particular opinion.

It is important, then, in order to have a clear declaration of the general will, that there should be no partial association in the State, and that every citizen should express only his own opinion. Such was the unique and sublime institution of the great Lycurgus. But if there are partial associations, it is necessary to multiply their number and prevent inequality, as Solon, Numa, and Servius did. These are the only proper precautions for ensuring that the general will may always be enlightened, and that the people may not be deceived.

THE LIMITS OF THE SOVEREIGN POWER

If the State or city is nothing but a moral person, the life of which consists in the union of its members, and if the most important of its cares is that of self-preservation, it needs a universal and compulsive force to move and dispose every part in the manner most expedient for the whole. As nature gives every man an absolute power over all his limbs, the social pact gives the body politic an absolute power over all its members; and it is this same power which, when directed by the general will, bears, as I said, the name of sovereignty.

But besides the public person, we have to consider the private persons who compose it, and whose life and liberty are naturally independent of it. The question, then, is to distinguish clearly between the respective rights of the citizens and of the sovereign, as well as between the duties which the former have to fulfil in their capacity as subjects and the natural rights which they ought to enjoy in their character as men.

It is admitted that whatever part of his power, property, and liberty each one alienates by the social compact is only that part of the whole of which the use is important to the community; but we must also admit that the sovereign alone is judge of what is important.

All the services that a citizen can render to the State he owes to it as soon as the sovereign demands them; but the sovereign, on its part, cannot impose on its subjects any burden which is useless to the community; it cannot even wish to do so, for, by the law of reason, just as by the law of nature, nothing is done without a cause.

The engagements which bind us to the social body are obligatory only because they are mutual; and their nature is such that in fulfilling them we cannot work for others without also working for ourselves. Why is the general will always right, and why do all invariably desire the prosperity of each, unless it is because there is no one but appropriates to himself this word *each* and thinks of himself in voting on behalf of all? This proves that equality of rights and the notion of justice that it produces are derived from the preference which each gives to himself, and consequently from man's nature; that the general will, to be truly such, should be so in its object as well as in its essence; that it ought to proceed from all in order to be applicable to all; and that it loses its natural rectitude when it tends to some individual and determinate object, because in that case, judging of what is unknown to us, we have no true principle of equity to guide us.

Indeed, so soon as a particular fact or right is in question with regard to a point which has not been regulated by an anterior general convention, the matter becomes contentious; it is a process in which the private persons interested are one of the parties and the public the other, but in which I perceive neither the law which must be followed, nor the judge who should decide. It would be ridiculous in such a case to wish to refer the matter for an express decision of the general will, which can be nothing but the decision of one of the parties, and which, consequently, is for the other party only a will that is foreign, partial, and inclined on such an occasion to injustice as well as liable to error. Therefore, just as a particular will cannot represent the general will, the general will in turn changes its nature when it has a particular end, and cannot, as general, decide about either a person or a fact. When the people of Athens, for instance, elected or deposed their chiefs, decreed honours to one, imposed penalties on another, and by multitudes of particular decrees exercised indiscriminately all the functions of government, the people no longer had any general will properly so called; they no longer acted as a sovereign power, but as magistrates. This will appear contrary to common ideas, but I must be allowed time to expound my own.

From this we must understand that what generalises the will is not so much the number of voices as the common interest which unites them; for, under this system, each necessarily submits to the conditions which he imposes on others—an admirable union of interest and justice, which gives to the deliberations of the community a spirit of equity that seems to disappear in the discussion of any private affair, for want of a common interest to unite and identify the ruling principle of the judge with that of the party.

By whatever path we return to our principle we always arrive at the same conclusion, viz. that the social compact establishes among the citizens such an equality that they all pledge themselves under the same conditions and ought all to enjoy the same rights. Thus, by the nature of the compact, every act of sovereignty, that is, every authentic act of the general will, binds or favours equally all the citizens; so that the sovereign knows only the body of the nation, and distinguishes none of those that compose it.

What, then, is an act of sovereignty properly so called? It is not an agreement between a superior and an inferior, but an agreement of the body with each of its members; a lawful agreement, because it has the social contract as its foundation; equitable, because it is common to all; useful, because it can have no other object than the general welfare; and stable, because it has the public force and the supreme power as a guarantee. So long as the subjects submit only to such conventions, they obey no one, but simply their own will; and to ask how far the respective rights of the sovereign and citizens extend is to ask up to what point the latter can make engagements among themselves, each with all and all with each.

Thus we see that the sovereign power, wholly absolute, wholly sacred, and wholly inviolable as it is, does not, and cannot, pass the limits of general conventions, and that every man can fully dispose of what is left to him of his property and liberty by these conventions; so that the sovereign never has a right to burden one subject more than another, because then the matter becomes particular and his power is no longer competent.

These distinctions once admitted, so untrue is it that in the social contract there is on the part of individuals any real renunciation, that their situation, as a result of this contract, is in reality preferable to what it was before, and that, instead of an alienation, they have only made an advantageous exchange of an uncertain and precarious mode of existence for a better and more assured one,

of natural independence for liberty, of the power to injure others
for their own safety, and of their strength, which others might overcome, for a right which the social union renders inviolable. Their
lives, also, which they have devoted to the State, are continually
protected by it; and in exposing their lives for its defence, what
do they do but restore what they have received from it? What do
they do but what they would do more frequently and with more
risk in the state of nature, when, engaging in inevitable struggles,
they would defend at the peril of their lives their means of preservation? All have to fight for their country in case of need, it is true;
but then no one ever has to fight for himself. Do we not gain, moreover, by incurring, for what ensures our safety, a part of the risks
that we should have to incur for ourselves individually, as soon as
we were deprived of it?

THE LAW

By the social compact we have given existence and life to the
body politic; the question now is to endow it with movement and
will by legislation. For the original act by which this body is formed
and consolidated determines nothing in addition as to what it must
do for its own preservation.

What is right and conformable to order is such by the nature of
things, and independently of human conventions. All justice comes
from God, He alone is the source of it; but could we receive it direct from so lofty a source, we should need neither government nor
laws. Without doubt there is a universal justice emanating from
reason alone; but this justice, in order to be admitted among us,
should be reciprocal. Regarding things from a human standpoint,
the laws of justice are inoperative among men for want of a natural
sanction; they only bring good to the wicked and evil to the just
when the latter observe them with every one, and no one observes
them in return. Conventions and laws, then, are necessary to couple
rights with duties and apply justice to its object. In the state of
nature, where everything is in common, I owe nothing to those to
whom I have promised nothing; I recognize as belonging to
others only what is useless to me. This is not the case in the civil
state, in which all rights are determined by law.

But then, finally, what is a law? So long as men are content to attach to this word only metaphysical ideas, they will continue to argue without being understood; and when they have stated what a law of nature is, they will know no better what a law of the State is.

I have already said that there is no general will with reference to a particular object. In fact, this particular object is either in the State or outside of it. If it is outside the State, a will which is foreign to it is not general in relation to it; and if it is within the State, it forms part of it; then there is formed between the whole and its part a relation which makes of it two separate beings, of which the part is one, and the whole, less this same part, is the other. But the whole less one part is not the whole, and so long as the relation subsists, there is no longer any whole, but two unequal parts; whence it follows that the will of the one is no longer general in relation to the other.

But when the whole people decree concerning the whole people, they consider themselves alone; and if a relation is then constituted, it is between the whole object under one point of view and the whole object under another point of view, without any division at all. Then the matter respecting which they decree is general like the will that decrees. It is this act that I call a law.

When I say that the object of the laws is always general, I mean that the law considers subjects collectively, and actions as abstract, never a man as an individual nor a particular action. Thus the law may indeed decree that there shall be privileges, but cannot confer them on any person by name; the law can create several classes of citizens, and even assign the qualifications which shall entitle them to rank in these classes, but it cannot nominate such and such persons to be admitted to them; it can establish a royal government and a hereditary succession, but cannot elect a king or appoint a royal family; in a word, no function which has reference to an individual object appertains to the legislative power.

From this standpoint we see immediately that it is no longer necessary to ask whose office it is to make laws, since they are acts of the general will; nor whether the prince is above the laws, since he is a member of the State; nor whether the law can be unjust, since no one is unjust to himself; nor how we are free and yet subject to the laws, since the laws are only registers of our wills.

We see, further, that since the law combines the universality of the will with the universality of the object, whatever any man prescribes on his own authority is not a law; and whatever the sovereign itself prescribes respecting a particular object is not a law, but a decree, not an act of sovereignty, but of magistracy.

I therefore call any State a republic which is governed by laws, under whatever form of administration it may be; for then only does the public interest predominate and the commonwealth count for something. Every legitimate government is republican; I will explain hereafter what government is.

Laws are properly only the conditions of civil association. The people, being subjected to the laws, should be the authors of them; it concerns only the associates to determine the conditions of association. But how will they be determined? Will it be by a common agreement, by a sudden inspiration? Has the body politic an organ for expressing its will? Who will give it the foresight necessary to frame its acts and publish them at the outset? Or how shall it declare them in the hour of need? How would a blind multitude, which often knows not what it wishes because it rarely knows what is good for it, execute of itself an enterprise so great, so difficult, as a system of legislation? Of themselves, the people always desire what is good, but do not always discern it. The general will is always right, but the judgment which guides it is not always enlightened. It must be made to see objects as they are, sometimes as they ought to appear; it must be shown the good path that it is seeking, and guarded from the seduction of private interests; it must be made to observe closely times and places, and to balance the attraction of immediate and palpable advantages against the danger of remote and concealed evils. Individuals see the good which they reject; the public desire the good which they do not see. All alike have need of guides. The former must be compelled to conform their wills to their reason; the people must be taught to know what they require. Then from the public enlightenment results the union of the understanding and the will in the social body; and from that the close co-operation of the parts, and, lastly, the maximum power of the whole. Hence arises the need of a legislator.

. . . . . .

THAT THE GENERAL WILL IS INDESTRUCTIBLE

So long as a number of men in combination are considered as a single body, they have but one will, which relates to the common preservation and to the general well-being. In such a case all the forces of the State are vigorous and simple, and its principles are clear and luminous; it has no confused and conflicting interests; the common good is everywhere plainly manifest and only good sense is required to perceive it. Peace, union, and equality are foes to political subtleties. Upright and simple-minded men are hard to deceive because of their simplicity; allurements and refined pretexts do not impose upon them; they are not even cunning enough to be dupes. When, in the happiest nation in the world, we see troops of peasants regulating the affairs of the State under an oak and always acting wisely, can we refrain from despising the refinements of other nations, who make themselves illustrious and wretched with so much art and mystery?

A State thus governed needs very few laws; and in so far as it becomes necessary to promulgate new ones, this necessity is universally recognized. The first man to propose them only gives expression to what all have previously felt, and neither factions nor eloquence will be needed to pass into law what every one has already resolved to do, so soon as he is sure that the rest will act as he does.

What deceives reasoners is that, seeing only States that are ill-constituted from the beginning, they are impressed with the impossibility of maintaining such a policy in those States; they laugh to think of all the follies to which a cunning knave, an insinuating speaker, can persuade the people of Paris or London. They know not that Cromwell would have been put to hard labour by the people of Berne, and the Duke of Beaufort flogged by the Genevese.

But when the social bond begins to be relaxed and the State weakened, when private interests begin to make themselves felt and small associations to exercise influence on the State, the common interest is injuriously affected and finds adversaries; unanimity no longer reigns in the voting; the general will is no longer the will of all; opposition and disputes arise, and the best counsel does not pass uncontested.

Lastly, when the State, on the verge of ruin, no longer subsists except in a vain and illusory form, when the social bond is broken in all hearts, when the basest interest shelters itself impudently under the sacred name of the public welfare, the general will becomes dumb; all, under the guidance of secret motives, no more express their opinions as citizens than if the State had never existed; and, under the name of laws, they deceitfully pass unjust decrees which have only private interest as their end.

Does it follow from this that the general will is destroyed or
corrupted? No; it is always constant, unalterable, and pure; but
it is subordinated to others which get the better of it. Each, de-
taching his own interest from the common interest, sees clearly
that he cannot completely separate it; but his share in the injury
done to the State appears to him as nothing in comparison with the
exclusive advantage which he aims at appropriating to himself.
This particular advantage being excepted, he desires the general
welfare for his own interests quite as strongly as any other. Even
in selling his vote for money, he does not extinguish in himself
the general will, but eludes it. The fault that he commits is to
change the state of the question, and to answer something different
from what he was asked; so that, instead of saying by a vote: "It
is beneficial to the State," he says: "It is beneficial to a certain man
or a certain party that such or such a motion should pass." Thus the
law of public order in assemblies is not so much to maintain in
them the general will as to ensure that it shall always be consulted
and always respond.

I might in this place make many reflections on the simple right
of voting in every act of sovereignty—a right which nothing can
take away from the citizens—and on that of speaking, proposing,
dividing, and discussing, which the government is always very careful to leave to its members only; but this important matter would
require a separate treatise, and I cannot say everything in this one.

VOTING

We see from the previous chapter that the manner in which
public affairs are managed may give a sufficiently trustworthy indication of the character and health of the body politic. The more
that harmony reigns in the assemblies, that is, the more the voting
approaches unanimity, the more also is the general will predominant; but long discussions, dissensions, and uproar proclaim the
ascendency of private interests and the decline of the State.

This is not so clearly apparent when two or more orders enter
into its constitution, as, in Rome, the patricians and plebeians,
whose quarrels often disturbed the *comitia,* even in the palmiest
days of the Republic; but this exception is more apparent than
real, for, at that time, by a vice inherent in the body politic, there
were, so to speak, two States in one; what is not true of the two

together is true of each separately. And, indeed, even in the most stormy times, the *plebiscita* of the people, when the Senate did not interfere with them, always passed peaceably and by a large majority of votes; the citizens having but one interest, the people had but one will.

At the other extremity of the circle unanimity returns; that is, when the citizens, fallen into slavery, have no longer either liberty or will. Then fear and flattery change votes into acclamations; men no longer deliberate, but adore or curse. Such was the disgraceful mode of speaking in the Senate under the Emperors. Sometimes it was done with ridiculous precautions. Tacitus observes that under Otho the senators, in overwhelming Vitellius with execrations, affected to make at the same time a frightful noise, in order that, if he happened to become master, he might not know what each of them had said.

From these different considerations are deduced the principles by which we should regulate the method of counting votes and of comparing opinions, according as the general will is more or less easy to ascertain and the State more or less degenerate.

There is but one law which by its nature requires unanimous consent, that is, the social compact; for civil association is the most voluntary act in the world; every man being born free and master of himself, no one can, under any pretext whatever, enslave him without his assent. To decide that the son of a slave is born a slave is to decide that he is not born a man.

If, then, at the time of the social compact, there are opponents of it, their opposition does not invalidate the contract, but only prevents them from being included in it; they are foreigners among citizens. When the State is established, consent lies in residence; to dwell in the territory is to submit to the sovereignty.

Excepting this original contract, the vote of the majority always binds all the rest, this being a result of the contract itself. But it will be asked how a man can be free and yet forced to conform to wills which are not his own. How are opponents free and yet subject to laws they have not consented to?

I reply that the question is wrongly put. The citizen consents to all the laws, even to those which are passed in spite of him, and even to those which punish him when he dares to violate any of them. The unvarying will of all the members of the State is the general will; it is through that that they are citizens and free.

When a law is proposed in the assembly of the people, what is asked of them is not exactly whether they approve the proposition or reject it, but whether it is conformable or not to the general will, which is their own; each one in giving his vote expresses his opinion thereupon; and from the counting of the votes is obtained the declaration of the general will. When, therefore, the opinion opposed to my own prevails, that simply shows that I was mistaken, and that what I considered to be the general will was not so. Had my private opinion prevailed, I should have done something other than I wished; and in that case I should not have been free.

This supposes, it is true, that all the marks of the general will are still in the majority; when they cease to be so, whatever side we take, there is no longer any liberty.

In showing before how particular wills were substituted for general wills in public resolutions, I have sufficiently indicated the means practicable for preventing this abuse; I will speak of it again hereafter. With regard to the proportional number of votes for declaring this will, I have also laid down the principles according to which it may be determined. The difference of a single vote destroys unanimity; but between unanimity and equality there are many unequal divisions, at each of which this number can be fixed according to the condition and requirements of the body politic.

Two general principles may serve to regulate these proportions: the one, that the more important and weighty the resolutions, the nearer should the opinion which prevails approach unanimity; the other, that the greater the despatch requisite in the matter under discussion, the more should we restrict the prescribed difference in the division of opinions; in resolutions which must be come to immediately the majority of a single vote should suffice. The first of these principles appears more suitable to laws, the second to affairs. Be that as it may, it is by their combination that are established the best proportions which can be assigned for the decision of a majority.

Adam Smith

═══════ 11 ═══════

The Wealth of Nations

The apostle of liberalism in economics, as Locke was in political theory, Adam Smith (1723–1790) was a Scottish professor of philosophy and one of the greatest economists of the modern era. Eccentric in personality and unprepossessing in appearance, Smith led an outwardly uneventful life. His intellectual point of departure was his discovery of an orderly and beneficent system operating behind the cruel, haphazard society of eighteenth-century Britain. Smith attacked the restrictive practices of mercantilism and wished to free the economy to operate in accordance with the laws of nature. His arguments served as the basis for nineteenth-century laissez-faire theories; however, proponents of those theories carried Smith's ideas to an extreme of which he would not have approved. Smith's major work, *An Inquiry into the Nature and Causes of the Wealth of Nations* (1776), became the bible of free enterprise and the competitive system. It was the first great work in political economy; it was also an encyclopedic survey of the economic life of Great Britain in the eighteenth century, a treatise on how to run a colonial empire, and an assault (with revolutionary import) on the mercantilistic system. In *The Wealth of Nations,* Smith expounded his belief in a natural economic order that was responsible for progress and continuously increasing productivity. The natural laws governing the market were those of individual, enlightened self-interest and competition, which, if allowed to operate freely, would be harmonized by an "invisible hand" for the ultimate good of society. He opposed any artificial controls or restrictions on the free working of the market. Smith was not an apologist for any one system or class, but industrial capitalists and their supporters later used his arguments to keep industry free from any form of government regulation. The selection given here brings out

Adam Smith, *An Inquiry into the Nature and Causes of the Wealth of Nations,* ed. J. E. T. Rogers (Oxford: Clarendon Press, 1869), I, 128, 134–36; II, 23–24, 28–30, 63, 68–69, 71–72, 115–17, 195–98, 244–48, 258–59, 272–73.

clearly Smith's economic individualism and his optimistic faith in the beneficence of free enterprise.

The property which every man has in his own labour, as it is the original foundation of all other property, so it is the most sacred and inviolable. The patrimony of a poor man lies in the strength and dexterity of his hands; and to hinder him from employing this strength and dexterity in what manner he thinks proper without injury to his neighbour, is a plain violation of this most sacred property. It is a manifest encroachment upon the just liberty both of the workman, and of those who might be disposed to employ him. As it hinders the one from working at what he thinks proper, so it hinders the others from employing whom they think proper. To judge whether he is fit to be employed, may surely be trusted to the discretion of the employers whose interest it so much concerns. The affected anxiety of the law-giver lest they should employ an improper person, is evidently as impertinent as it is oppressive.

. . .

The superiority which the industry of the towns has every-where in Europe over that of the country, is not altogether owing to corporations and corporation laws. It is supported by many other regulations. The high duties upon foreign manufactures and upon all goods imported by alien merchants, all tend to the same purpose. Corporation laws enable the inhabitants of towns to raise their prices, without fearing to be under-sold by the free competition of their own countrymen. Those other regulations secure them equally against that of foreigners. The enhancement of price occasioned by both is every-where finally paid by the landlords, farmers, and labourers of the country, who have seldom opposed the establishment of such monopolies. They have commonly neither inclination nor fitness to enter into combinations; and the clamour and sophistry of merchants and manufacturers easily persuade them that the private interest of a part, and of a subordinate part of the society, is the general interest of the whole.

People of the same trade seldom meet together, even for merriment and diversion, but the conversation ends in a conspiracy against the public, or in some contrivance to raise prices. It is impossible indeed to prevent such meetings, by any law which either could be executed, or would be consistent with liberty and justice. But though the law cannot hinder people of the same trade from sometimes assembling together, it ought to do nothing to facilitate such assemblies; much less to render them necessary.

. . .

The two principles being established, however, that wealth consisted in gold and silver, and that those metals could be brought into a country which had no mines only by the balance of trade, or by exporting to a greater value than it imported; it necessarily became the great object of political economy to diminish as much as possible the importation of foreign goods for home consumption, and to increase as much as possible the exportation of the produce of domestic industry. Its two great engines for enriching the country, therefore, were restraints upon importation, and encouragements to exportation.

The restraints upon importation were of two kinds.

First, Restraints upon the importation of such foreign goods for home consumption as could be produced at home, from whatever country they were imported.

Secondly, Restraints upon the importation of goods of almost all kinds from those particular countries with which the balance of trade was supposed to be disadvantageous.

Those different restraints consisted sometimes in high duties, and sometimes in absolute prohibitions.

Exportation was encouraged sometimes by drawbacks, sometimes by bounties, sometimes by advantageous treaties of commerce with foreign states, and sometimes by the establishment of colonies in distant countries.

Drawbacks were given upon two different occasions. When the home-manufactures were subject to any duty or excise, either the whole or a part of it was frequently drawn back upon their exportation; and when foreign goods liable to a duty were imported in order to be exported again, either the whole or a part of this duty was sometimes given back upon such exportation.

Bounties were given for the encouragement either of some beginning manufactures, or of such sorts of industry of other kinds as were supposed to deserve particular favour.

By advantageous treaties of commerce, particular privileges were procured in some foreign state for the goods and merchants of the country, beyond what were granted to those of other countries.

By the establishment of colonies in distant countries, not only particular privileges, but a monopoly was frequently procured for the goods and merchants of the country which established them.

The two sorts of restraints upon importation above-mentioned, together with these four encouragements to exportation, constitute the six principal means by which the commercial system proposes to increase the quantity of gold and silver in any country by turning the balance of trade in its favour.

. . .

What is the species of domestic industry which his capital can employ, and of which the produce is likely to be of the greatest value, every individual, it is evident, can, in his local situation, judge much better than any statesman or lawgiver can do for him. The statesman, who should attempt to direct private people in what manner they ought to employ their capitals, would not only load himself with a most unnecessary attention, but assume an authority which could safely be trusted, not only to no single person, but to no council or senate whatever, and which would nowhere be so dangerous as in the hands of a man who had folly and presumption enough to fancy himself fit to exercise it.

To give the monopoly of the home-market to the produce of domestic industry, in any particular art or manufacture, is in some measure to direct private people in what manner they ought to employ their capitals, and must, in almost all cases, be either a useless or a hurtful regulation. If the produce of domestic can be brought there as cheap as that of foreign industry, the regulation is evidently useless. If it cannot, it must generally be hurtful. It is the maxim of every prudent master of a family, never to attempt to make at home what it will cost him more to make than to buy. The taylor does not attempt to make his own shoes, but buys them of the shoemaker. The shoemaker does not attempt to make his own clothes, but employs a taylor. The farmer attempts to make neither the one nor the other, but employs those different artificers. All of them find it for their interest to employ their whole industry in a way in which they have some advantage over their neighbours, and to purchase with a part of its produce, or what is the same thing, with the price of a part of it, whatever else they have occasion for.

What is prudence in the conduct of every private family, can scarce be folly in that of a great kingdom. If a foreign country can supply us with a commodity cheaper than we ourselves can make it, better buy it of them with some part of the produce of our own industry, employed in a way in which we have some advantage. The general industry of the country, being always in proportion to the capital which employs it, will not thereby be diminished, no more than that of the above-mentioned artificers; but only left to find out the way in which it can be employed with the greatest advantage. It is certainly not employed to the greatest advantage, when it is thus directed towards an object which it can buy cheaper than it can make. The value of its annual produce is certainly more or less diminished, when it is thus turned away from producing commodities evidently of more value than the commodity which it is directed to produce. According to the supposition, that commodity could be purchased from foreign countries cheaper than it can be made at home. It could, therefore, have been purchased with a part only of the commodities, or, what is the same thing, with a part only of the price of the commodities, which the industry employed by an equal capital would have produced at home, had it been left to follow its natural course. The industry of the country, therefore, is thus turned away from a more, to a less advantageous employment, and the exchangeable value of its annual produce, instead of being increased, according to the intention of the lawgiver, must necessarily be diminished by every such regulation.

By means of such regulations, indeed, a particular manufacture may sometimes be acquired sooner than it could have been otherwise, and after a certain time may be made at home as cheap or cheaper than in the foreign country. But though the industry of the society may be thus carried with advantage into a particular channel sooner than it could have been otherwise, it will by no means follow that the sum total, either of its industry, or of its revenue, can ever be augmented by any such regulation. The industry of the society can augment only in proportion as its capital augments, and its capital can augment only in proportion to what can be gradually saved out of its revenue. But the immediate effect of every such regulation is to diminish its revenue, and what diminishes its revenue is certainly not very likely to augment its capital faster than it would have augmented of its own accord, had both capital and industry been left to find out their natural employments.

Though for want of such regulations the society should never acquire the proposed manufacture, it would not, upon that account, necessarily be the poorer in any one period of its duration. In every period of its duration its whole capital and industry might still have been employed, though upon different objects, in the manner that was most advantageous at the time. In every period its revenue might have been the greatest which its capital could afford, and both capital and revenue might have been augmented with the greatest possible rapidity.

Nothing, however, can be more absurd than this whole doctrine of the balance of trade, upon which, not only these restraints, but almost all the other regulations of commerce are founded. When two places trade with one another, this doctrine supposes that, if the balance be even, neither of them either loses or gains; but if it leans in any degree to one side, that one of them loses, and the other gains in proportion to its declension from the exact equilibrium. Both suppositions are false. A trade which is forced by means of bounties and monopolies, may be, and commonly is disadvantageous to the country in whose favour it is meant to be established, as I shall endeavour to shew hereafter. But that trade which, without force or constraint, is naturally and regularly carried on between any two places, is always advantageous, though not always equally so, to both.

By advantage or gain, I understand, not the increase of the quantity of gold and silver, but that of the exchangeable value of the annual produce of the land and labour of the country, or the increase of the annual revenue of its inhabitants.

The Portuguese, it is said, indeed, are better customers for our manufactures than the French, and should therefore be encouraged in preference to them. As they give us their custom, it is pretended, we should give them ours. The sneaking arts of underling tradesmen are thus erected into political maxims for the conduct of a great empire; for it is the most underling tradesmen only who make it a rule to employ chiefly their own customers. A great trader purchases his goods always where they are cheapest and best, without regard to any little interest of this kind.

By such maxims as these, however, nations have been taught that their interest consisted in beggaring all their neighbours. Each nation has been made to look with an invidious eye upon the prosperity of all the nations with which it trades, and to consider their gain as its own loss. Commerce, which ought naturally to be, among nations, as among individuals, a bond of union and friendship, has become the most fertile source of discord and animosity. The capricious ambition of kings and ministers has not, during the present and the preceding century, been more fatal to the repose of Europe, than the impertinent jealousy of merchants and manufacturers. The violence and injustice of the rulers of mankind is an ancient evil, for which, I am afraid, the nature of human affairs can scarce admit of a remedy. But the mean rapacity, the monopolizing spirit of merchants and manufacturers, who neither are, nor ought to be, the rulers of mankind, though it cannot perhaps be corrected, may very easily be prevented from disturbing the tranquillity of any body but themselves.

That it was the spirit of monopoly which originally both invented and propagated this doctrine, cannot be doubted; and they who first taught it were by no means such fools as they who believed it. In every country it always is and must be the interest of the great body of the people to buy whatever they want of those who sell it cheapest. The proposition is so very manifest, that it seems ridiculous to take any pains to prove it; nor could it ever have been called in question, had not the interested sophistry of merchants and manufacturers confounded the common sense of mankind. Their interest is, in this respect, directly opposite to that of the great body of the people. As it is the interest of the freemen of a corporation to hinder the rest of the inhabitants from employing any workmen but themselves, so it is the interest of the merchants and manufacturers of every country to secure to themselves the monopoly of the home market. Hence in Great Britain, and in most other European countries, the extraordinary duties upon almost all goods imported by alien marchants. Hence

the high duties and prohibitions upon all those foreign manufactures which can come into competition with our own. Hence
too the extraordinary restraints upon the importation of almost
all sorts of goods from those countries with which the balance of
trade is supposed to be disadvantageous; that is, from those against
whom national animosity happens to be most violently inflamed.

The wealth of a neighbouring nation, however, though dangerous in war and politics, is certainly advantageous in trade. In a
state of hostility it may enable our enemies to maintain fleets and
armies superior to our own; but in a state of peace and commerce
it must likewise enable them to exchange with us to a greater value,
and to afford a better market, either for the immediate produce
of our own industry, or for whatever is purchased with that produce. As a rich man is likely to be a better customer to the in-
dustrious people in his neighbourhood, than a poor, so is likewise
a rich nation. A rich man, indeed, who is himself a manufacturer,
is a very dangerous neighbour to all those who deal in the same
way. All the rest of the neighbourhood, however, by far the greatest number, profit by the good market which his expence affords
them. They even profit by his underselling the poorer workmen
who deal in the same way with him. The manufacturers of a rich
nation, in the same manner, may no doubt be very dangerous rivals
to those of their neighbours. This very competition, however, is
advantageous to the great body of the people, who profit greatly
besides by the good market which the great expence of such a
nation affords them in every other way.

．　．　．

There is no commercial country in Europe of which the approaching ruin has not frequently been foretold by the pretended
doctors of this system, from an unfavourable balance of trade.
After all the anxiety, however, which they have excited about this,
after all the vain attempts of almost all trading nations to turn that
balance in their own favour and against their neighbours, it does
not appear that any one nation in Europe has been in any respect
impoverished by this cause. Every town and country, on the contrary, in proportion as they have opened their ports to all nations,
instead of being ruined by this free trade, as the principles of the
commercial system would lead us to expect, have been enriched
by it. Though there are in Europe, indeed, a few towns which in

some respects deserve the name of free ports, there is no country which does so. Holland, perhaps, approaches the nearest to this character of any, though still very remote from it; and Holland, it is acknowledged, not only derives its whole wealth, but a great part of its necessary subsistence, from foreign trade.

. . .

Were all nations to follow the liberal system of free exportation and free importation, the different states into which a great continent was divided would so far resemble the different provinces of a great empire. As among the different provinces of a great empire the freedom of the inland trade appears, both from reason and experience, not only the best palliative of a dearth, but the most effectual preventative of a famine; so would the freedom of the exportation and importation trade be among the different states into which a great continent was divided. The larger the continent, the easier the communication through all the different parts of it, both by land and by water, the less would any one particular part of it ever be exposed to either of these calamities, the scarcity of any one country being more likely to be relieved by the plenty of some other. But very few countries have entirely adopted this liberal system. The freedom of the corn trade is almost every where more or less restrained, and, in many countries, is confined by such absurd regulations, as frequently aggravate the unavoidable misfortune of a dearth, into the dreadful calamity of a famine. The demand of such countries for corn may frequently become so great and so urgent, that a small state in their neighbourhood, which happened at the same time to be labouring under some degree of dearth, could not venture to supply them without exposing itself to the like dreadful calamity. The very bad policy of one country may thus render it in some measure dangerous and imprudent to establish what would otherwise be the best policy in another. The unlimited freedom of exportation, however, would be much less dangerous in great states, in which the growth being much greater, the supply could seldom be much affected by any quantity of corn that was likely to be exported. In a Swiss canton, or in some of the little states of Italy, it may, perhaps, sometimes be necessary to restrain the exportation of corn. In such great countries as France or England it scarce ever can. To hinder, besides, the farmer from sending his goods at all times to the best market, is evidently to sacrifice the ordinary laws of justice to an idea of public utility, to a sort of reasons of state; an act of legislative authority which ought to be exercised only, which can be pardoned only in cases of the most urgent necessity. The price at which the exportation of corn is prohibited, if it is ever to be prohibited, ought always to be a very high price.

The laws concerning corn may every where be compared to the laws concerning religion. The people feel themselves so much interested in what relates either to their subsistence in this life, or to their happiness in a life to come, that government must yield to their prejudices, and, in order to preserve the public tranquillity, establish that system which they approve of. It is upon this account, perhaps, that we so seldom find a reasonable system established with regard to either of those two capital objects.

.   .   .

It is thus that the single advantage which the monopoly procures to a single order of men, is in many different ways hurtful to the general interest of the country.

To found a great empire for the sole purpose of raising up a people of customers, may at first sight appear a project fit only for a nation of shopkeepers. It is, however, a project altogether unfit for a nation of shopkeepers; but extremely fit for a nation whose government is influenced by shopkeepers. Such statesmen, and such statesmen only, are capable of fancying that they will find some advantage in employing the blood and treasure of their fellow-citizens, to found and maintain such an empire. Say to a shopkeeper, Buy me a good estate, and I shall always buy my clothes at your shop, even though I should pay somewhat dearer than what I can have them for at other shops; and you will not find him very forward to embrace your proposal. But should any other person buy you such an estate, the shopkeeper would be much obliged to your benefactor if he would enjoin you to buy all your clothes at his shop. England purchased for some of her subjects, who found themselves uneasy at home, a great estate in a distant country. The price, indeed, was very small, and instead of thirty years purchase, the ordinary price of land in the present times, it amounted to little more than the expence of the different equipments which made the first discovery, reconnoitred the coast, and took a fictitious possession of the country. The land was good and of great extent, and the cultivators having plenty of good ground to work upon, and being for some time at liberty to sell their produce where they pleased, became in the course of little more than thirty or forty years (between 1620 and 1660) so numerous and thriving a people, that the shopkeepers and other traders of England wished to secure to themselves the monopoly of their custom. Without pretending, therefore, that they had paid any part, either of the original purchase-money, or of the subsequent expense of improvement, they petitioned the parliament that the cultivators of America might for the future be confined to their shop; first, for buying all the goods which they wanted from Europe; and, secondly, for selling all such parts of their own produce as those traders might find it convenient to buy. For they did not find it convenient to buy every part of it. Some parts of it imported into England might have interfered with some of the trades which they themselves carried on at home. Those particular parts of it therefore, they were willing that the colonists should sell where they could; the farther off the better; and upon that account proposed that their market should be confined to the countries south of Cape Finisterre. A clause in the famous act of navigation established this truly shopkeeper proposal into a law.

The maintenance of this monopoly has hitherto been the principal, or more properly perhaps the sole end and purpose of the dominion which Great Britain assumes over her colonies. In the exclusive trade, it is supposed, consists the great advantage of provinces, which have never yet afforded either revenue or military force for the support of the civil government, or the defence of the mother country. The monopoly is the principal badge of their dependency, and it is the sole fruit which has hitherto been gathered from that dependency. Whatever expence Great Britain has hitherto laid out in maintaining this dependency, has really been laid out in order to support this monopoly.

⋯

This whole expence is, in reality, a bounty which has been given in order to support a monopoly. The pretended purpose of it was to encourage the manufactures, and to increase the commerce of Great Britain. But its real effect has been to raise the rate of mercantile profit, and to enable our merchants to turn into a branch of trade, of which the returns are more slow and distant

than those of the greater part of other trades, a greater proportion of their capital than they otherwise would have done; two
events which if a bounty could have prevented, it might perhaps
have been very well worth while to give such a bounty.

Under the present system of management, therefore, Great Britain derives nothing but loss from the dominion which she assumes
over her colonies.

. . .

It is unnecessary, I imagine, to observe, how contrary such regulations are to the boasted liberty of the subject, of which we affect
to be so very jealous; but which, in this case, is so plainly sacrificed
to the futile interests of our merchants and manufacturers.

The laudable motive of all these regulations, is to extend our
own manufactures, not by their own improvement, but by the
depression of those of all our neighbours, and by putting an end,
as much as possible, to the troublesome competition of such odious
and disagreeable rivals. Our master manufacturers think it reasonable, that they themselves should have the monopoly of the
ingenuity of all their countrymen. Though by restraining, in some
trades, the number of apprentices which can be employed at one
time, and by imposing the necessity of a long apprenticeship in all
trades, they endeavour, all of them, to confine the knowledge of
their respective employments to as small a number as possible;
they are unwilling, however, that any part of this small number
should go abroad to instruct foreigners.

Consumption is the sole end and purpose of all production; and
the interest of the producer ought to be attended to, only so far as
it may be necessary for promoting that of the consumer. The
maxim is so perfectly self-evident, that it would be absurd to attempt to prove it. But in the mercantile system, the interest of the
consumer is almost constantly sacrificed to that of the producer;
and it seems to consider production, and not consumption, as the
ultimate end and object of all industry and commerce.

In the restraints upon the importation of all foreign commodities which can come into competition with those of our own
growth, or manufacture, the interest of the home-consumer is evidently sacrificed to that of the producer. It is altogether for the
benefit of the latter, that the former is obliged to pay that enhancement of price which this monopoly almost always occasions.

It is altogether for the benefit of the producer that bounties are granted upon the exportation of some of his productions. The home-consumer is obliged to pay, first, the tax which is necessary for paying the bounty, and secondly, the still greater tax which necessarily arises from the enhancement of the price of the commodity in the home market.

. . .

It cannot be very difficult to determine who have been the contrivers of this whole mercantile system; not the consumers, we may believe, whose interest has been entirely neglected; but the producers, whose interest has been so carefully attended to; and among this latter class our merchants and manufacturers have been by far the principal architects. In the mercantile regulations, which have been taken notice of in this chapter, the interest of our manufacturers has been most peculiarly attended to; and the interest, not so much of the consumers, as that of some other sets of producers, has been sacrificed to it.

. . .

M. Colbert, the famous minister of Louis XIV, was a man of probity, of great industry and knowledge of detail; of great experience and acuteness in the examination of public accounts, and of abilities, in short, every way fitted for introducing method and good order into the collection and expenditure of the public revenue. That minister had unfortunately embraced all the prejudices of the mercantile system, in its nature and essence a system of restraint and regulation, and such as could scarce fail to be agreeable to a laborious and plodding man of business, who had been accustomed to regulate the different departments of public offices, and to establish the necessary checks and controls for confining each to its proper sphere. The industry and commerce of a great country he endeavoured to regulate upon the same model as the departments of a public office; and instead of allowing every man to pursue his own interest his own way, upon the liberal plan of equality, liberty and justice, he bestowed upon certain branches of industry extraordinary privileges, while he laid others under as extraordinary restraints. He was not only disposed, like other European ministers, to encourage more the industry of the towns than that of the country; but, in order to support the industry of the towns, he was willing even to depress and keep down that of the country. In order to render provisions cheap to the inhabitants of the towns, and thereby to encourage manufactures and foreign commerce, he prohibited altogether the exportation of corn, and thus excluded the inhabitants of the country from every foreign market for by far the most important part of the produce of their industry. This prohibition, joined to the restraints imposed by the ancient provincial laws of France upon the transportation of corn from one province to another, and to the arbitrary and degrading taxes which are levied upon the cultivators in almost all the provinces, discouraged and kept down the agriculture of that country very much below the state to which it would naturally have risen in so very fertile a soil and so very happy a climate. This state of discouragement and depression was felt more or less in every different part of the country, and many different inquiries were set on foot concerning the causes of it. One of those causes appeared to be the preference given, by the institutions of M. Colbert, to the industry of the towns above that of the country.

. . .

Some speculative physicians seem to have imagined that the health of the human body could be preserved only by a certain precise regimen of diet and exercise, of which every, the smallest, violation necessarily occasioned some degree of disease or disorder proportioned to the degree of the violation. Experience, however, would seem to show, that the human body frequently preserves, to all appearance at least, the most perfect state of health under a vast variety of different regimens; even under some which are generally believed to be very far from being perfectly wholesome. But the healthful state of the human body, it would seem, contains in itself some unknown principle of preservation, capable either of preventing or of correcting, in many respects, the bad effects even of a very faulty regimen. Mr. Quesnai, who was himself a physician, and a very speculative physician, seems to have entertained a notion of the same kind concerning the political body, and to have imagined that it would thrive and prosper only under a certain precise regimen, the exact regimen of perfect liberty and perfect justice. He seems not to have considered that in the political body, the natural effort which every man is continually making to better his own condition, is a principle of preservation capable of preventing and correcting, in many respects, the bad effects of a political economy, in some degree both partial and oppressive. Such a political economy, though it no doubt retards more or less, is not always capable of stopping altogether the natural progress of a nation towards wealth and prosperity, and still less of making it go backwards. If a nation could not prosper without the enjoyment of perfect liberty and perfect justice, there is not in the world a nation which could ever have prospered. In the political body, however, the wisdom of nature has fortunately made ample provision for remedying many of the bad effects of the folly and injustice of man; in the same manner as it has done in the natural body, for remedying those of his sloth and intemperance.

• • •

It is thus that every system which endeavours, either, by extraordinary encouragements, to draw towards a particular species of industry a greater share of the capital of the society than what would naturally go to it; or, by extraordinary restraints, to force from a particular species of industry some share of the capital which would otherwise be employed in it; is in reality subversive of the great purpose which it means to promote. It retards, instead of accelerating, the progress of the society towards real wealth and greatness; and diminishes, instead of increasing, the real value of the annual produce of its land and labour.

All systems either of preference or of restraint, therefore, being thus completely taken away, the obvious and simple system of natural liberty establishes itself of its own accord. Every man, as long as he does not violate the laws of justice, is left perfectly free to pursue his own interest his own way, and to bring both his industry and capital into competition with those of any other man, or order of men. The sovereign is completely discharged from a duty, in the attempting to perform which he must always be exposed to innumerable delusions, and for the proper performance of which no human wisdom or knowledge could ever be sufficient; the duty of superintending the industry of private people, and of directing it towards the employments most suitable to the interest of the society. According to the system of natural liberty, the sovereign has only three duties to attend to; three duties of great importance, indeed, but plain and intelligible to common understandings: first, the duty of protecting the society from the violence and invasion of other independent societies; secondly, the duty of protecting, as far as possible, every member of the society from the injustice or oppression of every other member of it, or the duty of establishing an exact administration of justice; and, thirdly, the duty of erecting and maintaining certain public works and certain public institutions, which it can never be for the interest of any individual, or small number of individuals, to erect and maintain; because the profit could never repay the expence to any individual or small number of individuals, though it may frequently do much more than repay it to a great society.

Antoine Nicolas de Condorcet

━━━━━ 12 ━━━━━

The Progress of the Human Mind

Condemned as an enemy of the French Republic in 1793, and living as a fugitive from the Reign of Terror, Antoine Nicolas de Condorcet (1743–1794) was moved to put into writing the ideas for which he had lived and was prepared to die. Thus, out of the bloodstained chaos of the French Revolution came a "passionate affirmation of the rationalist faith," the *Sketch for a Historical Picture of the Progress of the Human Mind*. It was Condorcet's last testament to humanity; soon after it was completed, he was arrested and the next day was found dead in his cell, presumably a suicide by poison. In 1795, the work was published by the more moderate regime that succeeded the Terror, becoming, in effect, its declaration of revolutionary faith.

The *Sketch* was Condorcet's only work of note, but it was a distillation of all the ideas of this aristocratic intellectual and reformer. He was a religious skeptic and an outspoken adversary of the Church. He fought the influence of the hereditary nobility, despite his own noble birth. Condorcet's mind and efforts were devoted to scientific enlightenment and to social and political reform. He won fame as a mathematician, served as secretary of the Academy of Sciences, and became a leading member of the circle of philosopher-reformers around Voltaire. With the outbreak of the Revolution Condorcet plunged into political activity. As a moderate, he fell afoul of the radicals, but not before he had effectively championed his proposals, chiefly in the field of education.

The *Sketch* was just that, an outline of a larger work that Condorcet never lived to complete. It remains, however, the best and most moving expression of the Enlightenment gospel of progress. Suffused with a grand, historical optimism, it enshrines the idea of progress as a moral absolute.

Antoine Nicolas de Condorcet, *Sketch for a Historical Picture of the Progress of the Human Mind,* trans. June Barraclough (London: Weidenfeld, New York: Noonday Press, 1955), 4–5, 9–10, 127–28, 136–37, 139–41, 162–64, 173–76, 179–95, 199–202. Reprinted by permission of George Weidenfeld & Nicolson Ltd.

It sees the free exercise of man's irrepressible spirit of inquiry as liberating men everywhere from ignorance, poverty, and tyranny. Condorcet wrote in the belief that he stood on the threshold of the tenth and final stage of human history, the climax of man's progress, when reason and science would secure the natural rights of man in a world of peace, prosperity, and equality. Though this grandiose prophecy is far from fulfillment, Condorcet accurately foresaw many significant trends of modern social reform.

INTRODUCTION

Such is the aim of the work that I have undertaken, and its result will be to show by appeal to reason and fact that nature has set no term to the perfection of human faculties; that the perfectibility of man is truly indefinite; and that the progress of this perfectibility, from now onwards independent of any power that might wish to halt it, has no other limit than the duration of the globe upon which nature has cast us. This progress will doubtless vary in speed, but it will never be reversed as long as the earth occupies its present place in the system of the universe, and as long as the general laws of this system produce neither a general cataclysm nor such changes as will deprive the human race of its present faculties and its present resources.

The history of man from the time when alphabetical writing was known in Greece to the condition of the human race at the present day in the most enlightened countries of Europe is linked by an uninterrupted chain of facts and observations; and so at this point the picture of the march and progress of the human mind becomes truly historical. Philosophy has nothing more to guess, no more hypothetical surmises to make; it is enough to assemble and order the facts and to show the useful truths that can be derived from their connections and from their totality.

When we have shown all this, there will remain one last picture for us to sketch: that of our hopes, and of the progress reserved for future generations, which the constancy of the laws of nature seems to assure them. It will be necessary to indicate by what stages what must appear to us today a fantastic hope ought in time to become possible, and even likely; to show why, in spite of the transitory successes of prejudice and the support that it receives from the corruption of governments or peoples, truth alone will obtain a lasting victory; we shall demonstrate how nature has joined together indissolubly the progress of knowledge and that of liberty, virtue and respect for the natural rights of man; and how these, the only real goods that we possess, though so often separated that they have even been held to be incompatible, must on the contrary become inseparable from the moment when enlightenment has attained a certain level in a number of nations, and has penetrated throughout the whole mass of a great people whose language is universally known and whose commercial relations embrace the whole area of the globe. Once such a close accord had been established between all enlightened men, from then onwards all will be the friends of humanity, all will work together for its perfection and its happiness.

. . .

THE NINTH STAGE

This sketch of the progress of philosophy and of the dissemination of enlightenment, whose more general and more evident effects we have already examined, brings us up to the stage when the influence of progress upon public opinion, of public opinion upon nations or their leaders, suddenly ceases to be a slow, imperceptible affair, and produces a revolution in the whole order of several nations, a certain earnest of the revolution that must one day include in its scope the whole of the human race.

After long periods of error, after being led astray by vague or incomplete theories, publicists have at last discovered the true rights of man and how they can all be deduced from the single truth, that *man is a sentient being, capable of reasoning and of acquiring moral ideas.*

They have seen that the maintenance of these rights was the sole object of men's coming together in political societies, and that the social art is the art of guaranteeing the preservation of these rights and their distribution in the most equal fashion over the largest area. It was felt that in every society the means of assuring the rights of the individual should be submitted to certain common rules, but that the authority to choose these means and to determine these rules could belong only to the majority of the members of the society itself; for in making this choice the individual cannot follow his own reason without subjecting others to it, and the will of the majority is the only mark of truth that can be accepted by all without loss of equality.

.   .   .

Up till now we have shown the progress of philosophy only in the men who have cultivated, deepened and perfected it. It remains for us to show what have been its effects on public opinion; how reason, while it learnt to safeguard itself against the errors into which the imagination and respect for authority had so often led it, at last found a sure method of discovering and recognizing truth; and how at the same time it destroyed the prejudices of the masses which had for so long afflicted and corrupted the human race.

At last man could proclaim aloud his right, which for so long had been ignored, to submit all opinions to his own reason and to use in the search for truth the only instrument for its recognition that he has been given. Every man learnt with a sort of pride that nature had not for ever condemned him to base his beliefs on the opinions of others; the superstitions of antiquity and the abasement of reason before the transports of supernatural religion disappeared from society as from philosophy.

Soon there was formed in Europe a class of men who were concerned less with the discovery or development of the truth than with its propagation, men who whilst devoting themselves to the tracking down of prejudices in the hiding places where the priests, the schools, the governments and all long-established institutions had gathered and protected them, made it their life-work to destroy popular errors rather than to drive back the frontiers of human knowledge—an indirect way of aiding its progress which was not less fraught with peril, nor less useful.

In England Collins and Bolingbroke, in France Bayle, Fontenelle, Voltaire, Montesquieu and the schools founded by these famous men, fought on the side of truth, using in turn all the weapons with which learning, philosophy, wit and literary talent can furnish reason; using every mood from humour to pathos, every

literary form from the vast erudite encylopædia to the novel or
the broadsheet of the day; covering truth with a veil that spared
weaker eyes and excited one to guess what lay beyond it; skilfully
flattering prejudices so as to attack them the better; seldom threatening them, and then always either only one in its entirety or
several partially; sometimes conciliating the enemies of reason by
seeming to wish only for a half-tolerance in religious matters, only
for a half-freedom in politics; sparing despotism when tilting
against the absurdities of religion, and religion when abusing
tyranny; yet always attacking the principles of these two scourges
even when they seemed to be against only their more revolting or
ridiculous abuses, and laying their axes to the very roots of these
sinister trees when they appeared to be lopping off a few stray
branches; sometimes teaching the friends of liberty that superstition is the invincible shield behind which despotism shelters and
should therefore be the first victim to be sacrificed, the first chain to
be broken, and sometimes denouncing it to the despots as the real
enemy of their power, and frightening them with stories of its
secret machinations and its bloody persecutions; never ceasing to
demand the independence of reason and the freedom of the press
as the right and the salvation of mankind; protesting with inde-
fatigable energy against all the crimes of fanaticism and tyranny;
pursuing, in all matters of religion, administration, morals and
law, anything that bore the marks of tyranny, harshness or barbarism; invoking the name of nature to bid kings, captains, magistrates and priests to show respect for human life; laying to their
charge, with vehemence and severity, the blood their policy or their
indifference still spilled on the battlefield or on the scaffold; and
finally, taking for their battle cry—*reason, tolerance, humanity.*

· · ·

   The salutary influence of the new truths with which genius had
enriched philosophy, politics and public economy, and which had
been adopted more or less generally by enlightened men, was felt
far afield.
   The art of printing had spread so widely and had so greatly
increased the number of books published; the books that were
published catered so successfully for every degree of knowledge, or
industry, or income; they were so proportioned to every taste, or

cast of mind; they presented such easy and often such pleasant means of instruction; they opened so many doors to truth that it was no longer possible that they should all of them be closed again, that there was no class and no profession from which the truth could be withheld. And so, though there remained a great number of people condemned to ignorance either voluntary or enforced, the boundary between the cultivated and the uncultivated had been almost entirely effaced, leaving an insensible gradation between the two extremes of genius and stupidity.

Thus, an understanding of the natural rights of man, the belief that these rights are inalienable and indefeasible, a strongly expressed desire for liberty of thought and letters, of trade and industry, and for the alleviation of the people's suffering, for the proscription of all penal laws against religious dissenters and the abolition of torture and barbarous punishments, the desire for a milder system of criminal legislation and jurisprudence which should give complete security to the innocent, and for a simpler civil code, more in conformance with reason and nature, indifference in all matters of religion which now were relegated to the status of superstitions and political impostures, a hatred of hypocrisy and fanaticism, a contempt for prejudice, zeal for the propagation of enlightenment: all these principles, gradually filtering down from philosophical works to every class of society whose education went beyond the catechism and the alphabet, became the common faith, the badges of all those who were neither Machiavellians nor fools. In some countries these principles formed a public opinion sufficiently widespread for even the mass of the people to show a willingness to be guided by it and to obey it. For a feeling of humanity, a tender and active compassion for all the misfortunes that afflict the human race and a horror of anything that in the actions of public institutions, or governments, or individuals, adds new pains to those that are natural and inevitable, were the natural consequences of those principles; and this feeling exhaled from all the writings and all the speeches of the time, and already its happy influence had been felt in the laws and the public institutions, even of those nations still subject to despotism.

.   .   .

Such, in a word, has been the general progress of the sciences.

.   .   .

If we were to confine ourselves to showing the benefits that we have derived from the sciences in their immediate uses or in their applications to the arts, either for the well-being of individuals or for the prosperity of nations, we should display only a very small portion of their blessings.

The most important of these, perhaps, is to have destroyed prejudices and to have redirected the human intelligence, which had been obliged to follow the false directions imposed on it by the absurd beliefs that were implanted in each generation in infancy with the terrors of superstition and the fear of tyranny.

All errors in politics and morals are based on philosophical errors and these in turn are connected with scientific errors. There is not a religious system nor a supernatural extravagance that is not founded on ignorance of the laws of nature. The inventors, the defenders of these absurdities could not foresee the successive perfection of the human mind. Convinced that men in their day knew everything that they could ever know and would always believe what they then believed, they confidently supported their idle dreams on the current opinions of their country and their age.

Advances in the physical sciences are all the more fatal to these errors in that they often destroy them without appearing to attack them [, and that they can shower on those who defend them so obstinately the humiliating taunt of ignorance—*Translator*].

At the same time the habit of correct reasoning about the objects of these sciences, the precise ideas gained by their methods, and the means of recognizing or proving the truth of a belief should naturally lead us to compare the sentiment that forces us to accept well founded opinions credible for good reasons, with that which ties us to habitual prejudices or forces us to submit to authority. Such a comparison is enough to teach us to mistrust opinions of the latter kind, to convince us that we do not really believe them even when we boast of believing them, even when we profess them with the purest sincerity. This secret, once discovered, makes their destruction immediate and certain.

Finally this progress of the physical sciences which neither the passions nor self-interest can disturb, in which neither birth, nor profession, nor position are thought to confer on one the right to judge what one is not in a condition to understand, this inexorable progress cannot be contemplated by men of enlightenment without their wishing to make the other sciences follow the same path.

It offers them at every step a model to emulate and one by which they may judge of their own efforts, recognize the false roads on which they may have set out and preserve themselves equally from pyrrhonism, from credulity, from extreme diffidence, and from a too great submission even to the authority of learning and fame.

Admittedly, metaphysical analysis led to the same results but it gave only abstract principles, while now these same abstract principles, put into practice, are illuminated by example and fortified by success.

Up to this stage, the sciences had been the birthright of very few; they were now becoming common property and the time was at hand when their elements, their principles, and their simpler methods would become truly popular. For it was then, at last, that their application to the arts and their influence on men's judgment would become of truly universal utility.

. . .

THE TENTH STAGE

The future progress of the human mind

If man can, with almost complete assurance, predict phenomena when he knows their laws, and if, even when he does not, he can still, with great expectation of success, forecast the future on the basis of his experience of the past, why, then, should it be regarded as a fantastic undertaking to sketch, with some pretence to truth, the future destiny of man on the basis of his history? The sole foundation for belief in the natural sciences is this idea, that the general laws directing the phenomena of the universe, known or unknown, are necessary and constant. Why should this principle be any less true for the development of the intellectual and moral faculties of man than for the other operations of nature? Since beliefs founded on past experience of like conditions provide the only rule of conduct for the wisest of men, why should the philosopher be forbidden to base his conjectures on these same foundations, so long as he does not attribute to them a certainty superior to that warranted by the number, the constancy, and the accuracy of his observations?

Our hopes for the future condition of the human race can be

subsumed under three important heads: the abolition of inequality between nations, the progress of equality within each nation, and the true perfection of mankind. Will all nations one day attain that state of civilization which the most enlightened, the freest and the least burdened by prejudices, such as the French and the Anglo-Americans, have attained already? Will the vast gulf that separates these peoples from the slavery of nations under the rule of monarchs, from the barbarism of African tribes, from the ignorance of savages, little by little disappear?

Is there on the face of the earth a nation whose inhabitants have been debarred by nature herself from the enjoyment of freedom and the exercise of reason?

Are those differences which have hitherto been seen in every civilized country in respect of the enlightenment, the resources, and the wealth enjoyed by the different classes into which it is divided, is that inequality between men which was aggravated or perhaps produced by the earliest progress of society, are these part of civilization itself, or are they due to the present imperfections of the social art? Will they necessarily decrease and ultimately make way for a real equality, the final end of the social art, in which even the effects of the natural differences between men will be mitigated and the only kind of inequality to persist will be that which is in the interests of all and which favours the progress of civilization, of education, and of industry, without entailing either poverty, humiliation, or dependence? In other words, will men approach a condition in which everyone will have the knowledge necessary to conduct himself in the ordinary affairs of life, according to the light of his own reason, to preserve his mind free from prejudice, to understand his rights and to exercise them in accordance with his conscience and his creed; in which everyone will become able, through the development of his faculties, to find the means of providing for his needs; and in which at last misery and folly will be the exception, and no longer the habitual lot of a section of society?

Is the human race to better itself, either by discoveries in the sciences and the arts, and so in the means to individual welfare and general prosperity; or by progress in the principles of conduct or practical morality; or by a true perfection of the intellectual, moral, or physical faculties of man, an improvement which may result from a perfection either of the instruments used to heighten the intensity of these faculties and to direct their use or of the natural constitution of man?

In answering these three questions we shall find in the experience of the past, in the observation of the progress that the sciences and civilization have already made, in the analysis of the progress of the human mind and of the development of its faculties, the strongest reasons for believing that nature has set no limit to the realization of our hopes.

If we glance at the state of the world today we see first of all that in Europe the principles of the French constitution are already those of all enlightened men. We see them too widely propagated, too seriously professed, for priests and despots to prevent their gradual penetration even into the hovels of their slaves; there they will soon awaken in these slaves the remnants of their common sense and inspire them with that smouldering indignation which not even constant humiliation and fear can smother in the soul of the oppressed.

As we move from nation to nation, we can see in each what special obstacles impede this revolution and what attitudes of mind favour it. We can distinguish the nations where we may expect it to be introduced gently by the perhaps belated wisdom of their governments, and those nations where its violence intensified by their resistance must involve all alike in a swift and terrible convulsion.

Can we doubt that either common sense or the senseless discords of European nations will add to the effects of the slow but inexorable progress of their colonies, and will soon bring about the independence of the New World? And then will not the European population in these colonies, spreading rapidly over that enormous land, either civilize or peacefully remove the savage nations who still inhabit vast tracts of its land?

Survey the history of our settlements and commercial undertakings in Africa or in Asia, and you will see how our trade monopolies, our treachery, our murderous contempt for men of another colour or creed, the insolence of our usurpations, the intrigues or the exaggerated proselytic zeal of our priests, have destroyed the respect and good will that the superiority of our knowledge and the benefits of our commerce at first won for us in the eyes of the inhabitants. But doubtless the moment approaches when, no longer presenting ourselves as always either tyrants or corrupters, we shall become for them the beneficent instruments of their freedom.

. . .

The time will therefore come when the sun will shine only on free men who know no other master but their reason; when tyrants and slaves, priests and their stupid or hypocritical instruments will exist only in works of history and on the stage; and when we shall think of them only to pity their victims and their dupes; to maintain ourselves in a state of vigilance by thinking on their excesses; and to learn how to recognize and so to destroy, by force of reason, the first seeds of tyranny and superstition, should they ever dare to reappear amongst us.

In looking at the history of societies we shall have had occasion to observe that there is often a great difference between the rights that the law allows its citizens and the rights that they actually enjoy, and, again, between the equality established by political codes and that which in fact exists amongst individuals: and we shall have noticed that these differences were one of the principal causes of the destruction of freedom in the Ancient republics, of the storms that troubled them, and of the weakness that delivered them over to foreign tyrants.

These differences have three main causes: inequality in wealth; inequality in status between the man whose means of subsistence are hereditary and the man whose means are dependent on the length of his life, or, rather, on that part of his life in which he is capable of work; and, finally, inequality in education.

We therefore need to show that these three sorts of real inequality must constantly diminish without however disappearing altogether: for they are the result of natural and necessary causes which it would be foolish and dangerous to wish to eradicate; and one could not even attempt to bring about the entire disappearance of their effects without introducing even more fecund sources of inequality, without striking more direct and more fatal blows at the rights of man.

It is easy to prove that wealth has a natural tendency to equality, and that any excessive disproportion could not exist or at least would rapidly disappear if civil laws did not provide artificial ways of perpetuating and uniting fortunes; if free trade and in-

dustry were allowed to remove the advantages that accrued wealth
derives from any restrictive law or fiscal privilege; if taxes on
covenants, the restrictions placed on their free employment, their
subjection to tiresome formalities and the uncertainty and inevitable expense involved in implementing them did not hamper the
activity of the poor man and swallow up his meagre capital; if the
administration of the country did not afford some men ways of
making their fortune that were closed to other citizens; if prejudice and avarice, so common in old age, did not preside over the
making of marriages; and if, in a society enjoying simpler manners
and more sensible institutions, wealth ceased to be a means of
satisfying vanity and ambition, and if the equally misguided notions of austerity, which condemn spending money in the cultivation of the more delicate pleasures, no longer insisted on the hoard-
ing of all one's earnings.

.   .   .

We shall point out how [inequality] can be in great part eradi-
cated by guaranteeing people in old age a means of livelihood
produced partly by their own savings and partly by the savings
of others who make the same outlay, but who die before they
need to reap the reward; or, again, on the same principle of
compensation, by securing for widows and orphans an income
which is the same and costs the same for those families which suffer
an early loss and for those which suffer it later; or again by providing all children with the capital necessary for the full use of their
labour, available at the age when they start work and found a
family, a capital which increases at the expense of those whom premature death prevents from reaching this age. It is to the application of the calculus to the probabilities of life and the investment
of money that we owe the idea of these methods which have
already been successful, although they have not been applied in a
sufficiently comprehensive and exhaustive fashion to render them
really useful, not merely to a few individuals, but to society as a
whole, by making it possible to prevent those periodic disasters
which strike at so many families and which are such a recurrent
source of misery and suffering.

We shall point out that schemes of this nature, which can be
organized in the name of the social authority and become one of
its greatest benefits, can also be the work of private associations,

which will be formed without any real risk, once the principles for the proper working of these schemes have been widely diffused and the mistakes which have been the undoing of a large number of these associations no longer hold terrors for us.

. . .

The degree of equality in education that we can reasonably hope to attain, but that should be adequate, is that which excludes all dependence, either forced or voluntary. We shall show how this condition can be easily attained in the present state of human knowledge even by those who can study only for a small number of years in childhood, and then during the rest of their life in their few hours of leisure. We shall prove that, by a suitable choice of syllabus and of methods of education, we can teach the citizen everything that he needs to know in order to be able to manage his household, administer his affairs and employ his labour and his faculties in freedom; to know his rights and to be able to exercise them; to be acquainted with his duties and fulfill them satisfactorily; to judge his own and other men's actions according to his own lights and to be a stranger to none of the high and delicate feelings which honour human nature; not to be in a state of blind dependence upon those to whom he must entrust his affairs or the exercise of his rights; to be in a proper condition to choose and supervise them; to be no longer the dupe of those popular errors which torment man with superstitious fears and chimerical hopes; to defend himself against prejudice by the strength of his reason alone; and, finally, to escape the deceits of charlatans who would lay snares for his fortune, his health, his freedom of thought and his conscience under the pretext of granting him health, wealth and salvation.

From such time onwards the inhabitants of a single country will no longer be distinguished by their use of a crude or refined language; they will be able to govern themselves according to their own knowledge; they will no longer be limited to a mechanical knowledge of the procedures of the arts or of professional routine; they will no longer depend for every trivial piece of business, every insignificant matter of instruction on clever men who rule over them in virtue of their necessary superiority; and so they will attain a real equality, since differences in enlightenment or talent can no longer raise a barrier between men who understand

each other's feelings, ideas and language, some of whom may wish
to be taught by others but, to do so, will have no need to be controlled by them, or who may wish to confide the care of government to the ablest of their number but will not be compelled to
yield them absolute power in a spirit of blind confidence.

This kind of supervision has advantages even for those who do
not exercise it, since it is employed for them and not against them.
Natural differences of ability between men whose understanding
has not been cultivated give rise, even in savage tribes, to charlatans and dupes, to clever men and men readily deceived. These
same differences are truly universal, but now they are differences
only between men of learning and upright men who know the
value of learning without being dazzled by it; or between talent or
genius and the common sense which can appreciate and benefit
from them; so that even if these natural differences were greater,
and more extensive than they are, they would be only the more
influential in improving the relations between men and promoting
what is advantageous for their independence and happiness.

These various causes of equality do not act in isolation; they
unite, combine and support each other and so their cumulative
effects are stronger, surer and more constant. With greater equality
of education there will be greater equality in industry and so in
wealth; equality in wealth necessarily leads to equality in education: and equality between the nations and equality within a single
nation are mutually dependent.

So we might say that a well directed system of education rectifies
natural inequality in ability instead of strengthening it, just as
good laws remedy natural inequality in the means of subsistence,
and just as in societies where laws have brought about this same
equality, liberty, though subject to a regular constitution, will be
more widespread, more complete than in the total independence of
savage life. Then the social art will have fulfilled its aim, that of
assuring and extending to all men enjoyment of the common
rights to which they are called by nature.

The real advantages that should result from this progress, of
which we can entertain a hope that is almost a certainty, can have
no other term than that of the absolute perfection of the human
race; since, as the various kinds of equality come to work in its
favour by producing ampler sources of supply, more extensive education, more complete liberty, so equality will be more real and

will embrace everything which is really of importance for the happiness of human beings.

It is therefore only by examining the progress and the laws of this perfection that we shall be able to understand the extent or the limits of our hopes.

No-one has ever believed that the mind can gain knowledge of all the facts of nature or attain the ultimate means of precision in the measurement, or in the analysis of the facts of nature, the relations between objects and all the possible combinations of ideas. Even the relations between magnitudes, the mere notion of quantity or extension, taken in its fullest comprehension, gives rise to a system so vast that it will never be mastered by the human mind in its entirety, that there will always be a part of it, always indeed the larger part of it that will remain for ever unknown. People have believed that man can never know more than a part of the objects that the nature of his intelligence allows him to understand, and that he must in the end arrive at a point where the number and complexity of the objects that he already knows have absorbed all his strength so that any further progress must be completely impossible.

But since, as the number of known facts increases, the human mind learns how to classify them and to subsume them under more general facts, and, at the same time, the instruments and methods employed in their observation and their exact measurement acquire a new precision; since, as more relations between various objects become known, man is able to reduce them to more general relations, to express them more simply, and to present them in such a way that it is possible to grasp a greater number of them with the same degree of intellectual ability and the same amount of application; since, as the mind learns to understand more complicated combinations of ideas, simpler formulae soon reduce their complexity; so truths that were discovered only by great effort, that could at first only be understood by men capable of profound thought, are soon developed and proved by methods that are not beyond the reach of common intelligence. If the methods which have led to these new combinations of ideas are ever exhausted, if their application to hitherto unsolved questions should demand exertions greater than either the time or the capacity of the learned would permit, some method of a greater generality or simplicity will be found so that genius can continue undisturbed on its path. The strength and the limits of man's intelligence may remain unaltered; and yet the instruments that he uses will increase and improve, the language that fixes and determines his ideas will acquire greater breadth and precision and, unlike mechanics where an increase of force means a decrease of speed, the methods that lead genius to the discovery of truth increase at once the force and the speed of its operations.

Therefore, since these developments are themselves the necessary consequences of progress in detailed knowledge, and since the need for new methods in fact only arises in circumstances that give rise to new methods, it is evident that, within the body of the sciences of observation, calculation and experiment, the actual number of truths may always increase, and that every part of this body may develop, and yet man's faculties be of the same strength, activity and extent.

If we apply these general reflections to the various sciences, we can find in each of them examples of progressive improvement that will remove any doubts about what we may expect for the future. We shall point out in particular the progress that is both likely and imminent in those sciences which prejudice regards as all but exhausted. We shall give examples of the manner and extent of the precision and unity which could accrue to the whole system of human knowledge as the result of a more general and philosophical application of the sciences of calculation to the various branches of knowledge. We shall show how favourable to our hopes would be a more universal system of education by giving a greater number of people the elementary knowledge which could awaken their interest in a particular branch of study, and by providing conditions favourable to their progress in it; and how these hopes would be further raised, if more men possessed the means to devote themselves to these studies, for at present even in the most enlightened countries scarcely one in fifty of the people who have natural talents, receives the necessary education to develop them; and how, if this were done there would be a proportionate increase in the number of men destined by their discoveries to extend the boundaries of science.

We shall show how this equality in education and the equality which will come about between the different nations would accelerate the advance of these sciences whose progress depends on repeated observations over a large area; what benefits would thereby accrue to mineralogy, botany, zoology and meteorology; and what a vast disproportion holds in all these sciences between the poverty of existing methods which have nevertheless led to useful and important new truths, and the wealth of those methods which man would then be able to employ.

We shall show how even the sciences in which discovery is the fruit of solitary meditation would benefit from being studied by a greater number of people, in the matter of those improvements in detail which do not demand the intellectual energy of an inventor but suggest themselves to mere reflection.

If we turn now to the arts, whose theory depends on these same sciences, we shall find that their progress depending as it does on that of theory, can have no other limits; that the procedures of the different arts can be perfected and simplified in the same way as the methods of the sciences; new instruments, machines and looms can add to man's strength and can improve at once the quality and the accuracy of his productions, and can diminish the time and labour that has to be expended on them. The obstacles still in the way of this progress will disappear, accidents will be foreseen and prevented, the insanitary conditions that are due either to the work itself or to the climate will be eliminated.

A very small amount of ground will be able to produce a great quantity of supplies of greater utility or higher quality; more goods will be obtained for a smaller outlay; the manufacture of articles will be achieved with less wastage in raw materials and will make better use of them. Every type of soil will produce those things which satisfy the greatest number of needs; of several alternative ways of satisfying needs of the same order, that will be chosen which satisfies the greatest number of people and which requires least labour and least expenditure. So, without the need for sacrifice, methods of preservation and economy in expenditure will improve in the wake of progress in the arts of producing and preparing supplies and making articles from them.

So not only will the same amount of ground support more people, but everyone will have less work to do, will produce more, and satisfy his wants more fully.

With all this progress in industry and welfare which establishes a happier proportion between men's talents and their needs, each successive generation will have larger possessions, either as a result of this progress or through the preservation of the products of industry; and so, as a consequence of the physical constitution of the human race, the number of people will increase. Might there not then come a moment when these necessary laws begin to work in a contrary direction; when, the number of people in the world finally exceeding the means of subsistence, there will in consequence ensue a continual diminution of happiness and population, a true retrogression, or at best an oscillation between good and bad? In societies that have reached this stage will not this oscillation be a perennial source of more or less periodic disaster? Will it not show that a point has been attained beyond which all further improvement is impossible, that the perfectibility of the human race has after long years arrived at a term beyond which it may never go?

There is doubtless no-one who does not think that such a time is still very far from us; but will it ever arrive? It is impossible to pronounce about the likelihood of an event that will occur only when the human species will have necessarily acquired a degree of knowledge of which we can have no inkling. And who would take it upon himself to predict the condition to which the art of converting the elements to the use of man may in time be brought?

But even if we agree that the limit will one day arrive, nothing follows from it that is in the least alarming as far as either the happiness of the human race or its indefinite perfectibility is concerned; if we consider that, before all this comes to pass, the progress of reason will have kept pace with that of the sciences, and that the absurd prejudices of superstition will have ceased to corrupt and degrade the moral code by its harsh doctrines instead of purifying and elevating it, we can assume that by then men will know that, if they have a duty towards those who are not yet born, that duty is not to give them existence but to give them happiness; their aim should be to promote the general welfare of the human race or of the society in which they live or of the family to which they belong, rather than foolishly to encumber the world with useless and wretched beings. It is, then, possible that there should be a limit to the amount of food that can be produced, and, consequently, to the size of the population of the world, without this involving that untimely destruction of some of those creatures who have been given life, which is so contrary to nature and to social prosperity.

Since the discovery, or rather the exact analysis of the first principles of metaphysics, morals and politics is still recent and was preceded by the knowledge of a large number of detailed truths, the false notion that they have thereby attained their destination, has gained ready acceptance; men imagine that, because there are no more crude errors to refute, no more fundamental truths to establish, nothing remains to be done.

But it is easy to see how imperfect is the present analysis of man's moral and intellectual faculties; how much further the knowledge of his duties which presumes a knowledge of the influence of his actions upon the welfare of his fellow men and upon the society to which he belongs, can still be increased through a more profound, more accurate, more considered observation of that influence; how many questions have to be solved, how many social relations to be examined, before we can have precise knowledge of the individual rights of man and the rights that the state confers upon each in regard to all. Have we yet ascertained at all accurately the limits of the rights that exist between different societies in times of war, or that are enjoyed by society over its members in times of trouble and schism, or that belong to individuals, or spontaneous associations at the moment of their original, free formation or of their necessary disintegration?

If we pass on to the theory which ought to direct the application of particular principles and serve as the foundation for the social art, do we not see the necessity of acquiring a precision that these elementary truths cannot possess so long as they are absolutely general? Have we yet reached the point when we can reckon as the only foundation of law either justice or a proved and acknowledged utility instead of the vague, uncertain, arbitrary views of alleged political expediency? Are we yet in possession of any precise rules for selecting out of the almost infinite variety of possible systems in which the general principles of equality and natural rights are respected, those which will best secure the preservation of these rights, which will afford the freest scope for their exercise and their enjoyment, and which will moreover insure the leisure and welfare of individuals and the strength, prosperity and peace of nations?

The application of the calculus of combinations and probabilities to these sciences promises even greater improvement, since it is the only way of achieving results of an almost mathematical exactitude and of assessing the degree of their probability or likelihood. Sometimes, it is true, the evidence upon which these results are

based may lead us, without any calculation, at the first glance, to
some general truth and teach us whether the effect produced by
such-and-such a cause was or was not favourable, but if this evidence cannot be weighed and measured, and if these effects cannot
be subjected to precise measurement, then we cannot know exactly
how much good or evil they contain; or, again, if the good and
evil nearly balance each other, if the difference between them is
slight, we cannot pronounce with any certainty to which side the
balance really inclines. Without the application of the calculus it
would be almost impossible to choose with any certainty between
two combinations that have the same purpose and between which
there is no apparent difference in merit. Without the calculus these
sciences would always remain crude and limited for want of instruments delicate enough to catch the fleeting truth, of machines
precise enough to plumb the depths where so much that is of
value to science lies hidden.

However, such an application, notwithstanding the happy efforts
of certain geometers, is still in its earliest stages: and it will be left
to the generations to come to use this source of knowledge which
is as inexhaustible as the calculus itself, or as the number of combinations, relations and facts that may be included in its sphere of
operation.

. . .

Until men progress in the practice as well as in the science of
morality, it will be impossible for them to attain any insight into
either the nature and development of the moral sentiments, the
principles of morality, the natural motives that prompt their
actions, or their own true interests either as individuals or as members of society. Is not a mistaken sense of interest the most common cause of actions contrary to the general welfare? Is not the
violence of our passions often the result either of habits that we
have adopted through miscalculation, or of our ignorance how to
restrain them, tame them, deflect them, rule them?

Is not the habit of reflection upon conduct, of listening to the
deliverances of reason and conscience upon it, of exercising those
gentle feelings which identify our happiness with that of others,
the necessary consequence of a well-planned study of morality and
of a greater equality in the conditions of the social pact? Will not
the free man's sense of his own dignity and a system of education

built upon a deeper knowledge of our moral constitution, render common to almost every man those principles of strict and unsullied justice, those habits of an active and enlightened benevolence, of a fine and generous sensibility which nature has implanted in the hearts of all and whose flowering waits only upon the favourable influences of enlightenment and freedom? Just as the mathematical and physical sciences tend to improve the arts that we use to satisfy our simplest needs, is it not also part of the necessary order of nature that the moral and political sciences should exercise a similar influence upon the motives that direct our feelings and our actions?

What are we to expect from the perfection of laws and public institutions, consequent upon the progress of those sciences, but the reconciliation, the identification of the interests of each with the interests of all? Has the social art any other aim save that of destroying their apparent opposition? Will not a country's constitution and laws accord best with the rights of reason and nature when the path of virtue is no longer arduous and when the temptations that lead men from it are few and feeble?

Is there any vicious habit, any practice contrary to good faith, any crime, whose origin and first cause cannot be traced back to the legislation, the institutions, the prejudices of the country wherein this habit, this practice, this crime can be observed? In short will not the general welfare that results from the progress of the useful arts once they are grounded on solid theory, or from the progress of legislation once it is rooted in the truths of political science, incline mankind to humanity, benevolence and justice? In other words, do not all these observations which I propose to develop further in my book, show that the moral goodness of man, the necessary consequence of his constitution, is capable of indefinite perfection like all his other faculties, and that nature has linked together in an unbreakable chain truth, happiness and virtue?

Among the causes of the progress of the human mind that are of the utmost importance to the general happiness, we must number the complete annihilation of the prejudices that have brought about an inequality of rights between the sexes, an inequality fatal even to the party in whose favour it works. It is vain for us to look for a justification of this principle in any differences of physical organization, intellect or moral sensibility between men and women. This inequality has its origin solely in an abuse of strength, and all the later sophistical attempts that have been made to excuse it are vain.

We shall show how the abolition of customs authorized, laws dictated by this prejudice, would add to the happiness of family life, would encourage the practice of the domestic virtues on which all other virtues are based, how it would favour the progress of education, and how, above all, it would bring about its wider diffusion; for not only would education be extended to women as well as to men, but it can only really be taken proper advantage of when it has the support and encouragement of the the mothers of the family. Would not this belated tribute to equity and good sense, put an end to a principle only too fecund of injustice, cruelty and crime, by removing the dangerous conflict between the strongest and most irrepressible of all natural inclinations and man's duty or the interests of society? Would it not produce what has until now been no more than a dream, national manners of a mildness and purity, formed not by proud asceticism, not by hypocrisy, not by the fear of shame or religious terrors but by freely contracted habits that are inspired by nature and acknowledged by reason?

Once people are enlightened they will know that they have the right to dispose of their own life and wealth as they choose; they will gradually learn to regard war as the most dreadful of scourges, the most terrible of crimes. The first wars to disappear will be those into which usurpers have forced their subjects in defence of their pretended hereditary rights.

Nations will learn that they cannot conquer other nations without losing their own liberty; that permanent confederations are their only means of preserving their independence; and that they should seek not power but security. Gradually mercantile prejudices will fade away: and a false sense of commercial interest will lose the fearful power it once had of drenching the earth in blood and of ruining nations under pretext of enriching them. When at last the nations come to agree on the principles of politics and morality, when in their own better interests they invite foreigners to share equally in all the benefits men enjoy either through the bounty of nature or by their own industry, then all the causes that produce and perpetuate national animosities and poison national relations will disappear one by one; and nothing will remain to encourage or even to arouse the fury of war.

Organizations more intelligently conceived than those projects of eternal peace which have filled the leisure and consoled the hearts of certain philosophers, will hasten the progress of the brotherhood of nations, and wars between countries will rank with assassinations as freakish atrocities, humiliating and vile in the eyes of nature and staining with indelible opprobrium the country or the age whose annals record them.

.   .   .

All the causes that contribute to the perfection of the human race, all the means that ensure it must by their very nature exercise a perpetual influence and always increase their sphere of action. The proofs of this we have given and in the great work they will derive additional force from elaboration. We may conclude then that the perfectibility of man is indefinite. Meanwhile we have considered him as possessing the natural faculties and organization that he has at present. How much greater would be the certainty, how much vaster the scheme of our hopes if we could believe that these natural faculties themselves and this organization could also be improved? This is the last question that remains for us to ask ourselves.

Organic perfectibility or deterioration amongst the various strains in the vegetable and animal kingdom can be regarded as one of the general laws of nature. This law also applies to the human race. No-one can doubt that, as preventative medicine improves and food and housing become healthier, as a way of life is established that develops our physical powers by exercise without ruining them by excess, as the two most virulent causes of deterioration, misery and excessive wealth, are eliminated, the average length of human life will be increased and a better health and a stronger physical constitution will be ensured. The improvement of medical practice, which will become more efficacious with the progress of reason and of the social order, will mean the end of infectious and hereditary diseases and illnesses brought on by climate, food, or working conditions. It is reasonable to hope that all other diseases may likewise disappear as their distant causes are discovered. Would it be absurd then to suppose that this perfection of the human species might be capable of indefinite progress; that the day will come when death will be due only to extraordinary accidents or to the decay of the vital forces, and that ultimately the average span between birth and decay will have no assignable value? Certainly man will not become immortal, but will not the interval between the first breath that he draws and the time when in the natural course of events, without disease or accident, he expires, increase indefinitely?

. . .

Finally may we not extend such hopes to the intellectual and moral faculties? May not our parents, who transmit to us the benefits or disadvantages of their constitution, and from whom we receive our shape and features, as well as our tendencies to certain physical affections, hand on to us also that part of the physical organization which determines the intellect, the power of the brain, the ardour of the soul or the moral sensibility? Is it not probable that education, in perfecting these qualities, will at the same time influence, modify and perfect the organization itself? Analogy, investigation of the human faculties and the study of certain facts, all seem to give substance to such conjectures which would further push back the boundaries of our hopes.

These are the questions with which we shall conclude this final stage. How consoling for the philosopher who laments the errors, the crimes, the injustices which still pollute the earth and of which he is often the victim is this view of the human race, emancipated from its shackles, released from the empire of fate and from that of the enemies of its progress, advancing with a firm and sure step along the path of truth, virtue and happiness! It is the contemplation of this prospect that rewards him for all his efforts to assist the progress of reason and the defence of liberty. He dares to regard these strivings as part of the eternal chain of human destiny; and in this persuasion he is filled with the true delight of virtue and the pleasure of having done some lasting good which fate can never destroy by a sinister stroke of revenge, by calling back the reign of slavery and prejudice. Such contemplation is for him an asylum, in which the memory of his persecutors cannot pursue him; there he lives in thought with man restored to his natural rights and dignity, forgets man tormented and corrupted by greed, fear or envy; there he lives with his peers in an Elysium created by reason and graced by the purest pleasures known to the love of mankind.

Edmund Burke

13

Reflections on the Revolution in France

The liberal and democratic principles of the Enlightenment found explosive realization in the French Revolution, which in turn provoked a strong reaction against them. The most famous and most influential of these intellectual counterattacks was Edmund Burke's *Reflections on the Revolution in France* (1790). Burke (1729–1797) was a British politician and publicist who served in the House of Commons for many years and emerged as the spokesman of the landed aristocracy. In his view, the fixed social and political order of late eighteenth-century England, based on class distinctions, upper-class rule, and the Whig principles of 1688, was an excellent one, worthy of perpetuation. Burke saw the French Revolution, even as it got under way, as an attack on the whole social fabric. In the *Reflections,* written in the form of a letter to a resident of Paris, he warned that the Revolution's radical policies would lead ultimately to anarchy and military dictatorship. The essay was, however, more than a political pamphlet. It was a powerful, though unsystematic, critique of the rationalist theories of the Enlightenment and a statement of the basic principles of conservatism. Compounded of poetry, philosophy, religious mysticism, and socio-political analysis, the *Reflections* elaborated a theory of society as a complex organism evolving slowly in the fixed channels of historical tradition. Burke rejected what he considered the abstract vagaries of individual reason as the guide to social progress. He thought that man, individually and in the mass, was not basically rational, but a weak creature of irrational impulse who needed to be restrained by organized society. Property, religion, custom, and "prejudices" (or social myths) were the social controls necessary to preserve tolerable order. Burke, in short, was opposed to the rational optimism and the individualism of the Enlightenment. In time, his work became the bible of conservatism, an arsenal of arguments against social and democratic reform.

Edmund Burke, *Reflections on the Revolution in France,* in *The Works of Edmund Burke* (Boston: Little, Brown, 1881), III, 274–76, 295–99, 308–13, 344–48, 350–52, 358–59, 454–57, 559–60.

You will observe, that from Magna Charta to the Declaration of
Right, it has been the uniform policy of our Constitution to claim
and assert our liberties as an entailed inheritance derived to us
from our forefathers, and to be transmitted to our posterity,—as
an estate specially belonging to the people of this kingdom without
any reference whatever to any other more general or prior right.
By this means our Constitution preserves an unity in so great a
diversity of its parts. We have an inheritable crown, an inheritable
peerage, and a House of Commons and a people inheriting privileges, franchises, and liberties from a long line of ancestors.

This policy appears to me to be the result of profound reflection,—or rather the happy effect of following Nature, which is
wisdom without reflection, and above it. A spirit of innovation is
generally the result of a selfish temper and confined views. People
will not look forward to posterity, who never look backward to
their ancestors. Besides, the people of England well know that the
idea of inheritance furnishes a sure principle of conservation, and
a sure principle of transmission, without at all excluding a principle of improvement. It leaves acquisition free; but it secures
what it acquires. Whatever advantages are obtained by a state proceeding on these maxims are locked fast as in a sort of family set-
tlement, grasped as in a kind of mortmain forever. By a constitutional policy working after the pattern of Nature, we receive,
we hold, we transmit our government and our privileges, in the
same manner in which we enjoy and transmit our property and our
lives. The institutions of policy, the goods of fortune, the gifts of
Providence, are handed down to us, and from us, in the same
course and order. Our political system is placed in a just cor-
respondence and symmetry with the order of the world, and with
the mode of existence decreed to a permanent body composed of
transitory parts,—wherein, by the disposition of a stupendous
wisdom, moulding together the great mysterious incorporation of
the human race, the whole, at one time, is never old or middle-
aged or young, but, in a condition of unchangeable constancy,
moves on through the varied tenor of perpetual decay, fall, renova-
tion, and progression. Thus, by preserving the method of Nature
in the conduct of the state, in what we improve we are never wholly

new, in what we retain we are never wholly obsolete. By adhering in this manner and on those principles to our forefathers, we are guided, not by the superstition of antiquarians, but by the spirit of philosophic analogy. In this choice of inheritance we have given to our frame of polity the image of a relation in blood: binding up the Constitution of our country with our dearest domestic ties; adopting our fundamental laws into the bosom of our family affections; keeping inseparable, and cherishing with the warmth of all their combined and mutually reflected charities, our state, our hearths, our sepulchres, and our altars.

Through the same plan of a conformity to Nature in our artificial institutions, and by calling in the aid of her unerring and powerful instincts to fortify the fallible and feeble contrivances of our reason, we have derived several other, and those no small benefits, from considering our liberties in the light of an inheritance. Always acting as if in the presence of canonized forefathers, the spirit of freedom, leading in itself to misrule and excess, is tempered with an awful gravity. This idea of a liberal descent inspires us with a sense of habitual native dignity, which prevents that upstart insolence almost inevitably adhering to and disgracing those who are the first acquirers of any distinction. By this means our liberty becomes a noble freedom. It carries an imposing and majestic aspect. It has a pedigree and illustrating ancestors. It has its bearings and its ensigns armorial. It has its gallery of portraits, its monumental inscriptions, its records, evidences, and titles. We procure reverence to our civil institutions on the principle upon which Nature teaches us to revere individual men: on account of their age, and on account of those from whom they are descended. All your sophisters cannot produce anything better adapted to preserve a rational and manly freedom than the course that we have pursued, who have chosen our nature rather than our speculations, our breasts rather than our inventions, for the great conservatories and magazines of our rights and privileges.

. . .

Believe me, Sir, those who attempt to level never equalize. In all societies consisting of various descriptions of citizens, some description must be uppermost. The levellers, therefore, only change and pervert the natural order of things: they load the edifice of society by setting up in the air what the solidity of the structure requires to be on the ground. The associations of tailors and carpenters, of which the republic (of Paris, for instance) is composed, cannot be equal to the situation into which, by the worst of usurpations, and usurpation on the prerogatives of Nature, you attempt to force them.

The Chancellor of France, at the opening of the States, said, in a tone of oratorial flourish, that all occupations were honorable. If he meant only that no honest employment was disgraceful, he would not have gone beyond the truth. But in asserting that anything is honorable, we imply some distinction in its favor. The occupation of a hair-dresser, or of a working tallow-chandler, cannot be a matter of honor to any person,—to say nothing of a number of other more servile employments. Such descriptions of men ought not to suffer oppression from the state; but the state suffers oppression, if such as they, either individually or collectively, are permitted to rule. In this you think you are combating prejudice, but you are at war with Nature.

I do not, my dear Sir, conceive you to be of that sophistical, captious spirit, or of that uncandid dulness, as to require, for every general observation or sentiment, an explicit detail of the correctives and exceptions which reason will presume to be included in all the general propositions which come from reasonable men. You do not imagine that I wish to confine power, authority, and distinction to blood and names and titles. No, Sir. There is no qualification for government but virtue and wisdom, actual or presumptive. Wherever they are actually found, they have, in whatever state, condition, profession, or trade, the passport of Heaven to human place and honor. Woe to the country which would madly and impiously reject the service of the talents and virtues, civil, military, or religious, that are given to grace and to serve it; and would condemn to obscurity everything formed to diffuse lustre and glory around a state! Woe to that country, too, that, passing into the opposite extreme, considers a low education, a mean, contracted view of things, a sordid, mercenary occupation, as a preferable title to command! Everything ought to be open,— but not indifferently to every man. No rotation, no appointment by lot, no mode of election operating in the spirit of sortition or rotation, can be generally good in a government conversant in extensive objects; because they have no tendency, direct or indirect, to select the man with a view to the duty, or to accommodate the one to the other. I do not hesitate to say that the road to eminence and power, from obscure condition, ought not to be made too easy, nor a thing too much of course. If rare merit be the rarest of all rare things, it ought to pass through some sort of probation. The temple of honor ought to be seated on an eminence. If it be opened through virtue, let it be remembered, too, that virtue is never tried but by some difficulty and some struggle.

Nothing is a due and adequate representation of a state, that does not represent its ability, as well as its property. But as ability is a vigorous and active principle, and as property is sluggish, inert, and timid, it never can be safe from the invasions of ability, unless it be, out of all proportion, predominant in the representation. It must be represented, too, in great masses of accumulation, or it is not rightly protected. The characteristic essence of property, formed out of the combined principles of its acquisition and conservation, is to be *unequal*. The great masses, therefore, which excite envy, and tempt rapacity, must be put out of the possibility of danger. Then they form a natural rampart about the lesser properties in all their gradations. The same quantity of property which is by the natural course of things divided among many has not the same operation. Its defensive power is weakened as it is diffused. In this diffusion each man's portion is less than what, in the eagerness of his desires, he may flatter himself to obtain by dissipating the accumulations of others. The plunder of the few would, indeed, give but a share inconceivably small in the distribution to the many. But the many are not capable of making this calculation; and those who lead them to rapine never intend this distribution.

The power of perpetuating our property in our families is one of the most valuable and interesting circumstances belonging to it, and that which tends the most to the perpetuation of society itself. It makes our weakness subservient to our virtue; it grafts benevolence even upon avarice. The possessors of family wealth, and of the distinction which attends hereditary possession, (as most concerned in it,) are the natural securities for this transmission. With us the House of Peers is formed upon this principle. It is wholly composed of hereditary property and hereditary distinction, and made, therefore, the third of the legislature, and, in the last event, the sole judge of all property in all its subdivisions. The House of Commons, too, though not necessarily, yet in fact, is always so

composed, in the far greater part. Let those large proprietors be
what they will, (and they have their chance of being amongst the
best,) they are, at the very worst, the ballast in the vessel of the
commonwealth. For though hereditary wealth, and the rank which
goes with it, are too much idolized by creeping sycophants, and
the blind, abject admirers of power, they are too rashly slighted
in shallow speculations of the petulant, assuming, shortsighted
coxcombs of philosophy. Some decent, regulated preëminence,
some preference (not exclusive appropriation) given to birth, is
neither unnatural, nor unjust, nor impolitic.

It is said that twenty-four millions ought to prevail over two
hundred thousand. True; if the constitution of a kingdom be a
problem of arithmetic. This sort of discourse does well enough
with the lamp-post for its second: to men who *may* reason calmly
it is ridiculous. The will of the many, and their interest, must very
often differ; and great will be the difference when they make an
evil choice. A government of five hundred country attorneys and
obscure curates is not good for twenty-four millions of men, though
it were chosen by eight-and-forty millions; nor is it the better for
being guided by a dozen of persons of quality who have betrayed
their trust in order to obtain that power. At present, you seem in
everything to have strayed out of the high road of Nature.

. . .

Far am I from denying in theory, full as far is my heart from
withholding in practice, (if I were of power to give or to withhold,)
the *real* rights of men. In denying their false claims of right, I
do not mean to injure those which are real, and are such as their
pretended rights would totally destroy. If civil society be made for
the advantage of man, all the advantages for which it is made become his right. It is an institution of beneficence; and law itself is
only beneficence acting by a rule. Men have a right to live by
that rule; they have a right to justice, as between their fellows,
whether their fellows are in politic function or in ordinary occupation. They have a right to the fruits of their industry, and to the
means of making their industry fruitful. They have a right to the
acquisitions of their parents, to the nourishment and improvement
of their offspring, to instruction in life and to consolation in death.
Whatever each man can separately do, without trespassing upon
others, he has a right to do for himself; and he has a right to a

fair portion of all which society, with all its combinations of skill and force, can do in his favor. In this partnership all men have equal rights; but not to equal things. He that has but five shillings in the partnership has as good a right to it as he that has five hundred pounds has to his larger proportion; but he has not a right to an equal dividend in the product of the joint stock. And as to the share of power, authority, and direction which each individual ought to have in the management of the state, that I must deny to be amongst the direct original rights of man in civil society; for I have in my contemplation the civil social man, and no other. It is a thing to be settled by convention.

If civil society be the offspring of convention, that convention must be its law. That convention must limit and modify all the descriptions of constitution which are formed under it. Every sort of legislative, judicial, or executory power are its creatures. They can have no being in any other state of things; and how can any man claim, under the conventions of civil society, rights which do not so much as suppose its existence,—rights which are absolutely repugnant to it? One of the first motives to civil society, and which becomes one of its fundamental rules, is, *that no man should be judge in his own cause*. By this each person has at once divested himself of the first fundamental right of uncovenanted man, that is, to judge for himself, and to assert his own cause. He abdicates all right to be his own governor. He inclusively, in a great measure, abandons the right of self-defence, the first law of Nature. Men cannot enjoy the rights of an uncivil and of a civil state together. That he may obtain justice, he gives up his right of determining what it is in points the most essential to him. That he may secure some liberty, he makes a surrender in trust of the whole of it.

Government is not made in virtue of natural rights, which may and do exist in total independence of it,—and exist in much greater clearness, and in a much greater degree of abstract perfection: but their abstract perfection is their practical defect. By having a right to everything they want everything. Government is a contrivance of human wisdom to provide for human *wants*. Men have a right that these wants should be provided for by this wisdom. Among these wants is to be reckoned the want, out of civil society, of a sufficient restraint upon their passions. Society requires not only that the passions of individuals should be subjected, but that even in the mass and body, as well as in the individuals, the inclinations of men should frequently be thwarted, their will controlled, and their passions brought into subjection. This can only be done *by a power out of themselves,* and not, in the exercise of its function, subject to that will and to those passions which it is its office to bridle and subdue. In this sense the restraints on men, as well as their liberties, are to be reckoned among their rights. But as the liberties and the restrictions vary with times and circumstances, and admit of infinite modifications, they cannot be settled upon any abstract rule; and nothing is so foolish as to discuss them upon that principle.

The moment you abate anything from the full rights of men each to govern himself, and suffer any artificial, positive limitation upon those rights, from that moment the whole organization of government becomes a consideration of convenience. This it is which makes the constitution of a state, and the due distribution of its powers, a matter of the most delicate and complicated skill. It requires a deep knowledge of human nature and human necessities, and of the things which facilitate or obstruct the various ends which are to be pursued by the mechanism of civil institutions. The state is to have recruits to its strength and remedies to its distempers. What is the use of discussing a man's abstract right to food or medicine? The question is upon the method of procuring and administering them. In that deliberation I shall always advise to call in the aid of the farmer and the physician, rather than the professor of metaphysics.

The science of constructing a commonwealth, or renovating it, or reforming it, is, like every other experimental science, not to be taught *a priori.* Nor is it a short experience that can instruct us in that practical science; because the real effects of moral causes are not always immediate, but that which in the first instance is prejudicial may be excellent in its remoter operation, and its excellence may arise even from the ill effects it produces in the beginning. The reverse also happens; and very plausible schemes, with very pleasing commencements, have often shameful and lamentable conclusions. In states there are often some obscure and almost latent causes, things which appear at first view of little moment, on which a very great part of its prosperity or adversity may most essentially depend. The science of government being, therefore, so practical in itself, and intended for such practical purposes, a matter which requires experience, and even more experience than any person can gain in his whole life, however sagacious and observing he may be, it is with infinite caution that any man ought to venture upon pulling down an edifice which has answered in any tolerable degree for ages the common purposes of society, or on building it up again without having models and patterns of approved utility before his eyes.

These metaphysic rights entering into common life, like rays of light which pierce into a dense medium, are, by the laws of Nature, refracted from their straight line. Indeed, in the gross and complicated mass of human passions and concerns, the primitive rights of men undergo such a variety of refractions and reflections that it becomes absurd to talk of them as if they continued in the simplicity of their original direction. The nature of man is intricate; the objects of society are of the greatest possible complexity: and therefore no simple disposition or direction of power can be suitable either to man's nature or to the quality of his affairs. When I hear the simplicity of contrivance aimed at and boasted of in any new political constitutions, I am at no loss to decide that the artificers are grossly ignorant of their trade or totally negligent of their duty. The simple governments are fundamentally defective, to say no worse of them. If you were to contemplate society in but one point of view, all these simple modes of polity are infinitely captivating. In effect each would answer its single end much more perfectly than the more complex is able to attain all its complex purposes. But it is better that the whole should be imperfectly and anomalously answered than that while some parts are provided for with great exactness, others might be totally neglected, or perhaps materially injured, by the over-care of a favorite member.

The pretended rights of these theorists are all extremes; and in proportion as they are metaphysically true, they are morally and politically false. The rights of men are in a sort of *middle,* incapable of definition, but not impossible to be discerned. The rights of men in governments are their advantages; and these are often in balances between differences of good,—in compromises sometimes between good and evil, and sometimes between evil and evil. Political reason is a computing principle: adding, subtracting, multiplying, and dividing, morally, and not metaphysically or mathematically, true moral denominations.

By these theorists the right of the people is almost always sophistically confounded with their power. The body of the community, whenever it can come to act, can meet with no effectual resistance; but till power and right are the same, the whole body of them has no right inconsistent with virtue, and the first of all virtues, prudence. Men have no right to what is not reasonable, and to what is not for their benefit.

. . .

I almost venture to affirm that not one in a hundred amongst us participates in the "triumph" of the Revolution Society. If the king and queen of France and their children were to fall into our hands by the chance of war, in the most acrimonious of all hostilities, (I deprecate such an event, I deprecate such hostility,) they would be treated with another sort of triumphal entry into London. We formerly have had a king of France in that situation: you have read how he was treated by the victor in the field, and in what manner he was afterwards received in England. Four hundred years have gone over us; but I believe we are not materially changed since that period. Thanks to our sullen resistance to innovation, thanks to the cold sluggishness of our national character, we still bear the stamp of our forefathers. We have not (as I conceive) lost the generosity and dignity of thinking of the fourteenth century; nor as yet have we subtilized ourselves into savages. We are not the converts of Rousseau; we are not the disciples of Voltaire; Helvetius has made no progress amongst us. Atheists are not our preachers; madmen are not our lawgivers. We know that *we* have made no discoveries, and we think that no discoveries are to be made, in morality,—nor many in the great principles of government, nor in the ideas of liberty, which were understood long before we were born altogether as well as they will be after the grave has heaped its mould upon our presumption, and the silent tomb shall have imposed its law on our pert loquacity. In England we have not yet been completely embowelled of our natural entrails: we still feel within us, and we cherish and cultivate, those inbred sentiments which are the faithful guardians, the active monitors of our duty, the true supporters of all liberal and manly morals. We have not been drawn and trussed, in order that we may be filled, like stuffed birds in a museum, with chaff and rags, and paltry, blurred shreds of paper about the rights of man. We preserve the whole of our feelings still native and entire, unsophisticated by pedantry and infidelity. We have real hearts of flesh and blood beating in our bosoms. We fear God; we look up with awe to kings, with affection to Parliaments, with duty to magistrates, with reverence to priests, and with respect to nobility. Why? Because, when such ideas are brought before our minds, it is *natural* to be so affected; because all other feelings are false and spurious, and tend to corrupt our minds, to vitiate our primary morals, to render us unfit for rational liberty, and, by teaching us a servile, licentious, and abandoned insolence, to be our low sport for a few holidays, to make us perfectly fit for and justly deserving of slavery through the whole course of our lives.

You see, Sir, that in this enlightened age I am bold enough to confess that we are generally men of untaught feelings: that, instead of casting away all our old prejudices, we cherish them to a very considerable degree; and, to take more shame to ourselves, we cherish them because they are prejudices; and the longer they have lasted, and the more generally they have prevailed, the more we cherish them. We are afraid to put men to live and trade each on his own private stock of reason; because we suspect that the stock in each man is small, and that the individuals would do better to avail themselves of the general bank and capital of nations and of ages. Many of our men of speculation, instead of exploding general prejudices, employ their sagacity to discover the latent wisdom which prevails in them. If they find what they seek, (and they seldom fail,) they think it more wise to continue the prejudice, with the reason involved, than to cast away the coat of prejudice, and to leave nothing but the naked reason; because prejudice, with its reason, has a motive to give action to that reason, and an affection which will give it permanence. Prejudice is of ready application in the emergency; it previously engages the mind in a steady course of wisdom and virtue, and does not leave the man hesitating in the moment of decision, skeptical, puzzled, and unresolved. Prejudice renders a man's virtue his habit, and not a series of unconnected acts. Through just prejudice, his duty becomes a part of his nature.

Your literary men, and your politicians, and so do the whole clan of the enlightened among us, essentially differ in these points. They have no respect for the wisdom of others; but they pay it off by a very full measure of confidence in their own. With them

it is a sufficient motive to destroy an old scheme of things, because
it is an old one. As to the new, they are in no sort of fear with
regard to the duration of a building run up in haste; because duration is no object to those who think little or nothing has been
done before their time, and who place all their hopes in discovery.
They conceive, very systematically, that all things which give per-
petuity are mischievous, and therefore they are at inexpiable war
with all establishments. They think that government may vary like
modes of dress, and with as little ill effect; that there needs no
principle of attachment, except a sense of present conveniency, to
any constitution of the state. They always speak as if they were of
opinion that there is a singular species of compact between them
and their magistrates, which binds the magistrate, but which has
nothing reciprocal in it, but that the majesty of the people has a
right to dissolve it without any reason but its will. Their attachment to their country itself is only so far as it agrees with some of
their fleeting projects: it begins and ends with that scheme of
polity which falls in with their momentary opinion.

These doctrines, or rather sentiments, seem prevalent with your
new statesmen. But they are wholly different from those on which
we have always acted in this country.

·   ·   ·

We know, and, what is better, we feel inwardly, that religion is
the basis of civil society, and the source of all good, and of all comfort. In England we are so convinced of this, that there is no rust
of superstition, with which the accumulated absurdity of the human mind might have crusted it over in the course of ages, that
ninety-nine in a hundred of the people of England would not
prefer to impiety. We shall never be such fools as to call in an
enemy to the substance of any system to remove its corruptions, to
supply its defects, or to perfect its construction. If our religious
tenets should ever want a further elucidation, we shall not call on
Atheism to explain them. We shall not light up our temple from
that unhallowed fire. It will be illuminated with other lights. It
will be perfumed with other incense than the infectious stuff
which is imported by the smugglers of adulterated metaphysics.
If our ecclesiastical establishment should want a revision, it is not
avarice or rapacity, public or private, that we shall employ for the
audit or receipt or application of its consecrated revenue. Violently

condemning neither the Greek nor the Armenian, nor, since heats are subsided, the Roman system of religion, we prefer the Protestant: not because we think it has less of the Christian religion in it, but because, in our judgment, it has more. We are Protestants, not from indifference, but from zeal.

We know, and it is our pride to know, that man is by his constitution a religious animal; that atheism is against, not only our reason, but our instincts; and that it cannot prevail long. But if, in the moment of riot, and in a drunken delirium from the hot spirit drawn out of the alembic of hell, which in France is now so furiously boiling, we should uncover our nakedness, by throwing off that Christian religion which has hitherto been our boast and comfort, and one great source of civilization amongst us, and among many other nations, we are apprehensive (being well aware that the mind will not endure a void) that some uncouth, pernicious, and degrading superstition might take place of it.

For that reason, before we take from our establishment the natural, human means of estimation, and give it up to contempt, as you have done, and in doing it have incurred the penalties you well deserve to suffer, we desire that some other may be presented to us in the place of it. We shall then form our judgment.

On these ideas, instead of quarrelling with establishments, as some do, who have made a philosophy and a religion of their hostility to such institutions, we cleave closely to them. We are resolved to keep an established church, an established monarchy, an established aristocracy, and an established democracy, each in the degree it exists, and in no greater.

. . .

To avoid, therefore, the evils of inconstancy and versatility, ten thousand times worse than those of obstinacy and the blindest prejudice, we have consecrated the state, that no man should approach to look into its defects or corruptions but with due caution; that he should never dream of beginning its reformation by its subversion; that he should approach to the faults of the state as to the wounds of a father, with pious awe and trembling solicitude. By this wise prejudice we are taught to look with horror on those children of their country who are prompt rashly to hack that aged parent in pieces and put him into the kettle of magicians, in hopes that by their poisonous weeds and wild incantations they may regenerate the paternal constitution and renovate their father's life.

Society is, indeed, a contract. Subordinate contracts for objects of mere occasional interest may be dissolved at pleasure; but the state ought not to be considered as nothing better than a partnership agreement in a trade of pepper and coffee, calico or tobacco, or some other such low concern, to be taken up for a little temporary interest, and to be dissolved by the fancy of the parties. It is to be looked on with other reverence; because it is not a partnership in things subservient only to the gross animal existence of a temporary and perishable nature. It is a partnership in all science, a partnership in all art, a partnership in every virtue and in all perfection. As the ends of such a partnership cannot be obtained in many generations, it becomes a partnership not only between those who are living, but between those who are living, those who are dead, and those who are to be born. Each contract of each particular state is but a clause in the great primeval contract of eternal society, linking the lower with the higher natures, connecting the visible and invisible world, according to a fixed compact sanctioned by the inviolable oath which holds all physical and all moral natures each in their appointed place. This law is not subject to the will of those who, by an obligation above them, and infinitely superior, are bound to submit their will to that law.

．　．　．

It is this inability to wrestle with difficulty which has obliged the arbitrary Assembly of France to commence their schemes of reform with abolition and total destruction. But is it in destroying and pulling down that skill is displayed? Your mob can do this as well at least as your assemblies. The shallowest understanding, the rudest hand, is more than equal to that task. Rage and frenzy will pull down more in half an hour than prudence, deliberation, and foresight can build up in a hundred years. The errors and defects of old establishments are visible and palpable. It calls for little ability to point them out; and where absolute power is given, it requires but a word wholly to abolish the vice and the establishment together. The same lazy, but restless disposition, which loves sloth and hates quiet, directs these politicians, when they come to work for supplying the place of what they have destroyed. To make everything the reverse of what they have seen is quite as easy as to destroy. No difficulties occur in what has never been tried.

Criticism is almost baffled in discovering the defects of what has
not existed; and eager enthusiasm and cheating hope have all
the wide field of imagination, in which they may expatiate with
little or no opposition.

At once to preserve and to reform is quite another thing. When
the useful parts of an old establishment are kept, and what is super-
added is to be fitted to what is retained, a vigorous mind, steady,
persevering attention, various powers of comparison and combination, and the resources of an understanding fruitful in expedients
are to be exercised; they are to be exercised in a continued conflict
with the combined force of opposite vices, with the obstinacy that
rejects all improvement, and the levity that is fatigued and disgusted with everything of which it is in possession. But you may
object,—"A process of this kind is slow. It is not fit for an Assembly
which glories in performing in a few months the work of ages.
Such a mode of reforming, possibly, might take up many years."
Without question it might; and it ought. It is one of the excellences
of a method in which time is amongst the assistants, that its operation is slow, and in some cases almost imperceptible. If circumspection and caution are a part of wisdom, when we work only upon
inanimate matter, surely they become a part of duty too, when the
subject of our demolition and construction is not brick and timber,
but sentient beings, by the sudden alteration of whose state, condition, and habits, multitudes may be rendered miserable. But it
seems as if it were the prevalent opinion in Paris, that an unfeeling
heart and an undoubting confidence are the sole qualifications for
a perfect legislator. Far different are my ideas of that high office.
The true lawgiver ought to have a heart full of sensibility. He
ought to love and respect his kind, and to fear himself. It may be
allowed to his temperament to catch his ultimate object with an
intuitive glance; but his movements towards it ought to be deliberate. Political arrangement, as it is a work for social ends, is to
be only wrought by social means. There mind must conspire with
mind. Time is required to produce that union of minds which
alone can produce all the good we aim at. Our patience will
achieve more than our force. If I might venture to appeal to what
is so much out of fashion in Paris,—I mean to experience,—I should
tell you, that in my course I have known, and, according to my
measure, have coöperated with great men; and I have never yet
seen any plan which has not been mended by the observations of

those who were much inferior in understanding to the person who took the lead in the business. By a slow, but well-sustained progress, the effect of each step is watched; the good or ill success of the first gives light to us in the second; and so, from light to light, we are conducted with safety through the whole series. We see that the parts of the system do not clash. The evils latent in the most promising contrivances are provided for as they arise. One advantage is as little as possible sacrificed to another. We compensate, we reconcile, we balance. We are enabled to unite into a consistent whole the various anomalies and contending principles that are found in the minds and affairs of men. From hence arises, not an excellence in simplicity, but one far superior, an excellence in composition. Where the great interests of mankind are concerned through a long succession of generations, that succession ought to be admitted into some share in the councils which are so deeply to affect them. If justice requires this, the work itself requires the aid of more minds than one age can furnish. It is from this view of things that the best legislators have been often satisfied with the establishment of some sure, solid, and ruling principle in government,—a power like that which some of the philosophers have called a plastic Nature; and having fixed the principle, they have left it afterwards to its own operation.

.   .   .

The effects of the incapacity shown by the popular leaders in all the great members of the commonwealth are to be covered with the "all-atoning name" of Liberty. In some people I see great liberty, indeed; in many, if not in the most, an oppressive, degrading servitude. But what is liberty without wisdom and without virtue? It is the greatest of all possible evils; for it is folly, vice, and madness, without tuition or restraint. Those who know what virtuous liberty is cannot bear to see it disgraced by incapable heads, on account of their having high-sounding words in their mouths. Grand, swelling sentiments of liberty I am sure I do not despise. They warm the heart; they enlarge and liberalize our minds; they animate our courage in a time of conflict. Old as I am, I read the fine raptures of Lucan and Corneille with pleasure. Neither do I wholly condemn the little arts and devices of popularity. They facilitate the carrying of many points of moment; they keep the people together; they refresh the mind in its exertions; and they diffuse occasional gayety over the severe brow of moral freedom. Every politician ought to sacrifice to the Graces, and to join compliance with reason. But in such an undertaking as that in France all these subsidiary sentiments and artifices are of little avail. To make a government requires no great prudence. Settle the seat of power, teach obedience, and the work is done. To give freedom is still more easy. It is not necessary to guide; it only requires to let go the rein. But to form a *free government,* that is, to temper together these opposite elements of liberty and restraint in one consistent work, requires much thought, deep reflection, a sagacious, powerful, and combining mind. This I do not find in those who take the lead in the National Assembly. Perhaps they are not so miserably deficient as they appear. I rather believe it. It would put them below the common level of human understanding. But when the leaders choose to make themselves bidders at an auction of popularity, their talents, in the construction of the state, will be of no service. They will become flatterers instead of legislators,—the instruments, not the guides of the people. If any of them should happen to propose a scheme of liberty soberly limited, and defined with proper qualifications, he will be immediately outbid by his competitors, who will produce something more splendidly popular. Suspicions will be raised of his fidelity to his cause. Moderation will be stigmatized as the virtue of cowards, and compromise as the prudence of traitors,—until, in hopes of preserving the credit which may enable him to temper and moderate on some occasions, the popular leader is obliged to become active in propagating doctrines and establishing powers that will afterwards defeat any sober purpose at which he ultimately might have aimed.

Johann Wolfgang von Goethe

=== 14 ===

Faust

Johann Wolfgang von Goethe (1749–1832) was a universal genius whose
full and varied career reflected the romantic spirit of the nineteenth century. He was one of the greatest of German lyric poets. In his scientific
work, Goethe made important contributions to biology and advanced a
theory of evolution. As political adviser to the Duke of Saxe-Weimar from
1775 to the end of his life, Goethe proved a responsible and forward-look-
ing public servant. He also wrote novels and powerful dramas that influenced German and other European literature. In his varied activities and
his changing intellectual positions, Goethe epitomized the confused strains
of the transition from the neoclassicism of the eighteenth century to the
romanticism of the nineteenth. Indeed, he thought of himself as the
prophet of his time—the interpreter of the spiritual issues of his day; the
central idea of his life was the oneness of man and nature, the happy
unity of man and the world.

Goethe's masterpiece, *Faust,* was a reflection of the vicissitudes of his own
intellectual career as well as of the restless seeking, affirmations, and pro-
tests of his age. Part I, from which the following selection is taken, was
written between 1774 and 1808 (when it was published), while Goethe
was going through, successively, his sentimental "Storm and Stress" period,
his neoclassical phase, and his romantic phase. Part II was written during
the last twenty-five years of his life and was not published until the year
of his death.

There is still much dispute over the essential meaning of *Faust.* All
would agree that it is a great philosophical drama, whose theme is the
nature of man and his relation to the world. Goethe took the legend-
shrouded figure of the Renaissance scholar and man of magic and transformed him into a symbol of man's quest for truth—the universal rebel

From *Goethe's Faust,* translated by Louis MacNeice. Copyright 1951 by Louis
MacNeice. Reprinted by permission of Faber and Faber Ltd. and Oxford University Press, Inc. [Pp. 13–16, 19–22, 43–44, 54–65.]

seeking to achieve self-realization. Through experience of the most varied and intense kinds, made possible by a compact with the devil, Mephistopheles, Faust rejects the split between man and nature, between mind and soul, and between thought and action; thus he becomes one with all life. The drama involves the question of whether Faust's moral sense will be destroyed in the process. In the end he is saved, with his moral faculty intact: he finds ultimate satisfaction in serving God and his fellow man. Seen thus, Faust is the romantic hero incarnate and even, as some have said, the very symbol of the restless spirit of modern culture.

PROLOGUE IN HEAVEN

The Lord. The Heavenly Hosts. Mephistopheles following

(The Three Archangels step forward)

RAPHAEL

The chanting sun, as ever, rivals
The chanting of his brother spheres
And marches round his destined circuit—
A march that thunders in our ears.
His aspect cheers the Hosts of Heaven
Though what his essence none can say;
These inconceivable creations
Keep the high state of their first day.

GABRIEL

And swift, with inconceivable swiftness,
The earth's full splendour rolls around,
Celestial radiance alternating
With a dread night too deep to sound;
The sea against the rocks' deep bases
Comes foaming up in far-flung force,
And rock and sea go whirling onward
In the swift spheres' eternal course.

MICHAEL

And storms in rivalry are raging
From sea to land, from land to sea,
In frenzy forge the world a girdle
From which no inmost part is free.

The blight of lightning flaming yonder
Marks where the thunder-bolt will play;
And yet Thine envoys, Lord, revere
The gentle movement of Thy day.

CHOIR OF ANGELS

Thine aspect cheers the Hosts of Heaven
Though what Thine essence none can say,
And all Thy loftiest creations
Keep the high state of their first day.

(*Enter Mephistopheles*)

MEPHISTOPHELES

Since you, O Lord, once more approach and ask
If business down with us be light or heavy—
And in the past you've usually welcomed me—
That's why you see me also at your levee.
Excuse me, I can't manage lofty words—
Not though your whole court jeer and find me low;
My pathos certainly would make you laugh
Had you not left off laughing long ago.
Your suns and worlds mean nothing much to me;
How men torment themselves, that's all I see.
The little god of the world, one can't reshape, reshade him;
He is as strange to-day as that first day you made him.
His life would be not so bad, not quite,
Had you not granted him a gleam of Heaven's light;
He calls it Reason, uses it not the least
Except to be more beastly than any beast.
He seems to me—if your Honour does not mind—
Like a grasshopper—the long-legged kind—
That's always in flight and leaps as it flies along
And then in the grass strikes up its same old song.
I could only wish he confined himself to the grass!
He thrusts his nose into every filth, alas.

LORD

Mephistopheles, have you no other news?
Do you always come here to accuse?
Is nothing ever right in your eyes on earth?

MEPHISTOPHELES

No. Lord! I find things there as downright bad as ever.

I am sorry for men's days of dread and dearth;
Poor things, *my* wish to plague 'em isn't fervent.

LORD

Do you know Faust?

MEPHISTOPHELES

The Doctor?

LORD

Aye, my servant.

MEPHISTOPHELES

Indeed! He serves you oddly enough, I think.
The fool has no earthly habits in meat and drink.
The ferment in him drives him wide and far,
That he is mad he too has almost guessed;
He demands of heaven each fairest star
And of earth each highest joy and best,
And all that is new and all that is far
Can bring no calm to the deep-sea swell of his breast.

LORD

Now he may serve me only gropingly,
Soon I shall lead him into the light.
The gardener knows when the sapling first turns green
That flowers and fruit will make the future bright.

MEPHISTOPHELES

What do you wager? You will lose him yet,
Provided *you* give *me* permission
To steer him gently the course I set.

LORD

So long as he walks the earth alive,
So long you may try what enters your head;
Men make mistakes as long as they strive.

MEPHISTOPHELES

I thank you for that; as regards the dead,
The dead have never taken my fancy.
I favour cheeks that are full and rosy-red;
No corpse is welcome to my house;
I work as the cat does with the mouse.

LORD

Very well; you have my full permission.
Divert this soul from its primal source
And carry it, if you can seize it,

Down with you upon your course—
And stand ashamed when you must needs admit:
A good man with his groping intuitions
Still knows the path that is true and fit.

MEPHISTOPHELES

All right—but it won't last for long.
I'm not afraid my bet will turn out wrong.
And, if my aim prove true and strong,
Allow me to triumph wholeheartedly.
Dust shall be eat—and greedily—
Like my cousin the Snake renowned in tale and song.

LORD

That too you are free to give a trial;
I have never hated the likes of you.
Of all the spirits of denial
The joker is the last that I eschew.
Man finds relaxation too attractive—
Too fond too soon of unconditional rest;
Which is why I am pleased to give him a companion
Who lures and thrusts and must, as devil, be active.
But ye, true sons of Heaven, it is your duty
To take your joy in the living wealth of beauty.
The changing Essence which ever works and lives
Wall you around with love, serene, secure!
And that which floats in flickering appearance
Fix ye it firm in thoughts that must endure.

CHOIR OF ANGELS

Thine aspect cheers the Hosts of Heaven
Though what Thine essence none can say,
And all Thy loftiest creations
Keep the high state of their first day.

(*Heaven closes*)

MEPHISTOPHELES (*alone*)

I like to see the Old One now and then
And try to keep relations on the level.
It's really decent of so great a person
To talk so humanely even to the Devil.

NIGHT

*(In a high-vaulted narrow Gothic room Faust, restless,
in a chair at his desk)*

FAUST

Here stand I, ach, Philosophy
Behind me and Law and Medicine too
And, to my cost, Theology—
All these I have sweated through and through
And now you see me a poor fool
As wise as when I entered school!
They call me Master, they call me Doctor,
Ten years now I have dragged my college
Along by the nose through zig and zag
Through up and down and round and round
And this is all that I have found—
The impossibility of knowledge!
It is this that burns away my heart;
Of course I am cleverer than the quacks,
Than master and doctor, than clerk and priest,
I suffer no scruple or doubt in the least,
I have no qualms about devil or burning,
Which is just why all joy is torn from me,
I cannot presume to make use of my learning,
I cannot presume I could open my mind
To proselytize and improve mankind.

Besides, I have neither goods nor gold,
Neither reputation nor rank in the world;
No dog would choose to continue so!
Which is why I have given myself to Magic
To see if the Spirit may grant me to know
Through its force and its voice full many a secret,
May spare the sour sweat that I used to pour out
In talking of what I know nothing about,
May grant me to learn what it is that girds
The world together in its inmost being,
That the seeing its whole germination, the seeing
Its workings, may end my traffic in words.

O couldst thou, light of the full moon,
Look now thy last upon my pain,
Thou for whom I have sat belated
So many midnights here and waited
Till, over books and papers, thou
Didst shine, sad friend, upon my brow!
O could I but walk to and fro
On mountain heights in thy dear glow
Or float with spirits round mountain eyries
Or weave through fields thy glances glean
And freed from all miasmal theories
Bathe in thy dew and wash me clean!

Oh! Am I still stuck in this jail?
This God-damned dreary hole in the wall
Where even the lovely light of heaven
Breaks wanly through the painted panes!
Cooped up among these heaps of books
Gnawed by worms, coated with dust,
Round which to the top of the Gothic vault
A smoke-stained paper forms a crust.
Retorts and canisters lie pell-mell
And pyramids of instruments,
The junk of centuries, dense and mat—
Your world, man! World? They call it that!

And yet you ask why your poor heart
Cramped in your breast should feel such fear,
Why an unspecified misery
Should throw your life so out of gear?
Instead of the living natural world
For which God made all men his sons
You hold a reeking mouldering court
Among assorted skeletons.
Away! There is a world outside!
And this one book of mystic art
Which Nostradamus wrote himself,
Is this not adequate guard and guide?
By this you can tell the course of the stars,
By this, once Nature gives the word,
The soul begins to stir and dawn,

A spirit by a spirit heard.
In vain your barren studies here
Construe the signs of sanctity.
You Spirits, you are hovering near;
If you can hear me, answer me!

(He opens the book and perceives the sign of the Macro-cosm)

Ha! What a river of wonder at this vision
Bursts upon all my senses in one flood!
And I feel young, the holy joy of life
Glows new, flows fresh, through nerve and blood!
Was it a god designed this hieroglyph to calm
The storm which but now raged inside me,
To pour upon my heart such balm,
And by some secret urge to guide me
Where all the powers of Nature stand unveiled around me?
Am I a God? It grows so light!
And through the clear-cut symbol on this page
My soul comes face to face with all creating Nature.
At last I understand the dictum of the sage:
'The spiritual world is always open,
Your mind is closed, your heart is dead;
Rise, young man, and plunge undaunted
Your earthly breast in the morning red.'

(He contemplates the sign)

Into one Whole how all things blend,
Function and live within each other!
Passing gold buckets to each other
How heavenly powers ascend, descend!
The odour of grace upon their wings,
They thrust from heaven through earthly things
And as all sing so *the* All sings!
What a fine show! Aye, but only a show!
Infinite Nature, where can I tap thy veins?
Where are thy breasts, those well-springs of all life
On which hang heaven and earth,
Towards which my dry breast strains?
They well up, they give drink, but I feel drought and dearth.

(He turns the pages and perceives the sign of the Earth Spirit)

How differently this new sign works upon me!
Thy sign, thou Spirit of the Earth, 'tis thine
And thou are nearer to me.
At once I feel my powers unfurled,
At once I glow as from new wine
And feel inspired to venture into the world,
To cope with the fortunes of earth benign or malign,
To enter the ring with the storm, to grapple and clinch,
To enter the jaws of the shipwreck and never flinch.
Over me comes a mist,
The moon muffles her light,
The lamp goes dark.
The air goes damp. Red beams flash
Around my head. There blows
A kind of a shudder down from the vault
And seizes on me.
It is thou must be hovering round me, come at my prayers!
Spirit, unveil thyself!
My heart, oh my heart, how it tears!
And how each and all of my senses
Seem burrowing upwards towards new light, new breath!
I feel my heart has surrendered, I have no more defences.
Come then! Come! Even if it prove my death!

.   .   .

FAUST'S STUDY

(He enters with the poodle)

FAUST

I have forsaken field and meadow
Which night has laid in a deep bed,
Night that wakes our better soul
With a holy and foreboding dread.
Now wild desires are wrapped in sleep
And all the deeds that burn and break,
The love of Man is waking now,
The love of God begins to wake.

Poodle! Quiet! Don't run hither and thither!
Leave my threshold! Why are you snuffling there?
Lie down behind the stove and rest.
Here's a cushion; it's my best.
Out of doors on the mountain paths
You kept us amused by running riot;
But as my protégé at home
You'll only be welcome if you're quiet.

> Ah, when in our narrow cell
> The lamp once more imparts good cheer,
> Then in our bosom—in the heart
> That knows itself—then things grow clear.
> Reason once more begins to speak
> And the blooms of hope once more to spread;
> One hankers for the brooks of life,
> Ah, and for life's fountain head.

Don't growl, you poodle! That animal sound
Is not in tune with the holy music
By which my soul is girdled round.
We are used to human beings who jeer
At what they do not understand,
Who grouse at the good and the beautiful
Which often causes them much ado;
But must a dog snarl at it too?

But, ah, already, for all my good intentions
I feel contentment ebbing away in my breast.
Why must the stream so soon run dry
And we be left once more athirst?
I have experienced this so often;
Yet this defect has its compensation,
We learn to prize the supernatural
And hanker after revelation,
Which burns most bright and wins assent
Most in the New Testament.
I feel impelled to open the master text
And this once, with true dedication,
Take the sacred original
And make in my mother tongue my own translation.

(*He opens a Bible*)

It is written: In the beginning was the Word.
Here I am stuck at once. Who will help me on?
I am unable to grant the Word such merit,
I must translate it differently
If I am truly illumined by the spirit.
It is written: In the beginning was the Mind.
But why should my pen scour
So quickly ahead? Consider that first line well.
Is it the Mind that effects and creates all things?
It *should* read: In the beginning was the Power.
Yet, even as I am changing what I have writ,
Something warns me not to abide by it.
The spirit prompts me, I see in a flash what I need,
And write: In the beginning was the Deed!

.   .   .

(*The same room. Later*)

FAUST

Who's knocking? Come in! *Now* who wants to annoy me?

MEPHISTOPHELES (*outside door*)

It's I.

FAUST

　　Come in!

MEPHISTOPHELES (*outside door*)

　　　　　You must say 'Come in' three times.

FAUST

Come in then!

MEPHISTOPHELES (*entering*)

　　　　　Thank you; you overjoy me.

We two, I hope, we shall be good friends;
To chase those megrims of yours away
I am here like a fine young squire to-day,
In a suit of scarlet trimmed with gold
And a little cape of stiff brocade,
With a cock's feather in my hat
And at my side a long sharp blade,
And the most succinct advice I can give
Is that you dress up just like me,

So that uninhibited and free
You may find out what it means to live.

FAUST

The pain of earth's constricted life, I fancy,
Will pierce me still, whatever my attire;
I am too old for mere amusement,
Too young to be without desire.
How can the world dispel my doubt?
You must do without, you must do without!
That is the everlasting song
Which rings in every ear, which rings,
And which to us our whole life long
Every hour hoarsely sings.
I wake in the morning only to feel appalled,
My eyes with bitter tears could run
To see the day which in its course
Will not fulfil a wish for me, not one;
The day which whittles away with obstinate carping
All pleasures—even those of anticipation,
Which makes a thousand grimaces to obstruct
My heart when it is stirring in creation.
And again, when night comes down, in anguish
I must stretch out upon my bed
And again no rest is granted me,
For wild dreams fill my mind with dread.
The God who dwells within my bosom
Can make my inmost soul react;
The God who sways my every power
Is powerless with external fact.
And so existence weighs upon my breast
And I long for death and life—life I detest.

MEPHISTOPHELES

Yet death is never a wholly welcome guest.

FAUST

O happy is he whom death in the dazzle of victory
Crowns with the bloody laurel in the battling swirl!
Or he whom after the mad and breakneck dance
He comes upon in the arms of a girl!
O to have sunk away, delighted, deleted,
Before the Spirit of the Earth, before his might!

MEPHISTOPHELES

Yet I know someone who failed to drink
A brown juice on a certain night.

FAUST

Your hobby is espionage—is it not?

MEPHISTOPHELES

Oh I'm not omniscient—but I know a lot.

FAUST

Whereas that tumult in my soul
Was stilled by sweet familiar chimes
Which cozened the child that yet was in me
With echoes of more happy times,
I now curse all things that encompass
The soul with lures and jugglery
And bind it in this dungeon of grief
With trickery and flattery.
Cursed in advance be the high opinion
That serves our spirit for a cloak!
Cursed be the dazzle of appearance
Which bows our senses to its yoke!
Cursed be the lying dreams of glory,
The illusion that our name survives!
Cursed be the flattering things we own,
Servants and ploughs, children and wives!
Cursed be Mammon when with his treasures
He makes us play the adventurous man
Or when for our luxurious pleasures
He duly spreads the soft divan!
A curse on the balsam of the grape!
A curse on the love that rides for a fall!
A curse on hope! A curse on faith!
And a curse on patience most of all!

(*The invisible Spirits sing again*)

SPIRITS

Woe! Woe!
You have destroyed it,
The beautiful world;
By your violent hand
'Tis downward hurled!

A half-god has dashed it asunder!
From under
We bear off the rubble to nowhere
And ponder
Sadly the beauty departed.
Magnipotent
One among men,
Magnificent
Build it again,
Build it again in your breast!
Let a new course of life
Begin
With vision abounding
And new songs resounding
To welcome it in!

MEPHISTOPHELES

These are the juniors
Of my faction.
Hear how precociously they counsel
Pleasure and action.
Out and away
From your lonely day
Which dries your senses and your juices
Their melody seduces.

Stop playing with your grief which battens
Like a vulture on your life, your mind!
The worst of company would make you feel
That you are a man among mankind.
Not that it's really my proposition
To shove you among the common men;
Though I'm not one of the Upper Ten,
If you would like a coalition
With me for your career through life,
I am quite ready to fit in,
I'm yours before you can say knife.
I am your comrade;
If you so crave,
I am your servant, I am your slave.

FAUST

And what have I to undertake in return?

MEPHISTOPHELES

Oh it's early days to discuss what that is.

FAUST

No, no, the devil is an egoist
And ready to do nothing gratis
Which is to benefit a stranger.
Tell me your terms and don't prevaricate!
A servant like you in the house is a danger.

MEPHISTOPHELES

I will bind myself to your service in this world,
To be at your beck and never rest nor slack;
When we meet again on the other side,
In the same coin you shall pay me back.

FAUST

The other side gives me little trouble;
First batter this present world to rubble,
Then the other may rise—if that's the plan.
This earth is where my springs of joy have started,
And this sun shines on me when broken-hearted;
If I can first from them be parted,
Then let happen what will and can!
I wish to hear no more about it—
Whether there too men hate and love
Or whether in those spheres too, in the future,
There is a Below or an Above.

MEPHISTOPHELES

With such an outlook you can risk it.
Sign on the line! In these next days you will get
Ravishing samples of my arts;
I am giving you what never man saw yet.

FAUST

Poor devil, can *you* give anything ever?
Was a human spirit in its high endeavour
Even once understood by one of your breed?
Have you got food which fails to feed?
Or red gold which, never at rest,
Like mercury runs away through the hand?
A game at which one never wins?
A girl who, even when on my breast,
Pledges herself to my neighbour with her eyes?

The divine and lovely delight of honour
Which falls like a falling star and dies?
Show me the fruits which, before they are plucked, decay
And the trees which day after day renew their green!

MEPHISTOPHELES

Such a commission doesn't alarm me,
I have such treasures to purvey.
But, my good friend, the time draws on when we
Should be glad to feast at our ease on something good.

FAUST

If ever I stretch myself on a bed of ease,
Then I am finished! Is that understood?
If ever your flatteries can coax me
To be pleased with myself, if ever you cast
A spell of pleasure that can hoax me—
Then let *that* day be my last!
That's my wager!

MEPHISTOPHELES
Done!

FAUST
Let's shake!

If ever I say to the passing moment
'Linger a while! Thou art so fair!'
Then you may cast me into fetters,
I will gladly perish then and there!
Then you may set the death-bell tolling,
Then from my service you are free,
The clock may stop, its hand may fall,
And that be the end of time for me!

MEPHISTOPHELES

Think what you're saying, we shall not forget it.

FAUST

And you are fully within your rights;
I have made no mad or outrageous claim.
If I stay as I am, I am a slave—
Whether yours or another's, it's all the same.

MEPHISTOPHELES

I shall this very day at the College Banquet
Enter your service with no more ado,

But just one point—As a life-and-death insurance
I must trouble you for a line or two.

FAUST

So you, you pedant, you too like things in writing?
Have you never known a man? Or a man's word? Never?
Is it not enough that my word of mouth
Puts all my days in bond for ever?
Does not the world rage on in all its streams
And shall a promise hamper *me*?
Yet this illusion reigns within our hearts
And from it who would be gladly free?
Happy the man who can inwardly keep his word;
Whatever the cost, he will not be loath to pay!
But a parchment, duly inscribed and sealed,
Is a bogey from which all wince away.
The word dies on the tip of the pen
And wax and leather lord it then.
What do you, evil spirit, require?
Bronze, marble, parchment, paper?
Quill or chisel or pencil of slate?
You may choose whichever you desire.

MEPHISTOPHELES

How can you so exaggerate
With such a hectic rhetoric?
Any little snippet is quite good—
And you sign it with one little drop of blood.

FAUST

If that is enough and is some use,
One may as well pander to your fad.

MEPHISTOPHELES

Blood is a very special juice.

FAUST

Only do not fear that I shall break this contract.
What I promise is nothing more
Than what all my powers are striving for.
I have puffed myself up too much, it is only
Your sort that really fits my case.
The great Earth Spirit has despised me
And Nature shuts the door in my face.
The thread of thought is snapped asunder,

I have long loathed knowledge in all its fashions.
In the depths of sensuality
Let us now quench our glowing passions!
And at once make ready every wonder
Of unpenetrated sorcery!
Let us cast ourselves into the torrent of time,
Into the whirl of eventfulness,
Where disappointment and success,
Pleasure and pain may chop and change
As chop and change they will and can;
It is restless action makes the man.

MEPHISTOPHELES

No limit is fixed for you, no bound;
If you'd like to nibble at everything
Or to seize upon something flying round—
Well, may you have a run for your money!
But seize your chance and don't be funny!

FAUST

I've told you, it is no question of happiness.
The most painful joy, enamoured hate, enlivening
Disgust—I devote myself to all excess.
My breast, now cured of its appetite for knowledge,
From now is open to all and every smart,
And what is allotted to the whole of mankind
That will I sample in my inmost heart,
Grasping the highest and lowest with my spirit,
Piling men's weal and woe upon my neck,
To extend myself to embrace all human selves
And to founder in the end, like them, a wreck.

MEPHISTOPHELES

O believe *me,* who have been chewing
These iron rations many a thousand year,
No human being can digest
This stuff, from the cradle to the bier.
This universe—believe a devil—
Was made for no one but a god!
He exists in eternal light
But *us* he has brought into the darkness
While *your* sole portion is day and night.

FAUST

I will all the same!

MEPHISTOPHELES

That's very nice.
There's only one thing I find wrong;
Time is short, art is long.
You could do with a little artistic advice.
Confederate with one of the poets
And let him flog his imagination
To heap all virtues on your head,
A head with such a reputation:
Lion's bravery,
Stag's velocity,
Fire of Italy,
Northern tenacity.
Let *him* find out the secret art
Of combining craft with a noble heart
And of being in love like a young man,
Hotly, but working to a plan.
Such a person—*I'd* like to meet him;
'Mr. Microcosm' is how I'd greet him.

FAUST

What am I then if fate must bar
My efforts to reach that crown of humanity
After which all my senses strive?

MEPHISTOPHELES

You are in the end . . . what you are.
You can put on full-bottomed wigs with a million locks,
You can put on stilts instead of your socks,
You remain for ever what you are.

FAUST

I feel my endeavors have not been worth a pin
When I raked together the treasures of the human mind,
If at the end I but sit down to find
No new force welling up within.
I have not a hair's breadth more of height,
I am no nearer the Infinite.

MEPHISTOPHELES

My very good sir, you look at things
Just in the way that people do;

We must be cleverer than that
Or the joys of life will escape from you.
Hell! You have surely hands and feet,
Also a head and you-know-what;
The pleasures I gather on the wing,
Are they less mine? Of course they're not!
Suppose I can afford six stallions,
I can add that horse-power to my score
And dash along and be a proper man
As if my legs were twenty-four.
So good-bye to thinking! On your toes!
The world's before us. Quick! Here goes!
I tell you, a chap who's intellectual
Is like a beast on a blasted heath
Driven in circles by a demon
While a fine green meadow lies round beneath.

FAUST

How do we start?

MEPHISTOPHELES

We just say go—and skip.
But please get ready for this pleasure trip.

(Exit Faust)

Only look down on knowledge and reason,
The highest gifts that men can prize,
Only allow the spirit of lies
To confirm you in magic and illusion,
And then I have you body and soul.
Fate has given this man a spirit
Which is always pressing onwards, beyond control,
And whose mad striving overleaps
All joys of the earth between pole and pole.
Him shall I drag through the wilds of life
And through the flats of meaninglessness,
I shall make him flounder and gape and stick
And to tease his insatiableness
Hang meat and drink in the air before his watering lips;
In vain he will pray to slake his inner thirst,
And even had he not sold himself to the devil
He would be equally accursed.

(*Re-enter Faust*)

FAUST

And now, where are we going?

MEPHISTOPHELES

Wherever you please.

The small world, then the great for us.
With what pleasure and what profit
You will roister through the syllabus!

FAUST

But I, with this long beard of mine,
I lack the easy social touch,
I know the experiment is doomed;
Out in the world I never could fit in much.
I feel so small in company
I'll be embarrassed constantly.

MEPHISTOPHELES

My friend, it will solve itself, any such misgiving;
Just trust yourself and you'll learn the art of living.

FAUST

Well, then, how do we leave home?
Where are your grooms? Your coach and horses?

MEPHISTOPHELES

We merely spread this mantle wide,
It will bear us off on airy courses.
But do not on this noble voyage
Cumber yourself with heavy baggage.
A little inflammable gas which I'll prepare
Will lift us quickly into the air.
If we travel light we shall cleave the sky like a knife.
Congratulations on your new course of life!

15

Romantic Poetry

Romanticism was an intellectual style that flourished in the Western world from about 1780 to 1850. In literature, it was generally based on a faith in the value of the unseen and the ability of men to discover and express hidden truth by the use of imagination, emotion, and inspiration. Great art, in the romantic credo, was the expression, in new, appropriate language, of the basic moral and aesthetic, rather than factual, truths that would bring happiness to mankind. Specifically, this imaginative faith held to a belief in the surpassing goodness and glory of physical nature, in the primacy of the individual, and in the truth of the individual's subjective feelings. Romanticism was, at the same time, fascinated with the remote in space and time, with the dramatic and violent, and with the melancholy and terrible. Along with these affirmations, the romantics rejected the world as it was and rebelled against the social, intellectual, and aesthetic standards of their time.

Lyric poetry was the greatest literary expression of romanticism, and it has seldom been equaled in color, sensuousness, and imaginative scope. For the romantic rebels, the poem was an organic whole, expressing more than any paraphrase, and to be grasped only in terms of the unique world it had created. The poem sprang from the individual creator's mystical experience and had no basis in common social discourse.

The three poems reprinted below are prime examples of romantic lyric poetry. "Lines Composed a Few Miles Above Tintern Abbey" (1798) by William Wordsworth (1770–1850) reflects the poet's lifelong conviction that truth and joy lay in the union of the individual with external nature and that this experience could be made clear to others in artistic, symbolic forms. The poem itself is a quiet meditation expressed in smooth, rolling phrases of blank verse. It describes the development of the poet's responses to nature, from his childhood experience to his culminating religious communion with its beauty and harmony.

"Ode on a Grecian Urn," by John Keats (1795–1821), has the themes of

271

art and life. Written at the end of his short, tragic life (1820), it is an example of his self-discipline and craftsmanship as well as his sensuous appeal and the richness of his color and forms. Keats finds, in the scenes of life carved on an ancient urn, an expression of transcendent art that resolved the paradoxes of the arrested action: the life in death, past and present, poetry and reality, beauty and truth.

Walt Whitman (1819–1892) was a great American poet, a robust man of the people, and a romantic rebel. In the free-flowing verse and large rhythms of "Out of the Cradle Endlessly Rocking" (1859), he recaptures the intense melancholy of the childhood experience of lost love. This memory calls him to his poetic destiny whose fulfillment is death, which he joyfully hails as the continuum of life.

about Wordsworth mind – not nature own it uses only

WILLIAM WORDSWORTH: *Lines Composed*
a Few Miles Above Tintern Abbey,
on Revisiting the Banks of the Wye
During a Tour. July 13, 1798

Five years have past; five summers, with the length
Of five long winters! and again I hear
These waters, rolling from their mountain-springs
With a soft inland murmur.—Once again
Do I behold these steep and lofty cliffs,
That on a wild, secluded scene impress
Thoughts of more deep seclusion, and connect
The landscape with the quiet of the sky.
The day is come when I again repose
Here, under this dark sycamore, and view
These plots of cottage-ground, these orchard-tufts,
Which at this season, with their unripe fruits,
Are clad in one green hue, and lose themselves
'Mid groves and copses. Once again I see
These hedge-rows, hardly hedge-rows, little lines
Of sportive wood run wild: these pastoral farms,

William Wordsworth, "Lines Composed a Few Miles Above Tintern Abbey," in *The Poetical Works of William Wordsworth* (Boston: Houghton, Osgood, 1880), II, 186–91.

Green to the very door; and wreaths of smoke
Sent up, in silence, from among the trees!
With some uncertain notice, as might seem
Of vagrant dwellers in the houseless woods,
Or of some Hermit's cave, where by his fire
The Hermit sits alone.

           These beauteous forms,
Through a long absence, have not been to me
As is a landscape to a blind man's eye:
But oft, in lonely rooms, and 'mid the din
Of towns and cities, I have owed to them,
In hours of weariness, sensations sweet,
Felt in the blood, and felt along the heart;
And passing even into my purer mind,
With tranquil restoration:—feelings too
Of unremembered pleasure: such, perhaps,
As have no slight or trivial influence
On that best portion of a good man's life,
His little, nameless, unremembered acts
Of kindness and of love. Nor less, I trust,
To them I may have owed another gift,
Of aspect more sublime: that blessed mood,
In which the burden of the mystery,
In which the heavy and the weary weight
Of all this unintelligible world,
Is lightened:—that serene and blessed mood,
In which the affections gently lead us on,—
Until, the breath of this corporeal frame
And even the motion of our human blood
Almost suspended, we are laid asleep
In body, and become a living soul:
While with an eye made quiet by the power
Of harmony, and the deep power of joy,
We see into the life of things.
                       If this
Be but a vain belief, yet, oh! how oft—
In darkness and amid the many shapes
Of joyless daylight; when the fretful stir

Unprofitable, and the fever of the world,
Have hung upon the beatings of my heart—
How oft, in spirit, have I turned to thee,
O sylvan Wye! thou wanderer through the woods,
How often has my spirit turned to thee!

And now, with gleams of half-extinguished thought,
With many recognitions dim and faint,
And somewhat of a sad perplexity,
The picture of the mind revives again:
While here I stand, not only with the sense
Of present pleasure, but with pleasing thoughts
That in this moment there is life and food
For future years. And so I dare to hope,
Though changed, no doubt, from what I was when first
I came among these hills; when like a roe
I bounded o'er the mountains, by the sides
Of the deep rivers, and the lonely streams,
Wherever nature led: more like a man
Flying from something that he dreads, than one
Who sought the thing he loved. For nature then
(The coarser pleasures of my boyish days
And their glad animal movements all gone by)
To me was all in all.—I cannot paint
What then I was. The sounding cataract
Haunted me like a passion: the tall rock,
The mountain, and the deep and gloomy wood,
Their colors and their forms, were then to me
An appetite; a feeling and a love,
That had no need of a remoter charm
By thoughts supplied, nor any interest
Unborrowed from the eye.—That time is past,
And all its aching joys are now no more,
And all its dizzy raptures. Not for this
Faint I, nor mourn nor murmur; other gifts
Have followed; for such loss, I would believe,
Abundant recompense. For I have learned
To look on nature, not as in the hour
Of thoughtless youth; but hearing oftentimes
The still, sad music of humanity,

Nor harsh nor grating, though of ample power
To chasten and subdue. And I have felt
A presence that disturbs me with the joy   *Climax*
Of elevated thoughts; a sense sublime
Of something far more deeply interfused,
Whose dwelling is the light of setting suns,
And the round ocean, and the living air,   *God*
And the blue sky, and in the mind of man:
A motion and a spirit, that impels
All thinking things, all objects of all thought,
And rolls through all things. Therefore am I still
A lover of the meadows and the woods,
And mountains; and of all that we behold
From this green earth; of all the mighty world
Of eye, and ear,—both what they half create,
And what perceive; well pleased to recognize
In nature and the language of the sense,
The anchor of my purest thoughts, the nurse,
The guide, the guardian of my heart, and soul
Of all my moral being.
                            Nor perchance,
If I were not thus taught, should I the more
Suffer my genial spirits to decay:
For thou art with me here upon the banks
Of this fair river; thou my dearest Friend,
My dear, dear Friend; and in thy voice I catch
The language of my former heart, and read
My former pleasures in the shooting lights
Of thy wild eyes. O yet a little while
May I behold in thee what I was once,
My dear, dear Sister! and this prayer I make,
Knowing that Nature never did betray
The heart that loved her; 't is her privilege,
Through all the years of this our life, to lead
From joy to joy: for she can so inform
The mind that is within us, so impress
With quietness and beauty, and so feed
With lofty thoughts, that neither evil tongues,
Rash judgments, nor the sneers of selfish men,
Nor greetings where no kindness is, nor all

The dreary intercourse of daily life,
Shall e'er prevail against us, or disturb
Our cheerful faith, that all which we behold
Is full of blessings. Therefore let the moon
Shine on thee in thy solitary walk;
And let the misty mountain-winds be free
To blow against thee: and, in after years,
When these wild ecstasies shall be matured
Into a sober pleasure; when thy mind
Shall be a mansion for all lovely forms,
Thy memory be as a dwelling-place
For all sweet sounds and harmonies; O, then,
If solitude, or fear, or pain, or grief,
Should be thy portion, with what healing thoughts
Of tender joy wilt thou remember me,
And these my exhortations! Nor, perchance,—
If I should be where I no more can hear
Thy voice, nor catch from thy wild eyes these gleams
Of past existence,—wilt thou then forget
That on the banks of this delightful stream
We stood together; and that I, so long
A worshipper of Nature, hither came
Unwearied in that service: rather say
With warmer love,—oh! with far deeper zeal
Of holier love. Nor wilt thou then forget,
That after many wanderings, many years
Of absence, these steep woods and lofty cliffs,
And this green pastoral landscape, were to me
More dear, both for themselves and for thy sake!

JOHN KEATS: *Ode on a Grecian Urn*

Thou still unravish'd bride of quietness!
    Thou foster-child of Silence and slow Time,
Sylvan historian, who canst thus express
    A flowery tale more sweetly than our rhyme:
What leaf-fringed legend haunts about thy shape

John Keats, "Ode on a Grecian Urn," in *The Poetical Works of John Keats* (Boston: Little, Brown, 1854), 310–12.

Of deities or mortals, or of both,
In Tempe or the dales of Arcady?
What men or gods are these? what maidens loath?
What mad pursuit? What struggle to escape?
What pipes and timbrels? What wild ecstasy?

Heard melodies are sweet, but those unheard
Are sweeter; therefore, ye soft pipes, play on;
Not to the sensual ear, but, more endear'd,
Pipe to the spirit ditties of no tone:
Fair youth, beneath the trees, thou canst not leave
Thy song, nor ever can those trees be bare;
Bold Lover, never, never canst thou kiss,
Though winning near the goal—yet, do not grieve;
She cannot fade, though thou hast not thy bliss,
Forever wilt thou love, and she be fair!

Ah, happy, happy boughs! that cannot shed
Your leaves, nor ever bid the Spring adieu;
And, happy melodist, unwearied,
Forever piping songs forever new;
More happy love! more happy, happy love!
Forever warm and still to be enjoy'd,
Forever panting and forever young;
All breathing human passion far above,
That leaves a heart high sorrowful and cloy'd,
A burning forehead, and a parching tongue.

Who are these coming to the sacrifice?
To what green altar, O mysterious priest,
Lead'st thou that heifer lowing at the skies,
And all her silken flanks with garlands drest?
What little town by river or sea-shore,
Or mountain-built with peaceful citadel,
Is emptied of its folk, this pious morn?
And, little town, thy streets forevermore
Will silent be; and not a soul to tell
Why thou art desolate, can e'er return.

O Attic shape! Fair attitude! with brede
Of marble men and maidens overwrought,

With forest branches and the trodden weed;
　Thou, silent form! dost tease us out of thought
As doth eternity: Cold Pastoral!
　When old age shall this generation waste,
　　Thou shalt remain, in midst of other woe
　Than ours, a friend to man, to whom thou say'st,
"Beauty is truth, truth beauty,"—that is all
　Ye know on earth, and all ye need to know.

WALT WHITMAN: *Out of the Cradle*
Endlessly Rocking

Out of the cradle endlessly rocking,
Out of the mocking-bird's throat, the musical shuttle,
Out of the Ninth-month midnight,
Over the sterile sands and the fields beyond, where the child leaving
　his bed wander'd alone, bareheaded, barefoot,
Down from the shower'd halo,
Up from the mystic play of shadows twining and twisting as if they
　were alive,
Out from the patches of briers and blackberries,
From the memories of the bird that chanted to me,
From your memories sad brother, from the fitful risings and fallings
　I heard,
From under that yellow half-moon late-risen and swollen as if with
　tears,
From those beginning notes of yearning and love there in the mist,
From the thousand responses of my heart never to cease,
From the myriad thence-arous'd words,
From the word stronger and more delicious than any,
From such as now they start the scene revisiting,
As a flock, twittering, rising, or overhead passing,
Borne hither, ere all eludes me, hurriedly,
A man, yet by these tears a little boy again,
Throwing myself on the sand, confronting the waves,
I, chanter of pains and joys, uniter of here and hereafter,
Taking all hints to use them, but swiftly leaping beyond them,
A reminiscence sing.

Walt Whitman, "Out of the Cradle Endlessly Rocking," in *Leaves of Grass* (Phila-
delphia: McKay, 1884), 196–201.

Once Paumanok,
When the lilac-scent was in the air and Fifth-month grass was
    growing,
Up this seashore in some briers,
Two feather'd guests from Alabama, two together,
And their nest, and four light-green eggs spotted with brown,
And every day the he-bird to and fro near at hand,
And every day the she-bird crouch'd on her nest, silent, with bright
    eyes,
And every day I, a curious boy, never too close, never disturbing
    them,
Cautiously peering, absorbing, translating.

Shine! shine! shine!
Pour down your warmth, great sun!
While we bask, we two together.

Two together!
Winds blow south, or winds blow north,
Day come white, or night come black,
Home, or rivers and mountains from home,
Singing all time, minding no time,
While we two keep together.

Till of a sudden,
May-be kill'd, unknown to her mate,
One forenoon the she-bird crouch'd not on the nest,
Nor return'd that afternoon, nor the next,
Nor ever appear'd again.

And thenceforward all summer in the sound of the sea,
And at night under the full of the moon in calmer weather,
Over the hoarse surging of the sea,
Or flitting from brier to brier by day,
I saw, I heard at intervals the remaining one, the he-bird,
The solitary guest from Alabama.

Blow! blow! blow!
Blow up sea-winds along Paumanok's shore;
I wait and I wait till you blow my mate to me.

Yes, when the stars glisten'd,
All night long on the prong of a moss-scallop'd stake,

Down almost amid the slapping waves,
Sat the lone singer wonderful causing tears.

He call'd on his mate,
He pour'd forth the meanings which I of all men know.

Yes my brother I know,
The rest might not, but I have treasur'd every note,
For more than once dimly down to the beach gliding,
Silent, avoiding the moonbeams, blending myself with the shadows,
Recalling now the obscure shapes, the echoes, the sounds and
    sights after their sorts,
The white arms out in the breakers tirelessly tossing,
I, with bare feet, a child, the wind wafting my hair,
Listen'd long and long.

Listen'd to keep, to sing, now translating the notes,
Following you my brother.

Soothe! soothe! soothe!
Close on its wave soothes the wave behind,
And again another behind embracing and lapping, every one close,
But my love soothes not me, not me.

Low hangs the moon, it rose late,
It is lagging—O I think it is heavy with love, with love.

O madly the sea pushes upon the land,
With love, with love.

O night! do I not see my love fluttering out among the breakers?
What is that little black thing I see there in the white?

Loud! loud! loud!
Loud I call to you, my love!
High and clear I shoot my voice over the waves,
Surely you must know who is here, is here,
You must know who I am, my love.

Low-hanging moon!
What is that dusky spot in your brown yellow?
O it is the shape, the shape of my mate!
O moon do not keep her from me any longer.

Land! land! O land!
Whichever way I turn, O I think you could give me my mate back
    again if you only would,
For I am almost sure I see her dimly whichever way I look.

O rising stars!
Perhaps the one I want so much will rise, will rise with some of you.

O throat! O trembling throat!
Sound clearer through the atmosphere!
Pierce the woods, the earth,
Somewhere listening to catch you must be the one I want.

Shake out carols!
Solitary here, the night's carols!
Carols of lonesome love! death's carols!
Carols under that lagging, yellow, waning moon!
O under that moon where she droops almost down into the sea!
O reckless despairing carols.

But soft! sink low!
Soft! let me just murmur,
And do you wait a moment you husky-nois'd sea,
For somewhere I believe I heard my mate responding to me,
So faint, I must be still, be still to listen,
But not altogether still, for then she might not come immediately
    to me.

Hither my love!
Here I am! here!
With this just-sustain'd note I announce myself to you,
This gentle call is for you my love, for you.

Do not be decoy'd elsewhere,
That is the whistle of the wind, it is not my voice,
That is the fluttering, the fluttering of the spray,
Those are the shadows of leaves.

O darkness! O in vain!
O I am very sick and sorrowful.

O brown halo in the sky near the moon, drooping upon the sea!
O troubled reflection in the sea!

O throat! O throbbing heart!
And I singing uselessly, uselessly all the night.

O past! O happy life! O songs of joy!
In the air, in the woods, over fields,
Loved! loved! loved! loved! loved!
But my mate no more, no more with me!
We two together no more.

The aria sinking,
All else continuing, the stars shining,
The winds blowing, the notes of the bird continuous echoing,
With angry moans the fierce old mother incessantly moaning,
On the sands of Paumanok's shore gray and rustling,
The yellow half-moon enlarged, sagging down, drooping, the face
    of the sea almost touching,
The boy ecstatic, with his bare feet the waves, with his hair the
    atmosphere dallying,
The love in the heart long pent, now loose, now at last tumultuously
    bursting,
The aria's meaning, the ears, the soul, swiftly depositing,
The strange tears down the cheeks coursing,
The colloquy there, the trio, each uttering,
The undertone, the savage old mother incessantly crying,
To the boy's soul's questions sullenly timing, some drown'd secret
    hissing,
To the outsetting bard.

Demon or bird! (said the boy's soul,)
Is it indeed toward your mate you sing? or is it really to me?
For I, that was a child, my tongue's use sleeping, now I have heard
    you,
Now in a moment I know what I am for, I awake,
And already a thousand singers, a thousand songs, clearer, louder
    and more sorrowful than yours,
A thousand warbling echoes have started to life within me, never
    to die.

O you singer solitary, singing by yourself, projecting me,
O solitary me listening, never more shall I cease perpetuating you,
Never more shall I escape, never more the reverberations,
Never more the cries of unsatisfied love be absent from me,

Never again leave me to be the peaceful child I was before what
    there in the night,
By the sea under the yellow and sagging moon,
The messenger there arous'd, the fire, the sweet hell within,
The unknown want, the destiny of me.

O give me the clew! (it lurks in the night here somewhere,)
O if I am to have so much, let me have more!

A word then, (for I will conquer it,)
The word final, superior to all,
Subtle, sent up—what is it?—I listen;
Are you whispering it, and have been all the time, you sea-waves?
Is that it from your liquid rims and wet sands?

Whereto answering, the sea,
Delaying not, hurrying not,
Whisper'd me through the night, and very plainly before daybreak,
Lisp'd to me the low and delicious word death,
And again death, death, death, death,
Hissing melodious, neither like the bird nor like my arous'd child's
    heart,
But edging near as privately for me rustling at my feet,
Creeping thence steadily up to my ears and laving me softly all over,
Death, death, death, death, death.

Which I do not forget,
But fuse the song of my dusky demon and brother,
That he sang to me in the moonlight on Paumanok's gray beach,
With the thousand responsive songs at random,
My own songs awaked from that hour,
And with them the key, the word up from the waves,
The word of the sweetest song and all songs,
That strong and delicious word which, creeping to my feet,
(Or like some old crone rocking the cradle, swathed in sweet gar-
    ments, bending aside,)
The sea whisper'd me.

Alexis de Tocqueville

══════ 16 ══════

Democracy in America

Political and social democracy, as a logical extension of the principles of
liberalism, developed in the Western world in the course of the nineteenth
century and after. The earliest and fullest manifestation of these new developments came in the United States of America. Alexis de Tocqueville
(1805–1859), a French aristocrat, recognized this fact and, in 1830, left his
minor government post under the French monarchy to come to the United
States for a visit of some eighteen months to see the new society at work.
Ostensibly, he came to survey the American penal system and, indeed, produced a report on this subject. But the major results of his visit were the
two volumes of *Democracy in America* (1835, 1840), a thorough survey of
American society during the Age of Jackson.

    Democracy in America was well received in both Europe and America
and still remains the best work on this subject by any European observer.
But it was more than a scholarly travelogue. It was a shrewd and prophetic
analysis of democracy in action—the practical problems and implications of
social equality, public opinion, majority rule, democratic leadership, and
emerging industrialization. Tocqueville not only described but evaluated
what he saw. He judged democratic society by the standards of a moderate,
enlightened aristocrat, who appreciated the new order as the wave of the
future but was troubled by some of its aspects. Like Burke, Tocqueville
valued the conservative ideals of freedom and order, but, unlike him,
Tocqueville accepted the value of an open society based on popular liberty.
His central concern, therefore, was to reconcile individual freedom with
the conformity, materialism, and potential tyranny of an egalitarian order.
Tocqueville saw the solution in an enlightened and tempered self-interest
on the part of individuals and the diffusion of power among many interest
groups in a pluralistic system.

Alexis de Tocqueville, *Democracy in America*, trans. Henry Reeve, rev. ed. (London and New York: Colonial, 1900), I, 3, 6–7, 9–11, 13–14, 263–70; II, 11–13, 99–
103, 336–37, 339–44.

Amongst the novel objects that attracted my attention during my stay in the United States, nothing struck me more forcibly than the general equality of conditions. I readily discovered the prodigious influence which this primary fact exercises on the whole course of society, by giving a certain direction to public opinion, and a certain tenor to the laws; by imparting new maxims to the governing powers, and peculiar habits to the governed. I speedily perceived that the influence of this fact extends far beyond the political character and the laws of the country, and that it has no less empire over civil society than over the Government; it creates opinions, engenders sentiments, suggests the ordinary practices of life, and modifies whatever it does not produce. The more I advanced in the study of American society, the more I perceived that the equality of conditions is the fundamental fact from which all others seem to be derived, and the central point at which all my observations constantly terminated.

I then turned my thoughts to our own hemisphere, where I imagined that I discerned something analogous to the spectacle which the New World presented to me. I observed that the equality of conditions is daily progressing towards those extreme limits which it seems to have reached in the United States, and that the democracy which governs the American communities appears to be rapidly rising into power in Europe. I hence conceived the idea of the book which is now before the reader.

. . .

Nor is this phenomenon at all peculiar to France. Whithersoever we turn our eyes we shall witness the same continual revolution throughout the whole of Christendom. The various occurrences of national existence have everywhere turned to the advantage of democracy; all men have aided it by their exertions: those who have intentionally labored in its cause, and those who have served it unwittingly; those who have fought for it and those who have declared themselves its opponents, have all been driven along in the same track, have all labored to one end, some ignorantly and some unwillingly; all have been blind instruments in the hands of God.

The gradual development of the equality of conditions is therefore a providential fact, and it possesses all the characteristics of a divine decree: it is universal, it is durable, it constantly eludes all human interference, and all events as well as all men contribute to its progress. Would it, then, be wise to imagine that a social impulse which dates from so far back can be checked by the efforts of a generation? Is it credible that the democracy which has annihilated the feudal system and vanquished kings will respect the citizen and the capitalist? Will it stop now that it has grown so strong and its adversaries so weak? None can say which way we are going, for all terms of comparison are wanting: the equality of conditions is more complete in the Christian countries of the present day than it has been at any time or in any part of the world; so that the extent of what already exists prevents us from foreseeing what may be yet to come.

The whole book which is here offered to the public has been written under the impression of a kind of religious dread produced in the author's mind by the contemplation of so irresistible a revolution, which has advanced for centuries in spite of such amazing obstacles, and which is still proceeding in the midst of the ruins it has made.

· · ·

The scene is now changed . . . , the divisions which once severed mankind are lowered, property is divided, power is held in common, the light of intelligence spreads, and the capacities of all classes are equally cultivated; the State becomes democratic, and the empire of democracy is slowly and peaceably introduced into the institutions and the manners of the nation. I can conceive a society in which all men would profess an equal attachment and respect for the laws of which they are the common authors; in which the authority of the State would be respected as necessary, though not as divine; and the loyalty of the subject to its chief magistrate would not be a passion, but a quiet and rational persuasion. Every individual being in the possession of rights which he is sure to retain, a kind of manly reliance and reciprocal courtesy would arise between all classes, alike removed from pride and meanness. The people, well acquainted with its true interests, would allow that in order to profit by the advantages of society it is necessary to satisfy its demands. In this state of things the voluntary association of the citizens might supply the individual exertions of the nobles, and the community would be alike protected from anarchy and from oppression.

I admit that, in a democratic State thus constituted, society will not be stationary; but the impulses of the social body may be regulated and directed forwards; if there be less splendor than in the halls of an aristocracy, the contrast of misery will be less frequent also; the pleasures of enjoyment may be less excessive, but those of comfort will be more general; the sciences may be less perfectly cultivated, but ignorance will be less common; the impetuosity of the feelings will be repressed, and the habits of the nation softened; there will be more vices and fewer crimes. In the absence of enthusiasm and of an ardent faith, great sacrifices may be obtained from the members of a commonwealth by an appeal to their understandings and their experience; each individual will feel the same necessity for uniting with his fellow-citizens to protect his own weakness; and as he knows that if they are to assist he must co-operate, he will readily perceive that his personal interest is identified with the interest of the community. The nation, taken as a whole, will be less brilliant, less glorious, and perhaps less strong; but the majority of the citizens will enjoy a greater degree of prosperity, and the people will remain quiet, not because it despairs of amelioration, but because it is conscious of the advantages of its condition. If all the consequences of this state of things were not good or useful, society would at least have appropriated all such as were useful and good; and having once and for ever renounced the social advantages of aristocracy, mankind would enter into possession of all the benefits which democracy can afford.

But here it may be asked what we have adopted in the place of those institutions, those ideas, and those customs of our forefathers which we have abandoned. The spell of royalty is broken, but it has not been succeeded by the majesty of the laws; the people has learned to despise all authority, but fear now extorts a larger tribute of obedience than that which was formerly paid by reverence and by love.

I perceive that we have destroyed those independent beings which were able to cope with tyranny single-handed; but it is the Government that has inherited the privileges of which families, corporations, and individuals have been deprived; the weakness of the whole community has therefore succeeded that influence of a small body of citizens, which, if it was sometimes oppressive, was often conserva-

tive. The division of property has lessened the distance which separated the rich from the poor; but it would seem that the nearer
they draw to each other, the greater is their mutual hatred, and the
more vehement the envy and the dread with which they resist each
other's claims to power; the notion of Right is alike insensible to
both classes, and Force affords to both the only argument for the
present, and the only guarantee for the future. The poor man retains the prejudices of his forefathers without their faith, and their
ignorance without their virtues; he has adopted the doctrine of
self interest as the rule of his actions, without understanding the
science which controls it, and his egotism is no less blind than his
devotedness was formerly. If society is tranquil, it is not because it
relies upon its strength and its well-being, but because it knows its
weakness and its infirmities; a single effort may cost it its life;
everybody feels the evil, but no one has courage or energy enough
to seek the cure; the desires, the regret, the sorrows, and the joys of
the time produce nothing that is visible or permanent, like the
passions of old men which terminate in impotence.

We have, then, abandoned whatever advantages the old state of
things afforded, without receiving any compensation from our present condition; we have destroyed an aristocracy, and we seem inclined to survey its ruins with complacency, and to fix our abode in
the midst of them.

. . .

There is a country in the world where the great revolution which
I am speaking of seems nearly to have reached its natural limits;
it has been effected with ease and simplicity, say rather that this
country has attained the consequences of the democratic revolution which we are undergoing without having experienced the
revolution itself. The emigrants who fixed themselves on the shores
of America in the beginning of the seventeenth century severed the
democratic principle from all the principles which repressed it in
the old communities of Europe, and transplanted it unalloyed to
the New World. It has there been allowed to spread in perfect
freedom, and to put forth its consequences in the laws by influencing
the manners of the country.

It appears to me beyond a doubt that sooner or later we shall
arrive, like the Americans, at an almost complete equality of conditions. But I do not conclude from this that we shall ever be neces-

sarily led to draw the same political consequences which the Americans have derived from a similar social organization. I am far from supposing that they have chosen the only form of government which a democracy may adopt; but the identity of the efficient cause of laws and manners in the two countries is sufficient to account for the immense interest we have in becoming acquainted with its effects in each of them.

It is not, then, merely to satisfy a legitimate curiosity that I have examined America; my wish has been to find instruction by which we may ourselves profit. Whoever should imagine that I have intended to write a panegyric will perceive that such was not my design; nor has it been my object to advocate any form of government in particular, for I am of opinion that absolute excellence is rarely to be found in any legislation; I have not even affected to discuss whether the social revolution, which I believe to be irresistible, is advantageous or prejudicial to mankind; I have acknowledged this revolution as a fact already accomplished or on the eve of its accomplishment; and I have selected the nation, from amongst those which have undergone it, in which its devolment has been the most peaceful and the most complete, in order to discern its natural consequences, and, if it be possible, to distinguish the means by which it may be rendered profitable. I confess that in America I saw more than America; I sought the image of democracy itself, with its inclinations, its character, its prejudices, and its passions, in order to learn what we have to fear or to hope from its progress.

. . .

TYRANNY OF THE MAJORITY

I hold it to be an impious and an execrable maxim that, politically speaking, a people has a right to do whatsoever it pleases, and yet I have asserted that all authority originates in the will of the majority. Am I then, in contradiction with myself?

A general law—which bears the name of Justice—has been made and sanctioned, not only by a majority of this or that people, but by a majority of mankind. The rights of every people are consequently confined within the limits of what is just. A nation may be considered in the light of a jury which is empowered to represent society at large, and to apply the great and general law of justice. Ought such a jury, which represents society, to have more power than the society in which the laws it applies originate?

When I refuse to obey an unjust law, I do not contest the right which the majority has of commanding, but I simply appeal from the sovereignty of the people to the sovereignty of mankind. It has been asserted that a people can never entirely outstep the boundaries of justice and of reason in those affairs which are more peculiarly its own, and that consequently full power may fearlessly be given to the majority by which it is represented. But this language is that of a slave.

A majority taken collectively may be regarded as a being whose opinions, and most frequently whose interests, are opposed to those of another being, which is styled a minority. If it be admitted that a man, possessing absolute power, may misuse that power by wronging his adversaries, why should a majority not be liable to the same reproach? Men are not apt to change their characters by agglomeration; nor does their patience in the presence of obstacles increase with the consciousness of their strength. And for these reasons I can never willingly invest any number of my fellow-creatures with that unlimited authority which I should refuse to any one of them.

I do not think that it is possible to combine several principles in the same government, so as at the same time to maintain freedom, and really to oppose them to one another. The form of government which is usually termed mixed has always appeared to me to be a mere chimera. Accurately speaking there is no such thing as a mixed government (with the meaning usually given to that word), because in all communities some one principle of action may be discovered which preponderates over the others. England in the last century, which has been more especially cited as an example of this form of Government, was in point of fact an essentially aristocratic State, although it comprised very powerful elements of democracy; for the laws and customs of the country were such that the aristocracy could not but preponderate in the end, and subject the direction of public affairs to its own will. The error arose from too much attention being paid to the actual struggle which was going on between the nobles and the people, without considering the probable issue of the contest, which was in reality the important point. When a community really has a mixed government, that is to say, when it is equally divided between two adverse principles, it must either pass through a revolution or fall into complete dissolution.

I am therefore of opinion that some one social power must always be made to predominate over the others; but I think that liberty is endangered when this power is checked by no obstacles which may retard its course, and force it to moderate its own vehemence.

Unlimited power is in itself a bad and dangerous thing; human beings are not competent to exercise it with discretion, and God alone can be omnipotent, because His wisdom and His justice are always equal to His power. But no power upon earth is so worthy of honor for itself, or of reverential obedience to the rights which it represents, that I would consent to admit its uncontrolled and all-predominant authority. When I see that the right and the means of absolute command are conferred on a people or upon a king, upon an aristocracy or a democracy, a monarchy or a republic, I recognize the germ of tyranny, and I journey onward to a land of more hopeful institutions.

In my opinion the main evil of the present democratic institutions of the United States does not arise, as is often asserted in Europe, from their weakness, but from their overpowering strength; and I am not so much alarmed at the excessive liberty which reigns in that country as at the very inadequate securities which exist against tyranny.

When an individual or a party is wronged in the United States, to whom can he apply for redress? If to public opinion, public opinion constitutes the majority; if to the legislature, it represents the majority, and implicitly obeys its injunctions; if to the executive power, it is appointed by the majority, and remains a passive tool in its hands; the public troops consist of the majority under arms; the jury is the majority invested with the right of hearing judicial cases; and in certain States even the judges are elected by the majority. However iniquitous or absurd the evil of which you complain may be, you must submit to it as well as you can.

If, on the other hand, a legislative power could be so constituted as to represent the majority without necessarily being the slave of its passions; an executive, so as to retain a certain degree of uncontrolled authority; and a judiciary, so as to remain independent of the two other powers; a government would be formed which would still be democratic without incurring any risk of tyrannical abuse.

I do not say that tyrannical abuses frequently occur in America at the present day, but I maintain that no sure barrier is established against them, and that the causes which mitigate the government

are to be found in the circumstances and the manners of the country
more than in its laws.

. . .

POWER EXERCISED BY THE MAJORITY
IN AMERICA UPON OPINION

It is in the examination of the display of public opinion in the
United States that we clearly perceive how far the power of the
majority surpasses all the powers with which we are acquainted in
Europe. Intellectual principles exercise an influence which is so invisible, and often so inappreciable, that they baffle the toils of oppression. At the present time the most absolute monarchs in Europe
are unable to prevent certain notions, which are opposed to their
authority, from circulating in secret throughout their dominions,
and even in their courts. Such is not the case in America; as long as
the majority is still undecided, discussion is carried on; but as soon
as its decision is irrevocably pronounced, a submissive silence is observed, and the friends, as well as the opponents, of the measure
unite in assenting to its propriety. The reason of this is perfectly
clear: no monarch is so absolute as to combine all the powers of
society in his own hands, and to conquer all opposition with the
energy of a majority which is invested with the right of making and
of executing the laws.

The authority of a king is purely physical, and it controls the
actions of the subject without subduing his private will; but the
majority possesses a power which is physical and moral at the same
time; it acts upon the will as well as upon the actions of men, and
it represses not only all contest, but all controversy.

I know no country in which there is so little true independence
of mind and freedom of discussion as in America. In any constitutional state in Europe every sort of religious and political theory
may be advocated and propagated abroad; for there is no country
in Europe so subdued by any single authority as not to contain
citizens who are ready to protect the man who raises his voice in
the cause of truth from the consequences of his hardihood. If he is
unfortunate enough to live under an absolute government, the people is upon his side; if he inhabits a free country, he may find a
shelter behind the authority of the throne, if he require one. The

aristocratic part of society supports him in some countries, and the democracy in others. But in a nation where democratic institutions exist, organized like those of the United States, there is but one sole authority, one single element of strength and of success, with nothing beyond it.

In America the majority raises very formidable barriers to the liberty of opinion: within these barriers an author may write whatever he pleases, but he will repent it if he ever step beyond them. Not that he is exposed to the terrors of an auto-da-fé, but he is tormented by the slights and persecutions of daily obloquy. His political career is closed forever, since he has offended the only authority which is able to promote his success. Every sort of compensation, even that of celebrity, is refused to him. Before he published his opinions he imagined that he held them in common with many others; but no sooner has he declared them openly than he is loudly censured by his overbearing opponents, whilst those who think without having the courage to speak, like him, abandon him in silence. He yields at length, oppressed by the daily efforts he has been making, and he subsides into silence, as if he was tormented by remorse for having spoken the truth.

Fetters and headsmen were the coarse instruments which tyranny formerly employed; but the civilization of our age has refined the arts of despotism which seemed, however, to have been sufficiently perfected before. The excesses of monarchical power had devised a variety of physical means of oppression: the democratic republics of the present day have rendered it as entirely an affair of the mind as that will which it is intended to coerce. Under the absolute sway of an individual despot the body was attacked in order to subdue the soul, and the soul escaped the blows which were directed against it and rose superior to the attempt; but such is not the course adopted by tyranny in democratic republics; there the body is left free, and the soul is enslaved. The sovereign can no longer say, "You shall think as I do on pain of death;" but he says, "You are free to think differently from me, and to retain your life, your property, and all that you possess; but if such be your determination, you are henceforth an alien among your people. You may retain your civil rights, but they will be useless to you, for you will never be chosen by your fellow-citizens if you solicit their suffrages, and they will affect to scorn you if you solicit their esteem. You will remain among men, but you will be deprived of the rights of mankind. Your fellow-creatures will shun you like an impure being, and those who are most persuaded of your innocence will abandon you too, lest they should be shunned in their turn. Go in peace! I have given you your life, but it is an existence incomparably worse than death."

Monarchical institutions have thrown an odium upon despotism; let us beware lest democratic republics should restore oppression, and should render it less odious and less degrading in the eyes of the many, by making it still more onerous to the few.

Works have been published in the proudest nations of the Old World expressly intended to censure the vices and deride the follies of the times: Labruyère inhabited the palace of Louis XIV when he composed his chapter upon the Great, and Molière criticised the courtiers in the very pieces which were acted before the Court. But the ruling power in the United States is not to be made game of; the smallest reproach irritates its sensibility, and the slightest joke which has any foundation in truth renders it indignant; from the style of its language to the more solid virtues of its character, everything must be made the subject of encomium. No writer, whatever be his eminence, can escape from this tribute of adulation to his fellow-citizens. The majority lives in the perpetual practice of self-applause, and there are certain truths which the Americans can only learn from strangers or from experience.

If great writers have not at present existed in America, the reason is very simply given in these facts; there can be no literary genius without freedom of opinion, and freedom of opinion does not exist in America. The Inquisition has never been able to prevent a vast number of anti-religious books from circulating in Spain. The empire of the majority succeeds much better in the United States, since it actually removes the wish of publishing them. Unbelievers are to be met with in America, but, to say the truth, there is no public organ of infidelity. Attempts have been made by some governments to protect the morality of nations by prohibiting licentious books. In the United States no one is punished for this sort of works, but no one is induced to write them; not because all the citizens are immaculate in their manners, but because the majority of the community is decent and orderly.

In these cases the advantages derived from the exercise of this power are unquestionable, and I am simply discussing the nature of the power itself. This irresistible authority is a constant fact, and its judicious exercise is an accidental ocurrence.

. . .

OF THE PRINCIPAL SOURCE OF BELIEF
AMONG DEMOCRATIC NATIONS

When the ranks of society are unequal, and men unlike each other in condition, there are some individuals invested with all the power of superior intelligence, learning, and enlightenment, whilst the multitude is sunk in ignorance and prejudice. Men living at these aristocratic periods are therefore naturally induced to shape their opinions by the superior standard of a person or a class of persons, whilst they are averse to recognize the infallibility of the mass of the people.

The contrary takes place in ages of equality. The nearer the citizens are drawn to the common level of an equal and similar condition, the less prone does each man become to place implicit faith in a certain man or a certain class of men. But his readiness to believe the multitude increases, and opinion is more than ever mistress of the world. Not only is common opinion the only guide which private judgment retains amongst a democratic people, but amongst such a people it possesses a power infinitely beyond what it has elsewhere. At periods of equality men have no faith in one another, by reason of their common resemblance; but this very resemblance gives them almost unbounded confidence in the judgment of the public; for it would not seem probable, as they are all endowed with equal means of judging, but that the greater truth should go with the greater number.

When the inhabitant of a democratic country compares himself individually with all those about him, he feels with pride that he is the equal of any one of them; but when he comes to survey the totality of his fellows, and to place himself in contrast to so huge a body, he is instantly overwhelmed by the sense of his own insignificance and weakness. The same equality which renders him independent of each of his fellow-citizens taken severally, exposes him alone and unprotected to the influence of the greater number. The public has therefore among a democratic people a singular power, of which aristocratic nations could never so much as conceive an idea; for it does not persuade to certain opinions, but it enforces them, and infuses them into the faculties by a sort of enormous pressure of the minds of all upon the reason of each.

In the United States the majority undertakes to supply a multitude of ready-made opinions for the use of individuals, who are thus relieved from the necessity of forming opinions of their own. Everybody there adopts great numbers of theories, on philosophy, morals, and politics, without inquiry, upon public trust; and if we look to it very narrowly, it will be perceived that religion herself holds her sway there, much less as a doctrine of revelation than as a commonly received opinion. The fact that the political laws of the Americans are such that the majority rules the community with sovereign sway, materially increases the power which that majority naturally exercises over the mind. For nothing is more customary in man than to recognize superior wisdom in the person of his oppressor. This political omnipotence of the majority in the United States doubtless augments the influence which public opinion would obtain without it over the mind of each member of the community; but the foundations of that influence do not rest upon it. They must be sought for in the principle of equality itself, not in the more or less popular institutions which men living under that condition may give themselves. The intellectual dominion of the greater number would probably be less absolute amongst a democratic people governed by a king than in the sphere of a pure democracy, but it will always be extremely absolute; and by whatever political laws men are governed in the ages of equality, it may be foreseen that faith in public opinion will become a species of religion there, and the majority its ministering prophet.

Thus intellectual authority will be different, but it will not be diminished; and far from thinking that it will disappear, I augur that it may readily acquire too much preponderance, and confine the action of private judgment within narrower limits than are suited either to the greatness or the happiness of the human race. In the principle of equality I very clearly discern two tendencies: the one leading the mind of every man to untried thoughts, the other inclined to prohibit him from thinking at all. And I perceive how, under the dominion of certain laws, democracy would extinguish that liberty of the mind to which a democratic social condition is favorable; so that, after having broken all the bondage once imposed on it by ranks or by men, the human mind would be closely fettered to the general will of the greatest number.

If the absolute power of the majority were to be substituted by democratic nations, for all the different powers which checked or retarded overmuch the energy of individual minds, the evil would only have changed its symptoms. Men would not have found the means of independent life; they would simply have invented (no easy task) a new dress for servitude. There is—and I cannot repeat it too often—there is in this matter for profound reflection for those who look on freedom as a holy thing, and who hate not only the despot, but despotism. For myself, when I feel the hand of power lie heavy on my brow, I care but little to know who oppresses me; and I am not the more disposed to pass beneath the yoke, because it is held out to me by the arms of a million of men.

. . .

WHY DEMOCRATIC NATIONS SHOW A MORE ARDENT AND ENDURING LOVE OF EQUALITY THAN OF LIBERTY

The first and most intense passion which is engendered by the equality of conditions is, I need hardly say, the love of that same equality. My readers will therefore not be surprised that I speak of it before all others. Everybody has remarked that in our time, and especially in France, this passion for equality is every day gaining ground in the human heart. It has been said a hundred times that our contemporaries are far more ardently and tenaciously attached to equality than to freedom; but as I do not find that the causes of the fact have been sufficiently analyzed, I shall endeavor to point them out.

It is possible to imagine an extreme point at which freedom and equality would meet and be confounded together. Let us suppose that all the members of the community take a part in the government, and that each one of them has an equal right to take a part in it. As none is different from his fellows, none can exercise a tyrannical power: men will be perfectly free, because they will all be entirely equal; and they will all be perfectly equal, because they will be entirely free. To this ideal state democratic nations tend. Such is the completest form that equality can assume upon earth; but there

are a thousand others which, without being equally perfect, are
not less cherished by those nations.

The principle of equality may be established in civil society,
without prevailing in the political world. Equal rights may exist
of indulging in the same pleasures, of entering the same professions,
of frequenting the same places—in a word, of living in the same
manner and seeking wealth by the same means, although all men do
not take an equal share in the government. A kind of equality may
even be established in the political world, though there should be no
political freedom there. A man may be the equal of all his countrymen save one, who is the master of all without distinction, and who
selects equally from among them all the agents of his power. Several
other combinations might be easily imagined, by which very great
equality would be united to institutions more or less free, or even to
institutions wholly without freedom. Although men cannot become
absolutely equal unless they be entirely free, and consequently equality, pushed to its furthest extent, may be confounded with freedom,
yet there is good reason for distinguishing the one from the other.
The taste which men have for liberty, and that which they feel for
equality, are, in fact, two different things; and I am not afraid to add
that, amongst democratic nations, they are two unequal things.

Upon close inspection, it will be seen that there is in every age
some peculiar and preponderating fact with which all others are
connected; this fact almost always gives birth to some pregnant
idea or some ruling passion, which attracts to itself, and bears away
in its course, all the feelings and opinions of the time: it is like a
great stream, towards which each of the surrounding rivulets seems
to flow. Freedom has appeared in the world at different times and
under various forms; it has not been exclusively bound to any social
condition, and it is not confined to democracies. Freedom cannot,
therefore, form the distinguishing characteristic of democratic ages.
The peculiar and preponderating fact which marks those ages as its
own is the equality of conditions; the ruling passion of men in those
periods is the love of this equality. Ask not what singular charm the
men of democratic ages find in being equal, or what special reasons
they may have for clinging so tenaciously to equality rather than
to the other advantages which society holds out to them: equality is
the distinguishing characteristic of the age they live in; that, of itself, is enough to explain that they prefer it to all the rest.

But independently of this reason there are several others, which will at all times habitually lead men to prefer equality to freedom. If a people could ever succeed in destroying, or even in diminishing, the equality which prevails in its own body, this could only be accomplished by long and laborious efforts. Its social condition must be modified, its laws abolished, its opinions superseded, its habits changed, its manners corrupted. But political liberty is more easily lost; to neglect to hold it fast is to allow it to escape. Men therefore not only cling to equality because it is dear to them; they also adhere to it because they think it will last forever.

That political freedom may compromise in its excesses the tranquillity, the property, the lives of individuals, is obvious to the narrowest and most unthinking minds. But, on the contrary, none but attentive and clear-sighted men perceive the perils with which equality threatens us, and they commonly avoid pointing them out. They know that the calamities they apprehend are remote, and flatter themselves that they will only fall upon future generations, for which the present generation takes but little thought. The evils which freedom sometimes brings with it are immediate; they are apparent to all, and all are more or less affected by them. The evils which extreme equality may produce are slowly disclosed; they creep gradually into the social frame; they are only seen at intervals, and at the moment at which they become most violent habit already causes them to be no longer felt. The advantages which freedom brings are only shown by length of time; and it is always easy to mistake the cause in which they originate. The advantages of equality are instantaneous, and they may constantly be traced from their source. Political liberty bestows exalted pleasures, from time to time, upon a certain number of citizens. Equality every day confers a number of small enjoyments on every man. The charms of equality are every instant felt, and are within the reach of all; the noblest hearts are not insensible to them, and the most vulgar souls exult in them. The passion which equality engenders must therefore be at once strong and general. Men cannot enjoy political liberty unpurchased by some sacrifices, and they never obtain it without great exertions. But the pleasures of equality are self-proffered: each of the petty incidents of life seems to occasion them, and in order to taste them nothing is required but to live.

Democratic nations are at all times fond of equality, but there are certain epochs at which the passion they entertain for it swells to the height of fury. This occurs at the moment when the old social system, long menaced, completes its own destruction after a last intestine struggle, and when the barriers of rank are at length thrown down. At such times men pounce upon equality as their booty, and they cling to it as to some precious treasure which they fear to lose. The passion for equality penetrates on every side into men's hearts, expands there, and fills them entirely. Tell them not that by this blind surrender of themselves to an exclusive passion they risk their dearest interests: they are deaf. Show them not freedom escaping from their grasp, whilst they are looking another way: they are blind—or rather, they can discern but one sole object to be desired in the universe.

What I have said is applicable to all democratic nations: what I am about to say concerns the French alone. Amongst most modern nations, and especially amongst all those of the Continent of Europe, the taste and the idea of freedom only began to exist and to extend themselves at the time when social conditions were tending to equality, and as a consequence of that very equality. Absolute kings were the most efficient levellers of ranks amongst their subjects. Amongst these nations equality preceded freedom: equality was therefore a fact of some standing when freedom was still a novelty: the one had already created customs, opinions, and laws belonging to it, when the other, alone and for the first time, came into actual existence. Thus the latter was still only an affair of opinion and of taste, whilst the former had already crept into the habits of the people, possessed itself of their manners, and given a particular turn to the smallest actions of their lives. Can it be wondered that the men of our own time prefer the one to the other?

I think that democratic communities have a natural taste for freedom: left to themselves, they will seek it, cherish it, and view any privation of it with regret. But for equality, their passion is ardent, insatiable, incessant, invincible: they call for equality in freedom; and if they cannot obtain that, they still call for equality in slavery. They will endure poverty, servitude, barbarism—but they will not endure aristocracy. This is true at all times, and especially true in our own. All men and all powers seeking to cope with this irresistible passion, will be overthrown and destroyed by it. In our age, freedom cannot be established without it, and despotism itself cannot reign without its support.

• • •

WHAT SORT OF DESPOTISM DEMOCRATIC NATIONS HAVE TO FEAR

I believe that it is easier to establish an absolute and despotic government amongst a people in which the conditions of society are equal, than amongst any other; and I think that if such a government were once established amongst such a people, it would not only oppress men, but would eventually strip each of them of several of the highest qualities of humanity. Despotism therefore appears to me peculiarly to be dreaded in democratic ages. I should have loved freedom, I believe, at all times, but in the time in which we live I am ready to worship it. On the other hand, I am persuaded that all who shall attempt, in the ages upon which we are entering, to base freedom upon aristocratic privilege, will fail—that all who shall attempt to draw and to retain authority within a single class, will fail. At the present day no ruler is skilful or strong enough to found a despotism, by re-establishing permanent distinctions of rank amongst his subjects: no legislator is wise or powerful enough to preserve free institutions, if he does not take equality for his first principle and his watchword. All those of our contemporaries who would establish or secure the independence and the dignity of their fellow-men, must show themselves the friends of equality; and the only worthy means of showing themselves as such, is to be so: upon this depends the success of their holy enterprise. Thus the question is not how to reconstruct aristocratic society, but how to make liberty proceed out of that democratic state of society in which God has placed us.

These two truths appear to me simple, clear, and fertile in consequences; and they naturally lead me to consider what kind of free government can be established among a people in which social conditions are equal.

It results from the very constitution of democratic nations and from their necessities, that the power of government amongst them must be more uniform, more centralized, more extensive, more searching, and more efficient than in other countries. Society at large is naturally stronger and more active, individuals more subordinate and weak; the former does more, the latter less; and this is inevitably the case. It is not therefore to be expected that the range of private independence will ever be as extensive in democratic as in

aristocratic countries—nor is this to be desired; for, amongst aristocratic nations, the mass is often sacrificed to the individual, and the
prosperity of the greater number to the greatness of the few. It is
both necessary and desirable that the government of a democratic
people should be active and powerful: and our object should not
be to render it weak or indolent, but solely to prevent it from abusing its aptitude and its strength.

. . .

I think that men living in aristocracies may, strictly speaking,
do without the liberty of the press: but such is not the case with
those who live in democratic countries. To protect their personal
independence I trust not to great political assemblies, to parliamentary privilege, or to the assertion of popular sovereignty. All these
things may, to a certain extent, be reconciled with personal servitude
—but that servitude cannot be complete if the press is free: the press
is the chiefest democratic instrument of freedom.

Something analogous may be said of the judicial power. It is a
part of the essence of judicial power to attend to private interests,
and to fix itself with predilection on minute objects submitted to
its observation; another essential quality of judicial power is never
to volunteer its assistance to the oppressed, but always to be at the
disposal of the humblest of those who solicit it; their complaint,
however feeble they may themselves be, will force itself upon the
ear of justice and claim redress, for this is inherent in the very
constitution of the courts of justice. A power of this kind is therefore peculiarly adapted to the wants of freedom, at a time when the
eye and finger of the government are constantly intruding into the
minutest details of human actions, and when private persons are
at once too weak to protect themselves, and too much isolated for
them to reckon upon the assistance of their fellows. The strength of
the courts of law has ever been the greatest security which can be
offered to personal independence; but this is more especially the
case in democratic ages: private rights and interests are in constant
danger, if the judicial power does not grow more extensive and
more strong to keep pace with the growing equality of conditions.

Equality awakens in men several propensities extremely dangerous to freedom, to which the attention of the legislator ought constantly to be directed. I shall only remind the reader of the most
important amongst them. Men living in democratic ages do not

readily comprehend the utility of forms: they feel an instinctive contempt for them—I have elsewhere shown for what reasons. Forms excite their contempt and often their hatred; as they commonly aspire to none but easy and present gratifications, they rush onwards to the object of their desires, and the slightest delay exasperates them. This same temper, carried with them into political life, renders them hostile to forms, which perpetually retard or arrest them in some of their projects. Yet this objection which the men of democracies make to forms is the very thing which renders forms so useful to freedom; for their chief merit is to serve as a barrier between the strong and the weak, the ruler and the people, to retard the one, and give the other time to look about him. Forms become more necessary in proportion as the government becomes more active and more powerful, whilst private persons are becoming more indolent and more feeble. Thus democratic nations naturally stand more in need of forms than other nations, and they naturally respect them less. This deserves most serious attention. Nothing is more pitiful than the arrogant disdain of most of our contemporaries for questions of form; for the smallest questions of form have acquired in our time an importance which they never had before: many of the greatest interests of mankind depend upon them. I think that if the statesmen of aristocratic ages could sometimes contemn forms with impunity, and frequently rise above them, the statesmen to whom the government of nations is now confided ought to treat the very least among them with respect, and not neglect them without imperious necessity. In aristocracies the observance of forms was superstitious; amongst us they ought to be kept with a deliberate and enlightened deference.

Another tendency, which is extremely natural to democratic nations and extremely dangerous, is that which leads them to despise and undervalue the rights of private persons. The attachment which men feel to a right, and the respect which they display for it, is generally proportioned to its importance, or to the length of time during which they have enjoyed it. The rights of private persons amongst democratic nations are commonly of small importance, of recent growth, and extremely precarious—the consequence is that they are often sacrificed without regret, and almost always violated without remorse. But it happens that at the same period and amongst the same nations in which men conceive a natural contempt for the rights of private persons, the rights of society at large are naturally extended and consolidated: in other words, men become less attached to private rights at the very time at which it would be most necessary to retain and to defend what little remains of them. It is therefore most especially in the present democratic ages, that the true friends of the liberty and the greatness of man ought constantly to be on the alert to prevent the power of government from lightly sacrificing the private rights of individuals to the general execution of its designs. At such times no citizen is so obscure that it is not very dangerous to allow him to be oppressed—no private rights are so unimportant that they can be surrendered with impunity to the caprices of a government. The reason is plain:—if the private right of an individual is violated at a time when the human mind is fully impressed with the importance and the sanctity of such rights, the injury done is confined to the individual whose right is infringed; but to violate such a right, at the present day, is deeply to corrupt the manners of the nation and to put the whole community in jeopardy, because the very notion of this kind of right constantly tends amongst us to be impaired and lost.

* * *

I shall conclude by one general idea, which comprises not only all the particular ideas which have been expressed in the present chapter, but also most of those which it is the object of this book to treat of. In the ages of aristocracy which preceded our own, there were private persons of great power, and a social authority of extreme weakness. The outline of society itself was not easily discernible, and constantly confounded with the different powers by which the community was ruled. The principal efforts of the men of those times were required to strengthen, aggrandize, and secure the supreme power; and on the other hand, to circumscribe individual independence within narrower limits, and to subject private interests to the interests of the public. Other perils and other cares await the men of our age. Amongst the greater part of modern nations, the government, whatever may be its origin, its constitution, or its name, has become almost omnipotent, and private persons are falling, more and more, into the lowest stage of weakness and dependence. In olden society everything was different; unity and uniformity were nowhere to be met with. In modern society everything threatens to become so much alike, that the peculiar characteristics of each individual will soon be entirely lost in the general aspect of the world. Our forefathers were ever prone to make an improper use of the notion, that private rights ought to be respected; and we are naturally prone on the other hand to exaggerate the idea that the interest of a private individual ought always to bend to the interest of the many. The political world is metamorphosed: new remedies must henceforth be sought for new disorders. To lay down extensive, but distinct and settled limits, to the action of the government; to confer certain rights on private persons, and to secure to them the undisputed enjoyment of those rights; to enable individual man to maintain whatever independence, strength, and original power he still possesses; to raise him by the side of society at large, and uphold him in that position—these appear to me the main objects of legislators in the ages upon which we are now entering. It would seem as if the rulers of our time sought only to use men in order to make things great; I wish that they would try a little more to make great men; that they would set less value on the work, and more upon the workman; that they would never forget that a nation cannot long remain strong when every man belonging to it is individually weak, and that no form or combination of social polity has yet been devised, to make an energetic people out of a community of pusillanimous and enfeebled citizens.

I trace amongst our contemporaries two contrary notions which are equally injurious. One set of men can perceive nothing in the principle of equality but the anarchical tendencies which it engenders: they dread their own free agency—they fear themselves. Other thinkers, less numerous but more enlightened, take a different view: besides that track which starts from the principle of equality to terminate in anarchy, they have at last discovered the road which seems to lead men to inevitable servitude. They shape their souls beforehand to this necessary condition; and, despairing of remaining free, they already do obeisance in their hearts to the master who is soon to appear. The former abandon freedom, because they think it dangerous; the latter, because they hold it to be impossible. If I had entertained the latter conviction, I should not have written this book, but I should have confined myself to deploring in secret the destiny of mankind. I have sought to point out the dangers to which the principle of equality exposes the independence of man, because I firmly believe that these dangers are the most formidable, as well as the least foreseen, of all those which futurity holds in store: but I do not think that they are insurmountable. The men who live in the democratic ages upon which we are entering have naturally a taste for independence: they are naturally impatient of regulation, and they are wearied by the permanence even of the condition they themselves prefer. They are fond of power; but they are prone to despise and hate those who wield it, and they easily elude its grasp by their own mobility and insignificance. These propensities will always manifest themselves, because they originate in the groundwork of society, which will undergo no change: for a long time they will prevent the establishment of any despotism, and they will furnish fresh weapons to each succeeding generation which shall struggle in favor of the liberty of mankind. Let us then look forward to the future with that salutary fear which makes men keep watch and ward for freedom, not with that faint and idle terror which depresses and enervates the heart.

John Stuart Mill

17

On Liberty

The full flowering of liberal thought came in the work of John Stuart Mill (1806–1873), known as "the Aristotle of the Victorian Age" for his versatility and the reasonableness of his views. Mill was a liberal in politics who favored a democratic base for representation, an economist who balanced laissez faire and positive government, an empiricist in philosophy, and a secular humanist in religion. He was, in short, representative of the mind of middle-class England at its best in the mid-nineteenth century. Mills came to symbolize liberalism as a way of life, with its broad sympathies and its dedication to the improvement of mankind in freedom.

Mill's views were rooted in the doctrinaire rationalism of his father, James Mill, who rigidly directed his son's education in the principles of Jeremy Bentham's utilitarianism. In his twenties, however, the young Mill underwent a psychological crisis induced by his reading the romantic poets and philosophers. As a result, he rebelled against what seemed to him the barren, calculating rationalism of Bentham and adopted a more positive, complex, and flexible point of view. While receptive to the romantic and democratic currents of mid-century European thought, Mill remained dedicated to objective, rational methods and never forsook his belief in individualism. He was, at the same time, an active social reformer who worked for all the "good causes" of his day.

On Liberty (1859) was Mill's greatest contribution to social thought. It was an eloquent essay on "the nature and limits of the power which can be legitimately exercised by society over the individual," and it offered a rational defense of a balanced position between individual freedom and social necessity. For Mill, positive, individual liberty was necessary both to achieve the personal happiness of self-realization and the advancement of the welfare of society. He insisted, moreover, on the necessity for unrestricted competition of ideas as the social means for discovery of truth.

John Stuart Mill, *On Liberty* (London: John W. Parker & Son, 1859), 21–44, 94–99, 134–38, 140–41, 207.

Although Mill's view of society—as an atomistic aggregation of individuals
—is no longer consonant with reality, his views on intellectual freedom are
enduring ideals of the Western world.

The object of this Essay is to assert one very simple principle, as
entitled to govern absolutely the dealings of society with the individual in the way of compulsion and control, whether the means
used be physical force in the form of legal penalties, or the moral
coercion of public opinion. That principle is, that the sole end for
which mankind are warranted, individually or collectively, in interfering with the liberty of action of any of their number, is self-
protection. That the only purpose for which power can be rightfully exercised over any member of a civilized community, against
his will, is to prevent harm to others. His own good, either physical
or moral, is not a sufficient warrant. He cannot rightfully be compelled to do or forbear because it will be better for him to do so,
because it will make him happier, because, in the opinions of others,
to do so would be wise, or even right. These are good reasons for
remonstrating with him, or reasoning with him, or persuading him,
or entreating him, but not for compelling him, or visiting him with
any evil in case he do otherwise. To justify that, the conduct from
which it is desired to deter him, must be calculated to produce evil
to some one else. The only part of the conduct of any one, for which
he is amenable to society, is that which concerns others. In the part
which merely concerns himself, his independence is, of right, absolute. Over himself, over his own body and mind, the individual is
sovereign.

                                    •   •   •

It is proper to state that I forego any advantage which could be
derived to my argument from the idea of abstract right, as a thing
independent of utility. I regard utility as the ultimate appeal on
all ethical questions; but it must be utility in the largest sense,
grounded on the permanent interests of man as a progressive being.
Those interests, I contend, authorize the subjection of individual
spontaneity to external control, only in respect to those actions of
each, which concern the interest of other people. If any one does an

act hurtful to others, there is a *prima facie* case for punishing him, by law, or, where legal penalties are not safely applicable, by general disapprobation. There are also many positive acts for the benefit of others, which he may rightfully be compelled to perform; such as, to give evidence in a court of justice; to bear his fair share in the common defence, or in any other joint work necessary to the interest of the society of which he enjoys the protection; and to perform certain acts of individual beneficence, such as saving a fellow-creature's life, or interposing to protect the defenceless against ill-usage, things which whenever it is obviously a man's duty to do, he may rightfully be made responsible to society for not doing. A person may cause evil to others not only by his actions but by his inaction, and in either case he is justly accountable to them for the injury. The latter case, it is true, requires a much more cautious exercise of compulsion than the former. To make any one answerable for doing evil to others, is the rule; to make him answerable for not preventing evil, is, comparatively speaking, the exception. Yet there are many cases clear enough and grave enough to justify that exception. In all things which regard the external relations of the individual, he is *de jure* amenable to those whose interests are concerned, and if need be, to society as their protector. There are often good reasons for not holding him to the responsibility; but these reasons must arise from the special expediencies of the case: either because it is a kind of case in which he is on the whole likely to act better, when left to his own discretion, than when controlled in any way in which society have it in their power to control him; or because the attempt to exercise control would produce other evils, greater than those which it would prevent. When such reasons as these preclude the enforcement of responsibility, the conscience of the agent himself should step into the vacant judgment seat, and protect those interests of others which have no external protection; judging himself all the more rigidly, because the case does not admit of his being made accountable to the judgment of his fellow-creatures.

But there is a sphere of action in which society, as distinguished from the individual, has, if any, only an indirect interest; comprehending all that portion of a person's life and conduct which affects only himself, or if it also affects others, only with their free, voluntary, and undeceived consent and participation. When I say only himself, I mean directly, and in the first instance: for whatever affects himself, may affect others *through* himself; and the objection which may be grounded on this contingency, will receive consideration in the sequel. This, then, is the appropriate region of human liberty. It comprises, first, the inward domain of consciousness; demanding liberty of conscience, in the most comprehensive sense; liberty of thought and feeling; absolute freedom of opinion and sentiment on all subjects, practical or speculative, scientific, moral, or theological. The liberty of expressing and publishing opinions may seem to fall under a different principle, since it belongs to that part of the conduct of an individual which concerns other people; but, being almost of as much importance as the liberty of thought itself, and resting in great part on the same reasons, is practically inseparable from it. Secondly, the principle requires liberty of tastes and pursuits; of framing the plan of our life to suit our own character; of doing as we like, subject to such consequences as may follow: without impediment from our fellow-creatures, so long as what we do does not harm them, even though they should think our conduct foolish, perverse, or wrong. Thirdly, from this liberty of each individual, follows the liberty, within the same limits, of combination among individuals; freedom to unite, for any purpose not involving harm to others: the persons combining being supposed to be of full age, and not forced or deceived.

No society in which these liberties are not, on the whole, respected, is free, whatever may be its form of government; and none is completely free in which they do not exist absolute and unqualified. The only freedom which deserves the name, is that of pursuing our own good in our own way, so long as we do not attempt to deprive others of theirs, or impede their efforts to obtain it. Each is the proper guardian of his own health, whether bodily, or mental and spiritual. Mankind are greater gainers by suffering each other to live as seems good to themselves, than by compelling each to live as seems good to the rest.

Though this doctrine is anything but new, and, to some persons, may have the air of a truism, there is no doctrine which stands more directly opposed to the general tendency of existing opinion and practice. Society has expended fully as much effort in the attempt (according to its lights) to compel people to conform to its notions of personal, as of social excellence. The ancient commonwealths thought themselves entitled to practice, and the ancient philosophers countenanced, the regulation of every part of private conduct by public authority, on the ground that the State had a deep interest in the whole bodily and mental discipline of every one of its citizens; a mode of thinking which may have been admissible in small republics surrounded by powerful enemies, in constant peril of being subverted by foreign attack or internal commotion, and to which even a short interval of relaxed energy and self-command might so easily be fatal, that they could not afford to wait for the salutary permanent effects of freedom. In the modern world, the greater size of political communities, and above all, the separation between spiritual and temporal authority (which placed the direction of men's consciences in other hands than those which controlled their worldly affairs), prevented so great an interference by law in the details of private life; but the engines of moral repression have been wielded more strenuously against divergence from the reigning opinion in self-regarding, than even in social matters; religion, the most powerful of the elements which have entered into the formation of moral feeling, having almost always been governed either by the ambition of a hierarchy, seeking control over every department of human conduct, or by the spirit of Puritanism.

· · ·

Apart from the peculiar tenets of individual thinkers, there is also in the world at large an increasing inclination to stretch unduly the powers of society over the individual, both by the force of opinion and even by that of legislation: and as the tendency of all the changes taking place in the world is to strengthen society, and diminish the power of the individual, this encroachment is not one of the evils which tend spontaneously to disappear, but, on the contrary, to grow more and more formidable. The disposition of mankind, whether as rulers or as fellow-citizens, to impose their own opinions and inclinations as a rule of conduct on others, is so energetically supported by some of the best and by some of the worst feelings incident to human nature, that it is hardly ever kept under restraint by anything but want of power; and as the power is not declining, but growing, unless a strong barrier of moral conviction can be raised against the mischief, we must expect, in the present circumstances of the world, to see it increase.

It will be convenient for the argument, if, instead of at once entering upon the general thesis, we confine ourselves in the first instance to a single branch of it, on which the principle here stated is, if not fully, yet to a certain point, recognised by the current opinions. This one branch is the Liberty of Thought: from which it is impossible to separate the cognate liberty of speaking and of writing. Although these liberties, to some considerabe amount, form part of the political morality of all countries which profess religious toleration and free institutions, the grounds, both philosophical and practical, on which they rest, are perhaps not so familiar to the general mind, nor so thoroughly appreciated by many even of the leaders of opinion, as might have been expected. Those grounds, when rightly understood, are of much wider application than to only one division of the subject, and a thorough consideration of this part of the question will be found the best introduction to the remainder. Those to whom nothing which I am about to say will be new, may therefore, I hope, excuse me, if on the subject which for now three centuries has been so often discussed, I venture on one discussion more.

OF THE LIBERTY OF THOUGHT AND DISCUSSION

The time, it is to be hoped, is gone by, when any defence would be necessary of the 'liberty of the press' as one of the securities against corrupt or tyrannical government. No argument, we may suppose, can now be needed, against permitting a legislature or an executive, not identified in interest with the people, to prescribe opinions to them, and determine what doctrines or what arguments they shall be allowed to hear. This aspect of the question, besides, has been so often and so triumphantly enforced by preceding writers, that it needs not be specially insisted on in this place. Though the law of England, on the subject of the press, is as servile to this day as it was in the time of the Tudors, there is little danger of its being actually put in force against political discussion, except during some temporary panic, when fear of insurrection drives ministers and judges from their propriety; and, speaking generally, it is not, in constitutional countries, to be apprehended, that the government, whether completely responsible to the people or not, will often attempt to control the expression of opinion, except when in doing so it makes itself the organ of the general intolerance of the public. Let us suppose, therefore, that the government is entirely at one with the people, and never thinks of exerting any power of coercion unless in agreement with what it conceives to be their voice. But

I deny the right of the people to exercise such coercion, either by themselves or by their government. The power itself is illegitimate. The best government has no more title to it than the worst. It is as noxious, or more noxious, when exerted in accordance with public opinion, than when in opposition to it. If all mankind minus one, were of one opinion, and only one person were of the contrary opinion, mankind would be no more justified in silencing that one person, than he, if he had the power, would be justified in silencing mankind. Were an opinion a personal possession of no value except to the owner; if to be obstructed in the enjoyment of it were simply a private injury, it would make some difference whether the injury was inflicted only on a few persons or on many. But the peculiar evil of silencing the expression of an opinion is, that it is robbing the human race; posterity as well as the existing generation; those who dissent from the opinion, still more than those who hold it. If the opinion is right, they are deprived of the opportunity of exchanging error for truth: if wrong, they lose, what is almost as great a benefit, the clearer perception and livelier impression of truth, produced by its collision with error.

It is necessary to consider separately these two hypotheses, each of which has a distinct branch of the argument corresponding to it. We can never be sure that the opinion we are endeavouring to stifle is a false opinion; and if we were sure, stifling it would be an evil still.

First: the opinion which it is attempted to suppress by authority may possibly be true. Those who desire to suppress it, of course deny its truth; but they are not infallible. They have no authority to decide the question for all mankind, and exclude every other person from the means of judging. To refuse a hearing to an opinion, because they are sure that it is false, is to assume that their certainty is the same thing as absolute certainty. All silencing of discussion is an assumption of infallibility. Its condemnation may be allowed to rest on this common argument, not the worse for being common.

Unfortunately for the good sense of mankind, the fact of their fallibility is far from carrying the weight in their practical judgment, which is always allowed to it in theory; for while every one well knows himself to be fallible, few think it necessary to take any precautions against their own fallibility, or admit the supposition that any opinion, of which they feel very certain, may be one of the examples of the error to which they acknowledge themselves to be liable. Absolute princes, or others who are accustomed to unlimited deference, usually feel this complete confidence in their own opinions on nearly all subjects. People more happily situated, who sometimes hear their opinions disputed, and are not wholly unused to be set right when they are wrong, place the same unbounded reliance only on such of their opinions as are shared by all who surround them, or to whom they habitually defer: for in proportion to a man's want of confidence in his own solitary judgment, does he usually repose, with implicit trust, on the infallibility of 'the world' in general. And the world, to each individual, means the part of it with which he comes in contact; his party, his sect, his church, his class of society: the man may be called, by comparison, almost liberal and large-minded to whom it means anything so comprehensive as his own country or his own age. Nor is his faith in this collective authority at all shaken by his being aware that other ages, countries, sects, churches, classes, and parties have thought, and even now think, the exact reverse. He devolves upon his own world the responsibility of being in the right against the dissentient worlds of other people; and it never troubles him that mere accident has decided which of these numerous worlds is the object of his reliance, and that the same causes which make him a Churchman in London, would have made him a Buddhist or a Confucian in Pekin. Yet it is as evident in itself, as any amount of argument can make it, that ages are no more infallible than individuals; every age having held many opinions which subsequent ages have deemed not only false but absurd; and it is as certain that many opinions, now general, will be rejected by future ages, as it is that many, once general, are rejected by the present.

The objection likely to be made to this argument, would probably take some such form as the following. There is no greater assumption of infallibility in forbidding the propagation of error, than in any other thing which is done by public authority on its own judgment and responsibility. Judgment is given to men that they may use it. Because it may be used erroneously, are men to be told that they ought not to use it at all? To prohibit what they think pernicious, is not claiming exemption from error, but fulfilling the duty incumbent on them, although fallible, of acting on their conscientious conviction. If we were never to act on our opinions, because those opinions may be wrong, we should leave all our interests uncared for, and all our duties unperformed. An objection which applies to all conduct, can be no valid objection to any conduct in particular. It is the duty of governments, and of individuals, to form the truest opinions they can; to form them carefully, and never impose them upon others unless they are quite sure of being right. But when they are sure (such reasoners may say), it is not conscientiousness but cowardice to shrink from acting on their opinions, and allow doctrines which they honestly think dangerous to the welfare of mankind, either in this life or in another, to be scattered abroad without restraint, because other people, in less enlightened times, have persecuted opinions now believed to be true. Let us take care, it may be said, not to make the same mistake: but governments and nations have made mistakes in other things, which are not denied to be fit subjects for the exercise of authority: they have laid on bad taxes, made unjust wars. Ought we therefore to lay on no taxes, and, under whatever provocation, make no wars? Men, and governments, must act to the best of their ability. There is no such thing as absolute certainty, but there is assurance sufficient for the purposes of human life. We may, and must, assume our opinion to be true for the guidance of our own conduct: and it is assuming no more when we forbid bad men to pervert society by the propagation of opinions which we regard as false and pernicious.

I answer, that it is assuming very much more. There is the greatest difference between presuming an opinion to be true, because, with every opportunity for contesting it, it has not been refuted, and assuming its truth for the purpose of not permitting its refutation. Complete liberty of contradicting and disproving our opinion, is the very condition which justifies us in assuming its truth for purposes of action; and on no other terms can a being with human faculties have any rational assurance of being right.

When we consider either the history of opinion, or the ordinary conduct of human life, to what is it to be ascribed that the one and the other are no worse than they are? Not certainly to the inherent force of the human understanding; for, on any matter not self-evident, there are ninety-nine persons totally incapable of judging of it, for one who is capable; and the capacity of the hundredth person is only comparative; for the majority of the eminent men of every past generation held many opinions now known to be erroneous, and did or approved numerous things which no one will now justify. Why is it, then, that there is on the whole a preponderance among mankind of rational opinions and rational conduct? If there really is this preponderance—which there must be, unless human affairs are, and have always been, in an almost desperate state—it is owing to a quality of the human mind, the source of everything respectable in man either as an intellectual or as a moral being, namely, that his errors are corrigible. He is capable of rectifying his mistakes, by discussion and experience. Not by experience alone. There must be discussion, to show how experience is to be interpreted. Wrong opinions and practices gradually yield to fact and argument: but facts and arguments, to produce any effect on the mind, must be brought before it. Very few facts are able to tell their own story, without comments to bring out their meaning. The whole strength and value, then, of human judgment, depending on the one property, that it can be set right when it is wrong, reliance can be placed on it only when the means of setting it right are kept constantly at hand. In the case of any person whose judgment is really deserving of confidence, how has it become so? Because he has kept his mind open to criticism of his opinions and conduct. Because it has been his practice to listen to all that could be said against him; to profit by as much of it as was just, and expound to himself, and upon occasion to others, the fallacy of what was fallacious. Because he has felt, that the only way in which a human being can make some approach to knowing the whole of a subject, is by hearing what can be said about it by persons of every variety of opinion, and studying all modes in which it can be looked at by every character of mind. No wise man ever acquired his wisdom in any mode but this; nor is it in the nature of human intellect to become wise in any other manner. The steady habit of correcting and completing his own opinion by collating it with those of others, so far from causing doubt and hesitation in carrying it into practice, is the only stable foundation for a just reliance on it: for, being cognisant of all that can, at least obviously, be said against him, and having taken up his position against all gainsayers—knowing that he has sought for objections and difficulties, instead of avoiding them, and has shut out no light which can be thrown upon the subject from any quarter—he has a right to think his judgment better than that of any person, or any multitude, who have not gone through a similar process.

It is not too much to require that what the wisest of mankind, those who are best entitled to trust their own judgment, find necessary to warrant their relying on it, should be submitted to by that miscellaneous collection of a few wise and many foolish individuals, called the public. The most intolerant of churches, the Roman Catholic Church, even at the canonization of a saint, admits, and listens patiently to, a 'devil's advocate.' The holiest of men, it appears, cannot be admitted to posthumous honours, until all that the devil could say against him is known and weighed. If even the Newtonian philosophy were not permitted to be questioned, mankind could not feel as complete assurance of its truth as they now do. The beliefs which we have most warrant for, have no safeguard to rest on, but a standing invitation to the whole world to prove them unfounded. If the challenge is not accepted, or is accepted and the attempt fails, we are far enough from certainty still; but we have done the best that the existing state of human reason admits of; we have neglected nothing that could give the truth a chance of reaching us: if the lists are kept open, we may hope that if there be a better truth, it will be found when the human mind is capable of receiving it; and in the meantime we may rely on having attained such approach to truth, as is possible in our own day. This is the amount of certainty attainable by a fallible being, and this the sole way of attaining it.

Strange it is, that men should admit the validity of the arguments for free discussion, but object to their being 'pushed to an extreme;' not seeing that unless the reasons are good for an extreme case, they are not good for any case. Strange that they should imagine that they are not assuming infallibility, when they acknowledge that there should be free discussion on all subjects which can possibly be *doubtful,* but think that some particular principle or doctrine should be forbidden to be questioned because it is *so certain,* that is, because *they are certain* that it is certain. To call any proposition certain, while there is any one who would deny its certainty if permitted, but who is not permitted, is to assume that we ourselves, and those who agree with us, are the judges of certainty, and judges without hearing the other side.

In the present age—which has been described as 'destitute of faith, but terrified at scepticism'—in which people feel sure, not so much that their opinions are true, as that they should not know what to do without them—the claims of an opinion to be protected from public attack are rested not so much on its truth, as on its importance to society. There are, it is alleged, certain beliefs, so useful, not to say indispensable to well-being, that it is as much the duty of governments to uphold those beliefs, as to protect any other of the interests of society. In a case of such necessity, and so directly in the line of their duty, something less than infallibility may, it is maintained, warrant, and even bind, governments, to act on their own opinion, confirmed by the general opinion of mankind. It is also often argued, and still oftener thought, that none but bad men would desire to weaken these salutary beliefs; and there can be nothing wrong, it is thought, in restraining bad men, and prohibiting what only such men would wish to practice. This mode of thinking makes the justification of restraints on discussion not a question of the truth of doctrines, but of their usefulness; and flatters itself by that means to escape the responsibility of claiming to be an infallible judge of opinions. But those who thus satisfy themselves, do not perceive that the assumption of infallibility is merely shifted from one point to another. The usefulness of an opinion is itself matter of opinion: as disputable, as open to discussion, and requiring discussion as much, as the opinion itself. There is the same need of an infallible judge of opinions to decide an opinion to be noxious, as to decide it to be false, unless the opinion condemned has full opportunity of defending itself. And it will not do to say that the heretic may be allowed to maintain the utility or harmlessness of his opinion, though forbidden to maintain its truth. The truth of an opinion is part of its utility. If we would know whether or not it is desirable that a proposition should be believed, is it possible to exclude the consideration of whether or not it is true? In the opinion, not of bad men, but of the best men, no belief which is contrary to truth can be really useful: and can you prevent such men from urging that plea, when they are charged with culpability for denying some doctrine which they are told is useful, but which they believe to be false? Those who are on the side of received opinions, never fail to take all possible advantage of this plea; you do not find *them* handling the question of utility as if it could be completely abstracted from that of truth: on the contrary, it is, above all, because their doctrine is 'the truth,' that the knowledge or the belief of it is held to be so indispensable. There can be no fair discussion of the question of usefulness, when an argument so vital may be employed on one side, but not on the other. And in point of fact, when law or public feeling do not permit the truth of an opinion to be disputed, they are just as little tolerant of a denial of its usefulness. The utmost they allow is an extenuation of its absolute necessity, or of the positive guilt of rejecting it.

. . .

We have now recognised the necessity to the mental well-being of mankind (on which all their other well-being depends) of freedom of opinion, and freedom of the expression of opinion, on four distinct grounds; which we will now briefly recapitulate.

First, if any opinion is compelled to silence, that opinion may, for aught we can certainly know, be true. To deny this is to assume our own infallibility.

Secondly, though the silenced opinion be an error, it may, and very commonly does, contain a portion of truth; and since the general or prevailing opinion on any subject is rarely or never the whole truth, it is only by the collision of adverse opinions that the remainder of the truth has any chance of being supplied.

Thirdly, even if the received opinion be not only true, but the whole truth; unless it is suffered to be, and actually is, vigorously and earnestly contested, it will, by most of those who receive it, be held in the manner of a prejudice, with little comprehension or feeling of its rational grounds. And not only this, but, fourthly, the meaning of the doctrine itself will be in danger of being lost, or enfeebled, and deprived of its vital effect on the character and conduct: the dogma becoming a mere formal profession, inefficacious for good, but cumbering the ground, and preventing the growth of any real and heartfelt conviction, from reason or personal experience.

Before quitting the subject of freedom of opinion, it is fit to take some notice of those who say, that the free expression of all opinions should be permitted, on condition that the manner be temperate, and do not pass the bounds of fair discussion. Much might be said on the impossibility of fixing where these supposed bounds are to be placed; for if the test be offence to those whose opinion is attacked, I think experience testifies that this offence is given whenever the attack is telling and powerful, and that every opponent who pushes them hard, and whom they find it difficult to answer, appears to them, if he shows any strong feeling on the subject, an intemperate opponent. But this, though an important consideration in a practical point of view, merges in a more fundamental objection. Undoubtedly the manner of asserting an opinion, even though it be a true one, may be very objectionable, and may justly incur severe censure. But the principal offences of the kind are such as it is mostly impossible, unless by accidental self-betrayal, to bring home to conviction. The gravest of them is, to argue sophistically, to suppress facts or arguments, to misstate the elements of the case, or misrepresent the opposite opinion. But all this, even to the most aggravated degree, is so continually done in perfect good faith, by persons who are not considered, and in many other respects may not deserve to be considered, ignorant or incompetent, that it is rarely possible on adequate grounds conscientiously to stamp the misrepresentation as morally culpable; and still less could law presume to interfere with this kind of controversial misconduct. With regard to what is commonly meant by intemperate discussion, namely invective, sarcasm, personality, and the like, the denunciation of these weapons would deserve more sympathy if it were ever proposed to interdict them equally to both sides; but it is only desired to restrain the employment of them against the prevailing opinion: against the unprevailing they may not only be used without general disapproval, but will be likely to obtain for him who uses them the praise of honest zeal and righteous indignation. Yet whatever mischief arises from their use, is greatest when they are employed against the comparatively defenceless; and whatever unfair advantage can be derived by any opinion from this mode of asserting it, accrues almost exclusively to received opinions. The worst offence of this kind which can be committed by a polemic, is to stigmatize those who hold the contrary opinion as bad and immoral men. To calumny of this sort, those who hold any unpopular opinion are peculiarly exposed, because they are in general few and uninfluential, and nobody but themselves feels much interest in seeing justice done them; but this weapon is, from the nature of the case, denied to those who attack a prevailing opinion: they can neither use it with safety to themselves, nor, if they could, would it do anything but recoil on their own cause. In general, opinions contrary to those commonly received can only obtain a hearing by studied moderation of language, and the most cautious avoidance of unnecessary offence, from which they hardly ever deviate even in a slight degree without losing ground: while unmeasured vituperation employed on the side of the prevailing opinion, really does deter people from professing contrary opinions, and from listening to those who profess them. For the interest, therefore, of truth and justice, it is far more important to restrain this employment of vituperative language than the other; and, for example, if it were necessary to choose, there would be much more need to discourage offensive attacks on infidelity, than on religion. It is, however, obvious that law and authority have no business with restraining either, while opinion ought, in every instance, to determine its verdict by the circumstances of the individual case; condemning every one, on whichever side of the argument he places himself, in whose mode of advocacy either want of candour, or malignity, bigotry, or intolerance of feeling manifest themselves; but not inferring these vices from the side of the question to our own: and giving merited honour to every one, whatever opinion he may hold, who has calmness to see and honesty to state what his opponents and their opinions really are, exaggerating nothing to their discredit, keeping nothing back which tells, or can be supposed to tell, in their favour. This is the real morality of public discussion; and if often violated, I am happy to think that there are many controversialists who to a great extent observe it, and a still greater number who conscientiously strive towards it.

. . .

OF THE LIMITS TO THE AUTHORITY OF SOCIETY
OVER THE INDIVIDUAL

What, then, is the rightful limit to the sovereignty of the individual over himself? Where does the authority of society begin? How much of human life should be assigned to individuality, and how much to society?

Each will receive its proper share, if each has that which more particularly concerns it. To individuality should belong the part of life in which it is chiefly the individual that is interested; to society, the part which chiefly interests society.

Though society is not founded on a contract, and though no good purpose is answered by inventing a contract in order to deduce social obligations from it, every one who receives the protection of society owes a return for the benefit, and the fact of living in society renders it indispensable that each should be bound to observe a certain line of conduct towards the rest. This conduct consists, first, in not injuring the interests of one another; or rather certain in-

terests, which, either by express legal provision or by tacit understanding, ought to be considered as rights; and secondly, in each
person's bearing his share (to be fixed on some equitable principle)
of the labors and sacrifices incurred for defending the society or its
members from injury and molestation. These conditions society is
justified in enforcing, at all costs to those who endeavor to withhold
fulfilment. Nor is this all that society may do. The acts of an individual may be hurtful to others, or wanting in due consideration
for their welfare, without going the length of violating any of their
constituted rights. The offender may then be justly punished by
opinion, though not by law. As soon as any part of a person's conduct affects prejudicially the interests of others, society has jurisdiction over it, and the question whether the general welfare will or
will not be promoted by interfering with it, becomes open to discussion. But there is no room for entertaining any such question
when a person's conduct affects the interests of no persons besides
himself, or needs not affect them unless they like (all the persons
concerned being of full age and the ordinary amount of understanding). In all such cases there should be perfect freedom, legal
and social, to do the action and stand the consequences.

It would be a great misunderstanding of this doctrine, to suppose
that it is one of selfish indifference, which pretends that human
beings have no business with each other's conduct in life, and
that they should not concern themselves about the well-doing or
well-being of one another, unless their own interest is involved.
Instead of any diminution, there is need of a great increase of disinterested exertion to promote the good of others. But disinterested
benevolence can find other instruments to persuade people to their
good, than whips and scourges, either of the literal or the metaphorical sort. I am the last person to undervalue the self-regarding virtues;
they are only second in importance, if even second, to the social. It is
equally the business of education to cultivate both. But even education works by conviction and persuasion as well as by compulsion,
and it is by the former only that, when the period of education is
past, the self-regarding virtues should be inculcated. Human beings
owe to each other help to distinguish the better from the worse, and
encouragement to choose the former and avoid the latter. They
should be forever stimulating each other to increased exercise of
their higher faculties, and increased direction of their feelings and
aims towards wise instead of foolish, elevating instead of degrading,

objects and contemplations. But neither one person, nor any number of persons, is warranted in saying to another human creature of ripe years, that he shall not do with his life for his own benefit what he chooses to do with it. He is the person most interested in his own well-being: the interest which any other person, except in cases of strong personal attachment, can have in it, is trifling, compared with that which he himself has; the interest which society has in him individually (except as to his conduct to others) is fractional, and altogether indirect: while, with respect to his own feelings and circumstances, the most ordinary man or woman has means of knowledge immeasurably surpassing those that can be possessed by any one else. The interference of society to overrule his judgment and purposes in what only regards himself, must be grounded on general presumptions; which may be altogether wrong, and even if right, are as likely as not to be misapplied to individual cases, by persons no better acquainted with the circumstances of such cases than those are who look at them merely from without. In this department, therefore, of human affairs, Individuality has its proper field of action. In the conduct of human beings towards one another, it is necessary that general rules should for the most part be observed, in order that people may know what they have to expect; but in each person's own concerns, his individual spontaneity is entitled to free exercise. Considerations to aid his judgment, exhortations to strengthen his will, may be offered to him, even obtruded on him, by others; but he, himself, is the final judge. All errors which he is likely to commit against advice and warning, are far outweighed by the evil of allowing others to constrain him to what they deem his good.

*   *   *

What I contend for is, that the inconveniences which are strictly inseparable from the unfavorable judgment of others, are the only ones to which a person should ever be subjected for that portion of his conduct and character which concerns his own good, but which does not affect the interests of others in their relations with him. Acts injurious to others require a totally different treatment. Encroachment on their rights; infliction on them of any loss or damage not justified by his own rights; falsehood or duplicity in dealing with them; unfair or ungenerous use of advantages over them: even selfish abstinence from defending them against injury—

these are fit objects of moral reprobation, and, in grave cases, of moral retribution and punishment. And not only these acts, but the dispositions which lead to them, are properly immoral, and fit subjects of disapprobation which may rise to abhorrence. Cruelty of disposition; malice and ill-nature; that most anti-social and odious of all passions, envy; dissimulation and insincerity; irascibility on insufficient cause, and resentment disproportioned to the provocation; the love of domineering over others; the desire to engross more than one's share of advantages (the πλεονεξία of the Greeks); the pride which derives gratification from the abasement of others; the egotism which thinks self and its concerns more important than everything else, and decides all doubtful questions in his own favor;—these are moral vices, and constitute a bad and odious moral character: unlike the self-regarding faults previously mentioned, which are not properly immoralities, and to whatever pitch they may be carried, do not constitute wickedness. They may be proofs of any amount of folly, or want of personal dignity and self-respect; but they are only a subject of moral reprobation when they involve a breach of duty to others, for whose sake the individual is bound to have care for himself. What are called duties to ourselves are not socially obligatory, unless circumstances render them at the same time duties to others. The term duty to oneself, when it means anything more than prudence, means self-respect or self-development; and for none of these is any one accountable to his fellow-creatures, because for none of them is it for the good of mankind that he be held accountable to them.

·   ·   ·

The worth of a State, in the long run, is the worth of the individuals composing it; and a State which postpones the interests of *their* mental expansion and elevation, to a little more of administrative skill, or of that semblance of it which practice gives, in the details of business; a State which dwarfs its men, in order that they may be more docile instruments in its hands even for beneficial purposes, will find that with small men no great thing can really be accomplished; and that the perfection of machinery to which it has sacrificed everything, will in the end avail it nothing, for want of the vital power which, in order that the machine might work more smoothly, it has preferred to banish.

Georg Wilhelm Friedrich Hegel

═══ 18 ═══

Reason in History

Many elements of romanticism were incorporated into the work of Georg Wilhelm Friedrich Hegel (1770–1831), the greatest philosopher of the nineteenth century. His philosophical idealism, his emphasis on change and the sweep of history, his organic theory of society, and his rejection of the abstract, mechanical rationalism of the Enlightenment—all stamped him as a child of the romantic age. A university professor in Germany for most of his life, Hegel wrote in a complex and difficult style, but nevertheless dominated European philosophy in his lifetime by reason of the universal scope and power of his system. Subsequently, almost all great Western philosophies down to our own day, whether idealist or materialist, pragmatic or existentialist, radical or conservative, have had to come to terms with Hegel's ideas. In this respect, his work may be considered an intellectual bridge between the eighteenth and twentieth centuries.

Hegel was a philosophical idealist, for whom "Spirit" was the ultimate stuff and source of reality. All life was an evolutionary process in which mind and matter were united; the process was given direction by this underlying "Spirit" or "Absolute Mind." The inevitable goal of the "Spirit" working in natural and social phenomena was absolute freedom or self-realization. The mechanics of the process was a dialectical one, in which the clash of opposites (thesis and antithesis) generated a new and higher combination (synthesis), which then produced its own opposite, and so on, endlessly. Hegel's social thought followed from his basic philosophical views. History, for him, was not a mere series of events in the past but a creative force—the expression of the "World Spirit" realizing itself in historical change. For his own time, Hegel saw the national state as the true embodiment of universal reason, the only vehicle of progress toward true

From Georg Wilhelm Friedrich Hegel, *Reason in History,* edited by Robert S. Hartman, copyright 1953 by the Liberal Arts Press, Inc., reprinted by permission of the Liberal Arts Press Division of The Bobbs-Merrill Company, Inc. [This work is a new translation of Hegel's *The Philosophy of History.* Pp. 11, 12, 20, 22–23, 25–29, 49–50, 52–53, 68–71, 94–95.]

freedom. The individual's life and his very being were constituted by his social relations; hence he could achieve self-realization only by organic union with his society, his national state. It is easy to see how the intensely nationalistic tone of Hegel's social thought could be used to justify totalitarian rule, despite Hegel's own preference for a strong, constitutional state.

The Philosophy of History was not written by Hegel himself. It was a compilation of his own and his students' notes for lectures delivered at the University of Berlin between 1822 and 1831, and it was first published after his death in 1837. This selection—from the "Introduction" to the work—is a good summary of its general ideas.

The sole thought which philosophy brings to the treatment of history is the simple concept of *Reason:* that Reason is the law of the world and that, therefore, in world history, things have come about rationally. This conviction and insight is a presupposition of history as such; in philosophy itself it is not presupposed. Through its speculative reflection philosophy has demonstrated that Reason—and this term may be accepted here without closer examination of its relation to God—is both *substance and infinite power,* in itself the infinite material of all natural and spiritual life as well as the *infinite form,* the actualization of itself as content. It is *substance,* that is to say, that by which and in which all reality has its being and subsistence. It is infinite *power,* for Reason is not so impotent as to bring about only the ideal, the ought, and to remain in an existence outside of reality—who knows where—as something peculiar in the heads of a few people. It is the infinite *content* of all essence and truth, for it does not require, as does finite activity, the condition of external materials, of given data from which to draw nourishment and objects of its activity; it supplies its own nourishment and is its own reference. And it is infinite *form,* for only in its image and by its fiat do phenomena arise and begin to live. It is its own exclusive presupposition and absolutely final purpose, and itself works out this purpose from potentiality into actuality, from inward source to outward appearance, not only in the natural but also in the spiritual universe, in world history. That this *Idea* or *Reason* is the True, the Eternal, the Absolute Power and that it and nothing but it, its glory and majesty, manifests itself in the world—this, as we said before, has been proved in philosophy and is being presupposed here as proved.

. . .

Therefore, only the study of world history itself can show that it has proceeded rationally, that it represents the rationally necessary course of the World Spirit, the Spirit whose nature is indeed always one and the same, but whose one nature unfolds in the course of the world. This, as I said, must be the result of history. History itself must be taken as it is; we have to proceed historically, empirically.

. . .

The question of how Reason is determined in itself and what its relation is to the world coincides with the question, *What is the ultimate purpose of the world?* This question implies that the purpose is to be actualized and realized. Two things, then, must be considered: first, the content of this ultimate purpose, the determination as such, and, secondly, its realization.

To begin with, we must note that world history goes on within the realm of Spirit. The term "world" includes both physical and psychical nature. Physical nature does play a part in world history, and from the very beginning we shall draw attention to the fundamental natural relations thus involved. But Spirit, and the course of its development, is the substance of history. We must not contemplate nature as a rational system in itself, in its own particular domain, but only in its relation to Spirit. . . . Spirit, on the stage on which we observe it, that of world history, is in its most concrete reality. But nevertheless—or rather in order to understand also the general idea of this concrete existence of Spirit—we must set forth, first, some general definition of the *nature of Spirit.*

. . .

The nature of Spirit may be understood by a glance at its direct opposite—Matter. The essence of matter is gravity, the essence of Spirit—its substance—is Freedom. It is immediately plausible to everyone that, among other properties, Spirit also possesses Freedom. But philosophy teaches us that *all* the properties of Spirit exist only through Freedom. All are but means of attaining Freedom;

all seek and produce this and this alone. It is an insight of speculative philosophy that Freedom is the sole truth of Spirit. Matter
possesses gravity by virtue of its tendency toward a central point; it
is essentially composite, consisting of parts that exclude each other.
It seeks its unity and thereby its own abolition; it seeks its opposite.
If it would attain this it would be matter no longer, but would have
perished. It strives toward ideality, for in unity it exists ideally.
Spirit, on the contrary, is that which has its center in itself. It does
not have unity outside of itself but has found it; it is in itself and
with itself. Matter has its substance outside of itself; Spirit is Being-
within-itself (self-contained existence). But this, precisely, is Freedom. For when I am dependent, I refer myself to something else
which I am not; I cannot exist independently of something external.
I am free when I am within myself. This self-contained existence of
Spirit is self-consciousness, consciousness of self.

Two things must be distinguished in consciousness, first, *that* I
know and, secondly, *what* I know. In self-consciousness the two
coincide, for Spirit knows itself. It is the judgment of its own
nature and, at the same time, the operation of coming to itself, to
produce itself, to make itself (actually) into that which it is in itself
(potentially). Following this abstract definition it may be said that
world history is the exhibition of spirit striving to attain knowledge
of its own nature. As the germ bears in itself the whole nature of the
tree, the taste and shape of its fruit, so also the first traces of Spirit
virtually contain the whole of history.

• • •

The question of the *means* whereby Freedom develops itself into
a world leads us directly to the phenomenon of history. Although
Freedom as such is primarily an internal idea, the means it uses
are the external phenomena which in history present themselves
directly before our eyes. The first glance at history convinces
us that the actions of men spring from their needs, their passions,
their interests, their characters, and their talents. Indeed, it appears
as if in this drama of activities these needs, passions, and interests
are the sole springs of action and the main efficient cause. It is true
that this drama involves also universal purposes, benevolence, or
noble patriotism. But such virtues and aims are insignificant on
the broad canvas of history. We may, perhaps, see the ideal of
Reason actualized in those who adopt such aims and in the spheres

of their influence; but their number is small in proportion to the mass of the human race and their influence accordingly limited. Passions, private aims, and the satisfaction of selfish desires are, on the contrary, tremendous springs of action. Their power lies in the fact that they respect none of the limitations which law and morality would impose on them; and that these natural impulses are closer to the core of human nature than the artificial and troublesome discipline that tends toward order, self-restraint, law, and morality.

· · ·

The first thing we notice—something which has been stressed more than once before but which cannot be repeated too often, for it belongs to the central point of our inquiry—is the merely general and abstract nature of what we call principle, final purpose, destiny, or the nature and concept of Spirit. A principle, a law is something implicit, which as such, however true in itself, is not completely real (actual). Purposes, principles, and the like, are at first in our thoughts, our inner intention. They are not yet in reality. That which is in itself is a possibility, a faculty. It has not yet emerged out of its implicitness into existence. A second element must be added for it to become reality, namely, activity, actualization. The principle of this is the will, man's activity in general. It is only through this activity that the concept and its implicit ("being-in-themselves") determinations can be realized, actualized; for of themselves they have no immediate efficacy. The activity which puts them in operation and in existence is the need, the instinct, the inclination, and passion of man. When I have an idea I am greatly interested in transforming it into action, into actuality. In its realization through my participation I want to find my own satisfaction. A purpose for which I shall be active must in some way be my purpose; I must thereby satisfy my own desires, even though it may have ever so many aspects which do not concern me. This is the infinite right of the individual to find itself satisfied in its activity and labor. If men are to be interested in anything they must have "their heart" in it. Their feelings of self-importance must be satisfied.

· · ·

Two elements therefore enter into our investigation: first, the Idea, secondly, the complex of human passions; the one the warp, the other the woof of the vast tapestry of world history. Their contact and concrete union constitutes moral liberty in the state. We have already spoken of the Idea of freedom as the essence of Spirit and absolutely final purpose of history.

.   .   .

The [final] point, then, concerns the end to be attained by these means, that is, the form it assumes in the realm of the actual. We have spoken of means; but the carrying out of a subjective, limited aim also requires a *material* element, either already present or to be procured or to serve this actualization. Thus the question would arise: What is the material in which the final end of Reason is to be realized? It is first of all the subjective agent itself, human desires, subjectivity in general. In human knowledge and volition, as its material basis, the rational attains existence. We have considered subjective volition with its purpose, namely, the truth of reality, insofar as moved by a great world-historical passion. As a subjective will in limited passions it is dependent; it can gratify its particular desires only within this dependence. But the subjective will has also a substantial life, a reality where it moves in the region of essential being and has the essential itself as the object of its existence. This essential being is the union of the subjective with the rational will; it is the moral whole, the *State*. It is that actuality in which the individual has and enjoys his freedom, but only as knowing, believing, and willing the universal. This must not be understood as if the subjective will of the individual attained its gratification and enjoyment through the common will and the latter were a means for it—as if the individual limited his freedom among the other individuals, so that this common limitation, the mutual constraint of all, might secure a small space of liberty for each. (This would only be negative freedom.) Rather, law, morality, the State, and they alone, are the positive reality and satisfaction of freedom. The caprice of the individual is not freedom. It is this caprice which is being limited, the license of particular desires.

The subjective will, passion, is the force which actualizes and realizes. The Idea is the interior; the State is the externally existing, genuinely moral life. It is the union of the universal and essential with the subjective will, and as such it is *Morality*. The individual who lives in this unity has a moral life, a value which consists in this substantiality alone. Sophocles' Antigone says: "The divine commands are not of yesterday nor of today; no, they have an infinite existence, and no one can say whence they came." The laws of ethics are not accidental, but are rationality itself. It is the end of the State to make the substantial prevail and maintain itself in the actual doings of men and in their convictions. It is the absolute interest of Reason that this moral whole exist; and herein lies the justification and merit of heroes who have founded states, no matter how crude.

. . .

[The state] is the realization of Freedom, of the absolute, final purpose, and exists for its own sake. All the value man has, all spiritual reality, he has only through the state. For his spiritual reality is the knowing presence to him of his own essence, of rationality, of its objective, immediate actuality present in and for him. Only thus is he truly a consciousness, only thus does he partake in morality, in the legal and moral life of the state. For the True is the unity of the universal and particular will. And the universal in the state is in its laws, its universal and rational provisions. The state is the divine Idea as it exists on earth.

Thus the State is the definite object of world history proper. In it freedom achieves its objectivity and lives in the enjoyment of this objectivity. For law is the objectivity of Spirit; it is will in its true form. Only the will that obeys the law is free, for it obeys itself and, being in itself, is free. In so far as the state, our country, constitutes a community of existence, and as the subjective will of man subjects itself to the laws, the antithesis of freedom and necessity disappears. The rational, like the substantial, is necessary. We are free when we recognize it as law and follow it as the substance of our own being. The objective and the subjective will are then reconciled and form one and the same harmonious whole. For the ethos of the state is not of the moral, the reflective kind in which one's own conviction rules supreme. This latter is rather the peculiarity of the modern world. The true and antique morality is rooted in the principle that everybody stands in his place of duty. An Athenian citizen did what was required of him, as it were from instinct. But if I reflect on the object of my activity, I must have the consciousness that my will counts. Morality, however, is the duty, the substantial law, the second nature, as it has been rightly called; for the first nature of man is his immediate, animalic existence.

. . .

We have now learned the abstract characteristics of the nature of Spirit, the means which it uses to realize its Idea, and the form which its complete realization assumes in external existence, namely, the State. All that remains for this introduction is to consider the *course of world history.*

Historical change, seen abstractly, has long been understood generally as involving a progress toward the better, the more perfect. Change in nature, no matter how infinitely varied it is, shows only a cycle of constant repetition. In nature nothing new happens under the sun, and in this respect the multiform play of her products leads to boredom. One and the same permanent character continuously reappears, and all change reverts to it. Only the changes in the realm of Spirit create the novel. This characteristic of Spirit suggested to man a feature entirely different from that of nature—the desire toward *perfectibility.* This principle, which brings change itself under laws, has been badly received by religions such as the Catholic and also by states which desire as their true right to be static or at least stable. When the mutability of secular things, such as states, is conceded on principle, then religion, as religion of truth, is excluded. On the other hand, one leaves undecided whether changes, revolutions, and destructions of legitimate conditions are not due to accidents, blunders, and, in particular, the license and evil passions of men. Actually, perfectibility is something almost as undetermined as mutability in general; it is without aim and purpose and without a standard of change. The better, the more perfect toward which it is supposed to attain, is entirely undetermined.

The principle of *development* implies further that it is based on an inner principle, a presupposed potentiality, which brings itself into existence. This formal determination is essentially the Spirit whose scene, property, and sphere of realization is world history. It does not flounder about in the external play of accidents. On the contrary, it is absolutely determined and firm against them. It uses them for its own purposes and dominates them. But development is also a property of organic natural objects. Their existence is not merely dependent, subject to external influences. It proceeds from an inner immutable principle, a simple essence, which first exists as germ. From this simple existence it brings forth out of itself differentiations which connect it with other things. Thus it lives a life of continuous transformation. On the other hand, we may look at it from the opposite point of view and see in it the preservation of the organic principle and its form. Thus the organic individual produces itself; it makes itself actually into that which it is in itself (potentially). In the same way, Spirit is only that into which it makes itself, and it makes itself actually into that which it is in itself (potentially). The development of the organism proceeds in an immediate, direct (undialectic), unhindered manner. Nothing can interfere between the concept and its realization, the inherent nature of the germ and the adaptation of its existence to this nature. It is different with Spirit. The transition of its potentiality into actuality is mediated through consciousness and will. These are themselves first immersed in their immediate organic life; their first object and purpose is this natural existence as such. But the latter, through its animation by Spirit, becomes itself infinitely demanding, rich, and strong. Thus Spirit is at war with itself. It must overcome itself as its own enemy and formidable obstacle. Development, which in nature is a quiet unfolding, is in Spirit a hard, infinite struggle against itself. What Spirit wants is to attain its own concept. But it hides it from itself and is proud and full of enjoyment in this alienation from itself.

Historical development, therefore, is not the harmless and unopposed simple growth of organic life but hard, unwilling labor against itself. Furthermore, it is not mere formal self-development in general, but the production of an end of determined content. This end we have stated from the beginning: it is Spirit in its essence, the concept of freedom. This is the fundamental object and hence the leading principle of development. Through it the development receives meaning and significance—just as in Roman history Rome is the object and hence the guiding principle of the inquiry into past events. At the same time, however, the events arise out of this object and have meaning and content only with reference to it.

There are in world history several large periods which have passed away, apparently without further development. Their whole enormous gain of culture has been annihilated and, unfortunately, one had to start all over from the beginning in order to reach again one of the levels of culture which had been reached long ago—assisted, perhaps, by some ruins saved of old treasures—with a new, immeasurable effort of power and time, of crime and suffering. On the other hand, there are continuing developments, structures, and systems of culture in particular spheres, rich in kind and well-developed in every direction. The merely formal view of development can give preference neither to one course nor the other; nor can it account for the purpose of that decline of older periods. It must consider such events, and in particular such reversals, as external accidents. It can judge the relative advantages only according to indefinite viewpoints—viewpoints which are relative precisely because development *in general* is viewed as the one and only purpose.

World history, then, represents the phases in the development of the principle whose *content* is the consciousness of freedom. The analysis of its stages in general belongs to Logic. That of its particular, its concrete nature, belongs to the Philosophy of Spirit. Let us only repeat here that the first stage is the immersion of Spirit in natural life, the second its stepping out into the consciousness of its freedom. This first emancipation from nature is incomplete and partial; it issues from immediate naturalness, still refers to it, and hence is still incumbered by it as one of its elements. The third stage is the rising out of this still particular form of freedom into pure universality of freedom, where the spiritual essence attains the consciousness and feeling of itself. These stages are the fundamental principles of the universal process. Each is again, within itself, a process of its own formation. But the detail of this inner dialectic of transition must be left to the sequel.

All we have to indicate here is that Spirit begins with its infinite possibility, but *only* its possibility. As such it contains its absolute content within itself, as its aim and goal, which it attains only as result of its activity. Then and only then has Spirit attained its reality. Thus, in existence, progress appears as an advance from the imperfect to the more perfect. But the former must not only be taken in abstraction as the merely imperfect, but as that which contains at the same time its own opposite, the so-called perfect, as germ, as urge within itself. In the same way, at least in thought, possibility points to something which shall become real; more precisely, the Aristotelian *dynamis* is also *potentia,* force and power. The imperfect, thus, as the opposite of itself in itself, is its own antithesis, which on the one hand exists, but, on the other, is annulled and resolved. It is the urge, the impulse of spiritual life in itself, to break through the hull of nature, of sensuousness, of its own self-alienation, and to attain the light of consciousness, namely, its own self.

. . .

The result of this process, then, is that the Spirit in objectifying itself and thinking its own being, on the one hand, destroys this (particular) determination of its own being and, on the other hand, grasps its universality. It thus gives a new determination to its principle. The substantial determination of this national spirit is therewith changed; its principle passes into a new and higher one.

It is most important for the full understanding and comprehension of history to grasp and possess the thought of this transition. An individual as unity traverses various stages and remains the same individual. So also a people, up to the stage which is the universal stage of its spirit. In this consists the inner, the conceptual necessity of its change. Here we have the essence, the very soul of the philosophical understanding of history.

Spirit is essentially the result of its own activity. Its activity is transcending the immediately given, negating it, and returning into itself. We can compare it with the seed of a plant, which is both beginning and result of the plant's whole life. The powerlessness of life manifests itself precisely in this falling apart of beginning and end. Likewise in the lives of individuals and peoples. The life of a people brings a fruit to maturity, for its activity aims at actualizing its principle. But the fruit does not fall back into the womb of the people which has produced and matured it. On the contrary, it turns into a bitter drink for this people. The people cannot abandon it, for it has an unquenchable thirst for it. But imbibing the drink is the drinker's destruction, yet, at the same time the rise of a new principle.

We have already seen what the final purpose of this process is. The principles of the national spirits progressing through a necessary succession of stages are only moments of the one universal Spirit which through them elevates and completes itself into a self-comprehending *totality*.

Thus, in dealing with the idea of Spirit only and in considering the whole of world history as nothing but its manifestation, we are dealing only with the *present*—however long the past may be which we survey. The Idea is ever present, the Spirit immortal. This implies that the present stage of Spirit contains all previous stages within itself. These, to be sure, have unfolded themselves successively and separately, but Spirit still is what it has in itself always been. The differentiation of its stages is but the development of what it is in itself. The life of the ever-present Spirit is a cycle of stages, which, on the one hand, co-exist side by side, but, on the other hand, seem to be past. The moments which Spirit seems to have left behind, it still possesses in the depth of its present.

Karl Marx and Friedrich Engels

——————— 19 ———————

The Communist Manifesto

The development of the Industrial Revolution in the first half of the nineteenth century, with its grosser forms of exploitation of factory labor, gave rise to criticisms of the prevailing social and economic systems. The most thoroughgoing and influential attack was mounted in the 1840's by two young Germans, Karl Marx (1818–1883) and Friedrich Engels (1820–1895). Marx was a philosophy student turned journalist and revolutionary agitator, who was forced to flee from Germany and France. He finally settled in London in 1849, where he devoted the rest of his life to radical activities on an international scale and to writing a critical analysis of the capitalist economy. Marx worked in close collaboration with his friend and fellow radical, Engels, who used his inherited wealth to underwrite his impecunious colleague's activities. The two dedicated their lives to the overthrow of capitalist society and to its replacement by the new order of socialism or communism. Their chief weapon was the ideology that has come to be known as Marxism—a combination of philosophical, economic, and historical theory and revolutionary practice. Marxism has since become the official doctrine of the international socialist and communist movements and has also influenced the thought and practice of many non-Marxists. The underlying philosophy of Marxism was dialectical materialism, which, like Hegel's thought, viewed all existence as a process evolving in a rational pattern according to the "dialectic," the real "laws of motion" of nature, society, and thought. But it rejected Hegel's idealism and held matter to be the ultimate stuff of reality. It embodied a theory of history which saw all social change as basically determined by technological-economic forces ("the modes of production") and moving inevitably through conflict to the resolution of all contradictions in the final stage of communism.

Marx and Engels wished, however, to do more than understand the

Karl Marx and Friedrich Engels, *Manifesto of the Communist Party,* trans. Samuel Moore (New York: Socialist Labor Party, 1888), 7–21, 28.

world; they wished to change it. *The Communist Manifesto,* written in Paris in 1848 as a platform for a radical organization, was a call to arms as well as a summary of their basic social views. Its revolutionary appeal was made in the context of an outline of the history of Western Europe. Marx and Engels traced the evolution of socio-political systems in the past and projected this evolution into the future. For them, all historical change was characterized by the struggle of economic classes. The instrument for the final transformation of society was the proletariat, the class of industrial wage-earners. Once the proletariat achieved full consciousness of its role, it would organize economically and politically to overthrow the capitalist system. Though falling short of predictive accuracy, the *Manifesto,* as well as Marxism generally, has had a wide appeal because of the cogency of its analysis, its apocalyptic quality, and its assurance to the faithful of the inevitability of success.

A spectre is haunting Europe—the spectre of Communism. All the powers of old Europe have entered into a holy alliance to exorcise this spectre; Pope and Czar, Metternich and Guizot, French Radicals and German police-spies.

Where is the party in opposition that has not been decried as communistic by its opponents in power? Where the Opposition that has not hurled back the branding reproach of Communism, against the more advanced opposition parties, as well as against its reactionary adversaries?

Two things result from this fact.

1. Communism is already acknowledged by all European Powers to be itself a Power.

2. It is high time that Communists should openly, in the face of the whole world, publish their views, their aims, their tendencies, and meet this nursery tale of the Spectre of Communism with a Manifesto of the party itself.

To this end, Communists of various nationalities have assembled in London, and sketched the following manifesto, to be published in the English, French, German, Italian, Flemish and Danish languages.

BOURGEOIS AND PROLETARIANS

The history of all hitherto existing society is the history of class struggles.

Freeman and slave, patrician and plebeian, lord and serf, guild-master and journeyman, in a word, oppressor and oppressed, stood in constant opposition to one another, carried on an uninterrupted, now hidden, now open fight, a fight that each time ended, either in a revolutionary re-constitution of society at large, or in the common ruin of the contending classes.

In the earlier epochs of history, we find almost everywhere a complicated arrangement of society into various orders, a manifold graduation of social rank. In ancient Rome we have patricians, knights, plebeians, slaves; in the Middle Ages, feudal lords, vassals, guildmasters, journeymen, apprentices, serfs; in almost all of these classes, again, subordinate gradations.

The modern bourgeois society that has sprouted from the ruins of feudal society, has not done away with class antagonisms. It has but established new classes, new conditions of oppression, new forms of struggle in place of the old ones.

Our epoch, the epoch of the bourgeoisie, possesses, however, this distinctive feature: it has simplified the class antagonisms. Society as a whole is more and more splitting up into two great hostile camps, into two great classes directly facing each other: Bourgeoisie and Proletariat.

From the serfs of the Middle Ages sprang the chartered burghers of the earliest towns. From these burgesses the first elements of the bourgeoisie were developed.

The discovery of America, the rounding of the Cape, opened up fresh ground for the rising bourgeoisie. The East-Indian and Chinese markets, the colonization of America, trade with the colonies, the increase in the means of exchange and in commodities generally, gave to commerce, to navigation, to industry, an impulse never before known, and thereby, to the revolutionary element in the tottering feudal society, a rapid development.

The feudal system of industry, under which industrial production was monopolized by close guilds, now no longer sufficed for the growing wants of the new markets. The manufacturing system took its place. The guildmasters were pushed on one side by the manu-

facturing middle-class; division of labor between the different corpo-
rate guilds vanished in the face of division of labor in each single
workshop.

Meantime the markets kept ever growing, the demand, ever rising.
Even manufacture no longer sufficed. Thereupon, steam and machinery revolutionized industrial production. The place of manufacture was taken by the giant, Modern Industry, the place of the
industrial middle-class, by industrial millionaires, the leaders of
whole industrial armies, the modern bourgeois.

Modern industry has established the world-market, for which the
discovery of America paved the way. This market has given an immense development to commerce, to navigation, to communication
by land. This development has, in its turn, reacted on the extension
of industry; and in proportion as industry, commerce, navigation,
railways extended, in the same proportion the bourgeoisie developed, increased its capital, and pushed into the background every
class handed down from the Middle Ages.

We see, therefore, how the modern bourgeoisie is itself the product of a long course of development, of a series of revolutions in the
modes of production and of exchange.

Each step in the development of the bourgeoisie was accompanied
by a corresponding political advance of that class. An oppressed
class under the sway of the feudal nobility, an armed and self-govern-
ing association in the medieval commune, here independent urban
republic (as in Italy and Germany), there taxable "third estate" of
the monarchy (as in France), afterwards, in the period of manufacture proper, serving either the semi-feudal or the absolute monarchy
as a counterpoise against the nobility, and, in fact, corner stone of
the great monarchies in general, the bourgeoisie has at last, since
the establishment of Modern Industry and of the world-market, conquered for itself, in the modern representative State, exclusive political sway. The executive of the modern State is but a committee
for managing the common affairs of the whole bourgeoisie.

The bourgeoisie, historically, has played a most revolutionary
part.

The bourgeoisie, wherever it has got the upper hand, has put an
end to all feudal, patriarchal, idyllic relations. It has pitilessly torn
asunder the motley feudal ties that bound man to his "natural
superiors," and has left remaining no other nexus between man and
man than naked self-interest, than callous "cash payment." It has

drowned the most heavenly ecstasies of religious fervor, of chivalrous enthusiasm, of philistine sentimentalism, in the icy water of egotistical calculation. It has resolved personal worth into exchange value, and in place of the numberless indefeasible chartered freedoms, has set up that single, unconscionable freedom—Free Trade. In one word, for exploitation, veiled by religious and political illusions, it has substituted naked, shameless, direct, brutal exploitation.

The bourgeoisie has stripped of its halo every occupation hitherto honored and looked up to with reverent awe. It has converted the physician, the lawyer, the priest, the poet, the man of science, into its paid wage-laborers.

The bourgeoisie has torn away from the family its sentimental veil, and has reduced the family relation to a mere money relation.

The bourgeoisie has disclosed how it came to pass that the brutal display of vigor in the Middle Ages, which Reactionists so much admire, found its fitting complement in the most slothful indolence. It has been the first to show what man's activity can bring about. It has accomplished wonders far surpassing Egyptian pyramids, Roman aqueducts, and Gothic cathedrals; it has conducted expeditions that put in the shade all former Exoduses of nations and crusades.

The bourgeoisie cannot exist without constantly revolutionizing the instruments of production, and thereby the relations of production, and with them the whole relations of society. Conservation of the old modes of production in unaltered form, was, on the contrary, the first condition of existence for all earlier industrial classes. Constant revolutionizing of production, uninterrupted disturbance of all social conditions, everlasting uncertainty and agitation distinguish the bourgeois epoch from all earlier ones. All fixed, fast-frozen relations, with their train of ancient and venerable prejudices and opinions, are swept away, all new-formed ones become antiquated before they can ossify. All that is solid melts into air, all that is holy is profaned, and man is at last compelled to face with sober senses, his real conditions of life, and his relations with his kind.

The need of a constantly expanding market for its products chases the bourgeoisie over the whole surface of the globe. It must nestle everywhere, settle everywhere, establish connections everywhere.

The bourgeoisie has through its exploitation of the world-market given a cosmopolitan character to production and consumption in

every country. To the great chagrin of Reactionists, it has drawn
from under the feet of industry the national ground on which it
stood. All old-established national industries have been destroyed or
are daily being destroyed. They are dislodged by new industries,
whose introduction becomes a life and death question for all civilized nations, by industries that no longer work up indigenous raw
material, but raw material drawn from the remotest zones; industries
whose products are consumed, not only at home, but in every quarter of the globe. In place of the old wants, satisfied by the productions of the country, we find new wants, requiring for their satisfaction the products of distant lands and climes. In place of the old
local and national seclusion and self-sufficiency, we have intercourse
in every direction, universal inter-dependence of nations. And as in
material, so also in intellectual production. The intellectual creations of individual nations become common property. National one-
sidedness and narrow-mindedness become more and more impossible,
and from the numerous national and local literatures there arises
a world-literature.

The bourgeoisie, by the rapid improvement of all instruments of
production, by the immensely facilitated means of communication,
draws all, even the most barbarian, nations into civilization. The
cheap prices of its commodities are the heavy artillery with which it
batters down all Chinese walls, with which it forces the barbarians'
intensely obstinate hatred of foreigners to capitulate. It compels all
nations, on pain of extinction, to adopt the bourgeois mode of production; it compels them to introduce what it calls civilization into
their midst, i.e., to become bourgeois themselves. In a word, it creates
a world after its own image.

The bourgeoisie has subjected the country to the rule of the towns.
It has created enormous cities, has greatly increased the urban
population as compared with the rural, and has thus rescued a considerable part of the population from the idiocy of rural life. Just
as it has made the country dependent on the towns, so it has made
barbarian and semi-barbarian countries dependent on the civilized
ones, nations of peasants on nations of bourgeois, the East on the
West.

The bourgeoisie keeps more and more doing away with the
scattered state of the population, of the means of production, and of
property. It has agglomerated population, centralized means of
production, and has concentrated property in a few hands. The

necessary consequence of this was political centralization. Independent, or but loosely connected provinces, with separate interests, laws, governments, and systems of taxation, became lumped together in one nation, with one government, one code of laws, one national class-interest, one frontier and one customs-tariff.

The bourgeoisie, during its rule of scarce one hundred years, has created more massive and more colossal productive forces than have all preceding generations together. Subjection of Nature's forces to man, machinery, application of chemistry to industry and agriculture, steam-navigation, railways, electric telegraphs, clearing of whole continents for cultivation, canalization of rivers, whole populations conjured out of the ground—what earlier century had even a presentiment that such productive forces slumbered in the lap of social labor?

We see then: the means of production and of exchange on whose foundation the bourgeoisie built itself up, were generated in feudal society. At a certain stage in the development of these means of production and of exchange, the conditions under which feudal society produced and exchanged, the feudal organization of agriculture and manufacturing industry, in one word, the feudal relations of property became no longer compatible with the already developed productive forces; they became so many fetters. They had to burst asunder; they were burst asunder.

Into their places stepped free competition, accompanied by a social and political constitution adapted to it, and by the economical and political sway of the bourgeois class.

A similar movement is going on before our own eyes. Modern bourgeois society with its relations of production, of exchange and of property, a society that has conjured up such gigantic means of production and of exchange, is like the sorcerer, who is no longer able to control the powers of the nether world whom he has called up by his spells. For many a decade past the history of industry and commerce is but the history of the revolt of modern productive forces against modern conditions of production, against the property relations that are the conditions for the existence of the bourgeoisie and of its rule. It is enough to mention the commercial crises that by their periodical return put on its trial, each time more threateningly, the existence of the entire bourgeois society. In these crises a great part not only of the existing products, but also of the previously created productive forces, are periodically destroyed. In these crises there breaks out an epidemic that, in all earlier epochs, would have seemed an absurdity—the epidemic of over-production. Society suddenly finds itself put back into a state of momentary barbarism; it appears as if a famine, a universal war of devastation had cut off the supply of every means of subsistence; industry and commerce seem to be destroyed; and why? Because there is too much civilization, too much means of subsistence, too much industry, too much commerce. The productive forces at the disposal of society no longer tend to further the development of the conditions of bourgeois property; on the contrary, they have become too powerful for these conditions, by which they are fettered, and so soon as they overcome these fetters, they bring disorder into the whole of bourgeois society, endanger the existence of bourgeois property. The conditions of bourgeois society are too narrow to comprise the wealth created by them. And how does the bourgeoisie get over these crises? On the one hand by enforced destruction of a mass of productive forces; on the other, by the conquest of new markets, and by the more thorough exploitation of the old ones. That is to say, by paving the way for more extensive and more destructive crises, and by diminishing the means whereby crises are prevented.

The weapons with which the bourgeoisie felled feudalism to the ground are now turned against the bourgeoisie itself.

But not only has the bourgeoisie forged the weapons that bring death to itself; it has also called into existence the men who are to wield those weapons—the modern working-class—the proletarians.

In proportion as the bourgeoisie, i.e., capital, is developed, in the same proportion is the proletariat, the modern working-class, developed, a class of laborers, who live only so long as they find work, and who find work only so long as their labor increases capital. These laborers, who must sell themselves piecemeal, are a commodity, like every other article of commerce, and are consequently exposed to all the vicissitudes of competition, to all the fluctuations of the market.

Owing to the extensive use of machinery and to division of labor, the work of the proletarians has lost all individual character, and, consequently, all charm for the workman. He becomes an appendage of the machine, and it is only the most simple, most monotonous, and most easily acquired knack that is required of him. Hence, the cost of production of a workman is restricted, almost entirely, to the means of subsistence that he requires for his maintenance, and for the propagation of his race. But the price of a commodity, and also of labor, is equal to its cost of production. In proportion, therefore, as the repulsiveness of the work increases, the wage decreases. Nay more, in proportion as the use of machinery and division of labor increases, in the same proportion the burden of toil also increases, whether by prolongation of the working hours, by increase of the work enacted in a given time, or by increased speed of the machinery, etc.

Modern industry has converted the little workshop of the patriarchal master into the great factory of the industrial capitalist. Masses of laborers, crowded into the factory, are organized like soldiers. As privates of the industrial army they are placed under the command of a perfect hierarchy of officers and sergeants. Not only are they the slaves of the bourgeois class, and of the bourgeois State, they are daily and hourly enslaved by the machine, by the over-looker, and, above all, by the individual bourgeois manufacturer himself. The more openly this despotism proclaims gain to be its end and aim, the more petty, the more hateful and the more embittering it is.

The less the skill and exertion or strength implied in manual labor, in other words, the more modern industry becomes developed, the more is the labor of men superseded by that of women. Differences of age and sex have no longer any distinctive social validity for the working class. All are instruments of labor, more or less expensive to use, according to their age and sex.

No sooner is the exploitation of the laborer by the manufacturer, so far at an end, that he receives his wages in cash, than he is set upon by the other portions of the bourgeoisie, the landlord, the shopkeeper, the pawnbroker, etc.

The lower strata of the middle class—the small tradespeople, shopkeepers, and retired tradesmen generally, the handicraftsmen and peasants—all these sink gradually into the proletariat, partly because their diminutive capital does not suffice for the scale on which Modern Industry is carried on, and is swamped in the competition with the large capitalists, partly because their specialized skill is rendered worthless by new methods of production. Thus the proletariat is recruited from all classes of the population.

The proletariat goes through various stages of development. With its birth begins its struggle with the bourgeoisie. At first the contest is carried on by individual laborers, then by the workpeople of a factory, then by the operatives of one trade, in one locality, against the individual bourgeois who directly exploits them. They direct their attacks not against the bourgeois conditions of production, but against the instruments of production themselves; they destroy imported wares that compete with their labor, they smash to pieces machinery, they set factories ablaze, they seek to restore by force the vanished status of the workman of the Middle Ages.

At this stage the laborers still form an incoherent mass scattered over the whole country, and broken up by their mutual competition. If anywhere they unite to form more compact bodies, this is not yet the consequence of their own active union, but of the union of the bourgeoisie, which class, in order to attain its own political ends, is compelled to set the whole proletariat in motion, and is moreover yet, for a time, able to do so. At this stage, therefore, the proletarians do not fight their enemies, but the enemies of their enemies, the remnants of absolute monarchy, the landowners, the non-industrial bourgeois, the petty bourgeoisie. Thus the whole historical movement is concentrated in the hands of the bourgeoisie; every victory so obtained is a victory for the bourgeoisie.

But with the development of industry the proletariat not only increases in number, it becomes concentrated in greater masses, its strength grows, and it feels that strength more. The various interests and conditions of life within the ranks of the proletariat are more and more equalized, in proportion as machinery obliterates all distinctions of labor, and nearly everywhere reduces wages to the same low level. The growing competition among the bourgeois, and the resulting commercial crises, make the wages of the workers ever more fluctuating. The unceasing improvement of machinery, ever more rapidly developing, makes their livelihood more and more precarious; the collisions between individual workmen and individual bourgeois take more and more the character of collisions between two classes. Thereupon the workers begin to form combinations (Trades' Unions) against the bourgeois; they club together in order to keep up the rate of wages; they found permanent associations in order to make provision beforehand for these occasional revolts. Here and there the contest breaks out into riots.

Now and then the workers are victorious, but only for a time. The real fruit of their battles lies, not in the immediate result, but in the ever expanding union of the workers. This union is helped on by the improved means of communication that are created by modern industry, and that place the workers of different localities in contact with one another. It was just this contact that was needed to centralize the numerous local struggles, all of the same character, into one national struggle between classes. But every class struggle is a political struggle. And that union, to attain which the burghers of the Middle Ages, with their miserable highways, required centuries, the modern proletarians, thanks to railways, achieve in a few years.

This organization of the proletarians into a class, and consequently into a political party, is continually being upset again by the competition between the workers themselves. But it ever rises up again, stronger, firmer, mightier. It compels legislative recognition of particular interests of the workers, by taking advantage of the divisions among the bourgeoisie itself. Thus the ten-hour bill in England was carried.

Altogether collisions between the classes of the old society further, in many ways, the course of development of the proletariat. The bourgeoisie finds itself involved in a constant battle. At first with the aristocracy; later on, with those portions of the bourgeoisie itself, whose interests have become antagonistic to the progress of industry; at all times, with the bourgeoisie of foreign countries. In all these battles it sees itself compelled to appeal to the proletariat, to ask for its help, and thus, to drag it into the political arena. The bourgeoisie itself, therefore, supplies the proletariat with its own elements of political and general education, in other words, it furnishes the proletariat with weapons for fighting the bourgeoisie.

Further, as we have already seen, entire sections of the ruling classes are, by the advance of industry, precipitated into the proletariat, or are at least threatened in their conditions of existence. These also supply the proletariat with fresh elements of enlightenment and progress.

Finally, in times when the class-struggle nears the decisive hour, the process of dissolution going on within the ruling class, in fact, within the whole range of old society, assumes such a violent, glaring character, that a small section of the ruling class cuts itself adrift, and joins the revolutionary class, the class that holds the future in its hands. Just as, therefore, at an earlier period, a section of the nobility went over to the bourgeoisie, so now a portion of the bourgeoisie goes over to the proletariat, and in particular, a portion of the bourgeois ideologists, who have raised themselves to the level of comprehending theoretically the historical movements as a whole.

Of all the classes that stand face to face with the bourgeoisie today, the proletariat alone is a really revolutionary class. The other classes decay and finally disappear in the face of modern industry; the proletariat is its special and essential product.

The lower middle class, the small manufacturer, the shopkeeper, the artisan, the peasant, all these fight against the bourgeoisie, to save from extinction their existence as fractions of the middle class. They are, therefore, not revolutionary, but conservative. Nay more, they are reactionary, for they try to roll back the wheel of history. If by chance they are revolutionary, they are so, only in view of their impending transfer into the proletariat, they thus defend not their present, but their future interests, they desert their own standpoint to place themselves at that of the proletariat.

The "dangerous class," the social scum, that passively rotting mass thrown off by the lowest layers of old society, may, here and there, be swept into the movement by a proletarian revolution; its conditions of life, however, prepare it far more for the part of a bribed tool of reactionary intrigue.

In the conditions of the proletariat, those of old society at large are already virtually swamped. The proletarian is without property; his relation to his wife and children has no longer anything in common with the bourgeois family-relations; modern industrial labor, modern subjection to capital, the same in England as in France, in America as in Germany, has stripped him of every trace of national character. Law, morality, religion, are to him so many bourgeois prejudices, behind which lurk in ambush just as many bourgeois interests.

All the preceding classes that got the upper hand, sought to fortify their already acquired status by subjecting society at large to their conditions of appropriation. The proletarians cannot become masters of the productive forces of society, except by abolishing their own previous mode of appropriation, and thereby also every other previous mode of appropriation. They have nothing of their own to secure and to fortify; their mission is to destroy all previous securities for, and insurances of, individual property.

All previous historical movements were movements of minorities, or in the interest of minorities. The proletarian movement is the self-conscious, independent movement of the immense majority, in the interest of the immense majority. The proletariat, the lowest stratum of our present society, cannot stir, cannot raise itself up, without the whole superincumbent strata of official society being sprung into the air.

Though not in substance, yet in form, the struggle of the proletariat with the bourgeoisie is at first a national struggle. The proletariat of each country must, of course, first of all settle matters with its own bourgeoisie.

In depicting the most general phases of the development of the proletariat, we traced the more or less veiled civil war, raging within existing society, up to the point where that war breaks out into open revolution, and where the violent overthrow of the bourgeoisie lays the foundation for the sway of the proletariat.

Hitherto, every form of society has been based, as we have already seen, on the antagonism of oppressing and oppressed classes. But in order to oppress a class, certain conditions must be assured to it under which it can, at least, continue its slavish existence. The serf, in the period of serfdom, raised himself to membership in the commune, just as the petty bourgeois, under the yoke of feudal absolutism, managed to develop into a bourgeois. The modern laborer, on the contrary, instead of rising with the progress of industry, sinks deeper and deeper below the conditions of existence of his own class. He becomes a pauper, and pauperism develops more rapidly than population and wealth. And here it becomes evident, that the bourgeoisie is unfit any longer to be the ruling class in society, and to impose its conditions of existence upon society as an over-riding law. It is unfit to rule, because it is incompetent to assure an existence to its slave within his slavery, because it cannot help letting him sink into such a state that it has to feed him, instead of being fed by him. Society can no longer live under this bourgeoisie, in other words, its existence is no longer compatible with society.

The essential condition for the existence, and for the sway of the bourgeois class, is the formation and augmentation of capital; the condition for capital is wage-labor. Wage-labor rests exclusively on competition between the laborers. The advance of industry, whose involuntary promoter is the bourgeoisie, replaces the isolation of the laborers, due to competition, by their revolutionary combination, due to association. The development of Modern Industry, therefore, cuts from under its feet the very foundation on which the bourgeoisie produces and appropriates products. What the bourgeoisie therefore produces, above all, are its own grave-diggers. Its fall and the victory of the proletariat are equally inevitable.

PROLETARIANS AND COMMUNISTS

In what relation do the Communists stand to the proletarians as a whole?

The Communists do not form a separate party opposed to other working class parties.

They have no interests separate and apart from those of the proletariat as a whole.

They do not set up any sectarian principles of their own, by which to shape and mould the proletarian movement.

The Communists are distinguished from the other working class parties by this only: 1. In the national struggles of the proletarians of the different countries, they point out and bring to the front the common interests of the entire proletariat independently of all nationality. 2. In the various stages of development which the struggle of the working class against the bourgeoisie has to pass through, they always and everywhere represent the interests of the movement as a whole.

The Communists, therefore, are on the one hand, practically, the most advanced and resolute section of the working class parties of every country, that section which pushes forward all others; on the other hand, theoretically, they have over the great mass of the proletariat the advantage of clearly understanding the line of march, the conditions, and the ultimate general results of the proletarian movement.

The immediate aim of the Communists is the same as that of all the other proletarian parties: formation of the proletariat into a class, overthrow of the bourgeois supremacy, conquest of political power by the proletariat.

The theoretical conclusions of the Communists are in no way based on ideas or principles that have been invented, or discovered, by this or that would-be universal reformer.

They merely express, in general terms, actual relations springing from an existing class struggle, from a historical movement going on under our very eyes. The abolition of existing property relations is not at all a distinctive feature of Communism.

All property relations in the past have continually been subject to historical change consequent upon the change in historical conditions.

The French Revolution, for example, abolished feudal property in favor of bourgeois property.

The distinguishing feature of Communism is not the abolition of property generally, but the abolition of bourgeois property. But modern bourgeois private property is the final and most complete expression of the system of producing and appropriating products, that is based on class antagonism, on the exploitation of the many by the few.

In this sense, the theory of the Communists may be summed up in the single sentence: Abolition of private property.

We Communists have been reproached with the desire of abolishing the right of personally acquiring property as the fruit of a man's own labor, which property is alleged to be the ground work of all personal freedom, activity and independence.

Hard-won, self-acquired, self-earned property! Do you mean the property of the petty artisan and of the small peasant, a form of property that preceded the bourgeois form? There is no need to abolish that; the development of industry has to a great extent already destroyed it, and is still destroying it daily.

Or do you mean modern bourgeois private property?

But does wage-labor create any property for the laborer? Not a bit. It creates capital, i.e., that kind of property which exploits wage-labor, and which cannot increase except upon condition of getting a new supply of wage-labor for fresh exploitation. Property, in its present form, is based on the antagonism of capital and wage-labor. Let us examine both sides of this antagonism.

To be a capitalist, is to have not only a purely personal, but a social status in production. Capital is a collective product, and only by the united action of many members, nay, in the last resort, only by the united action of all members of society, can it be set in motion.

Capital is therefore not a personal, it is a social power.

When, therefore, capital is converted into common property, into the property of all members of society, personal property is not thereby transformed into social property. It is only the social character of the property that is changed. It loses its class-character.

Let us now take wage-labor.

The average price of wage-labor is the minimum wage, i.e., that quantum of the means of subsistence, which is absolutely requisite to keep the laborer in bare existence as a laborer. What, therefore, the wage-laborer appropriates by means of his labor, merely suffices to prolong and reproduce a bare existence. We by no means intend to abolish this personal appropriation of the products of labor, an appropriation that is made for the maintenance and reproduction of human life, and that leaves no surplus wherewith to command the labor of others. All that we want to do away with is the miserable character of this appropriation, under which the laborer lives merely to increase capital, and is allowed to live only in so far as the interest of the ruling class requires it.

In bourgeois society, living labor is but a means to increase accumulated labor. In communist society, accumulated labor is but a means to widen, to enrich, to promote the existence of the laborer.

In bourgeois society, therefore, the past dominates the present; in communist society, the present dominates the past. In bourgeois society capital is independent and has individuality, while the living person is dependent and has no individuality.

And the abolition of this state of things is called by the bourgeois, abolition of individuality and freedom! And rightly so. The abolition of bourgeois individuality, bourgeois independence, and bourgeois freedom is undoubtedly aimed at.

By freedom is meant, under the present bourgeois conditions of production, free trade, free selling and buying.

But if selling and buying disappears, free selling and buying disappears also. This talk about free selling and buying, and all the other "brave words" of our bourgeoisie about freedom in general, have a meaning, if any, only in contrast with restricted selling and buying, with the fettered traders of the Middle Ages, but have no meaning when opposed to the Communistic abolition of buying and selling, of the bourgeois conditions of production, and of the bourgeoisie itself.

You are horrified at our intending to do away with private property. But in your existing society, private property is already done away with for nine-tenths of the population; its existence for the few is solely due to its non-existence in the hands of those nine-tenths. You reproach us, therefore, with intending to do away with a form of property, the necessary condition for whose existence is, the non-existence of any property for the immense majority of society.

In one word, you reproach us with intending to do away with your property. Precisely so; that is just what we intend.

From the moment when labor can no longer be converted into capital, money, or rent, into a social power capable of being monopolized, i.e., from the moment when individual property can no longer be transformed into bourgeois property, into capital, from that moment, you say, individuality vanishes.

You must, therefore, confess that by "individual" you mean no other person than the bourgeois, than the middle-class owner of property. This person must, indeed, be swept out of the way, and made impossible.

Communism deprives no man of the power to appropriate the products of society: all that it does is to deprive him of the power to subjugate the labor of others by means of such appropriation.

It has been objected, that upon the abolition of private property all work will cease, and universal laziness will overtake us.

According to this, bourgeois society ought long ago to have gone to the dogs through sheer idleness; for those of its members who work, acquire nothing, and those who acquire anything, do not work. The whole of this objection is but another expression of the tautology: that there can no longer be any wage-labor when there is no longer any capital.

All objections urged against the Communistic mode of producing and appropriating material products, have, in the same way, been urged against the Communistic modes of producing and appropriating intellectual products. Just as, to the bourgeois, the disappearance of class property is the disappearance of production itself, so the disappearance of class culture is to him identical with the disappearance of all culture.

That culture, the loss of which he laments, is, for the enormous majority, a mere training to act as a machine.

But don't wrangle with us so long as you apply, to our intended abolition of bourgeois property, the standard of your bourgeois notions of freedom, culture, law, etc. Your very ideas are but the outgrowth of the conditions of your bourgeois production and bourgeois property, just as your jurisprudence is but the will of your class made into a law for all, a will, whose essential character and direction are determined by the economic conditions of existence of your class.

The selfish misconception that induces you to transform into eternal laws of nature and of reason, the social forms springing from your present mode of production and form of property—historical relations that rise and disappear in the progress of production—this misconception you share with every ruling class that has preceded you. What you see clearly in the case of ancient property, what you admit in the case of feudal property, you are of course forbidden to admit in the case of your own bourgeois form of property.

Abolition of the family! Even the most radical flare up at this infamous proposal of the Communists.

On what foundation is the present family, the bourgeois family, based? On capital, on private gain. In its completely developed form this family exists only among the bourgeoisie. But this state of things finds its complement in the practical absence of the family among the proletarians, and in public prostitution.

The bourgeois family will vanish as a matter of course when its complement vanishes, and both will vanish with the vanishing of capital.

Do you charge us with wanting to stop the exploitation of children by their parents? To this crime we plead guilty.

But, you will say, we destroy the most hallowed of relations, when we replace home education by social.

And your education! Is not that also social, and determined by the social conditions under which you educate, by the intervention, direct or indirect, of society by means of schools, etc.? The Communists have not invented the intervention of society in education; they do but seek to alter the character of that intervention, and to rescue education from the influence of the ruling class.

The bourgeois clap-trap about the family and education, about the hallowed co-relation of parent and child, becomes all the more disgusting, the more, by the action of Modern Industry, all family ties among the proletarians are torn asunder, and their children transformed into simple articles of commerce and instruments of labor.

But you Communists would introduce community of women, screams the whole bourgeoisie in chorus.

The bourgeois sees in his wife a mere instrument of production. He hears that the instruments of production are to be exploited in common, and, naturally, can come to no other conclusion, than that the lot of being common to all will likewise fall to the women.

He has not even a suspicion that the real point aimed at is to do away with the status of women as mere instruments of production.

For the rest, nothing is more ridiculous than the virtuous indignation of our bourgeois at the community of women which, they pretend, is to be openly and officially established by the Communists. The Communists have no need to introduce community of women; it has existed almost from time immemorial.

Our bourgeois, not content with having the wives and daughters of their proletarians at their disposal, not to speak of common prostitutes, take the greatest pleasure in seducing each other's wives.

Bourgeois marriage is in reality a system of wives in common and thus, at the most, what the Communists might possibly be reproached with, is that they desire to introduce, in substitution for a hypocritically concealed, an openly legalized community of women. For the rest, it is self-evident, that the abolition of the present system of production must bring with it the abolition of the community of women springing from that system, i.e., of prostitution both public and private.

The Communists are further reproached with desiring to abolish countries and nationalities.

The working men have no country. We cannot take from them what they have not got. Since the proletariat must first of all acquire political supremacy, must rise to be the leading class of the nation, must constitute itself the nation, it is, so far, itself national, though not in the bourgeois sense of the word.

National differences, and antagonisms between peoples, are daily more and more vanishing, owing to the development of the bourgeoisie, to freedom of commerce, to the world-market, to uniformity in the mode of production and in the conditions of life corresponding thereto.

The supremacy of the proletariat will cause them to vanish still faster. United action, of the leading civilized countries at least, is one of the first conditions for the emancipation of the proletariat.

In proportion as the exploitation of one individual by another is put an end to, the exploitation of one nation by another will also be put an end to. In proportion as the antagonism between classes within the nation vanishes, the hostility of one nation to another will come to an end.

The charges against Communism made from a religious, a philosophical, and generally, from an ideological standpoint, are not deserving of serious examination.

Does it require deep intuition to comprehend that man's ideas, views, and conceptions, in one word, man's consciousness, changes with every change in the conditions of his material existence, in his social relations and in his social life?

What else does the history of ideas prove, than that intellectual production changes in character in proportion as material production is changed? The ruling ideas of each age have ever been the ideas of its ruling class.

When people speak of ideas that revolutionize society, they do but express the fact, that within the old society, the elements of a new one have been created, and that the dissolution of the old ideas keeps even pace with the dissolution of the old conditions of existence.

When the ancient world was in its last throes, the ancient religions were overcome by Christianity. When Christian ideas succumbed in the 18th century to rationalist ideas, feudal society fought its death-battle with the then revolutionary bourgeoisie. The ideas of religious liberty and freedom of conscience, merely gave expression to the sway of free competition within the domain of knowledge.

"Undoubtedly," it will be said, "religious, moral, philosophical and juridical ideas have been modified in the course of historical development. But religion, morality, philosophy, political science, and law, constantly survived this change.

"There are, besides, eternal truths, such as Freedom, Justice, etc., that are common to all states of society. But Communism abolishes eternal truths, it abolishes all religion, and all morality, instead of constituting them on a new basis; it therefore acts in contradiction to all past historical experience."

What does this accusation reduce itself to? The history of all past society has consisted in the development of class antagonisms, antagonisms that assume different forms at different epochs.

But whatever form they may have taken, one fact is common to all past ages, viz., the exploitation of one part of society by the other. No wonder, then, that the social consciousness of past ages, despite all the multiplicity and variety it displays, moves within certain common forms, or general ideas, which cannot completely vanish except with the total disappearance of class antagonisms.

The Communist revolution is the most radical rupture with traditional property-relations; no wonder that its development involves the most radical rupture with traditional ideas.

But let us have done with the bourgeois objections to Communism.

We have seen above, that the first step in the revolution by the working class, is to raise the proletariat to the position of ruling class, to win the battle of democracy.

The proletariat will use its political supremacy, to wrest, by degrees, all capital from the bourgeoisie, to centralize all instruments of production in the hands of the State, i.e., of the proletariat organized as the ruling class; and to increase the total of productive forces as rapidly as possible.

Of course, in the beginning, this cannot be effected except by means of despotic inroads on the rights of property, and on the conditions of bourgeois production; by means of measures, therefore, which appear economically insufficient and untenable, but which, in the course of the movement, outstrip themselves, necessitate further inroads upon the old social order, and are unavoidable as a means of entirely revolutionizing the mode of production.

These measures will of course be different in different countries.

Nevertheless in the most advanced countries the following will be pretty generally applicable:

1. Abolition of property in land and application of all rents of land to public purposes.

2. A heavy progressive or graduated income tax.

3. Abolition of all right of inheritance.

4. Confiscation of the property of all emigrants and rebels.

5. Centralization of credit in the hands of the state, by means of a national bank with State capital and an exclusive monopoly.

6. Centralization of the means of communication and transport in the hands of the State.

7. Extension of factories and instruments of production owned by the State; the bringing into cultivation of waste lands, and the improvement of the soil generally in accordance with a common plan.

8. Equal liability of all to labor. Establishment of industrial armies, especially for agriculture.

9. Combination of agriculture with manufacturing industries; gradual abolition of the distinction between town and country, by a more equable distribution of population over the country.

10. Free education for all children in public schools. Abolition of children's factory labor in its present form. Combination of education with industrial production, etc., etc.

When, in the course of development, class distinctions have disappeared, and all production has been concentrated in the hands of a vast association of the whole nation, the public power will lose its political character. Political power, properly so called, is merely the organized power of one class for oppressing another. If the proletariat during its contest with the bourgeoisie is compelled, by the force of circumstances, to organize itself as a class, if, by means of a revolution, it makes itself the ruling class, and, as such, sweeps away by force the old conditions of production, then it will, along with these conditions, have swept away the conditions for the existence of class antagonisms, and of classes generally, and will thereby have abolished its own supremacy as a class.

In place of the old bourgeois society, with its classes and class antagonisms, we shall have an association, in which the free development of each is the condition for the free development of all.

*   *   *

POSITION OF THE COMMUNISTS IN RELATION TO THE VARIOUS EXISTING OPPOSITION PARTIES

The Communists fight for the attainment of the immediate aims, for the enforcement of the monetary interests of the working class; but in the movement of the present, they also represent and take care of the future of that movement. In France the Communists ally themselves with the Social-Democrats, against the conservative and radical bourgeoisie, reserving, however, the right to take up a critical position in regard to phrases and illusions traditionally handed down from the great Revolution.

*   *   *

In Germany they fight with the bourgeoisie whenever it acts in a revolutionary way, against the absolute monarchy, the feudal squirearchy, and the petty bourgeoisie.

But they never cease, for a single instant, to instill into the working class the clearest possible recognition of the hostile antagonism between bourgeoisie and proletariat, in order that the German workers may straightway use, as so many weapons against the bourgeoisie, the social and political conditions that the bourgeoisie must necessarily introduce along with its supremacy, and in order that, after the fall of the reactionary classes in Germany, the fight against the bourgeoisie itself may immediately begin.

The Communists turn their attention chiefly to Germany, because that country is on the eve of a bourgeois revolution, that is bound to be carried out under more advanced conditions of European civilization, and with a more developed proletariat, than that of England was in the seventeenth, and of France in the eighteenth century, and because the bourgeois revolution in Germany will be but the prelude to an immediately following proletarian revolution.

In short, the Communists everywhere support every revolutionary movement against the existing social and political order of things.

In all these movements they bring to the front, as the leading question in each, the property question, no matter what its degree of development at the time.

Finally, they labor everywhere for the union and agreement of the democratic parties of all countries.

The Communists disdain to conceal their views and aims. They openly declare that their ends can be attained only by the forcible overthrow of all existing social conditions. Let the ruling classes tremble at a Communistic revolution. The proletarians have nothing to lose but their chains. They have a world to win.

Working men of all countries, unite!

Charles Darwin

20

The Origin of Species

Charles Darwin (1809–1882) has, with good reason, been called "the Newton of Biology." His ideas not only revolutionized that discipline but re-
formed social thought generally around the concepts of evolutionary biology. Like Newton, Darwin is one of the giant figures in the intellectual development of the Western world. Darwin's central concept, it is important
to note, was not original with him. The idea of evolution was "in the air"
during the time that the young English naturalist was surveying the results
of his five-year trip to South America in the H.M.S. "Beagle" (1831–1836).
Geologists and biologists, as well as philosophers and social thinkers, had
already advanced the concept of developmental growth in their fields. Darwin, however, gave the theory a solid scientific basis and established it
beyond cavil by marshaling voluminous evidence in its favor. He was,
nevertheless, extremely diffident about publishing his conclusions, for fear
of offending religious scruples. The simultaneous, independent exposition
of organic evolution in 1858 by another biologist, Alfred Russel Wallace,
prodded Darwin into action. Thus he published in 1859 the results of his
own findings, *The Origin of Species by Means of Natural Selection, or the
Preservation of the Favored Races in the Struggle for Life.*

The title underlined Darwin's novel thesis that organic evolution had
taken place by natural selection and competitive struggle, in which successive small variations that made for survival eventually produced new
species. Even this explanation of the process had been suggested to him in
1838, when he read Thomas Malthus's *Essay on Population,* which described the pressure of population on the food supply. *The Origin of Species,* as well as Darwin's later work, *The Descent of Man* (1871), caused a
great outcry. His theory contradicted the Christian belief in special creation, it held man to be part of nature and subject to all its laws, and it

Charles Darwin, *The Origin of Species by Means of Natural Selection, or the
Preservation of the Favored Races in the Struggle for Life,* 6th ed. (New York:
Appleton, 1892), II, 267–68, 270–82, 287–306.

seemed to obliterate the distinction between body and mind. Darwin stood firm, however, and evolution was soon widely accepted both by scientists and the general public.

The implications of the evolutionary theory were equally important for political, economic, and moral thought. By analogy, all ideas, beliefs, and institutions were conceived to be in a state of flux, a view that seemed to destroy any rational basis for absolute standards and to equate the natural and the good. By making man part of nature engaged in a dramatic struggle for survival, Darwinism reinforced the perspectives of romanticism and encouraged the irrationalism of the last century. Some social thinkers used the theory to justify the competitive economic system, while others, like Marx, saw in it a rationale for the class struggle and progress toward socialism. Darwin himself never made these broader applications or ever went beyond the limits of his biological hypothesis. The organic theory of evolution still stands essentially as he stated it, with only those modifications made necessary by new discoveries in genetics, ecology, and paleontology.

As this whole volume is one long argument, it may be convenient to the reader to have the leading facts and inferences briefly recapitulated.

That many and serious objections may be advanced against the theory of descent with modification through variation and natural selection, I do not deny. I have endeavoured to give to them their full force. Nothing at first can appear more difficult to believe than that the more complex organs and instincts have been perfected, not by means superior to, though analogous with, human reason, but by the accumulation of innumerable slight variations, each good for the individual possessor. Nevertheless, this difficulty, though appearing to our imagination insuperably great cannot be considered real if we admit the following propositions, namely, that all parts of the organisation and instincts offer, at least, individual differences—that there is a struggle for existence leading to the preservation of profitable deviations of structure or instinct—and, lastly, that gradations in the state of perfection of each organ may have existed, each good of its kind. The truth of these propositions cannot, I think, be disputed.

It is, no doubt, extremely difficult even to conjecture by what gradations many structures have been perfected, more especially amongst broken and failing groups of organic beings, which have suffered much extinction; but we see so many strange gradations in nature, that we ought to be extremely cautious in saying that any organ or instinct, or any whole structure, could not have arrived at its present state by many graduated steps. There are, it must be admitted, cases of special difficulty opposed to the theory of natural selection; and one of the most curious of these is the existence in the same community of two or three defined castes of workers or sterile female ants; but I have attempted to show how these difficulties can be mastered.

. . .

Turning to geographical distribution, the difficulties encountered on the theory of descent with modification are serious enough. All the individuals of the same species, and all the species of the same genus, or even higher group, are descended from common parents; and therefore, in however distant and isolated parts of the world they may now be found, they must in the course of successive generations have travelled from some one point to all the others. We are often wholly unable even to conjecture how this could have been effected. Yet, as we have reason to believe that some species have retained the same specific form for very long periods of time, immensely long as measured by years, too much stress ought not to be laid on the occasional wide diffusion of the same species; for during very long periods there will always have been a good chance for wide migration by many means. A broken or interrupted range may often be accounted for by the extinction of the species in the intermediate regions. It cannot be denied that we are as yet very ignorant as to the full extent of the various climatal and geographical changes which have affected the earth during modern periods; and such changes will often have facilitated migration. As an example, I have attempted to show how potent has been the influence of the Glacial period on the distribution of the same and of allied species throughout the world. We are as yet profoundly ignorant of the many occasional means of transport. With respect to distinct species of the same genus inhabiting distant and isolated regions, as the process of modification has necessarily been slow, all the means of migration will have been possible during a very long period; and consequently the difficulty of the wide diffusion of the species of the same genus is in some degree lessened.

As according to the theory of natural selection an interminable number of intermediate forms must have existed, linking together all the species in each group by gradations as fine as are our existing varieties, it may be asked, Why do we not see these linking forms all around us? Why are not all organic beings blended together in an inextricable chaos? With respect to existing forms, we should remember that we have no right to expect (excepting in rare cases) to discover *directly* connecting links between them, but only between each and some extinct and supplanted form. Even on a wide area, which has during a long period remained continuous, and of which the climatic and other conditions of life change insensibly in proceeding from a district occupied by one species into another district occupied by a closely allied species, we have no just right to expect often to find intermediate varieties in the intermediate zones. For we have reason to believe that only a few species of a genus ever undergo change; the other species becoming utterly extinct and leaving no modified progeny. Of the species which do change, only a few within the same country change at the same time; and all modifications are slowly effected. I have also shown that the intermediate varieties which probably at first existed in the intermediate zones, would be liable to be supplanted by the allied forms on either hand; for the latter, from existing in greater numbers, would generally be modified and improved at a quicker rate than the intermediate varieties, which existed in lesser numbers; so that the intermediate varieties would, in the long run, be supplanted and exterminated.

On this doctrine of the extermination of an infinitude of connecting links, between the living and extinct inhabitants of the world, and at each successive period between the extinct and still older species, why is not every geological formation charged with such links? Why does not every collection of fossil remains afford plain evidence of the gradation and mutation of the forms of life? Although geological research has undoubtedly revealed the former existence of many links, bringing numerous forms of life much closer together, it does not yield the infinitely many fine gradations between past and present species required on the theory; and this is the most obvious of the many objections which may be urged against it. Why, again, do whole groups of allied species appear, though this appearance is often false, to have come in suddenly on the successive geological stages? Although we now know that

organic beings appeared on this globe, at a period incalculably remote, long before the lowest bed of the Cambrian system was deposited, why do we not find beneath this system great piles of strata
stored with the remains of the progenitors of the Cambrian fossils?
For on the theory, such strata must somewhere have been deposited
at these ancient and utterly unknown epochs of the world's history.

I can answer these questions and objections only on the supposition that the geological record is far more imperfect than most
geologists believe. The number of specimens in all our museums is
absolutely as nothing compared with the countless generations of
countless species which have certainly existed. The parent-form of
any two or more species would not be in all its characters directly
intermediate between its modified offspring, any more than the
rock-pigeon is directly intermediate in crop and tail between its
descendants, the pouter and fantail pigeons. We should not be able
to recognise a species as the parent of another and modified species,
if we were to examine the two ever so closely, unless we possessed
most of the intermediate links; and owing to the imperfection of
the geological record, we have no just right to expect to find so many
links. If two or three, or even more linking forms were discovered,
they would simply be ranked by many naturalists as so many new
species, more especially if found in different geological sub-stages,
let their differences be ever so slight. Numerous existing doubtful
forms could be named which are probably varieties; but who will
pretend that in future ages so many fossil links will be discovered,
that naturalists will be able to decide whether or not these doubtful forms ought to be called varieties? Only a small portion of the
world has been geologically explored. Only organic beings of certain classes can be preserved in a fossil condition, at least in any
great number. Many species when once formed never undergo any
further change but become extinct without leaving modified descendants; and the periods, during which species have undergone
modification, though long as measured by years, have probably been
short in comparison with the periods during which they retained the
same form. It is the dominant and widely ranging species which
vary most frequently and vary most, and varieties are often at first
local—both causes rendering the discovery of intermediate links in
any one formation less likely. Local varieties will not spread into
other and distant regions until they are considerably modified and
improved; and when they have spread, and are discovered in a

geological formation, they appear as if suddenly created there, and will be simply classed as new species. Most formations have been intermittent in their accumulation; and their duration has probably been shorter than the average duration of specific forms. Successive formations are in most cases separated from each other by blank intervals of time of great length; for fossiliferous formations thick enough to resist future degradation can as a general rule be accumulated only where much sediment is deposited on the subsiding bed of the sea. During the alternate periods of elevation and of stationary level the record will generally be blank. During these latter periods there will probably be more variability in the forms of life; during periods of subsidence, more extinction.

With respect to the absence of strata rich in fossils beneath the Cambrian formation, I can recur only to the hypothesis given in the tenth chapter; namely, that though our continents and oceans have endured for an enormous period in nearly their present relative positions, we have no reason to assume that this has always been the case; consequently formations much older than any now known may lie buried beneath the great oceans. With respect to the lapse of time not having been sufficient since our planet was consolidated for the assumed amount of organic change, and this objection, as urged by Sir William Thompson, is probably one of the gravest as yet advanced, I can only say, firstly, that we do not know at what rate species change as measured by years, and secondly, that many philosophers are not as yet willing to admit that we know enough of the constitution of the universe and of the interior of our globe to speculate with safety on its past duration.

That the geological record is imperfect all will admit; but that it is imperfect to the degree required by our theory, few will be inclined to admit. If we look to long enough intervals of time, geology plainly declares that species have all changed; and they have changed in the manner required by the theory, for they have changed slowly and in a graduated manner. We clearly see this in the fossil remains from consecutive formations invariably being much more closely related to each other, than are the fossils from widely separated formations.

Such is the sum of the several chief objections and difficulties which may be justly urged against the theory; and I have now briefly recapitulated the answers and explanations which, as far as I can see, may be given. I have felt these difficulties far too heavily

during many years to doubt their weight. But it deserves especial
notice that the more important objections relate to questions on
which we are confessedly ignorant; nor do we know how ignorant
we are. We do not know all the possible transitional gradations
between the simplest and the most perfect organs; it cannot be pretended that we know all the varied means of Distribution during
the long lapse of years, or that we know how imperfect is the
Geological Record. Serious as these several objections are, in my
judgment they are by no means sufficient to overthrow the theory
of descent with subsequent modification.

Now let us turn to the other side of the argument. Under domestication we see much variability, caused, or at least excited, by changed
conditions of life; but often in so obscure a manner, that we are
tempted to consider the variations as spontaneous. Variability is
governed by many complex laws,—by correlated growth, compensation, the increased use and disuse of parts, and the definite action
of the surrounding conditions. There is much difficulty in ascer-
taining how largely our domestic productions have been modified;
but we may safely infer that the amount has been large, and that
modifications can be inherited for long periods. As long as the conditions of life remain the same, we have reason to believe that a
modification, which has already been inherited for many generations, may continue to be inherited for an almost infinite number of
generations. On the other hand, we have evidence that variability
when it has once come into play, does not cease under domestication
for a very long period; nor do we know that it ever ceases, for new
varieties are still occasionally produced by our oldest domesticated
productions.

Variability is not actually caused by man; he only unintentionally
exposes organic beings to new conditions of life, and then nature
acts on the organisation and causes it to vary. But man can and
does select the variations given to him by nature, and thus accumulates them in any desired manner. He thus adapts animals and plants
for his own benefit or pleasure. He may do this methodically, or
he may do it unconsciously by preserving the individuals most useful
or pleasing to him without any intention of altering the breed. It
is certain that he can largely influence the character of a breed by
selecting, in each successive generation, individual differences so
slight as to be inappreciable except by an educated eye. This un-

conscious process of selection has been the great agency in the formation of the most distinct and useful domestic breeds. That many breeds produced by man have to a large extent the character of natural species, is shown by the inextricable doubts whether many of them are varieties or aboriginally distinct species.

There is no reason why the principles which have acted so efficiently under domestication should not have acted under nature. In the survival of favoured individuals and races, during the constantly-recurrent struggle for Existence, we see a powerful and ever-acting form of Selection. The struggle for existence inevitably follows from the high geometrical ratio of increase which is common to all organic beings. This high rate of increase is proved by calculation,—by the rapid increase of many animals and plants during a succession of peculiar seasons, and when naturalised in new countries. More individuals are born than can possible survive. A grain in the balance may determine which individuals shall live and which shall die,—which variety or species shall increase in number, and which shall decrease, or finally become extinct. As the individuals of the same species come in all respects into the closest competition with each other, the struggle will generally be most severe between them; it will be almost equally severe between the varieties of the same species, and next in severity between the species of the same genus. On the other hand the struggle will often be severe between beings remote in the scale of nature. The slightest advantage in certain individuals, at any age or during any season, over those with which they come into competition, or better adaptation in however slight a degree to the surrounding physical conditions, will, in the long run, turn the balance.

With animals having separated sexes, there will be in most cases a struggle between the males for the possession of the females. The most vigorous males, or those which have most successfully struggled with their conditions of life, will generally leave most progeny. But success will often depend on the males having special weapons, or means of defence, or charms; and a slight advantage will lead to victory.

As geology plainly proclaims that each land has undergone great physical changes, we might have expected to find that organic beings have varied under nature, in the same way as they have varied under domestication. And if there has been any variability under nature, it would be an unaccountable fact if natural selection had not come into play. It has often been asserted, but the assertion is incapable of proof, that the amount of variation under nature is a strictly limited quantity. Man, though acting on external characters alone and often capriciously, can produce within a short period a great result by adding up mere individual differences in his domestic productions; and every one admits that species present individual differences. But, besides such differences, all naturalists admit that natural varieties exist, which are considered sufficiently distinct to be worthy of record in systematic works. No one has drawn any clear distinction between individual differences and slight varieties; or between more plainly marked varieties and sub-species, and species. On separate continents, and on different parts of the same continent when divided by barriers of any kind, and on outlying islands, what a multitude of forms exist, which some experienced naturalists rank as varieties, others as geographical races or sub-species, and others as distinct, though closely allied species!

If then, animals and plants do vary, let it be ever so slightly or slowly, why should not variations or individual differences, which are in any way beneficial, be preserved and accumulated through natural selection, or the survival of the fittest? If man can by patience select variations useful to him, why, under changing and complex conditions of life, should not variations useful to nature's living products often arise, and be preserved or selected? What limit can be put to this power, acting during long ages and rigidly scrutinising the whole constitution, structure, and habits of each creature,—favouring the good and rejecting the bad? I can see no limit to this power, in slowly and beautifully adapting each form to the most complex relations of life. The theory of natural selection, even if we look no farther than this, seems to be in the highest degree probable. I have already recapitulated, as fairly as I could, the opposed difficulties and objections: now let us turn to the special facts and arguments in favour of the theory.

On the view that species are only strongly marked and permanent varieties, and that each species first existed as a variety, we can see why it is that no line of demarcation can be drawn between species, commonly supposed to have been produced by special acts of creation, and varieties which are acknowledged to have been produced by secondary laws. On this same view we can understand how it is that in a region where many species of a genus have been produced, and where they now flourish, these same species should present many varieties; for where the manufactory of species has been active, we might expect, as a general rule, to find it still in action; and this is the case if varieties be incipient species. Moreover, the species of the larger genera, which afford the greater number of varieties or incipient species, retain to a certain degree the character of varieties; for they differ from each other by a less amount of difference than do the species of smaller genera. The closely allied species also of the larger genera apparently have restricted ranges, and in their affinities they are clustered in little groups round other species—in both respects resembling varieties. These are strange relations on the view that each species was independently created, but are intelligible if each existed first as a variety.

As each species tends by its geometrical rate of reproduction to increase inordinately in number; and as the modified descendants of each species will be enabled to increase by as much as they become more diversified in habits and structure, so as to be able to seize on many and widely different places in the economy of nature, there will be a constant tendency in natural selection to preserve the most divergent offspring of any one species. Hence, during a long-continued course of modification, the slight differences characteristic of varieties of the same species, tend to be augmented into the greater differences characteristic of the species of the same genus. New and improved varieties will inevitably supplant and exterminate the older, less improved, and intermediate varieties; and thus species are rendered to a large extent defined and distinct objects. Dominant species belonging to the larger groups within each class tend to give birth to new and dominant forms; so that each large group tends to become still larger, and at the same time more divergent in character. But as all groups cannot thus go on increasing in size, for the world would not hold them, the more dominant groups beat the less dominant. This tendency in the large groups to go on increasing in size and diverging in character, together with the inevitable contingency of much extinction, explains the arrangement of all the forms of life in groups subordinate to groups, all within a few great classes, which has prevailed throughout all time. This grand fact of the grouping of all organic beings under what is called the Natural System, is utterly inexplicable on the theory of creation.

As natural selection acts solely by accumulating slight, successive, favourable variations, it can produce no great or sudden modifications; it can act only by short and slow steps. Hence, the canon of "Natura non facit saltum," which every fresh addition to our knowledge tends to confirm, is on this theory intelligible. We can see why throughout nature the same general end is gained by an almost infinite diversity of means, for every peculiarity when once acquired is long inherited, and structures already modified in many different ways have to be adapted for the same general purpose. We can, in short, see why nature is prodigal in variety, though niggard in innovation. But why this should be a law of nature if each species has been independently created no man can explain.

.   .   .

If we admit that the geological record is imperfect to an extreme degree, then the facts, which the record does give, strongly support the theory of descent with modification. New species have come on the stage slowly and at successive intervals; and the amount of change, after equal intervals of time, is widely different in different groups. The extinction of species and of whole groups of species, which has played so conspicuous a part in the history of the organic world, almost inevitably follows from the principle of natural selection; for old forms are supplanted by new and improved forms. Neither single species nor groups of species reappear when the chain of ordinary generation is once broken. The gradual diffusion of dominant forms, with the slow modification of their descendants, causes the forms of life, after long intervals of time, to appear as if they had changed simultaneously throughout the world. The fact of the fossil remains of each formation being in some degree intermediate in character between the fossils in the formations above and below, is simply explained by their intermediate position in the chain of descent. The grand fact that all extinct beings can be classed with all recent beings, naturally follows from the living and the extinct being the offspring of common parents. As species have generally diverged in character during their long course of descent and modification, we can understand why it is that the more ancient forms, or early progenitors of each group, so often occupy a position in some degree intermediate between existing groups. Recent forms are generally looked upon as being, on the whole, higher in the scale of organisation than ancient forms; and they must be higher, in so far as the later and more improved forms have conquered the older and less improved forms in the struggle for life; they have also generally had their organs more specialised for different functions. This fact is perfectly compatible with numerous beings still retaining simple and but little improved structures, fitted for simple conditions of life; it is likewise compatible with some forms having retrograded in organisation, by having become at each stage of descent better fitted for new and degraded habits of life. Lastly, the wonderful law of the long endurance of allied forms on the same continent, —of marsupials in Australia, of edentata in America, and other such cases,—is intelligible, for within the same country the existing and the extinct will be closely allied by descent.

Looking to geographical distribution, if we admit that there has been during the long course of ages much migration from one part of the world to another, owing to former climatal and geographical changes and to the many occasional and unknown means of dispersal, then we can understand, on the theory of descent with modification, most of the great leading facts in Distribution. We can see why there should be so striking a parallelism in the distribution of organic beings throughout space, and in their geological succession throughout time; for in both cases the beings have been connected by the bond of ordinary generation, and the means of modification have been the same. We see the full meaning of the wonderful fact, which has struck every traveller, namely, that on the same continent, under the most diverse conditions, under heat and cold, on mountain and lowland, on deserts and marshes, most of the inhabitants within each great class are plainly related; for they are the descendants of the same progenitors and early colonists. On this same principle of former migration, combined in most cases with modification, we can understand, by the aid of the Glacial period, the identity of some few plants, and the close alliance of many others, on the most distant mountains, and in the northern and southern temperate zones; and likewise the close alliance of some of the inhabitants of the sea in the northern and southern temperate latitudes, though separated by the whole intertropical ocean. Although two countries may present physical conditions as closely similar as the same species ever require, we need feel no surprise at their inhabitants being widely different, if they have been for a long period completely sundered from each other; for as the relation of organism to organism is the most important of all relations, and as the two countries will have received colonists at various periods and in different proportions, from some other country or from each other, the course of modification in the two areas will inevitably have been different.

· · ·

The fact, as we have seen, that all past and present organic beings can be arranged within a few great classes, in groups subordinate to groups, and with the extinct groups often falling in between the recent groups, is intelligible on the theory of natural selection with its contingencies of extinction and divergence of character. On these same principles we see how it is, that the mutual affinities of the forms within each class are so complex and circuitous. We see why certain characters are far more serviceable than others for classification;—why adaptive characters, though of paramount importance to the beings, are of hardly any importance in classification; why characters derived from rudimentary parts, though of no service to the beings, are often of high classificatory value; and why embryological characters are often the most valuable of all. The real affinities of all organic beings, in contradistinction to their adaptive resemblances, are due to inheritance or community of descent. The Natural System is a genealogical arrangement, with the acquired grades of difference, marked by the terms, varieties, species, genera, families, &c.; and we have to discover the lines of descent by the most permanent characters whatever they may be and of however slight vital importance.

The similar framework of bones in the hand of a man, wing of a bat, fin of the porpoise, and leg of the horse,—the same number of vertebrae forming the neck of the giraffe and of the elephant,— and innumerable other such facts, at once explain themselves on the theory of descent with slow and slight successive modifications. The similarity of pattern in the wing and in the leg of a bat, though used for such different purpose,—in the jaws and legs of a crab,—in the petals, stamens, and pistils of a flower, is likewise, to a large extent, intelligible on the view of the gradual modification of parts or organs, which were aboriginally alike in an early progenitor in each of these classes. On the principle of successive variations not always supervening at an early age, and being inherited at a corresponding not early period of life, we clearly see why the embryos of mammals, birds, reptiles, and fishes should be so closely similar, and so unlike the adult forms. We may cease marvelling at the embryo of an air-breathing mammal or bird having branchial slits and arteries running in loops, like those of a fish which has to breathe the air dissolved in water by the aid of well-developed branchiae.

Disuse, aided sometimes by natural selection, will often have reduced organs when rendered useless under changed habits or conditions of life; and we can understand on this view the meaning of rudimentary organs. But disuse and selection will generally act on each creature, when it has come to maturity and has to play its full part in the struggle for existence, and will thus have little power on an organ during early life; hence the organ will not be reduced or rendered rudimentary at this early age. The calf, for instance, has inherited teeth, which never cut through the gums of the upper jaw, from an early progenitor having well-developed teeth; and we may believe, that the teeth in the mature animal were formerly reduced by disuse, owing to the tongue and palate, or lips, having become excellently fitted through natural selection to browse without their aid; whereas in the calf, the teeth have been left unaffected, and on the principle of inheritance at corresponding ages have been inherited from a remote period to the present day. On the view of each organism with all its separate parts having been specially created, how utterly inexplicable is it that organs bearing the plain stamp of inutility, such as the teeth in the embryonic calf or the shrivelled wings under the soldered wing-covers of many beetles, should so frequently occur. Nature may be said to have taken pains to reveal her scheme of modification, by means of rudimentary organs, of embryological and homologous structures, but we are too blind to understand her meaning.

I have now recapitulated the facts and considerations which have thoroughly convinced me that species have been modified, during a long course of descent. This has been effected chiefly through the natural selection of numerous successive, slight, favourable variations; aided in an important manner by the inherited effects of the use and disuse of parts; and in an unimportant manner, that is in relation to adaptive structures, whether past or present, by the direct action of external conditions, and by variations which seem to us in our ignorance to arise spontaneously. It appears that I formerly underrated the frequency and value of these latter forms of variation, as leading to permanent modifications of structure independently of natural selection. But as my conclusions have lately been much misrepresented, and it has been stated that I attribute the modification of species exclusively to natural selection, I may be permitted to remark that in the first edition of this work, and subsequently, I placed in a most conspicuous position—namely, at the close of the Introduction—the following words: "I am convinced that natural selection has been the main but not the exclusive means of modification." This has been of no avail. Great is the power of steady misrepresentation; but the history of science shows that fortunately this power does not long endure.

It can hardly be supposed that a false theory would explain, in so satisfactory a manner as does the theory of natural selection, the several large classes of facts above specified. It has recently been objected that this is an unsafe method of arguing; but it is a method used in judging of the common events of life, and has often been used by the greatest natural philosophers. The undulatory theory of light has thus been arrived at; and the belief in the revolution of the earth on its own axis was until lately supported by hardly any direct evidence. It is no valid objection that science as yet throws no light on the far higher problem of the essence or origin of life. Who can explain what is the essence of the attraction of gravity? No one now objects to following out the results consequent on this unknown element of attraction; notwithstanding that Leibnitz formerly accused Newton of introducing "occult qualities and miracles into philosophy."

I see no good reason why the views given in this volume should shock the religious feelings of any one. It is satisfactory, as showing how transient such impressions are, to remember that the greatest discovery ever made by man, namely, the law of the attraction of gravity, was also attacked by Leibnitz, "as subversive of natural, and inferentially of revealed, religion." A celebrated author and divine has written to me that "he has gradually learnt to see that it is just as noble a conception of the Deity to believe that He created a few original forms capable of self-development into other and needful forms, as to believe that He required a fresh act of creation to supply the voids caused by the action of His laws."

Why, it may be asked, until recently did nearly all the most eminent living naturalists and geologists disbelieve in the mutability of species. It cannot be asserted that organic beings in a state of nature are subject to no variation; it cannot be proved that the amount of variation in the course of long ages is a limited quantity; no clear distinction has been, or can be, drawn between species and well-marked varieties. It cannot be maintained that species when intercrossed are invariably sterile, and varieties invariably fertile; or that sterility is a special endowment and sign of creation. The belief that species were immutable productions was almost unavoidable as long as the history of the world was thought to be of short duration; and now that we have acquired some idea of the lapse of time, we are too apt to assume, without proof, that the geological record is so perfect that it would have afforded us plain evidence of the mutation of species, if they had undergone mutation.

But the chief cause of our natural unwillingness to admit that one species has given birth to other and distinct species, is that we are always slow in admitting great changes of which we do not see the steps. The difficulty is the same as that felt by so many geologists, when Lyell first insisted that long lines of inland cliffs had been formed, and great valleys excavated, by the agencies which we see still at work. The mind cannot possibly grasp the full meaning of the term of even a million years; it cannot add up and perceive the full effects of many slight variations, accumulated during an almost infinite number of generations.

Although I am fully convinced of the truth of the views given in this volume under the form of an abstract, I by no means expect to convince experienced naturalists whose minds are stocked with a multitude of facts all viewed, during a long course of years, from a point of view directly opposite to mine. It is so easy to hide our ignorance under such expressions as the "plan of creation," "unity of design," &c., and to think that we give an explanation when we only re-state a fact. Any one whose disposition leads him to attach more weight to unexplained difficulties than to the explanation of a certain number of facts will certainly reject the theory. A few naturalists, endowed with much flexibility of mind, and who have already begun to doubt the immutability of species, may be influenced by this volume; but I look with confidence to the future,— to young and rising naturalists, who will be able to view both sides of the question with impartiality. Whoever is led to believe that species are mutable will do good service by conscientiously expressing his conviction; for thus only can the load of prejudice by which this subject is overwhelmed be removed.

Several eminent naturalists have of late published their belief that a multitude of reputed species in each genus are not real species; but that other species are real, that is, have been independently created. This seems to me a strange conclusion to arrive at. They admit that a multitude of forms, which till lately they themselves thought were special creations, and which are still thus looked at by the majority of naturalists, and which consequently have all the external characteristic features of true species,—they admit that these have been produced by variation, but they refuse to extend the same view to other and slightly different forms. Nevertheless they do not pretend that they can define, or even conjecture, which are the created forms of life, and which are those produced by secondary laws. They admit variation as a *vera causa* in one case, they arbitrarily reject it in another, without assigning any distinction in the two cases. The day will come when this will be given as a curious illustration of the blindness of preconceived opinion. These authors seem no more startled at a miraculous act of creation than at an ordinary birth. But do they really believe that at innumerable periods in the earth's history certain elemental atoms have been commanded suddenly to flash into living tissues? Do they believe that at each supposed act of creation one individual or many were produced? Were all the infinitely numerous kinds of animals and plants created as eggs or seed, or as full grown? and in the case of mammals, were they created bearing the false marks of nourishment from the mother's womb? Undoubtedly some of these same questions cannot be answered by those who believe in the appearance or creation of only a few forms of life, or of some one form alone. It has been maintained by several authors that it is as easy to believe in the creation of a million beings as of one; but Maupertuis' philosophical axiom "of least action" leads the mind more willingly to admit the smaller number; and certainly we ought not to believe that innumerable beings within each great class have been created with plain, but deceptive, marks of descent from a single parent.

As a record of a former state of things, I have retained in the foregoing paragraphs, and elsewhere, several sentences which imply that naturalists believe in the separate creation of each species; and I have been much censured for having thus expressed myself. But undoubtedly this was the general belief when the first edition of the present work appeared. I formerly spoke to very many naturalists on the subject of evolution, and never once met with any sympathetic agreement. It is probable that some did then believe in evolution, but they were either silent, or expressed themselves so ambiguously that it was not easy to understand their meaning. Now things are wholly changed, and almost every naturalist admits the great principle of evolution. There are, however, some who still think that species have suddenly given birth, through quite unexplained means, to new and totally different forms: but, as I have attempted to show, weighty evidence can be opposed to the admission of great and abrupt modifications. Under a scientific point of view, and as leading to further investigation, but little advantage is gained by believing that new forms are suddenly developed in an inexplicable manner from old and widely different forms, over the old belief in the creation of species from the dust of the earth.

It may be asked how far I extend the doctrine of the modification of species. The question is difficult to answer, because the more distinct the forms are which we consider, by so much the arguments in favour of community of descent become fewer in number and less in force. But some arguments of the greatest weight extend very far. All the members of whole classes are connected together by a chain of affinities, and all can be classed on the same principle, in groups subordinate to groups. Fossil remains sometimes tend to fill up very wide intervals between existing orders.

Organs in a rudimentary condition plainly show that an early progenitor had the organ in a fully developed condition; and this in some cases implies an enormous amount of modification in the descendants. Throughout whole classes various structures are formed on the same pattern, and at a very early age the embryos closely resemble each other. Therefore I cannot doubt that the theory of descent with modification embraces all the members of the same great class or kingdom. I believe that animals are descended from at most only four or five progenitors, and plants from an equal or lesser number.

Analogy would lead me one step farther, namely, to the belief that all animals and plants are descended from some one prototype. But analogy may be a deceitful guide. Nevertheless all living things have much in common, in their chemical composition, their cellular structure, their laws of growth, and their liability to injurious influences. We see this even in so trifling a fact as that the same poison often similarly affects plants and animals; or that the poison secreted by the gall-fly produces monstrous growths on the wild rose or oak-tree. With all organic beings, excepting perhaps some of the very lowest, sexual reproduction seems to be essentially similar. With all, as far as is at present known, the germinal vesicle is the same; so that all organisms start from a common origin. If we look even to the two main divisions—namely, to the animal and vegetable kingdoms—certain low forms are so far intermediate in character that naturalists have disputed to which kingdom they should be referred. As Professor Asa Gray has remarked, "the spores and other reproductive bodies of many of the lower algae may claim to have first a characteristically animal, and then an unequivocally vegetable existence." Therefore, on the principle of natural selection with divergence of character, it does not seem incredible that, from some such low and intermediate form, both animals and plants may have been developed; and, if we admit this, we must likewise admit that all the organic beings which have ever lived on this earth may be descended from some one primordial form. But this inference is chiefly grounded on analogy, and it is immaterial whether or not it be accepted. No doubt it is possible, as Mr. G. H. Lewes has urged, that at the first commencement of life many different forms were evolved; but if so, we may conclude that only a very few have left modified descendants. For, as I have recently remarked in regard to the members of each great kingdom, such as the Vertebrata, Articulata, &c., we have distinct evidence in their embryological, homologous, and rudimentary structures, that within each kingdom all the members are descended from a single progenitor.

When the views advanced by me in this volume, and by Mr. Wallace, or when analogous views on the origin of species are generally admitted, we can dimly foresee that there will be a considerable revolution in natural history. Systematists will be able to pursue their labours as at present; but they will not be incessantly haunted by the shadowy doubt whether this or that form be a true species. This, I feel sure and I speak after experience, will be no slight relief. The endless disputes whether or not some fifty species of British brambles are good species will cease. Systematists will have only to decide (not that this will be easy) whether any form be sufficiently constant and distinct from other forms, to be capable of definition; and if definable, whether the differences be sufficiently important to deserve a specific name. This latter point will become a far more essential consideration than it is at present; for differences, however slight, between any two forms, if not blended by intermediate gradations, are looked at by most naturalists as sufficient to raise both forms to the rank of species.

Hereafter we shall be compelled to acknowledge that the only distinction between species and well-marked varieties is, that the latter are known, or believed, to be connected at the present day by intermediate gradations whereas species were formerly thus connected. Hence, without rejecting the consideration of the present existence of intermediate gradations between any two forms, we shall be led to weigh more carefully and to value higher the actual amount of difference between them. It is quite possible that forms now generally acknowledged to be merely varieties may hereafter be thought worthy of specific names; and in this case scientific and common language will come into accordance. In short, we shall have to treat species in the same manner as those naturalists treat genera, who admit that genera are merely artificial combinations made for convenience. This may not be a cheering prospect; but we shall at least be freed from the vain search for the undiscovered and undiscoverable essence of the term species.

The other and more general departments of natural history will rise greatly in interest. The terms used by naturalists, of affinity, relationship, community of type, paternity, morphology, adaptive characters, rudimentary and aborted organs, &c., will cease to be metaphorical, and will have a plain signification. When we no longer look at an organic being as a savage looks at a ship, as something wholly beyond his comprehension; when we regard every production of nature as one which has had a long history; when we contemplate every complex structure and instinct as the summing up of many contrivances, each useful to the possessor, in the same way as any great mechanical invention is the summing up of the labour, the experience, the reason, and even the blunders of numerous workmen; when we thus view each organic being, how far more interesting—I speak from experience—does the study of natural history become!

A grand and almost untrodden field of inquiry will be opened, on the causes and laws of variation, on correlation, on the effects of use and disuse, on the direct action of external conditions, and so forth. The study of domestic productions will rise immensely in value. A new variety raised by man will be a more important and interesting subject for study than one more species added to the infinitude of already recorded species. Our classifications will come to be, as far as they can be so made, genealogies; and will then truly give what may be called the plan of creation. The rules for classifying will no doubt become simpler when we have a definite object in view. We possess no pedigrees or armorial bearings; and we have to discover and trace the many diverging lines of descent in our natural genealogies, by characters of any kind which have long been inherited. Rudimentary organs will speak infallibly with respect to the nature of long-lost structures. Species and groups of species which are called aberrant, and which may fancifully be called living fossils, will aid us in forming a picture of the ancient forms of life. Embryology will often reveal to us the structure, in some degree obscured, of the prototypes of each great class.

When we can feel assured that all the individuals of the same species, and all the closely allied species of most genera, have within a not very remote period descended from one parent, and have migrated from some one birth-place; and when we better know the many means of migration, then, by the light which geology now throws, and will continue to throw, on former changes of climate and of the level of the land, we shall surely be enabled to trace in an admirable manner the former migrations of the inhabitants of the whole world. Even at present, by comparing the differences between the inhabitants of the sea on the opposite sides of a continent, and the nature of the various inhabitants on that continent in relation to their apparent means of immigration, some light can be thrown on ancient geography.

The noble science of Geology loses glory from the extreme imperfection of the record. The crust of the earth with its imbedded remains must not be looked at as a well-filled museum, but as a poor collection made at hazard and at rare intervals. The accumulation of each great fossiliferous formation will be recognised as having depended on an unusual concurrence of favourable circumstances, and the blank intervals between the successive stages as having been of vast duration. But we shall be able to gauge with some security the duration of these intervals by a comparison of the preceding and succeeding organic forms. We must be cautious in attempting to correlate as strictly contemporaneous two formations, which do not include many identical species, by the general succession of the forms of life. As species are produced and exterminated by slowly acting and still existing causes, and not by miraculous acts of creation; and as the most important of all causes of organic change is one which is almost independent of altered and perhaps suddenly altered physical conditions, namely, the mutual relation of organism to organism,—the improvement of one organism entailing the improvement or the extermination of others; it follows, that the amount of organic change in the fossils of consecutive formations probably serves as a fair measure of the relative, though not actual lapse of time. A number of species, however, keeping in a body might remain for a long period unchanged, whilst within the same period several of these species by migrating into new countries and coming into competition with foreign associates, might become modified; so that we must not overrate the accuracy of organic change as a measure of time.

In the future I see open fields for far more important researches. Psychology will be securely based on the foundation already well laid by Mr. Herbert Spencer, that of the necessary acquirement of each mental power and capacity by gradation. Much light will be thrown on the origin of man and his history.

Authors of the highest eminence seem to be fully satisfied with the view that each species has been independently created. To my mind it accords better with what we know of the laws impressed on matter by the Creator, that the production and extinction of the past and present inhabitants of the world should have been due to secondary causes, like those determining the birth and death of the individual. When I view all beings not as special creations, but as the lineal descendants of some few beings which lived long before the first bed of the Cambrian system was deposited, they seem to me to become ennobled. Judging from the past, we may safely infer that not one living species will transmit its unaltered likeness to a distant futurity. And of the species now living very few will transmit progeny of any kind to a far distant futurity; for the manner in which all organic beings are grouped, shows that the greater number of species in each genus, and all the species in many genera, have left no descendants, but have become utterly extinct. We can so far take a prophetic glance into futurity as to foretell that it will be the common and widely-spread species, belonging to the larger and dominant groups within each class, which will ultimately prevail and procreate new and dominant species. As all the living forms of life are the lineal descendants of those which lived long before the Cambrian epoch, we may feel certain that the ordinary succession by generation has never once been broken, and that no cataclysm has desolated the whole world. Hence we may look with some confidence to a secure future of great length. And as natural selection works solely by and for the good of each being, all corporeal and mental endowments will tend to progress towards perfection.

It is interesting to contemplate a tangled bank, clothed with many plants of many kinds, with birds singing on the bushes, with various insects flitting about, and with worms crawling through the damp earth, and to reflect that these elaborately constructed forms, so different from each other, and dependent upon each other in so complex a manner, have all been produced by laws acting around us. These laws, taken in the largest sense, being Growth with Reproduction; Inheritance which is almost implied by reproduction; Variability from the indirect and direct action of the conditions of life, and from use and disuse: a Ratio of Increase so high as to lead to a Struggle for Life, and as a consequence to Natural Selection, entailing Divergence of Character and the Extinction of less-improved forms. Thus, from the war of nature, from famine and death, the most exalted object which we are capable of conceiving, namely, the production of the higher animals, directly follows. There is grandeur in this view of life, with its several powers, having been originally breathed by the Creator into a few forms or into one; and that, whilst this planet has gone cycling on according to the fixed law of gravity, from so simple a beginning endless forms most beautiful and most wonderful have been, and are being evolved.

Fyodor Dostoevsky

---- *21* ----

The Brothers Karamazov:
The Grand Inquisitor

The contemporary era, with its concern for the irrational, unconscious springs of human behavior, with its doubts and rejection of the old certainties, may be said to have begun in the last quarter of the nineteenth century. Fyodor Dostoevsky (1821–1881), the great Russian novelist, was the literary herald of the new age, and it is significant that his genius was not truly appreciated until half a century after his death. Today he is considered one of the greatest artists and thinkers of the Western world, the one who first laid bare the chaos in men's minds and souls that prefigured the intellectual confusion of the twentieth century.

Dostoevsky's art is inseparable from his ideas. In his novels, he cast these ideas in artistic form, and his characters are symbols of universal truths. Although he wrote in a simple, direct style, the novels have an intricate, agitated quality that produces a disturbing emotional effect in the reader. Dostoevsky was a literary realist, but he probed beneath the surface of realistic detail into the tortured, innermost recesses of his characters. His work thus focused on the morbid aspects of human behavior and feeling, on evil and suffering. Dostoevsky saw men as both corrupt and capable of greatness; he felt that their salvation lay in faith in God and in His revelation through suffering, forgiveness, and love. Dostoevsky was, however, no simple believer. His faith arose from doubts and contradictions and was shaped by a sense of man's unending tragic quest.

Dostoevsky's novels reflected the tragic course of his own life and the torments of his restless mind and passionate nature. From childhood on, death, disease, and suffering pervaded his life. While in exile in Siberia as a result of his radical social views, he experienced a religious conversion. His religious feelings led him to identify with the masses of Russian peas-

Reprinted with permission of The Macmillan Company from *The Brothers Karamazov* by F. Dostoevsky. [Trans. Constance Garnett (New York, 1951), 253–72.] First published in 1912 by William Heinemann Ltd.

ants and to preach a gospel of mystical Russian nationalism. At the same
time, he attacked the bourgeois civilization of Western Europe, with its
rationalism and materialism, as decadent and doomed to destruction.
Dostoevsky was not only the prophet of the irrational: he was the enemy
of reason.

The Brothers Karamazov (1880), from which the following selection is
taken, is Dostoevsky's greatest novel. A tragic tale of a middle-class Russian
family, its theme is the search for faith through struggle against evil. "The
Grand Inquisitor" is a legend composed by Ivan Karamazov, a rationalist
and unbeliever, and told to his brother, Alyosha, a saintly figure living in a
monastery. Essentially, it is an allegory of man's tragic predicament, in
which he strives for true freedom but fears and rejects it in favor of the
happiness and security of obedience to authority. The story has also been
taken as a prophetic attack on authoritarian ideologies and systems and on
secular rationalism.

"Even this must have a preface—that is, a literary preface," laughed
Ivan, "and I am a poor hand at making one. You see, my action
takes place in the sixteenth century, and at that time, as you probably learnt at school, it was customary in poetry to bring down
heavenly powers on earth. Not to speak of Dante, in France clerks,
as well as the monks in the monasteries, used to give regular per-
formances in which the Madonna, the saints, the angels, Christ,
and God Himself were brought on the stage. In those days it was
done in all simplicity. In Victor Hugo's 'Notre Dame de Paris'
an edifying and gratuitous spectacle was provided for the people in
the Hotel de Ville of Paris in the reign of Louis XI in honor of
the birth of the dauphin. It was called Le bon jugement de la très
sainte et gracieuse Vierge Marie, and she appears herself on the
stage and pronounces her bon jugement. Similar plays, chiefly from
the Old Testament, were occasionally performed in Moscow, too,
up to the times of Peter the Great. But besides plays there were all
sorts of legends and ballads scattered about the world, in which
the saints and angels and all the powers of Heaven took part when
required. In our monasteries the monks busied themselves in translating, copying, and even composing such poems—and even under
the Tatars. There is, for instance, one such poem (of course, from
the Greek), 'The Wanderings of Our Lady Through Hell,' with

descriptions as bold as Dante's. Our Lady visits Hell, and the Archangel Michael leads her through the torments. She sees the sinners and their punishment. There she sees among others one noteworthy set of sinners in a burning lake; some of them sink to the bottom of the lake so that they can't swim out, and 'these God forgets'—an expression of extraordinary depth and force. And so Our Lady, shocked and weeping, falls before the throne of God and begs for mercy for all in Hell—for all she has seen there, and indiscriminately. Her conversation with God is immensely interesting. She beseeches Him, she will not desist, and when God points to the hands and feet of her Son, nailed to the Cross, and asks, 'How can I forgive His tormentors?' she bids all the saints, all the martyrs, all the angels and archangels to fall down with her and pray for mercy on all without distinction. It ends by her winning from God a respite of suffering every year from Good Friday till Trinity day, and the sinners at once raise a cry of thankfulness from Hell, chanting, 'Thou art just, O Lord, in this judgment.' Well, my poem would have been of that kind if it had appeared at that time. He comes on the scene in my poem, but He says nothing, only appears and passes on. Fifteen centuries have passed since He promised to come in His glory, fifteen centuries since His prophet wrote, 'Behold, I come quickly'; 'Of that day and that hour knoweth no man, neither the Son, but the Father,' as He Himself predicted on earth. But humanity awaits him with the same faith and with the same love. Oh, with greater faith, for it is fifteen centuries since man has ceased to see signs from Heaven.

> *No signs from Heaven come today*
> *To add to what the heart doth say.*

There was nothing left but faith in what the heart doth say. It is true there were many miracles in those days. There were saints who performed miraculous cures; some holy people, according to their biographies, were visited by the Queen of Heaven herself. But the devil did not slumber, and doubts were already arising among men of the truth of these miracles. And just then there appeared in the north of Germany a terrible new heresy. 'A huge star like to a torch' (that is, to a church) 'fell on the sources of the waters and they became bitter.' These heretics began blasphemously denying miracles. But those who remained faithful were all the more ardent in their faith. The tears of humanity rose up to Him as

before, awaiting His coming, loved Him, hoped for Him, yearned
to suffer and die for Him as before. And so many ages mankind had
prayed with faith and fervor, 'O Lord our God, hasten Thy coming,' so many ages called upon Him, that in His infinite mercy He
deigned to come down to His servants. Before that day He had
come down, He had visited some holy men, martyrs, and hermits, as
is written in their 'Lives.' Among us, Tyutchev, with absolute faith
in the truth of his words, bore witness that

> *Bearing the Cross, in slavish dress,*
> *Weary and worn, the Heavenly King*
> *Our mother, Russia, came to bless,*
> *And through our land went wandering.*

And that certainly was so, I assure you.

"And behold, He deigned to appear for a moment to the people,
to the tortured, suffering people, sunk in iniquity, but loving Him
like children. My story is laid in Spain, in Seville, in the most terrible time of the Inquisition, when fires were lighted every day to
the glory of God, and 'in the splendid *auto da fé* the wicked heretics
were burnt.' Oh, of course, this was not the coming in which He
will appear according to His promise at the end of time in all His
heavenly glory, and which will be sudden 'as lightning flashing from
east to west.' No, He visited His children only for a moment, and
there where the flames were crackling round the heretics. In His
infinite mercy He came once more among men in that human shape
in which He walked among men for three years fifteen centuries ago.
He came down to the 'hot pavement' of the southern town in
which on the day before almost a hundred heretics had, *ad majorem
gloriam Dei,* been burnt by the cardinal, the Grand Inquisitor, in a
magnificent *auto da fé,* in the presence of the king, the court, the
knights, the cardinals, the most charming ladies of the court, and
the whole population of Seville.

"He came softly, unobserved, and yet, strange to say, every one
recognized Him. That might be one of the best passages in the poem.
I mean, why they recognized Him. The people are irresistibly
drawn to Him, they surround Him, they flock about Him, follow
Him. He moves silently in their midst with a gentle smile of infinite compassion. The sun of love burns in His heart, light and
power shine from His eyes, and their radiance, shed on the people,
stirs their hearts with responsive love. He holds out His hands to

them, blesses them, and a healing virtue comes from contact with Him, even with His garments. An old man in the crowd, blind from childhood, cries out, 'O Lord, heal me and I shall see Thee!' and, as it were, scales fall from his eyes and the blind man sees Him. The crowd weeps and kisses the earth under His feet. Children throw flowers before Him, sing, and cry hosannah. 'It is He—it is He!' all repeat. 'It must be He, it can be no one but Him!' He stops at the steps of the Seville cathedral at the moment when the weeping mourners are bringing in a little open white coffin. In it lies a child of seven, the only daughter of a prominent citizen. The dead child lies hidden in flowers. 'He will raise your child,' the crowd shouts to the weeping mother. The priest, coming to meet the coffin, looks perplexed and frowns, but the mother of the dead child throws herself at His feet with a wail. 'If it is Thou, raise my child!' she cries, holding out her hands to Him. The procession halts, the coffin is laid on the steps at His feet. He looks with compassion, and His lips once more softly pronounce, 'Maiden, arise!' and the maiden arises. The little girl sits up in the coffin and looks round, smiling with wide-open wondering eyes, holding a bunch of white roses they had put in her hand.

"There are cries, sobs, confusion among the people, and at that moment the cardinal himself, the Grand Inquisitor, passes by the cathedral. He is an old man, almost ninety, tall and erect, with a withered face and sunken eyes, in which there is still a gleam of light. He is not dressed in his gorgeous cardinal's robes, as he was the day before, when he was burning the enemies of the Roman Church—at that moment he was wearing his coarse, old, monk's cassock. At a distance behind him come his gloomy assistants and slaves and the 'holy guard.' He stops at the sight of the crowd and watches it from a distance. He sees everything; he sees them set the coffin down at His feet, sees the child rise up, and his face darkens. He knits his thick grey brows and his eyes gleam with a sinister fire. He holds out his finger and bids the guards take Him. And such is his power, so completely are the people cowed into submission and trembling obedience to him, that the crowd immediately makes way for the guards, and in the midst of death-like silence they lay hands on Him and lead Him away. The crowd instantly bows down to the earth, like one man, before the old inquisitor. He blesses the people in silence and passes on. The guards lead their prisoner to the close, gloomy, vaulted prison in the ancient

palace of the Holy Inquisition and shut Him in it. The day passes
and is followed by the dark, burning 'breathless' night of Seville.
The air is 'fragrant with laurel and lemon.' In the pitch darkness
the iron door of the prison is suddenly opened and the Grand Inquisitor himself comes in with a light in his hand. He is alone; the
door is closed at once behind him. He stands in the doorway and for
a minute or two gazes into His face. At last he goes up slowly, sets
the light on the table and speaks.

"'Is it Thou? Thou?' but receiving no answer, he adds at once,
'Don't answer, be silent. What canst Thou say, indeed? I know too
well what Thou wouldst say. And Thou hast no right to add anything to what Thou hadst said of old. Why, then, art Thou come
to hinder us? For Thou hast come to hinder us, and Thou knowest that. But dost Thou know what will be tomorrow? I know not
who Thou art and care not to know whether it is Thou or only a
semblance of Him, but tomorrow I shall condemn Thee and burn
Thee at the stake as the worst of heretics. And the very people who
have today kissed Thy feet, tomorrow at the faintest sign from me
will rush to heap up the embers of Thy fire. Knowest Thou that?
Yes, maybe Thou knowest it,' he added with thoughtful penetration,
never for a moment taking his eyes off the Prisoner."

"I don't quite understand, Ivan. What does it mean?" Alyosha,
who had been listening in silence, said with a smile. "Is it simply a
wild fantasy, or a mistake on the part of the old man—some impossible *qui pro quo*?"

"Take it as the last," said Ivan, laughing, "if you are so corrupted
by modern realism and can't stand anything fantastic. If you like it
to be a case of mistaken identity, let it be so. It is true," he went on,
laughing, "the old man was ninety, and he might well be crazy
over his set idea. He might have been struck by the appearance of
the Prisoner. It might, in fact, be simply his ravings, the delusion
of an old man of ninety, over-excited by the *auto da fé* of a hundred
heretics the day before. But does it matter to us after all whether
it was a mistake of identity or a wild fantasy? All that matters is
that the old man should speak out, should speak openly of what
he has thought in silence for ninety years."

"And the Prisoner too is silent? Does He look at him and not
say a word?"

"That's inevitable in any case," Ivan laughed again. "The old
man has told Him He hasn't the right to add anything to what

He has said of old. One may say it is the most fundamental feature of Roman Catholicism, in my opinion at least. 'All has been given by Thee to the Pope,' they say, 'and all, therefore, is still in the Pope's hands, and there is no need for Thee to come now at all. Thou must not meddle for the time, at least.' That's how they speak and write, too—the Jesuits, at any rate. I have read it myself in the works of their theologians. 'Hast Thou the right to reveal to us one of the mysteries of that world from which Thou hast come?' my old man asks Him, and answers the question for Him. 'No, Thou has not; that Thou mayest not add to what has been said of old, and mayest not take from men the freedom which Thou didst exalt when Thou wast on earth. Whatsoever Thou revealest anew will encroach on men's freedom of faith; for it will be manifest as a miracle, and the freedom of their faith was dearer to Thee than anything in those days fifteen hundred years ago. Didst Thou not often say then, "I will make you free"? But now Thou hast seen these "free" men,' the old man adds suddenly, with a pensive smile. 'Yes, we've paid dearly for it,' he goes on, looking sternly at Him, 'but at last we have completed that work in Thy name. For fifteen centuries we have been wrestling with Thy freedom, but now it is ended and over for good. Dost Thou not believe that it's over for good? Thou lookest meekly at me and deignest not even to be wroth with me. But let me tell Thee that now, to-day, people are more persuaded than ever that they have perfect freedom, yet they have brought their freedom to us and laid it humbly at our feet. But that has been our doing. Was this what Thou didst? Was this Thy freedom?' "

"I don't understand again," Alyosha broke in. "Is he ironical, is he jesting?"

"Not a bit of it! He claims it as a merit for himself and his Church that at last they have vanquished freedom and have done so to make men happy. 'For now' (he is speaking of the Inquisition, of course) 'for the first time it has become possible to think of the happiness of men. Man was created a rebel; and how can rebels be happy? Thou wast warned,' he says to Him. 'Thou hast had no lack of admonitions, and warnings, but Thou didst not listen to those warnings; Thou didst reject the only way by which men might be made happy. But, fortunately, departing Thou didst hand on the work to us. Thou hast promised, Thou hast established by Thy word, Thou hast given to us the right to bind and to unbind, and now, of course, Thou canst not think of taking it away. Why, then, hast Thou come to hinder us?' "

"And what's the meaning of 'no lack of admonitions and warnings'?" asked Alyosha.

"Why, that's the chief part of what the old man must say.

" 'The wise and dread Spirit, the spirit of self-destruction and nonexistence,' the old man goes on, 'the great spirit talked with Thee in the wilderness, and we are told in the books that he "tempted" Thee. Is that so? And could anything truer be said than what he revealed to Thee in three questions and what Thou didst reject, and what in the books is called "the temptation"? And yet if there has ever been on earth a real stupendous miracle, it took place on that day, on the day of the three temptations. The statement of those three questions was itself the miracle. If it were possible to imagine simply for the sake of argument that those three questions of the dread spirit had perished utterly from the books, and that we had to restore them and to invent them anew, and to do so had gathered together all the wise men of the earth—rulers, chief priests, learned men, philosophers, poets—and had set them the task to invent three questions, such as would not only fit the occasion, but express in three words, three human phrases, the whole future history of the world and of humanity—dost Thou believe that all the wisdom of the earth united could have invented anything in depth and force equal to the three questions which were actually put to Thee then by the wise and mighty spirit in the wilderness? From those questions alone, from the miracle of their statement, we can see that we have here to do not with the fleeting human intelligence, but with the absolute and eternal. For in those three questions the whole subsequent history of mankind is, as it were, brought together into one whole, and foretold, and in them are united all the unsolved historical contradictions of human nature. At the time it could not be so clear, since the future was unknown; but now that fifteen hundred years have passed, we see that everything in those three questions was so justly divined and foretold, and has been so truly fulfilled, that nothing can be added to them or taken from them.

" 'Judge Thyself who was right—Thou or he who questioned Thee then? Remember the first question; its meaning, in other words, was this: "Thou wouldst go into the world, and art going with empty hands, with some promise of freedom which men in their simplicity and their natural unruliness cannot even understand, which they fear and dread—for nothing has ever been more insupportable for a man and a human society than freedom. But seest Thou these stones in this parched and barren wilderness? Turn them into bread, and mankind will run after Thee like a flock of sheep, grateful and obedient, though forever trembling, lest Thou withdraw Thy hand and deny them Thy bread." But Thou wouldst not deprive man of freedom and didst reject the offer, thinking, what is that freedom worth, if obedience is bought with bread? Thou didst reply that man lives not by bread alone. But dost Thou know that for the sake of that earthly bread the spirit of the earth will rise up against Thee and will strive with Thee and overcome Thee, and all will follow him, crying, "Who can compare with this beast? He has given us fire from heaven!" Dost Thou know that the ages will pass, and humanity will proclaim by the lips of their sages that there is no crime, and therefore no sin; there is only hunger? "Feed men, and then ask of them virtue!" that's what they'll write on the banner which they will raise against Thee, and with which they will destroy Thy temple. Where Thy temple stood will rise a new building; the terrible tower of Babel will be built again, and though, like the one of old, it will not be finished, yet Thou mightest have prevented that new tower and have cut short the sufferings of men for a thousand years; for they will come back to us after a thousand years of agony with their tower. They will seek us again, hidden underground in the catacombs, for we shall be again persecuted and tortured. They will find us and cry to us, "Feed us, for those who have promised us fire from heaven haven't given it!" And then we shall finish building their tower, for he finishes the building who feeds them. And we alone shall feed them in Thy name, declaring falsely that it is in Thy name. Oh, never, never can they feed themselves without us! No science will give them bread so long as they remain free. In the end they will lay their freedom at our feet, and say to us, "Make us your slaves, but feed us." They will understand themselves, at last, that freedom and bread enough for all are inconceivable together, for never, never will they be able to share between them! They will be convinced, too, that they can never be free, for they are weak, vicious, worthless and rebellious. Thou didst promise them the bread of Heaven, but, I repeat again, can it compare with earthly bread in the eyes of the weak, ever-sinful and ignoble race of man? And if for the sake of the bread of Heaven

thousands and tens of thousands shall follow Thee, what is to become of the millions and tens of thousands of millions of creatures
who will not have the strength to forego the earthly bread for the
sake of the heavenly? Or dost Thou care only for the tens of
thousands of the great and strong, while the millions, numerous as
the sands of the sea, who are weak but love Thee, must exist
only for the sake of the great and strong? No, we care for the weak,
too. They are sinful and rebellious, but in the end they too will become obedient. They will marvel at us and look on us as gods,
because we are ready to endure the freedom which they have found
so dreadful and to rule over them—so awful it will seem to them to
be free. But we shall tell them that we are Thy servants and rule
them in Thy name. We shall deceive them again, for we will not let
Thee come to us again. That deception will be our suffering, for
we shall be forced to lie.

" 'This is the significance of the first question in the wilderness,
and this is what Thou hast rejected for the sake of that freedom
which Thou hast exalted above everything. Yet in this question
lies hidden the great secret of this world. Choosing "bread," Thou
wouldst have satisfied the universal and everlasting craving of humanity—to find someone to worship. So long as man remains free
he strives for nothing so incessantly and so painfully as to find someone to worship. But man seeks to worship what is established
beyond dispute, so that all men would agree at once to worship it.
For these pitiful creatures are concerned not only to find what
one or the other can worship, but to find something that all would
believe in and worship; what is essential is that all may be *together*
in it. This craving for *community* of worship is the chief misery of
every man individually and of all humanity from the beginning of
time. For the sake of common worship they've slain each other
with the sword. They have set up gods and challenged one another,
"Put away your gods and come and worship ours, or we will kill
you and your gods!" And so it will be to the end of the world, even
when gods disappear from the earth; they will fall down before idols
just the same. Thou didst know, Thou couldst not but have known,
this fundamental secret of human nature, but Thou didst reject the
one infallible banner which was offered Thee to make all men bow
down to Thee alone—the banner of earthly bread; and Thou hast
rejected it for the sake of freedom and the bread of Heaven. Behold what Thou didst further. And all again in the name of freedom!

I tell Thee that man is tormented by no greater anxiety than to find someone quickly to whom he can hand over the gift of freedom with which the ill-fated creature is born. But only one who can appease their conscience can take over their freedom. In bread there was offered Thee an invincible banner; give bread, and man will worship Thee, for nothing is more certain than bread. But if someone else gains possession of his conscience—oh! then he will cast away Thy bread and follow after him who has ensnared his conscience. In that Thou wast right. For the secret of man's being is not only to live but to have something to live for. Without a stable conception of the object of life, man would not consent to go on living, and would rather destroy himself than remain on earth, though he had bread in abundance. That is true. But what happened? Instead of taking men's freedom from them, Thou didst make it greater than ever! Didst Thou forget that man prefers peace, and even death, to freedom of choice in the knowledge of good and evil? Nothing is more seductive for man than his freedom of conscience, but nothing is a greater cause of suffering. And behold, instead of giving a firm foundation for setting the conscience of man at rest forever, Thou didst choose all that is exceptional, vague and enigmatic; Thou didst choose what was utterly beyond the strength of men, acting as though Thou didst not love them at all—Thou who didst come to give Thy life for them! Instead of taking possession of man's freedom, Thou didst increase it, and burdened the spiritual kingdom of mankind with its sufferings forever. Thou didst desire man's free love, that he should follow Thee freely, enticed and taken captive by Thee. In place of the rigid, ancient law, man must hereafter with free heart decide for himself what is good and what is evil, having only Thy image before him as his guide. But didst Thou not know he would at last reject even Thy image and Thy truth, if he is weighed down with the fearful burden of free choice? They will cry aloud at last that the truth is not in Thee, for they could not have been left in greater confusion and suffering than Thou hast caused, laying upon them so many cares and unanswerable problems.

" 'So that, in truth, Thou didst Thyself lay the foundation for the destruction of Thy kingdom, and no one is more to blame for it. Yet what was offered Thee? There are three powers, three powers alone, able to conquer and to hold captive forever the conscience of these impotent rebels for their happiness—those forces are miracle,

mystery and authority. Thou hast rejected all three and hast set the
example for doing so. When the wise and dread spirit set Thee on
the pinnacle of the temple and said to Thee, "If Thou wouldst know
whether Thou art the Son of God then cast Thyself down, for it is
written: the angels shall hold him up lest he fall and bruise himself, and Thou shalt know then whether Thou art the Son of God
and shalt prove then how great is Thy faith in Thy Father." But
Thou didst refuse and wouldst not cast Thyself down. Oh! of course,
Thou didst proudly and well like God; but the weak, unruly race
of men, are they gods? Oh, Thou didst know then that in taking
one step, in making one movement to cast Thyself down, Thou
wouldst be tempting God and have lost all Thy faith in Him, and
wouldst have been dashed to pieces against that earth which Thou
didst come to save. And the wise spirit that tempted Thee would
have rejoiced. But I ask again, are there many like Thee? And
couldst Thou believe for one moment that men, too, could face such
a temptation? Is the nature of men such that they can reject miracle,
and at the great moments of their life, the moments of their deepest,
most agonizing spiritual difficulties, cling only to the free verdict
of the heart? Oh, Thou didst know that Thy deed would be recorded in books, would be handed down to remote times and the
utmost ends of the earth, and Thou didst hope that man, following
Thee, would cling to God and not ask for a miracle. But Thou
didst not know that when man rejects miracle he rejects God too;
for man seeks not so much God as the miraculous. And as man
cannot bear to be without the miraculous, he will create new
miracles of his own for himself, and will worship deeds of sorcery
and witchcraft, though he might be a hundred times over a rebel,
heretic and infidel. Thou didst not come down from the Cross when
they shouted to Thee, mocking and reviling Thee, "Come down
from the Cross and we will believe that Thou art He." Thou didst
not come down, for again Thou wouldst not enslave man by a
miracle, and didst crave faith given freely, not based on miracle.
Thou didst crave for free love and not the base raptures of the
slave before the might that has overawed him forever. But Thou
didst think too highly of men therein, for they are slaves, of course,
though rebellious by nature. Look round and judge; fifteen centuries
have passed; look upon them. Whom hast Thou raised up to Thyself? I swear, man is weaker and baser by nature than Thou hast
believed him! Can he, can he do what Thou didst? By showing him

so much respect, Thou didst, as it were, cease to feel for him, for Thou didst ask far too much from him—Thou who hast loved him more than Thyself! Respecting him less, Thou wouldst have asked less of him. That would have been more like love, for his burden would have been lighter. He is weak and vile. What though he is everywhere now rebelling against our power, and proud of his rebellion? It is the pride of a child and a schoolboy. They are little children rioting and barring out the teacher at school. But their childish delight will end; it will cost them dear. They will cast down temples and drench the earth with blood. But they will see at last, the foolish children, that, though they are rebels, they are impotent rebels, unable to keep up their own rebellion. Bathed in their foolish tears, they will recognize at last that He who created them rebels must have meant to mock at them. They will say this in despair, and their utterance will be a blasphemy which will make them more unhappy still, for man's nature cannot bear blasphemy, and in the end always avenges it on itself. And so unrest, confusion and unhappiness—that is the present lot of man after Thou didst bear so much for their freedom! Thy great prophet tells in vision and in image that he saw all those who took part in the first resurrection and that there were of each tribe twelve thousand. But if there were so many of them, they must have been not men but gods. They had borne Thy cross, they had endured scores of years in the barren, hungry wilderness, living upon locusts and roots—and Thou mayest indeed point with pride at those children of freedom, of free love, of free and splendid sacrifice for Thy name. But remember that they were only some thousands; and what of the rest? And how are the other weak ones to blame, because they could not endure what the strong have endured? How is the weak soul to blame that it is unable to receive such terrible gifts? Canst Thou have simply come to the elect and for the elect? But if so, it is a mystery and we cannot understand it. And if it is a mystery, we too have a right to preach a mystery, and to teach them that it's not the free judgment of their hearts, not love, that matters, but a mystery which they must follow blindly, even against their conscience. So we have done. We have corrected Thy work and have founded it upon *miracle, mystery* and *authority*. And men rejoiced that they were again led like sheep, and that the terrible gift that had brought them such suffering was, at last, lifted from their hearts. Were we right teaching them this? Speak! Did we not love mankind, so meekly acknowledging their feebleness, lovingly lightening their burden, and permitting their weak nature even sin with our sanction? Why hast Thou come now to hinder us? And why dost Thou look silently and searchingly at me with Thy mild eyes? Be angry. I don't want Thy love, for I love Thee not. And what use is it for me to hide anything from Thee? Don't I know to Whom I am speaking? All that I can say is known to Thee already. And is it for me to conceal from Thee our mystery? Perhaps it is Thy will to hear it from my lips. Listen, then. We are not working with Thee, but with *him*—that is our mystery. It's long—eight centuries—since we have been on *his* side and not on Thine. Just eight centuries ago, we took from him what Thou didst reject with scorn, that last gift he offered Thee, showing Thee all the kingdoms of the earth. We took from him Rome and the sword of Caesar, and proclaimed ourselves sole rulers of the earth, though hitherto we have not been able to complete our work. But whose fault is that? Oh, the work is only beginning, but it has begun. It has long to await completion and the earth has yet much to suffer, but we shall triumph and shall be Caesars, and then we shall plan the universal happiness of man. But Thou mightest have taken even the sword of Caesar. Why didst Thou reject that last gift? Hadst Thou accepted that last counsel of the mighty spirit, Thou wouldst have accomplished all that man seeks on earth—that is, someone to worship, someone to keep his conscience, and some means of uniting all in one unanimous and harmonious ant heap, for the craving for universal unity is the third and last anguish of men. Mankind as a whole has always striven to organize a universal state. There have been many great nations with great histories, but the more highly they were developed the more unhappy they were, for they felt more acutely than other people the craving for world-wide union. The great conquerors, Timours and Genghis Khans, whirled like hurricanes over the face of the earth, striving to subdue its people, and they too were but the unconscious expression of the same craving for universal unity. Hadst Thou taken the world and Caesar's purple, Thou wouldst have founded the universal state and have given universal peace. For who can rule men if not he who holds their conscience and their bread in his hands? We have taken the sword of Caesar, and in taking it, of course, have rejected Thee and followed *him*. Oh, ages are yet to come of the confusion of free thought, of their science and cannibalism. For having begun to build their tower of Babel without us, they will end, of course, with cannibalism. But then the beast will crawl to us and lick our feet and spatter them with tears of blood. And we shall sit upon the beast and raise the cup, and on it will be written, "Mystery." But then, and only then, the reign of peace and happiness will come for men. Thou art proud of Thine elect, but Thou hast only the elect, while we give rest to all. And besides, how many of those elect, those mighty ones who could become elect, have grown weary waiting for Thee, and have transferred and will transfer the powers of their spirit and the warmth of their heart to the other camp, and end by raising their *free* banner against Thee. Thou didst Thyself lift up that banner. But with us all will be happy and will no more rebel, nor destroy one another as under Thy freedom. Oh, we shall persuade them that they will only become free when they renounce their freedom to us and submit to us. And shall we be right or shall we be lying? They will be convinced that we are right, for they will remember the horrors of slavery and confusion to which Thy freedom brought them. Freedom, free thought and science, will lead them into such straits and will bring them face to face with such marvels and insoluble mysteries that some of them, the fierce and rebellious, will destroy themselves; others, rebellious but weak, will destroy one another, while the rest, weak and unhappy, will crawl fawning to our feet and whine to us: "Yes, you were right, you alone possess His mystery, and we come back to you, save us from ourselves!"

" 'Receiving bread from us, they will see clearly that we take the bread made by their hands from them, to give it to them, without any miracle. They will see that we do not change the stones to bread, but in truth they will be more thankful for taking it from our hands than for the bread itself! For they will remember only too well that in old days, without our help, even the bread they made turned to stones in their hands, while since they have come back to us, the very stones have turned to bread in their hands. Too, too well they know the value of complete submission! And until men know that, they will be unhappy. Who is most to blame for their not knowing it, speak? Who scattered the flock and sent it astray on unknown paths? But the flock will come together again and will submit once more, and then it will be once for all. Then we shall give them the quiet humble happiness of weak creatures such as they are by nature. Oh, we shall persuade them at last not to be proud, for Thou didst lift them up and thereby taught them to be proud. We shall show them that they are weak, that they are only pitiful children, but that childlike happiness is the sweetest of all. They will become timid and will look to us and huddle close to us in fear, as chicks to the hen. They will marvel at us and will be awe-stricken before us, and will be proud at our being so powerful and clever, that we have been able to subdue such a turbulent flock of thousands of millions. They will tremble impotently before our wrath, their minds will grow fearful, they will be quick to shed tears like women and children, but they will be just as ready at a sign from us to pass to laughter and rejoicing. to happy mirth and childish song. Yes, we shall set them to work, but in their leisure hours we shall make their life like a child's game, with children's songs and innocent dance. Oh, we shall allow them even sin; they are weak and helpless, and they will love us like children because we allow them to sin. We shall tell them that every sin will be expiated, if it is done with our permission, that we allow them to sin because we love them, and the punishment for these sins we take upon ourselves. And we shall take it upon ourselves, and they will adore us as their saviors who have taken on themselves their sins before God. And they will have no secrets from us. We shall allow or forbid them to live with their wives and mistresses, to have or not to have children—according to whether they have been obedient or disobedient—and they will submit to us gladly and cheerfully. The most painful secrets of their conscience, all, all they will bring to us, and we shall have an answer for all. And they will be glad to believe our answer, for it will save them from the great anxiety and terrible agony they endure at present in making a free decision for themselves. And all will be happy, all the millions of creatures, except the hundred thousand who rule over them. For only we, we who guard the mystery, shall be unhappy. There will be thousands of millions of happy babes, and a hundred thousand sufferers who have taken upon themselves the curse of the knowledge of good and evil. Peacefully they will die, peacefully they will expire in Thy name, and beyond the grave they will find nothing but death. But we shall keep the secret, and for their happiness we shall allure them with the reward of heaven and eternity. Though if there were anything in the other world, it certainly would not be for such as they. It is prophesied that Thou wilt come again in victory, Thou wilt come with Thy chosen, the proud and strong, but we will say that they have only saved themselves, but we have saved all. We are told that the harlot who sits upon the beast, and holds in her hands the *mystery*, shall be put to shame, that the weak will rise up again, and will rend her royal purple and will strip naked her loathsome body. But then I will stand up and point out to Thee the thousand millions of happy children who have known no sin. And we who have taken their sins upon us for their happiness will stand up before Thee and say: "Judge us if Thou canst and darest." Know that I fear Thee not. Know that I too have been in the wilderness, I too have lived on roots and locusts, I too prized the freedom with which Thou hast blessed men, and I too was striving to stand among Thy elect, among the strong and powerful, thirsting "to make up the number." But I awakened and would not serve madness. I turned back and joined the ranks of those *who have corrected Thy work*. I left the proud and went back to the humble, for the happiness of the humble. What I say to Thee will come to pass, and our dominion will be built up. I repeat, tomorrow Thou shalt see that obedient flock who at a sign from me will hasten to heap up the hot cinders about the pile on which I shall burn Thee for coming to hinder us. For if anyone has ever deserved our fires, it is Thou. Tomorrow I shall burn Thee. *Dixi.*' "

Ivan stopped. He was carried away as he talked and spoke with excitement; when he had finished, he suddenly smiled.

Alyosha had listened in silence; toward the end he was greatly moved and seemed several times on the point of interrupting, but restrained himself. Now his words came with a rush.

"But . . . that's absurd!" he cried, flushing. "Your poem is in praise of Jesus, not in blame of Him—as you meant it to be. And who will believe you about freedom? Is that the way to understand it? That's not the idea of it in the Orthodox Church. . . . That's Rome, and not even the whole of Rome, it's false—those are the worst of the Catholics, the Inquisitors, the Jesuits! . . . And there could not be such a fantastic creature as your Inquisitor. What are these sins of mankind they take on themselves? Who are these keepers of the mystery who have taken some curse upon themselves for the happiness of mankind? When have they been seen? We know the Jesuits, they are spoken ill of, but surely they are not what you describe? They are not that at all, not at all. . . . They are simply the Romish army for the earthly sovereignty of the world in the future, with the Pontiff of Rome for Emperor . . . that's their ideal, but there's no sort of mystery or lofty melancholy about it. . . . It's simple lust of power, of filthy earthly gain, of domination—something like a universal serfdom with them as masters—that's all they stand for. They don't even believe in God, perhaps. Your suffering Inquisitor is a mere fantasy."

"Stay, stay," laughed Ivan, "how hot you are! A fantasy you say, let it be so! Of course it's a fantasy. But allow me to say: do you really think that the Roman Catholic movement of the last centuries is actually nothing but the lust of power, of filthy earthly gain? Is that Father Païssy's teaching?"

"No, no, on the contrary, Father Païssy did once say something the same as you . . . but of course it's not the same, not a bit the same," Alyosha hastily corrected himself.

"A precious admission, in spite of your 'not a bit the same.' I ask you why your Jesuits and Inquisitors have united simply for vile material gain? Why can there not be among them one martyr oppressed by great sorrow and loving humanity? You see, only suppose that there was one such man among all those who desire nothing but filthy material gain—if there's only one like my old Inquisitor, who had himself eaten roots in the desert and made frenzied efforts to subdue his flesh to make himself free and perfect. But yet all his life he loved humanity, and suddenly his eyes were opened, and he saw that it is no great moral blessedness to attain perfection and freedom, if at the same time one gains the conviction that billions of God's creatures have been created as a mockery, that they will never be capable of using their freedom, that these poor rebels can never turn into giants to complete the tower, that it was not for such geese that the great idealist dreamt his dream of harmony. Seeing all that, he turned back and joined—the clever people. Surely that could have happened?"

"Joined whom, what clever people?" cried Alyosha, completely carried away. "They have no such great cleverness and no mysteries and secrets. . . . Perhaps nothing but atheism, that's all their secret. Your Inquisitor does not believe in God, that's his secret!"

"What if it is so! At last you have guessed it. It's perfectly true that that's the whole secret, but isn't that suffering, at least for a man like that, who has wasted his whole life in the desert and yet could not shake off his incurable love of humanity? In his old age he reached the clear conviction that nothing but the advice of the great dread spirit could build up any tolerable sort of life for the feeble, unruly, 'incomplete, empirical creatures created in jest.' And so, convinced of this, he sees that he must follow the council of the wise spirit, the dread spirit of death and destruction, and therefore accept lying and deception, and lead men consciously to death and destruction, and yet deceive them all the way so that they may not notice where they are being led, that the poor, blind creatures may at least on the way think themselves happy. And note, the deception is in the name of Him in Whose ideal the old man had so fervently believed all his life long. Is not that tragic? And if only one such stood at the head of the whole army 'filled with the lust of power only for the sake of filthy gain'—would not one such be enough to make a tragedy? More than that, one such standing at the head is enough to create the actual leading idea of the Roman Church with all its armies and Jesuits, its highest idea. I tell you frankly that I firmly believe that there has always been such a man among those who stood at the head of the movement. Who knows, there may have been some such even among the Roman Popes. Who knows, perhaps the spirit of that accursed old man who loves mankind so obstinately in his own way is to be found even now in a whole multitude of such old men, existing not by chance but by agreement, as a secret league formed long ago for the guarding of the mystery, to guard it from the weak and the unhappy, so as to make them happy. No doubt it is so, and so it must be indeed. I fancy that even among the Masons there's something of the same mystery at the bottom, and that that's why the Catholics so detest the Masons as their rivals breaking up the unity of the idea, while it is so essential that there should be one flock and one shepherd. . . . But from the way I defend my idea I might be an author impatient of your criticism. Enough of it."

"You are perhaps a Mason yourself!" broke suddenly from Alyosha. "You don't believe in God," he added, speaking this time very sorrowfully. He fancied besides that his brother was looking at him ironically. "How does your poem end?" he asked, suddenly looking down. "Or was it the end?"

"I meant it to end like this: When the Inquisitor ceased speaking, he waited some time for his Prisoner to answer him. His silence weighed down upon him. He saw the Prisoner had listened intently all the time, looking gently in his face and evidently not wishing to reply. The old man longed for Him to say something, however bitter

and terrible. But He suddenly approached the old man in silence
and softly kissed him on his bloodless, aged lips. That was all his
answer. The old man shuddered. His lips moved. He went to the
door, opened it, and said to him: 'Go, and come no more. . . .
Come not at all, never, never!' And he let him out into the dark
alleys of the town. The Prisoner went away."

"And the old man?"

"The kiss glows in his heart, but the old man adheres to his
idea."

"And you with him, you too?" cried Alyosha, mournfully.

Ivan laughed.

"Why, it's all nonsense, Alyosha. It's only a senseless poem of a
senseless student, who could never write two lines of verse. Why do
you take it so seriously? Surely you don't suppose I am going straight
off to the Jesuits, to join the men who are correcting His work? Good
Lord, it's no business of mine. I told you, all I want is to live on to
thirty, and then . . . dash the cup to the ground!"

"But the little sticky leaves, and the precious tombs, and the blue
sky, and the woman you love! How will you live, how will you love
them?" Alyosha cried sorrowfully. "With such a hell in your heart
and your head, how can you? No, that's just what you are going
away for, to join them . . . if not, you will kill yourself, you can't
endure it!"

"There is a strength to endure everything," Ivan said with a
cold smile.

"What strength?"

"The strength of the Karamazovs—the strength of the Karamazov
baseness."

"To sink into debauchery, to stifle your soul with corruption,
yes?"

"Possibly even that . . . only perhaps till I am thirty I shall
escape it, and then—"

"How will you escape it? By what will you escape it? That's impossible with your ideas."

"In the Karamazov way, again."

" 'Everything is lawful,' you mean? Everything is lawful, is that
it?"

Ivan scowled, and all at once turned strangely pale.

"Ah, you've caught up yesterday's phrase, which so offended
Miüsov—and which Dmitri pounced upon so naïvely and para-

phrased!" he smiled queerly. "Yes, if you like, 'everything is lawful' since the word has been said. I won't deny it. And Mitya's version isn't bad."

Alyosha looked at him in silence.

"I thought that going away from here I have you at least," Ivan said suddenly, with unexpected feeling; "but now I see that there is no place for me even in your heart, my dear hermit. The formula, 'all is lawful,' I won't renounce—will you renounce me for that, yes?"

Alyosha got up, went to him and softly kissed him on the lips.

"That's plagiarism," cried Ivan, highly delighted. "You stole that from my poem. Thank you, though. Get up, Alyosha, it's time we were going, both of us."

They went out, but stopped when they reached the entrance of the restaurant.

"Listen, Alyosha," Ivan began in a resolute voice, "if I am really able to care for the sticky little leaves, I shall only love them remembering you. It's enough for me that you are somewhere here, and I shan't lose my desire for life yet. Is that enough for you? Take it as a declaration of love if you like. And now you go to the right and I to the left. And it's enough, do you hear—enough! I mean even if I don't go away tomorrow (I think I certainly shall go) and we meet again, don't say a word more on these subjects. I beg that particularly. And about Dmitri, too, I ask you especially never speak to me again," he added, with sudden irritation; "it's all exhausted, it has all been said over and over again, hasn't it? And I'll make you one promise in return for it. When, at thirty, I want to 'dash the cup to the ground,' wherever I may be I'll come to have one more talk with you, even though it were from America—you may be sure of that. I'll come on purpose. It will be very interesting to have a look at you, to see what you'll be by that time. It's rather a solemn promise, you see. And we really may be parting for seven years or ten. Come, go now to your Pater Seraphicus, he is dying. If he dies without you, you will be angry with me for having kept you. Good-bye, kiss me once more; that's right, now go."

Friedrich Nietzsche

— 22 —

Beyond Good and Evil

Friedrich Nietzsche (1844–1900) said that Dostoevsky was the only one who had taught him anything about human nature. And, as was the case with the Russian, Nietzsche's true greatness has been recognized only in recent years, when he has been acclaimed as the prophet of existentialism and psychoanalytic doctrine. The earlier views of Nietzsche as a brilliant but incoherent iconoclast and as the mad prophet of German Nazism have been abandoned as distortions. Today, he is accorded a place as one of the original thinkers of the Western tradition; he is one of the first to recognize the absurdity of human existence as the necessary basis for creative life and to stress the importance of irrational and illusional factors in shaping human behavior.

Nietzsche did not build a grand philosophical system. His ideas were expressed in an elusive style, as brilliant aphorisms or in short paragraphs; nevertheless, they framed a consistent and searching point of view. They are the work of a lonely, sensitive man with profound convictions and integrity, whose life was marked by suffering and disease, culminating in insanity. It was as though Nietzsche strove by intellectual energy to overcome the obstacles of his life and to derive bold, new visions from his plight. As a result, his work has a supercharged quality that does not always make for clarity, but allows him to strike off brilliant insights into the nature and condition of man.

Like Dostoevsky, Nietzsche hated the ugliness and materialism of European society in the late nineteenth century. He rejected all its sanctities and certainties—democracy, Christianity, science, the life of reason—as meaningless perversions which, he thought, were leading it to a dark fate. Europe could be saved only by a revolution in all the accepted values, only by understanding the deepest feelings of human beings and harness-

Friedrich Nietzsche, *Beyond Good and Evil*, trans. Helen Zimmern (New York: Macmillan, 1907), 5–9, 13–14, 20–22, 33–34, 43, 46–48, 56–61, 223–32, 234–41, 247–49, 255–56. Reprinted by permission of George Allen & Unwin Ltd.

ing them by an act of will to creative ends. Nietzsche's affirmative values were those of the determined individuals ("supermen"), who, through disciplined struggle, sacrifice, and suffering, would make every moment in life count and for whom the good life was rooted in the mystery of existence. His attacks on bourgeois civilization and his advocacy of relentless struggle against the "herd" who accepted the values of that civilization served to inspire Social Darwinists, Fascists, and National Socialists. But these groups, in making Nietzsche their idol, violated the spirit of his ideas by taking them out of context. Nietzsche, in fact, clearly expressed his abhorrence of racism and German nationalism, and his point of view was the very antithesis of the totalitarian philosophy.

Beyond Good and Evil (1886) is perhaps the clearest statement of Nietzsche's philosophy: his distrust of reason, his uncompromising anti-intellectualism, and his rejection of all the moral values of a Christian, democratic civilization. His views cannot always be understood or accepted, but neither can they be ignored.

PREJUDICES OF PHILOSOPHERS

The Will to Truth, which is to tempt us to many a hazardous enterprise, the famous Truthfulness of which all philosophers have hitherto spoken with respect, what questions has this Will to Truth not laid before us! What strange, perplexing, questionable questions! It is already a long story; yet it seems as if it were hardly commenced. Is it any wonder if we at last grow distrustful, lose patience, and turn impatiently away? That this Sphinx teaches us at last to ask questions ourselves? *Who* is it really that puts questions to us here? *What* really is this "Will to Truth" in us? In fact we made a long halt at the question as to the origin of this Will—until at last we came to an absolute standstill before a yet more fundamental question. We inquired about the *value* of this Will. Granted that we want the truth: *why not rather* untruth? And uncertainty? Even ignorance? The problem of the value of truth presented itself before us—or was it we who presented ourselves before the problem? Which of us is the Oedipus here? Which the Sphinx? It would seem to be a rendezvous of questions and notes of interrogation. And could it be believed that it at last seems to us as if the problem had never been propounded before, as if we were the first to discern it, get a sight of it, and *risk raising* it. For there is risk in raising it, perhaps there is no greater risk.

"How could anything originate out of its opposite? For example, truth out of error? or the Will to Truth out of the will to deception? or the generous deed out of selfishness? or the pure sun-bright vision of the wise man out of covetousness? Such genesis is impossible; whoever dreams of it is a fool, nay, worse than a fool; things of the highest value must have a different origin, an origin of *their own—*in this transitory, seductive, illusory, paltry world, in this turmoil of delusion and cupidity, they cannot have their source. But rather in the lap of Being, in the intransitory, in the concealed God, in the 'Thing-in-itself'—*there* must be their source, and nowhere else!"— This mode of reasoning discloses the typical prejudice by which metaphysicians of all times can be recognised, this mode of valuation is at the back of all their logical procedure; through this "belief" of theirs, they exert themselves for their "knowledge," for something that is in the end solemnly christened "the Truth." The fundamental belief of metaphysicians is *the belief in antitheses of values*. It never occurred even to the wariest of them to doubt here on the very threshold (where doubt, however, was most necessary); though they had made a solemn vow, *"de omnibus dubitandum."* For it may be doubted, firstly, whether antitheses exist at all; and secondly, whether the popular valuations and antitheses of value upon which metaphysicians have set their seal, are not perhaps merely superficial estimates, merely provisional perspectives, besides being probably made from some corner, perhaps from below— "frog perspectives," as it were, to borrow an expression current among painters. In spite of all the value which may belong to the true, the positive, and the unselfish, it might be possible that a higher and more fundamental value for life generally should be assigned to pretence, to the will to delusion, to selfishness, and cupidity. It might even be possible that *what* constitutes the value of those good and respected things, consists precisely in their being insidiously related, knotted, and crocheted to these evil and apparently opposed things—perhaps even in being essentially identical with them. Perhaps! But who wishes to concern himself with such dangerous "Perhapses"! For that investigation one must await the advent of a new order of philosophers, such as will have other tastes and inclinations, the reverse of those hitherto prevalent—philos-

ophers of the dangerous "Perhaps" in every sense of the term. And to speak in all seriousness, I see such new philosophers beginning to appear.

Having kept a sharp eye on philosophers, and having read between their lines long enough, I now say to myself that the greater part of conscious thinking must be counted amongst the instinctive functions, and it is so even in the case of philosophical thinking; one has here to learn anew, as one learned anew about heredity and "innateness." As little as the act of birth comes into consideration in the whole process and procedure of heredity, just as little is "being-conscious" *opposed* to the instinctive in any decisive sense; the greater part of the conscious thinking of a philosopher is secretly influenced by his instincts, and forced into definite channels. And behind all logic and its seeming sovereignty of movement, there are valuations, or to speak more plainly, physiological demands, for the maintenance of a definite mode of life. For example, that the certain is worth more than the uncertain, that illusion is less valuable than "truth": such valuations, in spite of their regulative importance for *us,* might notwithstanding be only superficial valuations, special kinds of *niaiserie,* such as may be necessary for the maintenance of beings such as ourselves. Supposing, in effect, that man is not just the "measure of things." . . .

The falseness of an opinion is not for us any objection to it: it is here, perhaps, that our new language sounds most strangely. The question is, how far an opinion is life-furthering, life-preserving, species-preserving, perhaps species-rearing; and we are fundamentally inclined to maintain that the falsest opinions (to which the synthetic judgments *a priori* belong), are the most indispensable to us; that without a recognition of logical fictions, without a comparison of reality with the purely *imagined* world of the absolute and immutable, without a constant counterfeiting of the world by means of numbers, man could not live—that the renunciation of false opinions would be a renunciation of life, a negation of life. *To recognise untruth as a condition of life:* that is certainly to impugn the traditional ideas of value in a dangerous manner, and a philosophy which ventures to do so, has thereby alone placed itself beyond good and evil.

• • •

You desire to *live* "according to Nature"? Oh, you noble Stoics, what fraud of words! Imagine to yourselves a being like Nature, boundlessly extravagant, boundlessly indifferent, without purpose or consideration, without pity or justice, at once fruitful and barren and uncertain: imagine to yourselves *indifference* as a power—how *could* you live in accordance with such indifference? To live—is not that just endeavouring to be otherwise than this Nature? Is not living valuing, preferring, being unjust, being limited, endeavouring to be different? And granted that your imperative, "living according to Nature," means actually the same as "living according to life"— how could you do *differently?* Why should you make a principle out of what you yourselves are, and must be? In reality, however, it is quite otherwise with you: while you pretend to read with rapture the canon of your law in Nature, you want something quite the contrary, you extraordinary stage-players and self-deluders! In your pride you wish to dictate your morals and ideals to Nature, to Nature herself, and to incorporate them therein; you insist that it shall be Nature "according to the Stoa," and would like everything to be made after your own image, as a vast, eternal glorification and generalisation of Stoicism! With all your love for truth, you have forced yourselves so long, so persistently, and with such hypnotic rigidity to see Nature *falsely,* that is to say, Stoically, that you are no longer able to see it otherwise—and to crown all, some unfathomable superciliousness gives you the Bedlamite hope that *because* you are able to tyrannise over yourselves—Stoicism is self-tyranny—Nature will also allow herself to be tyrannised over: is not the Stoic a *part* of Nature? . . . But this is an old and everlasting story: what happened in old times with the Stoics still happens to-day, as soon as ever a philosophy begins to believe in itself. It always creates the world in its own image; it cannot do otherwise; philosophy is this tyrannical impulse itself, the most spiritual Will to Power, the will to "creation of the world," the will to the *causa prima.*

• • •

Psychologists should bethink themselves before putting down the instinct of self-preservation as the cardinal instinct of an organic being. A living thing seeks above all to *discharge* its strength—life itself is *Will to Power;* self-preservation is only one of the indirect and most frequent *results* thereof. In short, here, as everywhere else, let us beware of *superfluous* teleological principles!—one of which is the instinct of self-preservation (we owe it to Spinoza's inconsistency). It is thus, in effect, that method ordains, which must be essentially economy of principles.

It is perhaps just dawning on five or six minds that natural philosophy is only a world-exposition and world-arrangement (according to us, if I may say so!) and *not* a world-explanation; but in so far as it is based on belief in the senses, it is regarded as more, and for a long time to come must be regarded as more—namely, as an explanation. It has eyes and fingers of its own, it has ocular evidence and palpableness of its own: this operates fascinatingly, persuasively, and *convincingly* upon an age with fundamentally plebeian tastes—in fact, it follows instinctively the canon of truth of eternal popular sensualism. What is clear, what is "explained"? Only that which can be seen and felt—one must pursue every problem thus far. Obversely, however, the charm of the Platonic mode of thought, which was an *aristocratic* mode, consisted precisely in *resistance to* obvious sense-evidence—perhaps among men who enjoyed even stronger and more fastidious senses than our contemporaries, but who knew how to find a higher triumph in remaining masters of them: and this by means of pale, cold, grey conceptional networks which they threw over the motley whirl of the senses—the mob of the senses, as Plato said. In this overcoming of the world, and interpreting of the world in the manner of Plato, there was an *enjoyment* different from that which the physicists of to-day offer us—and likewise the Darwinists and antiteleologists among the physiological workers, with their principle of the "smallest possible effort," and the greatest possible blunder. "Where there is nothing more to see or to grasp, there is also nothing more for men to do" —that is certainly an imperative different from the Platonic one, but it may notwithstanding be the right imperative for a hardy, laborious race of machinists and bridge-builders of the future, who have nothing but *rough* work to perform.

. . .

All psychology hitherto has run aground on moral prejudices and timidities, it has not dared to launch out into the depths. In so far as it is allowable to recognise in that which has hitherto been written, evidence of that which has hitherto been kept silent, it seems as if nobody had yet harboured the notion of psychology as the Morphology and *Development-doctrine of the Will to Power,* as I conceive of it. The power of moral prejudices has penetrated deeply into the most intellectual world, the world apparently most indifferent and unprejudiced, and has obviously operated in an injurious, obstructive, blinding, and distorting manner. A proper physio-psychology has to contend with unconscious antagonism in the heart of the investigator, it has "the heart" against it: even a doctrine of the reciprocal conditionalness of the "good" and the "bad" impulses, causes (as refined immorality) distress and aversion in a still strong and manly conscience—still more so, a doctrine of the derivation of all good impulses from bad ones. If, however, a person should regard even the emotions of hatred, envy, covetousness, and imperiousness as life-conditioning emotions, as factors which must be present, fundamentally and essentially, in the general economy of life (which must, therefore, be further developed if life is to be further developed), he will suffer from such a view of things as from sea-sickness. And yet this hypothesis is far from being the strangest and most painful in this immense and almost new domain of dangerous knowledge; and there are in fact a hundred good reasons why every one should keep away from it who *can* do so! On the other hand, if one has once drifted hither with one's bark, well! very good! now let us set our teeth firmly! let us open our eyes and keep our hand fast on the helm! We sail away right *over* morality, we crush out, we destroy perhaps the remains of our own morality by daring to make our voyage thither—but what do *we* matter! Never yet did a *profounder* world of insight reveal itself to daring travellers and adventurers, and the psychologist who thus "makes a sacrifice"—it is *not* the *sacrifizio dell' intelletto,* on the contrary!—will at least be entitled to demand in return that psychology shall once more be recognised as the queen of the sciences, for whose service and equipment the other sciences exist. For psychology is once more the path to the fundamental problems.

. . .

It is the business of the very few to be independent; it is a privilege of the strong. And whoever attempts it, even with the best right, but without being *obliged* to do so, proves that he is probably not only strong, but also daring beyond measure. He enters into a labyrinth, he multiplies a thousandfold the dangers which life in itself already brings with it; not the least of which is that no one

can see how and where he loses his way, becomes isolated, and is
torn piecemeal by some minotaur of conscience. Supposing such a
one comes to grief, it is so far from the comprehension of men that
they neither feel it, nor sympathise with it. And he cannot any
longer go back! He cannot even go back again to the sympathy of
men!

. . .

Throughout the longest period of human history—one calls it
the prehistoric period—the value or non-value of an action was inferred from its *consequences;* the action in itself was not taken into
consideration, any more than its origin; but pretty much as in
China at present, where the distinction or disgrace of a child re-
dounds to its parents, the retro-operating power of success or failure
was what induced men to think well or ill of an action. Let us
call this period the *pre-moral* period of mankind; the imperative,
"know thyself!" was then still unknown.—In the last ten thousand
years, on the other hand, on certain large portions of the earth, one
has gradually got so far, that one no longer lets the consequences of
an action, but its origin, decide with regard to its worth: a great
achievement as a whole, an important refinement of vision and of
criterion, the unconscious effect of the supremacy of aristocratic
values and of the belief in "origin," the mark of a period which
may be designated in the narrower sense as the *moral* one: the first
attempt at self-knowledge is thereby made. Instead of the consequences, the origin—what an inversion of perspective! And assuredly an inversion effected only after long struggle and wavering!
To be sure, an ominous new superstition, a peculiar narrowness of
interpretation, attained supremacy precisely thereby: the origin of
an action was interpreted in the most definite sense possible, as
origin out of an *intention;* people were agreed in the belief that the
value of an action lay in the value of its intention. The intention
as the sole origin and antecedent history of an action: under the
influence of this prejudice moral praise and blame have been bestowed, and men have judged and even philosophised almost up to
the present day.—Is it not possible, however, that the necessity may
now have arisen of again making up our minds with regard to the
reversing and fundamental shifting of values, owing to a new self-
consciousness and acuteness in man—is it not possible that we may
be standing on the threshold of a period which to begin with, would

be distinguished negatively as *ultra-moral:* nowadays when, at least amongst us immoralists, the suspicion arises that the decisive value of an action lies precisely in that which is *not intentional,* and that all its intentionalness, all that is seen, sensible, or "sensed" in it, belongs to its surface or skin—which, like every skin, betrays something, but *conceals* still more? In short, we believe that the intention is only a sign or symptom, which first requires an explanation—a sign, moreover, which has too many interpretations, and consequently hardly any meaning in itself alone: that morality, in the sense in which it has been understood hitherto, as intention-morality, has been a prejudice, perhaps a prematureness or preliminariness, probably something of the same rank as astrology and alchemy, but in any case something which must be surmounted. The surmounting of morality, in a certain sense even the self-surmounting of morality—let that be the name for the long secret labour which has been reserved for the most refined, the most upright, and also the most wicked consciences of to-day, as the living touchstones of the soul.

It cannot be helped: the sentiment of surrender, of sacrifice for one's neighbour, and all self-renunciation-morality, must be mercilessly called to account, and brought to judgment; just as the aesthetics of "disinterested contemplation," under which the emasculation of art nowadays seeks insidiously enough to create itself a good conscience. There is far too much witchery and sugar in the sentiments "for others" and *"not* for myself," for one not needing to be doubly distrustful here, and for one asking promptly: "Are they not perhaps—*deceptions?"*—That they *please—*him who has them, and him who enjoys their fruit, and also the mere spectator—that is still no argument in their *favour,* but just calls for caution. Let us therefore be cautious!

*   *   *

One must subject oneself to one's own tests that one is destined for independence and command, and do so at the right time. One must not avoid one's tests, although they constitute perhaps the most dangerous game one can play, and are in the end tests made only before ourselves and before no other judge. Not to cleave to any person, be it even the dearest—every person is a prison and also a recess. Not to cleave to a fatherland, be it even the most suffering and necessitous—it is even less difficult to detach one's heart from a victorious fatherland. Not to cleave to a sympathy, be it even for higher men, into whose peculiar torture and helplessness chance has given us an insight. Not to cleave to a science, though it tempt one with the most valuable discoveries, apparently specially reserved for *us*. Not to cleave to one's own liberation, to the voluptuous distance and remoteness of the bird, which always flies further aloft in order always to see more under it—the danger of the flier. Not to cleave to our own virtues, nor become as a whole a victim to any of our specialities, to our "hospitality" for instance, which is the danger of dangers for highly developed and wealthy souls, who deal prodigally, almost indifferently with themselves, and push the virtue of liberality so far that it becomes a vice. One must know how *to conserve oneself*—the best test of independence.

A new order of philosophers is appearing; I shall venture to baptize them by a name not without danger. As far as I understand them, as far as they allow themselves to be understood—for it is their nature to *wish* to remain something of a puzzle—these philosophers of the future might rightly, perhaps also wrongly, claim to be designated as *"tempters."* This name itself is after all only an attempt, or, if it be preferred, a temptation.

Will they be new friends of "truth," these coming philosophers? Very probably, for all philosophers hitherto have loved their truths. But assuredly they will not be dogmatists. It must be contrary to their pride, and also contrary to their taste, that their truth should still be truth for every one—that which has hitherto been the secret wish and ultimate purpose of all dogmatic efforts. "My opinion is *my* opinion: another person has not easily a right to it"—such a philosopher of the future will say, perhaps. One must renounce the bad taste of wishing to agree with many people. "Good" is no longer good when one's neighbour takes it into his mouth. And how could there be a "common good"! The expression contradicts itself; that which can be common is always of small value. In the end things must be as they are and have always been—the great things remain for the great, the abysses for the profound, the delicacies and thrills for the refined, and, to sum up shortly, everything rare for the rare.

Need I say expressly after all this that they will be free, *very* free spirits, these philosophers of the future—as certainly also they will not be merely free spirits, but something more, higher, greater, and fundamentally different, which does not wish to be misunderstood and mistaken? But while I say this, I feel under *obligation* almost as much to them as to ourselves (we free spirits who are their heralds and forerunners), to sweep away from ourselves altogether a stupid old prejudice and misunderstanding, which, like a fog, has too long made the conception of "free spirit" obscure. In every country of Europe, and the same in America, there is at present something which makes an abuse of this name: a very narrow, prepossessed, enchained class of spirits, who desire almost the opposite of what our intentions and instincts prompt—not to mention that in respect to the *new* philosophers who are appearing, they must still more be closed windows and bolted doors. Briefly and regrettably, they belong to the *levellers,* these wrongly named "free spirits" —as glib-tongued and scribe-fingered slaves of the democratic taste and its "modern ideas": all of them men without solitude, without personal solitude, blunt honest fellows to whom neither courage nor honourable conduct ought to be denied; only, they are not free, and are ludicrously superficial, especially in their innate partiality for seeing the cause of almost *all* human misery and failure in the old forms in which society has hitherto existed—a notion which happily inverts the truth entirely! What they would fain attain with all their strength, is the universal, green-meadow happiness of the herd, together with security, safety, comfort, and alleviation of life for every one; their two most frequently chanted songs and doctrines are called "Equality of Rights" and "Sympathy with all Sufferers" —and suffering itself is looked upon by them as something which must be *done away with.* We opposite ones, however, who have opened our eye and conscience to the question how and where the plant "man" has hitherto grown most vigorously, believe that this has always taken place under the opposite conditions, that for this end the dangerousness of his situation had to be increased enormously, his inventive faculty and dissembling power (his "spirit") had to develop into subtlety and daring under long oppression and compulsion, and his Will to Life had to be increased to the unconditioned Will to Power:—we believe that severity, violence, slavery, danger in the street and in the heart, secrecy, stoicism, tempter's art and devilry of every kind,—that everything wicked, terrible, tyrannical, predatory, and serpentine in man, serves as well for the elevation of the human species as its opposite:—we do not even say enough when we only say *this much;* and in any case we find ourselves here, both with our speech and our silence, at the *other* extreme of all modern ideology and gregarious desirability, as their antipodes perhaps? What wonder that we "free spirits" are not exactly the most communicative spirits? that we do not wish to betray in every respect *what* a spirit can free itself from, and *where* perhaps it will then be driven? And as to the import of the dangerous formula, "Beyond Good and Evil," with which we at least avoid confusion, we *are* something else than *"libres-penseurs," "liberi pensatori,"* "free-thinkers," and whatever these honest advocates of "modern ideas" like to call themselves. Having been at home, or at least guests, in many realms of the spirit; having escaped again and again from the gloomy, agreeable nooks in which preferences and prejudices, youth, origin, the accident of men and books, or even the weariness of travel seemed to confine us; full of malice against the seductions of dependency which lie concealed in honours, money, positions, or exaltation of the senses; grateful even for distress and the vicissitudes of illness, because they always free us from some rule, and its "prejudice," grateful to the God, devil, sheep, and worm in us; inquisitive to a fault, investigators to the point of cruelty, with unhesitating fingers for the intangible, with teeth and stomachs for the most indigestible, ready for any business that requires sagacity and acute senses, ready for every adventure, owing to an excess of "free will"; with anterior and posterior souls, into the ultimate intentions of which it is difficult to pry, with foregrounds and backgrounds to the end of which no foot may run; hidden ones under the mantles of light, appropriators, although we resemble heirs and spendthrifts, arrangers and collectors from morning till night, misers of our wealth and our full-crammed drawers, economical in learning and forgetting, inventive in scheming; sometimes proud of tables of categories, sometimes pedants, sometimes night-owls of work even in full day; yea, if necessary, even scarecrows—and it is necessary nowadays, that is to say, inasmuch as we are the born, sworn, jealous friends of *solitude,* of our own profoundest midnight and midday solitude:—such kind of men are we, we free spirits! And perhaps *ye* are also something of the same kind, ye coming ones? ye *new* philosophers?

WHAT IS NOBLE?

Every elevation of the type "man," has hitherto been the work of an aristocratic society—and so will it always be—a society believing in a long scale of gradations of rank and differences of worth among human beings, and requiring slavery in some form or other. Without the *pathos of distance,* such as grows out of the incarnated difference of classes, out of the constant outlooking and downlooking of the ruling caste on subordinates and instruments, and out of their equally constant practice of obeying and commanding, of keeping down and keeping at a distance—that other more mysterious pathos could never have arisen, the longing for an ever new widening of distance within the soul itself, the formation of ever higher, rarer, further, more extended, more comprehensive states, in short, just the elevation of the type "man," the continued "self-surmounting of man," to use a moral formula in a supermoral sense. To be sure, one must not resign oneself to any humanitarian illusions about the history of the origin of an aristocratic society (that is to say, of the preliminary condition for the elevation of the type "man"): the truth is hard. Let us acknowledge unprejudicedly how every higher civilisation hitherto has *originated!* Men with a still natural nature, barbarians in every terrible sense of the word, men of prey, still in possession of unbroken strength of will and desire for power, threw themselves upon weaker, more moral, more peaceful races (perhaps trading or cattle-rearing communities), or upon old mellow civilisations in which the final vital force was flickering out in brilliant fireworks of wit and depravity. At the commencement, the noble caste was always the barbarian caste: their superiority did not consist first of all in their physical, but in their psychical power—they were more *complete* men (which at every point also implies the same as "more complete beasts").

Corruption—as the indication that anarchy threatens to break out among the instincts, and that the foundation of the emotions, called "life," is convulsed—is something radically different according to the organisation in which it manifests itself. When, for instance, an aristocracy like that of France at the beginning of the Revolution, flung away its privileges with sublime disgust and sacrificed itself to an excess of its moral sentiments, it was corruption:—it was really

only the closing act of the corruption which had existed for centuries, by virtue of which that aristocracy had abdicated step by step
its lordly prerogatives and lowered itself to a *function* of royalty
(in the end even to its decoration and parade-dress). The essential
thing, however, in a good and healthy aristocracy is that it should
not regard itself as a function either of the kingship or the commonwealth, but as the *significance* and highest justification thereof—that
it should therefore accept with a good conscience the sacrifice of a
legion of individuals, who, *for its sake,* must be suppressed and reduced to imperfect men, to slaves and instruments. Its fundamental
belief must be precisely that society is *not* allowed to exist for its
own sake, but only as a foundation and scaffolding, by means of
which a select class of beings may be able to elevate themselves to
their higher duties, and in general to a higher *existence:* like those
sun-seeking climbing plants in Java—they are called *Sipo Matador,*
—which encircle an oak so long and so often with their arms, until
at last, high above it, but supported by it, they can unfold their
tops in the open light, and exhibit their happiness.

To refrain mutually from injury, from violence, from exploitation, and put one's will on a par with that of others: this may result
in a certain rough sense in good conduct among individuals when
the necessary conditions are given (namely, the actual similarity of
the individuals in amount of force and degree of worth, and their
co-relation within one organisation). As soon, however, as one wished
to take this principle more generally, and if possible even as *the
fundamental principle of society,* it would immediately disclose
what it really is—namely, a Will to the *denial* of life, a principle
of dissolution and decay. Here one must think profoundly to the
very basis and resist all sentimental weakness: life itself is *essentially*
appropriation, injury, conquest of the strange and weak, suppression, severity, obtrusion of peculiar forms, incorporation, and at
the least, putting it mildest, exploitation;—but why should one for
ever use precisely these words on which for ages a disparaging purpose has been stamped? Even the organisation within which, as
was previously supposed, the individuals treat each other as equal
—it takes place in every healthy aristocracy—must itself, if it be a living and not a dying organisation, do all that towards other bodies,
which the individuals within it refrain from doing to each other:
it will have to be the incarnated Will to Power, it will endeavour

to grow, to gain ground, attract to itself and acquire ascendency—not owing to any morality or immorality, but because it *lives*, and because life *is* precisely Will to Power. On no point, however, is the ordinary consciousness of Europeans more unwilling to be corrected than on this matter; people now rave everywhere, even under the guise of science, about coming conditions of society in which "the exploiting character" is to be absent:—that sounds to my ears as if they promised to invent a mode of life which should refrain from all organic functions. "Exploitation" does not belong to a depraved, or imperfect and primitive society: it belongs to the *nature* of the living being as a primary organic function; it is a consequence of the intrinsic Will to Power, which is precisely the Will to Life.— Granting that as a theory this is a novelty—as a reality it is the *fundamental fact* of all history: let us be so far honest towards ourselves!

In a tour through the many finer and coarser moralities which have hitherto prevailed or still prevail on the earth, I found certain traits recurring regularly together and connected with one another, until finally two primary types revealed themselves to me, and a radical distinction was brought to light. There is *master-morality* and *slave-morality;*—I would at once add, however, that in all higher and mixed civilisations, there are also attempts at the reconciliation of the two moralities; but one finds still oftener the confusion and mutual misunderstanding of them, indeed, sometimes their close juxtaposition—even in the same man, within one soul. The distinctions of moral values have either originated in a ruling caste, pleasantly conscious of being different from the ruled—or among the ruled class, the slaves and dependents of all sorts. In the first case, when it is the rulers who determine the conception "good," it is the exalted, proud disposition which is regarded as the distinguishing feature, and that which determines the order of rank. The noble type of man separates from himself the beings in whom the opposite of this exalted, proud disposition displays itself: he despises them. Let it at once be noted that in this first kind of morality the antithesis "good" and "bad" means practically the same as "noble" and "despicable";—the antithesis "good" and *"evil"* is of a different origin. The cowardly, the timid, the insignificant, and those thinking merely of narrow utility are despised; moreover, also, the distrustful, with their constrained glances, the self-abasing, the dog-like kind of men who let themselves be abused, the mendicant flatterers, and above all the liars:—it is a fundamental belief of all aristocrats that the common people are untruthful. "We truthful ones"—the nobility in ancient Greece called themselves. It is obvious that everywhere the designations of moral value were at first applied to *men,* and were only derivatively and at a later period applied to *actions;* it is a gross mistake, therefore, when historians of morals start with questions like, "Why have sympathetic actions been praised?" The noble type of man regards *himself* as a determiner of values; he does not require to be approved of; he passes the judgment: "What is injurious to me is injurious in itself"; he knows that it is he himself only who confers honour on things; he is a *creator of values.* He honours whatever he recognises in himself: such morality is self-glorification. In the foreground there is the feeling of plenitude, of power, which seeks to overflow, the happiness of high tension, the consciousness of a wealth which would fain give and bestow:—the noble man also helps the unfortunate, but not —or scarcely—out of pity, but rather from an impulse generated by the superabundance of power. The noble man honours in himself the powerful one, him also who has power over himself, who knows how to speak and how to keep silence, who takes pleasure in subjecting himself to severity and hardness, and has reverence for all that is severe and hard. "Wotan placed a hard heart in my breast," says an old Scandinavian Saga: it is thus rightly expressed from the soul of a proud Viking. Such a type of man is even proud of *not* being made for sympathy; the hero of the Saga therefore adds warningly: "He who has not a hard heart when young, will never have one." The noble and brave who think thus are the furthest removed from the morality which sees precisely in sympathy, or in acting for the good of others, or in *désintéressement,* the characteristic of the moral; faith in oneself, pride in oneself, a radical enmity and irony towards "selflessness," belong as definitely to noble morality, as do a careless scorn and precaution in presence of sympathy and the "warm heart."—It is the powerful who *know* how to honour, it is their art, their domain for invention. The profound reverence for age and for tradition—all law rests on this double reverence,—the belief and prejudice in favour of ancestors and unfavourable to newcomers, is typical in the morality of the powerful; and if, reversely, men of "modern ideas" believe almost instinctively in "progress" and the "future," and are more and more lacking in respect for

old age, the ignoble origin of these "ideas" has complacently betrayed itself thereby. A morality of the ruling class, however, is more
especially foreign and irritating to present-day taste in the sternness
of its principle that one has duties only to one's equals; that one
may act towards beings of a lower rank, towards all that is foreign,
just as seems good to one, or "as the heart desires," and in any
case "beyond good and evil": it is here that sympathy and similar
sentiments can have a place. The ability and obligation to exercise
prolonged gratitude and prolonged revenge—both only within the
circle of equals,—artfulness in retaliation, *raffinement* of the idea in
friendship, a certain necessity to have enemies (as outlets for the
emotions of envy, quarrelsomeness, arrogance—in fact, in order to be
a good *friend*): all these are typical characteristics of the noble
morality, which, as has been pointed out, is not the morality of
"modern ideas," and is therefore at present difficult to realise, and
also to unearth and disclose.—It is otherwise with the second type
of morality, *slave-morality*. Supposing that the abused, the oppressed, the suffering, the unemancipated, the weary, and those uncertain of themselves, should moralise, what will be the common element in their moral estimates? Probably a pessimistic suspicion with
regard to the entire situation of man will find expression, perhaps a
condemnation of man, together with his situation. The slave has
an unfavourable eye for the virtues of the powerful; he has a scepticism and distrust, a *refinement* of distrust of everything "good"
that is there honoured—he would fain persuade himself that the very
happiness there is not genuine. On the other hand, *those* qualities
which serve to alleviate the existence of sufferers are brought into
prominence and flooded with light; it is here that sympathy, the
kind, helping hand, the warm heart, patience, diligence, humility,
and friendliness attain to honour; for here these are the most useful
qualities, and almost the only means of supporting the burden of
existence. Slave-morality is essentially the morality of utility. Here is
the seat of the origin of the famous antithesis "good" and *"evil"*:
—power and dangerousness are assumed to reside in the evil, a certain dreadfulness, subtlety, and strength, which do not admit of
being despised. According to slave-morality, therefore, the "evil"
man arouses fear; according to master-morality, it is precisely the
"good" man who arouses fear and seeks to arouse it, while the bad
man is regarded as the despicable being. The contrast attains its
maximum when, in accordance with the logical consequences of

slave-morality, a shade of depreciation—it may be slight and well-intentioned—at last attaches itself even to the "good" man of this morality; because, according to the servile mode of thought, the good man must in any case be the *safe* man: he is good-natured, easily deceived, perhaps a little stupid, *un bonhomme.* Everywhere that slave-morality gains the ascendency, language shows a tendency to approximate the significations of the words "good" and "stupid." —A last fundamental difference: the desire for *freedom,* the instinct for happiness and the refinements of the feeling of liberty belong as necessarily to slave-morals and morality, as artifice and enthusiasm in reverence and devotion are the regular symptoms of an aristocratic mode of thinking and estimating.—Hence we can understand without further detail why love *as a passion*—it is our European speciality—must absolutely be of noble origin; as is well known, its invention is due to the Provençal poet-cavaliers, those brilliant ingenious men of the *"gai saber,"* to whom Europe owes so much, and almost owes itself.

. . .

A *species* originates, and a type becomes established and strong in the long struggle with essentially constant *unfavourable* conditions. On the other hand, it is known by the experience of breeders that species which receive superabundant nourishment, and in general a surplus of protection and care, immediately tend in the most marked way to develop variations, and are fertile in prodigies and monstrosities (also in monstrous vices). Now look at an aristocratic commonwealth, say an ancient Greek *polis,* or Venice, as a voluntary or involuntary contrivance for the purpose of *rearing* human beings; there are there men beside one another, thrown upon their own resources, who want to make their species prevail, chiefly because they *must* prevail, or else run the terrible danger of being exterminated. The favour, the superabundance, the protection are there lacking under which variations are fostered; the species needs itself as species, as something which, precisely by virtue of its hardness, its uniformity, and simplicity of structure, can in general prevail and make itself permanent in constant struggle with its neighbours, or with rebellious or rebellion-threatening vassals. The most varied experience teaches it what are the qualities to which it principally owes the fact that it still exists, in spite of all Gods and men, and has hitherto been victorious: these qualities it calls virtues, and these virtues alone it develops to maturity. It does so with severity, indeed it desires severity; every aristocratic morality is intolerant in the education of youth, in the control of women, in the marriage customs, in the relations of old and young, in the penal laws (which have an eye only for the degenerating): it counts intolerance itself among the virtues, under the name of "justice." A type with few, but very marked features, a species of severe, warlike, wisely silent, reserved and reticent men (and as such, with the most delicate sensibility for the charm and *nuances* of society) is thus established, unaffected by the vicissitudes of generations; the constant struggle with uniform *unfavourable* conditions is, as already remarked, the cause of a type becoming stable and hard. Finally, however, a happy state of things results, the enormous tension is relaxed; there are perhaps no more enemies among the neighbouring peoples, and the means of life, even of the enjoyment of life, are present in superabundance. With one stroke the bond and constraint of the old discipline severs: it is no longer regarded as necessary, as a condition of existence—if it would continue, it can only do so as a form of *luxury,* as an archaïsing *taste.* Variations, whether they be deviations (into the higher, finer, and rarer), or deteriorations and monstrosities, appear suddenly on the scene in the greatest exuberance and splendour; the individual dares to be individual and detach himself. At this turning-point of history there manifest themselves, side by side, and often mixed and entangled together, a magnificent, manifold, virgin-forest-like up-growth and up-striving, a kind of *tropical tempo* in the rivalry of growth, and an extraordinary decay and self-destruction, owing to the savagely opposing and seemingly exploding egoisms, which strive with one another "for sun and light," and can no longer assign any limit, restraint, or forbearance for themselves by means of the hitherto existing morality. It was this morality itself which piled up the strength so enormously, which bent the bow in so threatening a manner:— it is now "out of date," it is getting "out of date." The dangerous and disquieting point has been reached when the greater, more manifold, more comprehensive life *is lived beyond* the old morality; the "individual" stands out, and is obliged to have recourse to his own law-giving, his own arts and artifices for self-preservation, self-elevation, and self-deliverance. Nothing but new "Whys," nothing but new "Hows," no common formulas any longer, misunderstanding and disregard in league with each other, decay, deterioration, and the loftiest desires frightfully entangled, the genius of the race overflowing from all the cornucopias of good and bad, a portentous simultaneousness of Spring and Autumn, full of new charms and mysteries peculiar to the fresh, still inexhausted, still unwearied corruption. Danger is again present, the mother of morality, great danger; this time shifted into the individual, into the neighbour and friend, into the street, into their own child, into their own heart, into all the most personal and secret recesses of their desires and volitions. What will the moral philosophers who appear at this time have to preach? They discover, these sharp onlookers and loafers, that the end is quickly approaching, that everything around them decays and produces decay, that nothing will endure until the day after to-morrow, except one species of man, the incurably *mediocre*. The mediocre alone have a prospect of continuing and propagating themselves—they will be the men of the future, the sole survivors; "be like them! become mediocre!" is now the only morality which has still a significance, which still obtains a hearing.—But it is difficult to preach this morality of mediocrity! it can never avow what it is and what it desires! it has to talk of moderation and dignity and duty and brotherly love—it will have difficulty *in concealing its irony!*

There is an *instinct for rank,* which more than anything else is already the sign of a *high* rank; there is a *delight* in the *nuances* of reverence which leads one to infer noble origin and habits. The refinement, goodness, and loftiness of a soul are put to a perilous test when something passes by that is of the highest rank, but is not yet protected by the awe of authority from obstrusive touches and incivilities: something that goes its way like a living touchstone, undistinguished, undiscovered, and tentative, perhaps voluntarily veiled and disguised. He whose task and practice it is to investigate souls, will avail himself of many varieties of this very art to determine the ultimate value of a soul, the unalterable, innate order of rank to which it belongs: he will test it by its *instinct for reverence.* *Différence engendre haine:* the vulgarity of many a nature spurts up suddenly like dirty water, when any holy vessel, any jewel from closed shrines, any book bearing the marks of great destiny, is brought before it; while on the other hand, there is an involuntary silence, a hesitation of the eye, a cessation of all gestures, by which it is indicated that a soul *feels* the nearness of what is worthiest of respect. The way in which, on the whole, the reverence for the *Bible* has hitherto been maintained in Europe, is perhaps the best example of discipline and refinement of manners which Europe owes to Christianity: books of such profoundness and supreme significance require for their protection an external tyranny of authority, in order to acquire the *period* of thousands of years which is necessary to exhaust and unriddle them. Much has been achieved when the sentiment has been at last instilled into the masses (the shallow-pates and the boobies of every kind) that they are not allowed to touch everything, that there are holy experiences before which they must take off their shoes and keep away the unclean hand—it is almost their highest advance towards humanity. On the contrary, in the so-called cultured classes, the believers in "modern ideas," noth-ing is perhaps so repulsive as their lack of shame, the easy insolence of eye and hand with which they touch, taste, and finger everything; and it is possible that even yet there is more *relative* nobility of taste, and more tact for reverence among the people, among the lower classes of the people, especially among peasants, than among the newspaper-reading *demimonde* of intellect, the cultured class.

· · ·

At the risk of displeasing innocent ears, I submit that egoism belongs to the essence of a noble soul, I mean the unalterable belief that to a being such as "we," other beings must naturally be in subjection, and have to sacrifice themselves. The noble soul ac-cepts the fact of his egoism without question, and also without con-sciousness of harshness, constraint, or arbitrariness therein, but rather as something that may have its basis in the primary law of things:—if he sought a designation for it he would say: "It is justice itself." He acknowledges under certain circumstances, which made him hesitate at first, that there are other equally privileged ones; as soon as he has settled this question of rank, he moves among those equals and equally privileged ones with the same assurance, as regards modesty and delicate respect, which he enjoys in inter-course with himself—in accordance with an innate heavenly mech-anism which all the stars understand. It is an *additional* instance of his egoism, this artfulness and self-limitation in intercourse with his equals—every star is a similar egoist; he honours *himself* in them, and in the rights which he concedes to them, he has no doubt that the exchange of honours and rights, as the *essence* of all intercourse, belongs also to the natural condition of things. The noble soul gives as he takes, prompted by the passionate and sensitive instinct of requital, which is at the root of his nature. The notion of "favour" has, *inter pares,* neither significance nor good repute; there may be a sublime way of letting gifts as it were light upon one from above, and of drinking them thirstily like dew-drops; but for those arts and displays the noble soul has no aptitude. His egoism hinders him here: in general, he looks "aloft" unwillingly—he looks either *forward,* horizontally and deliberately, or downwards—*he knows that he is on a height.*

. . .

The intellectual haughtiness and loathing of every man who has suffered deeply—it almost determines the order of rank *how* deeply men can suffer—the chilling certainty, with which he is thoroughly imbued and coloured, that by virtue of his suffering he *knows more* than the shrewdest and wisest can ever know, that he has been familiar with, and "at home" in, many distant, dreadful worlds of which "*you* know nothing"!—this silent intellectual haughtiness of the sufferer, this pride of the elect of knowledge, of the "initiated," of the almost sacrificed, finds all forms of disguise necessary to protect itself from contact with officious and sympathising hands, and in general from all that is not its equal in suffering. Profound suffering makes noble; it separates.

. . .

A man who strives after great things, looks upon every one whom he encounters on his way either as a means of advance, or a delay and hindrance—or as a temporary resting-place. His peculiar lofty *bounty* to his fellow-men is only possible when he attains his elevation and dominates. Impatience, and the consciousness of being always condemned to comedy up to that time—for even strife is a comedy, and conceals the end, as every means does—spoil all intercourse for him; this kind of man is acquainted with solitude, and what is most poisonous in it.

. . .

—What is noble? What does the word "noble" still mean for us nowadays? How does the noble man betray himself, how is he recognised under this heavy overcast sky of the commencing plebian-

ism, by which everything is rendered opaque and leaden?—It is not
his actions which establish his claim—actions are always ambiguous,
always inscrutable; neither is it his "works." One finds nowadays
among artists and scholars plenty of those who betray by their works
that a profound longing for nobleness impels them; but this very
need of nobleness is radically different from the needs of the noble
soul itself, and is in fact the eloquent and dangerous sign of the
lack thereof. It is not the works, but the *belief* which is here decisive
and determines the order of rank—to employ once more an old
religious formula with a new and deeper meaning,—it is some fundamental certainty which a noble soul has about itself, something
which is not to be sought, is not to be found, and perhaps, also, is
not to be lost.—*The noble soul has reverence for itself.*—

Henri Bergson

23

Creative Evolution

During the first two decades of the twentieth century, Henri Bergson (1859–1941) enjoyed an extraordinary popularity both in philosophical circles and among the general educated public. He was hailed as the prophet of human freedom and creativity who grounded his teachings in experimental science. His lectures as professor of philosophy in Paris were crowded social events. His ideas generated lively discussion and controversy, and his fame was capped by the award of the Nobel Prize for literature in 1927. Bergson, however, outlived his day of glory. When new findings outmoded the biological and psychological basis of his work, his philosophy lost much of its relevance and was generally rejected. Bergson's ideas have, nevertheless, recently assumed renewed importance as contemporary thinkers have followed through on the new vistas he opened up. Elements of Bergsonism have found expression in Alfred N. Whitehead's "process" philosophy, in existentialism's "moment of decisive choice," in the "stream of consciousness" method of novelists, in the aesthetics of abstract and expressionist art, and in pragmatism's philosophy of action.

In his heyday, Bergson was the foremost spokesman of the anti-intellectual revolt in Western thought. He attacked and rejected the dominant scientific mechanism and determinism, the age-old rationalist tradition, and the Aristotelian-Christian teleological view. He affirmed the superiority of intuition—the immediate perceptive experience—to the analytic function of the intellect. The latter was, Bergson thought, incapable of accounting for human decision and moral action. Intuition was the faculty of comprehending the ultimate reality of organic life, that vital impulse (*élan vital*), which was the dynamic core of the evolutionary process. This reality was neither in space nor in abstract clock-time, but in "time lived," the flux of consciousness ("duration"). It was a process, rather than a series of separate states or things, in which each moment was unique, free, and creative.

Creative Evolution (1907), Bergson's most influential work, is an elaborate exposition of his system. William James hailed it as a "marvel." A poetic rather than a systematic expression, bordering on mysticism, the work is more important for its suggestive insights than for the logical cogency of its argument; its greatest significance has been for the moral, aesthetic, and religious ideas of our time.

The existence of which we are most assured and which we know best is unquestionably our own, for of every other object we have notions which may be considered external and superficial, whereas, of ourselves, our perception is internal and profound. What, then, do we find? In this privileged case, what is the precise meaning of the word "exist"? Let us recall here briefly the conclusions of an earlier work.

I find, first of all, that I pass from state to state. I am warm or cold, I am merry or sad, I work or I do nothing, I look at what is around me or I think of something else. Sensations, feelings, volitions, ideas—such are the changes into which my existence is divided and which color it in turns. I change, then, without ceasing. But this is not saying enough. Change is far more radical than we are at first inclined to suppose.

For I speak of each of my states as if it formed a block and were a separate whole. I say indeed that I change, but the change seems to me to reside in the passage from one state to the next: of each state, taken separately, I am apt to think that it remains the same during all the time that it prevails. Nevertheless, a slight effort of attention would reveal to me that there is no feeling, no idea, no volition which is not undergoing change every moment: if a mental state ceased to vary, its duration would cease to flow. Let us take the most stable of internal states, the visual perception of a motionless external object. The object may remain the same, I may look at it from the same side, at the same angle, in the same light; nevertheless the vision I now have of it differs from that which I have just had, even if only because the one is an instant older than the other. My memory is there, which conveys something of the past into the present. My mental state, as it advances on the road of time, is continually swelling with the duration which it accumulates: it goes on increasing—rolling upon itself, as a snowball on the snow. Still more is this the case with states more deeply internal, such as sensations, feelings, desires, etc., which do not correspond, like a simple visual perception, to an unvarying external object. But it is expedient to disregard this uninterrupted change, and to notice it only when it becomes sufficient to impress a new attitude on the body, a new direction on the attention. Then, and then only, we find that our state has changed. The truth is that we change without ceasing, and that the state itself is nothing but change.

This amounts to saying that there is no essential difference between passing from one state to another and persisting in the same state. If the state which "remains the same" is more varied than we think, on the other hand the passing from one state to another resembles, more than we imagine, a single state being prolonged; the transition is continuous. But, just because we close our eyes to the unceasing variation of every psychical state, we are obliged, when the change has become so considerable as to force itself on our attention, to speak as if a new state were placed alongside the previous one. Of this new state we assume that it remains unvarying in its turn, and so on endlessly. The apparent discontinuity of the psychical life is then due to our attention being fixed on it by a series of separate acts: actually there is only a gentle slope; but in following the broken line of our acts of attention, we think we perceive separate steps. True, our psychic life is full of the unforeseen. A thousand incidents arise, which seem to be cut off from those which precede them, and to be disconnected from those which follow. Discontinuous though they appear, however, in point of fact they stand out against the continuity of a background on which they are designed, and to which indeed they owe the intervals that separate them; they are the beats of the drum which break forth here and there in the symphony. Our attention fixes on them because they interest it more, but each of them is borne by the fluid mass of our whole psychical existence. Each is only the best illuminated point of a moving zone which comprises all that we feel or think or will—all, in short, that we are at any given moment. It is this entire zone which in reality makes up our state. Now, states thus defined cannot be regarded as distinct elements. They continue each other in an endless flow.

But, as our attention has distinguished and separated them artificially, it is obliged next to reunite them by an artificial bond. It imagines, therefore, a formless ego, indifferent and unchangeable, on which it threads the psychic states which it has set up as independent entities. Instead of a flux of fleeting shades merging into each other, it perceives distinct and, so to speak, solid colors, set side by side like the beads of a necklace; it must perforce then suppose a thread, also itself solid, to hold the beads together. But if this colorless substratum is perpetually colored by that which covers it, it is for us, in its indeterminateness, as if it did not exist, since we only perceive what is colored, or, in other words, psychic states. As a matter of fact, this substratum has no reality; it is merely a symbol intended to recall unceasingly to our consciousness the artificial character of the process by which the attention places clean-cut states side by side, where actually there is a continuity which unfolds. If our existence were composed of separate states with an impassive ego to unite them, for us there would be no duration. For an ego which does not change does not *endure,* and a psychic state which remains the same so long as it is not replaced by the following state does not *endure* either. Vain, therefore, is the attempt to range such states beside each other on the ego supposed to sustain them: never can these solids strung upon a solid make up that duration which flows. What we actually obtain in this way is an artificial imitation of the internal life, a static equivalent which will lend itself better to the requirements of logic and language, just because we have eliminated from it the element of real time. But, as regards the psychical life unfolding beneath the symbols which conceal it, we readily perceive that time is just the stuff it is made of.

There is, moreover, no stuff more resistant nor more substantial. For our duration is not merely one instant replacing another; if it were, there would never be anything but the present—no prolonging of the past into the actual, no evolution, no concrete duration. Duration is the continuous progress of the past which gnaws into the future and which swells as it advances. And as the past grows without ceasing, so also there is no limit to its preservation. Memory, as we have tried to prove, is not a faculty of putting away recollections in a drawer, or of inscribing them in a register. There is no register, no drawer, there is not even, properly speaking, a faculty, for a faculty works intermittently, when it will or when it can, whilst the piling up of the past upon the past goes on without relaxation. In reality, the past is preserved by itself, automatically. In its entirety, probably, it follows us at every instant; all that we have felt, thought and willed from our earliest infancy is there, leaning over the present which is about to join it, pressing against the portals of consciousness that would fain leave it outside. The cerebral mechanism is arranged just so as to drive back into the unconscious almost the whole of this past, and to admit beyond the threshold only that which can cast light on the present situation or further the action now being prepared—in short, only that which can give *useful* work. At the most, a few superfluous recollections may succeed in smuggling themselves through the half-open door. These memories, messengers from the unconscious, remind us of what we are dragging behind us unawares. But, even though we may have no distinct idea of it, we feel vaguely that our past remains present to us. What are we, in fact, what is our *character,* if not the condensation of the history that we have lived from our birth—nay, even before our birth, since we bring with us prenatal dispositions? Doubtless we think with only a small part of our past, but it is with our entire past, including the original bent of our soul, that we desire, will and act. Our past, then, as a whole, is made manifest to us in its impulse; it is felt in the form of tendency, although a small part of it only is known in the form of idea.

From this survival of the past it follows that consciousness cannot go through the same state twice. The circumstances may still be the same, but they will act no longer on the same person, since they find him at a new moment of his history. Our personality, which is being built up each instant with its accumulated experience, changes without ceasing. By changing, it prevents any state, although superficially identical with another, from ever repeating it in its very depth. That is why our duration is irreversible. We could not live over again a single moment, for we should have to begin by effacing the memory of all that had followed. Even could we erase this memory from our intellect, we could not from our will.

Thus our personality shoots, grows and ripens without ceasing. Each of its moments is something new added to what was before. We may go further: it is not only something new, but something unforeseeable. Doubtless, my present state is explained by what was in me and by what was acting on me a moment ago. In analyzing it I should find no other elements. But even a superhuman intelligence would not have been able to foresee the simple indivisible form which gives to these purely abstract elements their concrete organization. For to foresee consists of projecting into the future what has been perceived in the past, or of imagining for a later time a new grouping, in a new order, of elements already perceived. But that which has never been perceived, and which is at the same time simple, is necessarily unforeseeable. Now such is the case with each of our states, regarded as a moment in a history that is gradually unfolding: it is simple, and it cannot have been already perceived, since it concentrates in its indivisibility all that has been perceived and what the present is adding to it besides. It is an original moment of a no less original history.

The finished portrait is explained by the features of the model, by the nature of the artist, by the colors spread out on the palette; but, even with the knowledge of what explains it, no one, not even the artist, could have foreseen exactly what the portrait would be, for to predict it would have been to produce it before it was produced—an absurd hypothesis which is its own refutation. Even so with regard to the moments of our life, of which we are the artisans. Each of them is a kind of creation. And just as the talent of the painter is formed or deformed—in any case, is modified—under the very influence of the works he produces, so each of our states, at the moment of its issue, modifies our personality, being indeed the new form that we are just assuming. It is then right to say that what we do depends on what we are; but it is necessary to add also that we are, to a certain extent, what we do, and that we are creating ourselves continually. This creation of self by self is the more complete, the more one reasons on what one does. For reason does not proceed in such matters as in geometry, where impersonal premises are given once for all, and an impersonal conclusion must perforce be drawn. Here, on the contrary, the same reasons may dictate to different persons, or to the same person at different moments, acts profoundly different, although equally reasonable. The truth is that they are not quite the same reasons, since they are not those of the same person, nor of the same moment. That is why we cannot deal with them in the abstract, from outside, as in geometry, nor solve for another the problems by which he is faced in life. Each must solve them from within, on his own account. But we need not go more deeply into this. We are seeking only the precise meaning that our consciousness gives to this word "exist," and we find that, for a conscious being, to exist is to change, to change is to mature, to mature is to go on creating oneself endlessly. Should the same be said of existence in general?

. . .

Now, the more we fix our attention on this continuity of life, the more we see that organic evolution resembles the evolution of a consciousness, in which the past presses against the present and causes the upspringing of a new form of consciousness, incommensurable with its antecedents. That the appearance of a vegetable or animal species is due to specific causes, nobody will gainsay. But this can only mean that if, after the fact, we could know these causes in detail, we could explain by them the form that has been produced; foreseeing the form is out of the question. It may perhaps be said that the form could be foreseen if we could know, in all their details, the conditions under which it will be produced. But these conditions are built up into it and are part and parcel of its being; they are peculiar to that phase of its history in which life finds itself at the moment of producing the form: how could we know beforehand a situation that is unique of its kind, that has never yet occurred and will never occur again? Of the future, only that is foreseen which is like the past or can be made up again with elements like those of the past. Such is the case with astronomical, physical and chemical facts, with all facts which form part of a system in which elements supposed to be unchanging are merely put together, in which the only changes are changes of position, in which there is no theoretical absurdity in imagining that things are restored to their place; in which, consequently, the same total phenomenon, or at least the same elementary phenomena, can be repeated. But an original situation, which imparts something of its own originality to its elements, that is to say, to the partial views that are taken of it, how can such a situation be pictured as given before it is actually produced? All that can be said is that, once produced, it will be explained by the elements that analysis will then carve out of it. Now, what is true of the production of a new species is also true of the production of a new individual, and, more generally, of any moment of any living form. For, though the variation must reach a certain importance and a certain generality in order to give rise to a new species, it is being produced every moment, continuously and insensibly, in every living being. And it is evident that even the sudden "mutations" which we now hear of are possible only if a process of incubation, or rather of maturing, is going on throughout a series of generations that do not seem to change. In this sense it might be said of life, as of consciousness, that at every moment it is creating something.

But against this idea of the absolute originality and unforeseeability of forms our whole intellect rises in revolt. The essential function of our intellect, as the evolution of life has fashioned it, is to be a light for our conduct, to make ready for our action on things, to foresee, for a given situation, the events, favorable or unfavorable, which may follow thereupon. Intellect therefore instinctively selects in a given situation whatever is like something already known; it seeks this out, in order that it may apply its principle that "like produces like." In just this does the prevision of the future by common sense consist. Science carries this faculty to the highest possible degree of exactitude and precision, but does not alter its essential character. Like ordinary knowledge, in dealing with things science is concerned only with the aspect of *repetition*. Though the whole be original, science will always manage to analyze it into elements or aspects which are approximately a reproduction of the past. Science can work only on what is supposed to repeat itself—that is to say, on what is withdrawn, by hypothesis, from the action of real time. Anything that is irreducible and irreversible in the successive moments of a history eludes science. To get a notion of this irreducibility and irreversibility, we must break with scientific habits which are adapted to the fundamental requirements of thought, we must do violence to the mind, go counter to the natural bent of the intellect. But that is just the function of philosophy.

In vain, therefore, does life evolve before our eyes as a continuous creation of unforeseeable form: the idea always persists that form, unforeseeability and continuity are mere appearance—the outward reflection of our own ignorance. What is presented to the senses as a continuous history would break up, we are told, into a series of successive states. "What gives you the impression of an original state resolves, upon analysis, into elementary facts, each of which is the repetition of a fact already known. What you call an unforeseeable form is only a new arrangement of old elements. The elementary causes, which in their totality have determined this arrangement, are themselves old causes repeated in a new order. Knowledge of the elements and of the elementary causes would have made it possible to foretell the living form which is their sum and their resultant. When we have resolved the biological aspect of phenomena into physico-chemical factors, we will leap, if necessary, over physics and chemistry themselves; we will go from masses to molecules, from molecules to atoms, from atoms to corpuscles: we must indeed at last come to something that can be treated as a kind of solar system, astronomically. If you deny it, you oppose the very principle of scientific mechanism, and you arbitrarily affirm that living matter is not made of the same elements as other matter."—We reply that we do not question the fundamental identity of inert matter and organized matter. The only question is whether the natural systems which we call living beings must be assimilated to the artificial systems that science cuts out within inert matter, or whether they must not rather be compared to that natural system which is the whole of the universe. That life is a kind of mechanism I cordially agree. But is it the mechanism of parts artificially isolated within the whole of the universe, or is it the mechanism of the real whole? The real whole might well be, we conceive, an indivisible continuity. The systems we cut out within it would, properly speaking, not then be *parts* at all; they would be *partial views* of the whole. And, with these partial views put end to end, you will not make even a beginning of the reconstruction of the whole, any more than, by multiplying photographs of an object in a thousand different aspects, you will reproduce the object itself. So of life and of the physico-chemical phenomena to which you endeavor to reduce it. Analysis will undoubtedly resolve the process of organic creation into an ever-growing number of physico-chemical phenomena, and chemists and physicists will have to do, of course, with nothing but these. But it does not follow that chemistry and physics will ever give us the key to life.

A very small element of a curve is very near being a straight line. And the smaller it is, the nearer. In the limit, it may be termed a part of the curve or a part of the straight line, as you please, for in each of its points a curve coincides with its tangent. So likewise "vitality" is tangent, at any and every point, to physical and chemical forces; but such points are, as a fact, only views taken by a mind which imagines stops at various moments of the movement that generates the curve. In reality, life is no more made of physico-chemical elements than a curve is composed of straight lines.

• • •

We see that the intellect, so skilful in dealing with the inert, is awkward the moment it touches the living. Whether it wants to treat the life of the body or the life of the mind, it proceeds with the rigor, the stiffness and the brutality of an instrument not designed for such use. The history of hygiene or of pedagogy teaches us much in this matter. When we think of the cardinal, urgent and constant need we have to preserve our bodies and to raise our souls, of the special facilities given to each of us, in this field, to experiment continually on ourselves and on others, of the palpable injury by which the wrongness of a medical of pedagogical practise is both made manifest and punished at once, we are amazed at the stupidity and especially at the persistence of errors. We may easily find their origin in the natural obstinacy with which we treat the living like the lifeless and think all reality, however fluid, under the form of the sharply defined solid. We are at ease only in the discontinuous, in the immobile, in the dead. *The intellect is characterized by a natural inability to comprehend life.*

Instinct, on the contrary, is molded on the very form of life. While intelligence treats everything mechanically, instinct proceeds, so to speak, organically. If the consciousness that slumbers in it should awake, if it were wound up into knowledge instead of being wound off into action, if we could ask and it could reply, it would give up to us the most intimate secrets of life. For it only carries out further the work by which life organizes matter—so that we cannot say, as has often been shown, where organization ends and where instinct begins. When the little chick is breaking its shell with a peck of its beak, it is acting by instinct, and yet it does but carry on the movement which has borne it through embryonic life. Inversely, in the course of embryonic life itself (especially when the embryo lives freely in the form of a larva), many of the acts accomplished must be referred to instinct. The most essential of the primary instincts are really, therefore, vital processes. The potential consciousness that accompanies them is generally actualized only at the outset of the act, and leaves the rest of the process to go on by itself. It would only have to expand more widely, and then dive into its own depth completely, to be one with the generative force of life.

. . .

Instinct is sympathy. If this sympathy could extend its object and also reflect upon itself, it would give us the key to vital operations—just as intelligence, developed and disciplined, guides us into matter. For—we cannot too often repeat it—intelligence and instinct are turned in opposite directions, the former towards inert matter, the latter towards life. Intelligence, by means of science, which is its work, will deliver up to us more and more completely the secret of physical operations; of life it brings us, and moreover only claims to bring us, a translation in terms of inertia. It goes all round life, taking from outside the greatest possible number of views of it, drawing it into itself instead of entering into it. But it is to the very inwardness of life that *intuition* leads us—by intuition I mean instinct that has become disinterested, self-conscious, capable of reflecting upon its object and of enlarging it indefinitely.

That an effort of this kind is not impossible, is proved by the existence in man of an aesthetic faculty along with normal perception. Our eye perceives the features of the living being, merely as assembled, not as mutually organized. The intention of life, the simple movement that runs through the lines, that binds them together and gives them significance, escapes it. This intention is just what the artist tries to regain, in placing himself back within the object by a kind of sympathy, in breaking down, by an effort of intuition, the barrier that space puts up between him and his model. It is true that this aesthetic intuition, like external perception, only attains the individual. But we can conceive an inquiry turned in the same direction as art, which would take life *in general* for its object, just as physical science, in following to the end the direction pointed out by external perception, prolongs the individual facts into general laws. No doubt this philosophy will never obtain a knowledge of its object comparable to that which science has of its own. Intelligence remains the luminous nucleus around which instinct, even enlarged and purified into intuition, forms only a vague nebulosity. But, in default of knowledge properly so called, reserved to pure intelligence, intuition may enable us to grasp what it is that intelligence fails to give us, and indicate the means of supplementing it. On the one hand, it will utilize the mechanism of intelligence itself to show how intellectual molds cease to be strictly applicable; and on the other hand, by its own work, it will suggest to us the vague feeling, if nothing more, of what must take the place of intellectual molds. Thus, intuition may bring the intellect to recognize that life does not quite go into the category of the many nor yet into that of the one; that neither mechanical causality nor finality can give a sufficient interpretation of the vital process. Then, by the sympathetic communication which it establishes between us and the rest of the living, by the expansion of our consciousness which it brings about, it introduces us into life's own domain, which is reciprocal interpenetration, endlessly continued creation. But, though it thereby transcends intelligence, it is from intelligence that has come the push that has made it rise to the point it has reached. Without intelligence, it would have remained in the form of instinct, riveted to the special object of its practical interest, and turned outward by it into movements of locomotion.

* * *

Everything is obscure in the idea of creation if we think of *things* which are created and a *thing* which creates, as we habitually do, as the understanding cannot help doing. We shall show the origin of this illusion in our next chapter. It is natural to our intellect, whose function is essentially practical, made to present to us things and states rather than changes and acts. But things and states are only views, taken by our mind, of becoming. There are no things, there are only actions. More particularly, if I consider the world in which we live, I find that the automatic and strictly determined evolution of this well-knit whole is action which is unmaking itself, and that the unforeseen forms which life cuts out in it, forms capable of being themselves prolonged into unforeseen movements, represent the action that is making itself. Now, I have every reason to believe that the other worlds are analogous to ours, that things happen there in the same way. And I know they were not all constructed at the same time, since observation shows me, even to-day, nebulae in course of concentration. Now, if the same kind of action is going on everywhere, whether it is that which is unmaking itself or whether it is that which is striving to remake itself, I simply express this probable similitude when I speak of a centre from which worlds shoot out like rockets in a fire-works display—provided, however, that I do not present this centre as a *thing,* but as a continuity of shooting out. God thus defined, has nothing of the already made; He is unceasing life, action, freedom. Creation, so conceived, is not a mystery; we experience it in ourselves when we act freely. That new things can join things already existing is absurd, no doubt, since the *thing* results from a solidification performed by our understanding, and there are never any things other than those that the understanding has thus constituted. To speak of things creating themselves would therefore amount to saying that the understanding presents to itself more than it presents to itself—a self-contradictory affirmation, an empty and vain idea. But that action increases as it goes on, that it creates in the measure of its advance, is what each of us finds when he watches himself act. Things are constituted by the instantaneous cut which the understanding practices, at a given moment, on a flux of this kind, and what is mysterious when we compare the cuts together becomes clear when we relate them to the flux.

• • •

Radical . . . is the difference between animal consciousness, even the most intelligent, and human consciousness. For consciousness corresponds exactly to the living being's power of choice; it is co-extensive with the fringe of possible action that surrounds the real action: consciousness is synonymous with invention and with freedom. Now, in the animal, invention is never anything but a variation on the theme of routine. Shut up in the habits of the species, it succeeds, no doubt, in enlarging them by its individual initiative; but it escapes automatism only for an instant, for just the time to create a new automatism. The gates of its prison close as soon as they are opened; by pulling at its chain it succeeds only in stretching it. With man, consciousness breaks the chain. In man, and in man alone, it sets itself free. The whole history of life until man has been that of the effort of consciousness to raise matter, and of the more or less complete overwhelming of consciousness by the matter which has fallen back on it. The enterprise was paradoxical, if, indeed, we may speak here otherwise than by metaphor of enterprise and of effort. It was to create with matter, which is necessity itself, an instrument of freedom, to make a machine which should triumph over mechanism, and to use the determinism of nature to pass through the meshes of the net which this very determinism had spread. But, everywhere except in man, consciousness has let itself be caught in the net whose meshes it tried to pass through: it has remained the captive of the mechanisms it has set up. Automatism, which it tries to draw in the direction of freedom, winds about it and drags it down. It has not the power to escape, because the energy it has provided for acts is almost all employed in maintaining the infinitely subtle and essentially unstable equilibrium into which it has brought matter. But man not only maintains his machine, he succeeds in using it as he pleases. Doubtless he owes this to the superiority of his brain, which enables him to build an unlimited number of motor mechanisms, to oppose new habits to the old ones unceasingly, and, by dividing automatism against itelf, to rule it. He owes it to his language, which furnishes consciousness with an immaterial body in which to incarnate itself and thus exempts it from dwelling exclusively on material bodies, whose flux would soon drag it along and finally swallow it up. He owes it to social life, which stores and preserves efforts as language stores thought, fixes thereby a mean level to which individuals must raise themselves at the outset, and by this initial stimulation prevents the average man from slumbering and drives the superior man to mount still higher. But our brain, our society, and our language are only the external and various signs of one and the same internal superiority. They tell, each after its manner, the unique, exceptional success which life has won at a given moment of its evolution. They express the difference of kind, and not only of degree, which separates man from the rest of the animal world. They let us guess that, while at the end of the vast spring-board from which life has taken its leap, all the others have stepped down, finding the cord stretched too high, man alone has cleared the obstacle.

It is in this quite special sense that man is the "term" and the "end" of evolution. Life, we have said, transcends finality as it transcends the other categories. It is essentially a current sent through matter, drawing from it what it can. There has not, therefore, properly speaking, been any project or plan. On the other hand, it is abundantly evident that the rest of nature is not for the sake of man: we struggle like the other species, we have struggled against other species. Moreover, if the evolution of life had encountered other accidents in its course, if, thereby, the current of life had been otherwise divided, we should have been, physically and morally, far different from what we are. For these various reasons it would be wrong to regard humanity, such as we have it before our eyes, as pre-figured in the evolutionary movement. It cannot even be said to be the outcome of the whole of evolution, for evolution has been accomplished on several divergent lines, and while the human species is at the end of one of them, other lines have been followed with other species at their end. It is in a quite different sense that we hold humanity to be the ground of evolution.

From our point of view, life appears in its entirety as an immense wave which, starting from a centre, spreads outwards, and which on almost the whole of its circumference is stopped and converted into oscillation: at one single point the obstacle has been forced, the impulsion has passed freely. It is this freedom that the human form registers. Everywhere but in man, consciousness has had to come to a stand; in man alone it has kept on its way. Man, then, continues the vital movement indefinitely, although he does not draw along with him all that life carries in itself. On other lines of evolution there have traveled other tendencies which life implied, and of which, since everything interpenetrates, man has, doubtless, kept something, but of which he has kept only very little. *It is as if a vague and formless being, whom we may call, as we will,* man *or* superman, *had sought to realize himself, and had succeeded only by abandoning a part of himself on the way.* The losses are represented by the rest of the animal world, and even by the vegetable world, at least in what these have that is positive and above the accidents of evolution.

From this point of view, the discordances of which nature offers us the spectacle are singularly weakened. The organized world as a whole becomes as the soil on which was to grow either man himself or a being who morally must resemble him. The animals, however distant they may be from our species, however hostile to it, have none the less been useful traveling companions, on whom consciousness has unloaded whatever encumbrances it was dragging along, and who have enabled it to rise, in man, to heights from which it sees an unlimited horizon open again before it.

It is true that it has not only abandoned cumbersome baggage on the way; it has also had to give up valuable goods. Consciousness, in man, is pre-eminently intellect. It might have been, it ought, so it seems, to have been also intuition. Intuition and intellect represent two opposite directions of the work of consciousness: intuition goes in the very direction of life, intellect goes in the inverse direction, and thus finds itself naturally in accordance with the movement of matter. A complete and perfect humanity would be that in which these two forms of conscious activity should attain their full development. And, between this humanity and ours, we may conceive any number of possible stages, corresponding to all the degrees imaginable of intelligence and of intuition. In this lies the part of contingency in the mental structure of our species. A different evolution might have led to a humanity either more intellectual still or more intuitive. In the humanity of which we are a part, intuition is, in fact, almost completely sacrificed to intellect. It seems that to conquer matter, and to reconquer its own self, consciousness has had to exhaust the best part of its power. This conquest, in the particular conditions in which it has been accomplished, has required that consciousness should adapt itself to the habits of matter and concentrate all its attention on them, in fact determine itself more especially as intellect. Intuition is there, however, but vague and above all discontinuous. It is a lamp almost extinguished, which only glimmers now and then, for a few moments at most. But it glimmers wherever a vital interest is at stake. On our personality, on our liberty, on the place we occupy in the whole of nature, on our origin and perhaps also on our destiny, it throws a light feeble and vacillating, but which none the less pierces the darkness of the night in which the intellect leaves us.

These fleeting intuitions, which light up their object only at distant intervals, philosophy ought to seize, first to sustain them, then to expand them and so unite them together. The more it advances in this work, the more will it perceive that intuition is mind itself, and, in a certain sense, life itself: the intellect has been cut out of it by a process resembling that which has generated matter. Thus is revealed the unity of the spiritual life. We recognize it only when we place ourselves in intuition in order to go from intuition to the intellect, for from the intellect we shall never pass to intuition.

Philosophy introduces us thus into the spiritual life. And it shows us at the same time the relation of the life of the spirit to that of the body. The great error of the doctrines on the spirit has been the idea that by isolating the spiritual life from all the rest, by suspending it in space as high as possible above the earth, they were placing it beyond attack, as if they were not thereby simply exposing it to be taken as an effect of mirage! Certainly they are right to listen to conscience when conscience affirms human freedom; but the intellect is there, which says that the cause determines its effect, that like conditions like, that all is repeated and that all is given. They are right to believe in the absolute reality of the person and in his independence toward matter; but science is there, which shows the interdependence of conscious life and cerebral activity. They are right to attribute to man a privileged place in nature, to hold that the distance is infinite between the animal and man; but the history of life is there, which makes us witness the genesis of species by gradual transformation, and seems thus to reintegrate man in animality. When a strong instinct assures the probability of personal survival, they are right not to close their ears to its voice; but if there exist "souls" capable of an independent life, whence do they come? When, how and why do they enter into this body which we see arise, quite naturally, from a mixed cell derived from the bodies of its two parents? All these questions will remain unanswered, a philosophy of intuition will be a negation of science, will be sooner or later swept away by science, if it does not resolve to see the life of the body just where it really is, on the road that leads to the life of the spirit. But it will then no longer have to do with definite living beings. Life as a whole, from the initial impulsion that thrust it into the world, will appear as a wave which rises, and which is opposed by the descending movement of matter. On the greater part of its surface, at different heights, the current is converted by matter into a vortex. At one point alone it passes freely, dragging with it the obstacle which will weigh on its progress but will not stop it. At this point is humanity; it is our privileged situation. On the other hand, this rising wave is consciousness, and, like all consciousness, it includes potentialities without number which interpenetrate and to which consequently neither the category of unity nor that of multiplicity is appropriate, made as they both are for inert matter. The matter that it bears along with it, and in the interstices of which it inserts itself, alone can divide it into distinct individualities. On flows the current, running through human generations, subdividing itself into individuals. This subdivision was vaguely indicated in it, but could not have been made clear without matter. Thus souls are continually being created, which, nevertheless, in a certain sense pre-existed. They are nothing else than the little rills into which the great river of life divides itself, flowing through the body of humanity. The movement of the stream is distinct from the river bed, although it must adopt its winding course. Consciousness is distinct from the organism it animates, although it must undergo its vicissitudes. As the possible actions which a state of consciousness indicates are at every instant beginning to be carried out in the nervous centres, the brain underlies at every instant the motor indications of the state of consciousness; but the interdependency of consciousness and brain is limited to this; the destiny of consciousness is not bound up on that account with the destiny of cerebral matter. Finally, consciousness is essentially free; it is freedom itself; but it cannot pass through matter without settling on it, without adapting itself to it: this adaptation is what we call intellectuality; and the intellect, turning itself back toward active, that is to say free, consciousness, naturally makes it enter into the conceptual forms into which it is accustomed to see matter fit. It will therefore always perceive freedom in the form of necessity; it will always neglect the part of novelty or of creation inherent in the free act; it will always substitute for action itself an imitation artificial, approximative, obtained by compounding the old with the old and the same with the same. Thus, to the eyes of a philosophy that attempts to reabsorb intellect in intuition, many difficulties vanish or become light. But such a doctrine does not only facilitate speculation; it gives us also more power to act and to live. For, with it, we feel ourselves no longer isolated in humanity, humanity no longer seems isolated in the nature that it dominates. As the smallest grain of dust is bound up with our entire solar system, drawn along with it in that undivided movement of descent which is materiality itself, so all organized beings, from the humblest to the highest, from the first origins of life to the time in which we are, and in all places as in all times, do but evidence a single impulsion, the inverse of the movement of matter, and in itself indivisible. All the living hold together, and all yield to the same tremendous push. The animal takes its stand on the plant, man bestrides animality, and the whole of humanity, in space and in time, is one immense army galloping beside and before and behind each of us in an overwhelming charge able to beat down every resistance and clear the most formidable obstacles, perhaps even death.

Sigmund Freud

24

Civilization and Its Discontents

Along with Marx and Darwin, Sigmund Freud (1856–1939) has shaped the contemporary outlook on man and the world. What others had offered as poetic insights, Freud established by clinical observation and persuasive reasoning, as well as by speculative leaps of the imagination. He provided a naturalistic explanation of the vital role of unconscious elements in human behavior and destroyed the old view of the self as a conscious rational entity. His great influence is apparent in modern psychiatry, literature, art, and social thought.

An Austrian-Jewish physician, who was himself zealous in the observance of conventional middle-class moralities, Freud began his career in a rather unrevolutionary manner: in his treatment of the mentally disturbed, he used methods that were firmly in the tradition of nineteenth-century positivistic science. Increasingly, however, Freud came to rely on imaginative insights and on literary myths and symbols to clarify the deepest springs of behavior. He nevertheless maintained his faith in reason as the indispensable means of finding the truths that would make men free.

Freud extended his findings from the study of neurotics to normal individuals and to society as a whole. He explained all human behavior as the result of instinctual drives, such as the sexual and aggressive urges, that are suppressed because they are unpleasant or socially disapproved. He saw the mind as the battleground of warring impulses ("id" and "superego"), where only a compromise effected by the suppression of some of them can produce the realistic adjustment necessary for normal living. Neuroses and insanity result from the failure of the rational, conscious personality ("ego") to make such an adjustment, and their cure can come only from the restoration of memory that provides self-knowledge (psychoanalysis).

Reprinted from *Civilization and Its Discontents* by Sigmund Freud, newly translated from the German and edited by James Strachey. By permission of W. W. Norton & Co., Inc. and The Hogarth Press Ltd. Copyright © 1961 by James Strachey, first American edition 1962. [Pp. 22–35, 55–59, 61–63, 65–66, 69–75, 86–92.]

For Freud, the guilt feelings accompanying the suppression of instinctual drives were the motive force of social organization or culture. This is the core of his theory of the relation of the individual to society, which he elaborated in *Civilization and Its Discontents* (1930). Society or culture, he maintained, repressed man's urges at painful cost, but such constraint was the very condition of progress; for if these urges were given free play, man would destroy himself. Freud has been attacked for the naturalistic determinism implicit in his views as well as for his pessimism about the possibilities of human progress. It is certain, however, that he has enlarged the dimensions of man's knowledge of himself and thereby made possible a controlled liberation of human energies.

The question of the purpose of human life has been raised countless times; it has never yet received a satisfactory answer and perhaps does not admit of one. Some of those who have asked it have added that if it should turn out that life has *no* purpose, it would lose all value for them. But this threat alters nothing. It looks, on the contrary, as though one had a right to dismiss the question, for it seems to derive from the human presumptuousness, many other manifestations of which are already familiar to us. Nobody talks about the purpose of the life of animals, unless, perhaps, it may be supposed to lie in being of service to man. But this view is not tenable either, for there are many animals of which man can make nothing, except to describe, classify and study them; and innumerable species of animals have escaped even this use, since they existed and became extinct before man set eyes on them. Once again, only religion can answer the question of the purpose of life. One can hardly be wrong in concluding that the idea of life having a purpose stands and falls with the religious system.

We will therefore turn to the less ambitious question of what men themselves show by their behaviour to be the purpose and intention of their lives. What do they demand of life and wish to achieve in it? The answer to this can hardly be in doubt. They strive after happiness; they want to become happy and to remain so. This endeavour has two sides, a positive and a negative aim. It aims, on the one hand, at an absence of pain and unpleasure, and, on the other, at the experiencing of strong feelings of pleasure. In its narrower sense the word 'happiness' only relates to the last. In conformity with this dichotomy in his aims, man's activity develops in two directions, according as it seeks to realize—in the main, or even exclusively—the one or the other of these aims.

As we see, what decides the purpose of life is simply the programme of the pleasure principle. This principle dominates the operation of the mental apparatus from the start. There can be no doubt about its efficacy, and yet its programme is at loggerheads with the whole world, with the macrocosm as much as with the microcosm. There is no possibility at all of its being carried through; all the regulations of the universe run counter to it. One feels inclined to say that the intention that man should be 'happy' is not included in the plan of 'Creation.' What we call happiness in the strictest sense comes from the (preferably sudden) satisfaction of needs which have been dammed up to a high degree, and it is from its nature only possible as an episodic phenomenon. When any situation that is desired by the pleasure principle is prolonged, it only produces a feeling of mild contentment. We are so made that we can derive intense enjoyment only from a contrast and very little from a state of things. Thus our possibilities of happiness are already restricted by our constitution. Unhappiness is much less difficult to experience. We are threatened with suffering from three directions: from our own body, which is doomed to decay and dissolution and which cannot even do without pain and anxiety as warning signals; from the external world, which may rage against us with overwhelming and merciless forces of destruction; and finally from our relations to other men. The suffering which comes from this last source is perhaps more painful to us than any other. We tend to regard it as a kind of gratuitous addition, although it cannot be any less fatefully inevitable than the suffering which comes from elsewhere.

It is no wonder if, under the pressure of these possibilities of suffering, men are accustomed to moderate their claims to happiness—just as the pleasure principle itself, indeed, under the influence of the external world, changed into the more modest reality principle—, if a man thinks himself happy merely to have escaped unhappiness or to have survived his suffering, and if in general the task of avoiding suffering pushes that of obtaining pleasure into the background. Reflection shows that the accomplishment of this task can be attempted along very different paths; and all these paths have been recommended by the various schools of worldly wisdom and put into practice by men. An unrestricted satisfaction of every need presents itself as the most enticing method of conducting one's life, but it means putting enjoyment before caution, and soon brings its own punishment. The other methods, in which avoidance of unpleasure is the main purpose, are differentiated according to the source of unpleasure to which their attention is chiefly turned. Some of these methods are extreme and some moderate; some are one-sided and some attack the problem simultaneously at several points. Against the suffering which may come upon one from human relationships the readiest safeguard is voluntary isolation, keeping oneself aloof from other people. The happiness which can be achieved along this path is, as we see, the happiness of quietness. Against the dreaded external world one can only defend oneself by some kind of turning away from it, if one intends to solve the task by oneself. There is, indeed, another and better path: that of becoming a member of the human community, and, with the help of a technique guided by science, going over to the attack against nature and subjecting her to the human will. Then one is working with all for the good of all. But the most interesting methods of averting suffering are those which seek to influence our own organism. In the last analysis, all suffering is nothing else than sensation; it only exists in so far as we feel it, and we only feel it in consequence of certain ways in which our organism is regulated.

The crudest, but also the most effective among these methods of influence is the chemical one—intoxication.

* * *

The service rendered by intoxicating media in the struggle for happiness and in keeping misery at a distance is so highly prized as a benefit that individuals and peoples alike have given them an established place in the economics of their libido. We owe to such media not merely the immediate yield of pleasure, but also a greatly desired degree of independence from the external world. For one knows that, with the help of this 'drowner of cares' one can at any time withdraw from the pressure of reality and find refuge in a world of one's own with better conditions of sensibility. As is well known, it is precisely this property of intoxicants which also determines their danger and their injuriousness. They are responsible, in certain circumstances, for the useless waste of a large quota of energy which might have been employed for the improvement of the human lot.

. . .

Another technique for fending off suffering is the employment of the displacements of libido which our mental apparatus permits of and through which its function gains so much in flexibility. The task here is that of shifting the instinctual aims in such a way that they cannot come up against frustration from the external world. In this, sublimation of the instincts lends its assistance. One gains the most if one can sufficiently heighten the yield of pleasure from the sources of psychical and intellectual work. When that is so, fate can do little against one. A satisfaction of this kind, such as an artist's joy in creating, in giving his phantasies body, or a scientist's in solving problems or discovering truths, has a special quality which we shall certainly one day be able to characterize in metapsychological terms. At present we can only say figuratively that such satisfactions seem 'finer and higher.' But their intensity is mild as compared with that derived from the sating of crude and primary instinctual impulses; it does not convulse our physical being. And the weak point of this method is that it is not applicable generally: it is accessible to only a few people. It presupposes the possession of special dispositions and gifts which are far from being common to any practical degree. And even to the few who do possess them, this method cannot give complete protection from suffering. It creates no impenetrable armour against the arrows of fortune, and it habitually fails when the source of suffering is a person's own body.

While this procedure already clearly shows an intention of making oneself independent of the external world by seeking satisfaction in internal, psychical processes, the next procedure brings out those features yet more strongly. In it, the connection with reality is still further loosened; satisfaction is obtained from illusions, which are recognized as such without the discrepancy between them and reality being allowed to interfere with enjoyment. The region from which these illusions arise is the life of the imagination; at the time when the development of the sense of reality took place, this region was expressly exempted from the demands of reality-testing and was set apart for the purpose of fulfilling wishes which were difficult to carry out. At the head of these satisfactions through phantasy stands the enjoyment of works of art—an enjoyment which, by the agency of the artist, is made accessible even to those who are not themselves creative. People who are receptive to the influence of art cannot set too high a value on it as a source of pleasure and consolation in life. Nevertheless the mild narcosis induced in us by art can do no more than bring about a transient withdrawal from the pressure of vital needs, and it is not strong enough to make us forget real misery.

Another procedure operates more energetically and more thoroughly. It regards reality as the sole enemy and as the source of all suffering, with which it is impossible to live, so that one must break off all relations with it if one is to be in any way happy. The hermit turns his back on the world and will have no truck with it. But one can do more than that; one can try to re-create the world, to build up in its stead another world in which its most unbearable features are eliminated and replaced by others that are in conformity with one's own wishes. But whoever, in desperate defiance, sets out upon this path to happiness will as a rule attain nothing. Reality is too strong for him. He becomes a madman, who for the most part finds no one to help him in carrying through his delusion. It is asserted, however, that each one of us behaves in some one respect like a paranoic, corrects some aspect of the world which is unbearable to him by the construction of a wish and introduces this delusion into reality. A special importance attaches to the case in which this attempt to procure a certainty of happiness and a protection against suffering through a delusional remoulding of reality is made by a considerable number of people in common. The religions of mankind must be classed among the mass-delusions of this kind. No one, needless to say, who shares a delusion ever recognizes it as such.

I do not think that I have made a complete enumeration of the methods by which men strive to gain happiness and keep suffering away and I know, too, that the material might have been differently arranged. One procedure I have not yet mentioned—not because I have forgotten it but because it will concern us later in another connection. And how could one possibly forget, of all others, this technique in the art of living? It is conspicuous for a most remarkable combination of characteristic features. It, too, aims of course at making the subject independent of Fate (as it is best to call it), and to that end it locates satisfaction in internal mental processes, making use, in so doing, of the displaceability of the libido of which we have already spoken. But it does not turn away from the external world; on the contrary, it clings to the objects belonging to that world and obtains happiness from an emotional relationship to them. Nor is it content to aim at an avoidance of unpleasure—a goal, as we might call it, of weary resignation; it passes this by without heed and holds fast to the original, passionate striving for a positive fulfilment of happiness. And perhaps it does in fact come nearer to this goal than any other method. I am, of course, speaking of the way of life which makes love the centre of everything, which looks for all satisfaction in loving and being loved. A psychical attitude of this sort comes naturally enough to all of us; one of the forms in which love manifests itself—sexual love— has given us our most intense experience of an overwhelming sensation of pleasure and has thus furnished us with a pattern for our search for happiness. What is more natural than that we should persist in looking for happiness along the path on which we first encountered it? The weak side of this technique of living is easy to see; otherwise no human being would have thought of abandoning this path to happiness for any other. It is that we are never so defenceless against suffering as when we love, never so helplessly unhappy as when we have lost our loved object or its love. But this does not dispose of the technique of living based on the value of love as a means to happiness. There is much more to be said about it.

We may go on from here to consider the interesting case in which happiness in life is predominantly sought in the enjoyment of beauty, wherever beauty presents itself to our senses and our judgement—the beauty of human forms and gestures, of natural objects and landscapes and of artistic and even scientific creations. This aesthetic attitude to the goal of life offers little protection against the threat of suffering, but it can compensate for a great deal. The enjoyment of beauty has a peculiar, mildly intoxicating quality of feeling. Beauty has no obvious use; nor is there any clear cultural necessity for it. Yet civilization could not do without it. The science of aesthetics investigates the conditions under which things are felt as beautiful, but it has been unable to give any explanation of the nature and origin of beauty, and, as usually happens, lack of success is concealed beneath a flood of resounding and empty words. Psychoanalysis, unfortunately, has scarcely anything to say about beauty either. All that seems certain is its derivation from the field of sexual feeling. The love of beauty seems a perfect example of an impulse inhibited in its aim. 'Beauty' and 'attraction' are originally attributes of the sexual object. It is worth remarking that the genitals themselves, the sight of which is always exciting, are nevertheless hardly ever judged to be beautiful; the quality of beauty seems, instead, to attach to certain secondary sexual characters.

In spite of the incompleteness [of my enumeration], I will venture on a few remarks as a conclusion to our enquiry. The programme of becoming happy, which the pleasure principle imposes on us, cannot be fulfilled; yet we must not—indeed, we cannot—give up our efforts to bring it nearer to fulfilment by some means or other. Very different paths may be taken in that direction, and we may give priority either to the positive aspect of the aim, that of gaining pleasure, or to its negative one, that of avoiding unpleasure. By none of these paths can we attain all that we desire. Happiness, in the reduced sense in which we recognize it as possible, is a problem of the economics of the individual's libido. There is no golden rule which applies to everyone: every man must find out for himself in what particular fashion he can be saved. All kinds of different factors will operate to direct his choice. It is a question of how much real satisfaction he can expect to get from the external world, how far he is led to make himself independent of it, and, finally, how much strength he feels he has for altering the world to suit his wishes. In this, his psychical constitution will play a decisive part, irrespectively of the external circumstances. The man who is predominantly erotic will give first preference to his emotional relationships to other people; the narcissistic man, who inclines to be self-sufficient, will seek his main satisfactions in his internal mental processes; the man of action will never give up the external world on which he can try out his strength. As regards the second of these types, the nature of his talents and the amount of instinctual sublimation open to him will decide where he shall locate his interests. Any choice that is pushed to an extreme will be penalized by exposing the individual to the dangers which arise if a technique of living that has been chosen as an exclusive one should prove inadequate. Just as a cautious business-man avoids tying up all his capital in one concern, so, perhaps, worldly wisdom will advise us not to look for the whole of our satisfaction from a single aspiration. Its success is never certain, for that depends on the convergence of many factors, perhaps on none more than on the capacity of the psychical constitution to adapt its function to the environment and then to exploit that environment for a yield of pleasure. A person who is born with a specially unfavourable instinctual constitution, and who has not properly undergone the transformation and rearrangement of his libidinal components which is indispensable for later achievements, will find it hard to obtain happiness from his external situation, especially if he is faced with tasks of some difficulty. As a last technique of living, which will at least bring him substitutive satisfactions, he is offered that of a flight into neurotic illness—a flight which he usually accomplishes when he is still young. The man who sees his pursuit of happiness come to nothing in later years can still find consolation in the yield of pleasure of chronic intoxication; or he can embark on the desperate attempt at rebellion seen in a psychosis.

Religion restricts this play of choice and adaptation, since it imposes equally on everyone its own path to the acquisition of happiness and protection from suffering. Its technique consists in depressing the value of life and distorting the picture of the real world in a delusional manner—which presupposes an intimidation of the intelligence. At this price, by forcibly fixing them in a state of psychical infantilism and by drawing them into a mass-delusion, religion succeeds in sparing many people an individual neurosis. But hardly anything more. There are, as we have said, many paths which *may* lead to such happiness as is attainable by men, but there is none which does so for certain. Even religion cannot keep its promise. If the believer finally sees himself obliged to speak of God's 'inscrutable decrees,' he is admitting that all that is left to him as a last possible consolation and source of pleasure in his suffering is an unconditional submission. And if he is prepared for that, he could probably have spared himself the *détour* he has made.

Our enquiry concerning happiness has not so far taught us much that is not already common knowledge. And even if we proceed from it to the problem of why it is so hard for men to be happy, there seems no greater prospect of learning anything new. We have given the answer already by pointing to the three sources from which our suffering comes: the superior power of nature, the feebleness of our own bodies and the inadequacy of the regulations which adjust the mutual relationships of human beings in the family, the state and society. In regard to the first two sources, our judgement cannot hesitate long. It forces us to acknowledge those sources of suffering and to submit to the inevitable. We shall never completely master nature; and our bodily organism, itself a part of that nature, will always remain a transient structure with a limited capacity for adaptation and achievement. This recognition does not have a paralysing effect. On the contrary, it points the direction for our activity. If we cannot remove all suffering, we can remove some, and we can mitigate some: the experience of many thousands of years has convinced us of that. As regards the third source, the social source of suffering, our attitude is a different one. We do not admit it at all; we cannot see why the regulations made by ourselves should not, on the contrary, be a protection and a benefit for every one of us. And yet, when we consider how unsuccessful we have been in precisely this field of prevention of suffering, a suspicion dawns on us that here, too, a piece of unconquerable nature may lie behind—this time a piece of our own psychical constitution.

When we start considering this possibility, we come upon a contention which is so astonishing that we must dwell upon it. This contention holds that what we call our civilization is largely responsible for our misery, and that we should be much happier if we gave it up and returned to primitive conditions. I call this contention astonishing because, in whatever way we may define the concept of civilization, it is a certain fact that all the things with which we seek to protect ourselves against the threats that emanate from the sources of suffering are part of that very civilization.

How has it happened that so many people have come to take up this strange attitude of hostility to civilization? I believe that the basis of it was a deep and long-standing dissatisfaction with the then existing state of civilization and that on that basis a condemnation of it was built up, occasioned by certain specific historical events. I think I know what the last and the last but one of those occasions were. I am not learned enough to trace the chain of them far back enough in the history of the human species; but a factor of this kind hostile to civilization must already have been at work in the victory of Christendom over the heathen religions. For it was very closely related to the low estimation put upon earthly life by the Christian doctrine. The last but one of these occasions was when the progress of voyages of discovery led to contact with primitive peoples and races. In consequence of insufficient observation and a mistaken view of their manners and customs, they appeared to Europeans to be leading a simple, happy life with few wants, a life such as was un-attainable by their visitors with their superior civilization. Later experience has corrected some of these judgements. In many cases the observers had wrongly attributed to the absence of complicated cultural demands what was in fact due to the bounty of nature and the ease with which the major human needs were satisfied. The last occasion is especially familiar to us. It arose when people came to know about the mechanism of the neuroses, which threaten to undermine the modicum of happiness enjoyed by civilized men. It was discovered that a person becomes neurotic because he cannot tolerate the amount of frustration which society imposes on him in the service of its cultural ideals, and it was inferred from this that the abolition or reduction of those demands would result in a return to possibilities of happiness.

There is also an added factor of disappointment. During the last few generations mankind has made an extraordinary advance in the natural sciences and in their technical application and has estab-lished his control over nature in a way never before imagined. The single steps of this advance are common knowledge and it is unnec-essary to enumerate them. Men are proud of those achievements, and have a right to be. But they seem to have observed that this newly-won power over space and time, this subjugation of the forces of nature, which is the fulfilment of a longing that goes back thou-sands of years, has not increased the amount of pleasurable satis-faction which they may expect from life and has not made them feel happier. From the recognition of this fact we ought to be content to conclude that power over nature is not the *only* precondition of human happiness, just as it is not the *only* goal of cultural endeavour; we ought not to infer from it that technical progress is without value for the economics of our happiness. One would like to ask: is there, then, no positive gain in pleasure, no unequivocal increase in my feeling of happiness, if I can, as often as I please, hear the voice of a child of mine who is living hundreds of miles away or if I can learn in the shortest possible time after a friend has reached his destination that he has come through the long and difficult voyage unharmed? Does it mean nothing that medicine has succeeded in enormously reducing infant mortality and the danger of infection for women in childbirth, and, indeed, in considerably lengthening the average life of a civilized man? And there is a long list that might be added to benefits of this kind which we owe to the much-despised era of scientific and technical advances. But here the voice of pessimistic criticism makes itself heard and warns us that most of these satisfactions follow the model of the 'cheap enjoyment' extolled in the anecdote—the enjoyment obtained by putting a bare leg from under the bedclothes on a cold winter night and drawing it in again. If there had been no railway to conquer distances, my child would never have left his native town and I should need no telephone to hear his voice; if travelling across the ocean by ship had not been introduced, my friend would not have embarked on his sea-voyage and I should not need a cable to relieve my anxiety about him. What is the use of reducing infantile mortality when it is precisely that reduction which imposes the greatest restraint on us in the begetting of children, so that, taken all round, we nevertheless rear no more children than in the days before the reign of hygiene, while at the same time we have created difficult conditions for our sexual life in marriage, and have probably worked against the beneficial effects of natural selection? And, finally, what good to us is a long life if it is difficult and barren of joys, and if it is so full of misery that we can only welcome death as a deliverer?

· · ·

Psycho-analytic work has shown us that it is precisely these frustrations of sexual life which people known as neurotics cannot tolerate. The neurotic creates substitutive satisfactions for himself in his symptoms, and these either cause him suffering in themselves or become sources of suffering for him by raising difficulties in his relations with his environment and the society he belongs to. The latter fact is easy to understand; the former presents us with a new problem. But civilization demands other sacrifices besides that of sexual satisfaction.

We have treated the difficulty of cultural development as a general difficulty of development by tracing it to the inertia of the libido, to its disinclination to give up an old position for a new one. We are saying much the same thing when we derive the antithesis between civilization and sexuality from the circumstance that sexual love is a relationship between two individuals in which a third can only be superfluous or disturbing, whereas civilization depends on relationships between a considerable number of individuals. When a love-relationship is at its height there is no room left for any interest in the environment; a pair of lovers are sufficient to themselves, and do not even need the child they have in common to make them happy. In no other case does Eros so clearly betray the core of his being, his purpose of making one out of more than one; but when he has achieved this in the proverbial way through the love of two human beings, he refuses to go further.

So far, we can quite well imagine a cultural community consisting of double individuals like this, who, libidinally satisfied in themselves, are connected with one another through the bonds of common work and common interests. If this were so, civilization would not have to withdraw any energy from sexuality. But this desirable state of things does not, and never did, exist. Reality shows us that civilization is not content with the ties we have so far allowed it. It aims at binding the members of the community together in a libidinal way as well and employs every means to that end. It favours every path by which strong identifications can be established between the members of the community, and it summons up aim-inhibited libido on the largest scale so as to strengthen the communal bond by relations of friendship. In order for these aims to be fulfilled, a restriction upon sexual life is unavoidable. But we are unable to understand what the necessity is which forces civilization along this path and which causes its antagonism to sexuality. There must be some disturbing factor which we have not yet discovered.

The clue may be supplied by one of the ideal demands, as we have called them, of civilized society. It runs: 'Thou shalt love thy neighbour as thyself.' It is known throughout the world and is undoubtedly older than Christianity, which puts it forward as its proudest claim. Yet it is certainly not very old; even in historical times it was still strange to mankind. Let us adopt a naïve attitude towards it, as though we were hearing it for the first time; we shall be unable then to suppress a feeling of surprise and bewilderment. Why should we do it? What good will it do us? But, above all, how shall we achieve it? How can it be possible? My love is something valuable to me which I ought not to throw away without reflection. It imposes duties on me for whose fulfilment I must be ready to make sacrifices. If I love someone, he must deserve it in some way. (I leave out of account the use he may be to me, and also his possible significance for me as a sexual object, for neither of these two kinds of relationship comes into question where the precept to love my neighbour is concerned.) He deserves it if he is so like me in important ways that I can love myself in him; and he deserves it if he is so much more perfect than myself that I can love my ideal of my own self in him. Again, I have to love him if he is my friend's son, since the pain my friend would feel if any harm came to him would be my pain too—I should have to share it. But if he is a stranger to me and if he cannot attract me by any worth of his own or any significance that he may already have acquired for my emotional life, it will be hard for me to love him. Indeed, I should be wrong to do so, for my love is valued by all my own people as a sign of my preferring them, and it is an injustice to them if I put a stranger on a par with them. But if I am to love him (with this universal love) merely because he, too, is an inhabitant of this earth, like an insect, an earth-worm or a grass-snake, then I fear that only a small modicum of my love will fall to his share—not by any possibility as much as, by the judgment of my reason, I am entitled to retain for myself. What is the point of a precept enunciated with so much solemnity if its fulfilment cannot be recommended as reasonable?

On closer inspection, I find still further difficulties. Not merely is this stranger in general unworthy of my love; I must honestly confess that he has more claim to my hostility and even my hatred. He seems not to have the least trace of love for me and shows me not the slightest consideration. If it will do him any good he has no hesitation in injuring me, nor does he ask himself whether the amount of advantage he gains bears any proportion to the extent of the harm he does to me. Indeed, he need not even obtain an advantage; if he can satisfy any sort of desire by it, he thinks nothing of jeering at me, insulting me, slandering me and showing his superior power; and the more secure he feels and the more helpless I am, the more certainly I can expect him to behave like this to me. If he behaves differently, if he shows me consideration and forbearance as a stranger, I am ready to treat him in the same way, in any case and quite apart from any precept. Indeed, if this grandiose commandment had run 'Love thy neighbour as thy neighbour loves thee,' I should not take exception to it. And there is a second commandment, which seems to me even more incomprehensible and arouses still stronger opposition in me. It is 'Love thine enemies.' If I think it over, however, I see that I am wrong in treating it as a greater imposition. At bottom it is the same thing.

I think I can now hear a dignified voice admonishing me: 'It is precisely because your neighbour is not worthy of love, and is on the contrary your enemy, that you should love him as yourself.' I then understand that the case is one like that of *Credo quia absurdum.*

Now it is very probable that my neighbour, when he is enjoined to love me as himself, will answer exactly as I have done and will repel me for the same reasons. I hope he will not have the same objective grounds for doing so, but he will have the same idea as I have. Even so, the behaviour of human beings shows differences, which ethics, disregarding the fact that such differences are determined, classifies as 'good' or 'bad.' So long as these undeniable differences have not been removed, obedience to high ethical demands entails damage to the aims of civilization, for it puts a positive premium on being bad. One is irresistibly reminded of an incident in the French Chamber when capital punishment was being debated. A member had been passionately supporting its abolition and his speech was being received with tumultuous applause, when a voice from the hall called out: 'Que messieurs les assassins commencent!'

The element of truth behind all this, which people are so ready to disavow, is that men are not gentle creatures who want to be loved, and who at the most can defend themselves if they are attacked; they are, on the contrary, creatures among whose instinctual endowments is to be reckoned a powerful share of aggressiveness. As a result, their neighbour is for them not only a potential helper or sexual object, but also someone who tempts them to satisfy their aggressiveness on him, to exploit his capacity for work without compensation, to use him sexually without his consent, to seize his possessions, to humiliate him, to cause him pain, to torture and to kill him. *Homo homini lupus.* Who, in the face of all his experience of life and of history, will have the courage to dispute this assertion? As a rule this cruel aggressiveness waits for some provocation or puts itself at the service of some other purpose, whose goal might also have been reached by milder measures. In circumstances that are favourable to it, when the mental counter-forces which ordinarily inhibit it are out of action, it also manifests itself spontaneously and reveals man as a savage beast to whom consideration towards his own kind is something alien. Anyone who calls to mind the atrocities committed during the racial migrations or the invasions of the Huns, or by the people known as Mongols under

Jenghiz Khan and Tamerlane, or at the capture of Jerusalem by the pious Crusaders, or even, indeed, the horrors of the recent World War—anyone who calls these things to mind will have to bow humbly before the truth of this view.

The existence of this inclination to aggression, which we can detect in ourselves and justly assume to be present in others, is the factor which disturbs our relations with our neighbour and which forces civilization into such a high expenditure [of energy]. In consequence of this primary mutual hostility of human beings, civilized society is perpetually threatened with disintegration. The interest of work in common would not hold it together; instinctual passions are stronger than reasonable interests. Civilization has to use its utmost efforts in order to set limits to man's aggressive instincts and to hold the manifestations of them in check by psychical reaction-formations. Hence, therefore, the use of methods intended to incite people into identifications and aim-inhibited relationships of love, hence the restriction upon sexual life, and hence too the ideal's commandment to love one's neighbour as oneself—a commandment which is really justified by the fact that nothing else runs so strongly counter to the original nature of man. In spite of every effort, these endeavours of civilization have not so far achieved very much. It hopes to prevent the crudest excesses of brutal violence by itself assuming the right to use violence against criminals, but the law is not able to lay hold of the more cautious and refined manifestations of human aggressiveness. The time comes when each one of us has to give up as illusions the expectations which, in his youth, he pinned upon his fellowmen, and when he may learn how much difficulty and pain has been added to his life by their ill-will. At the same time, it would be unfair to reproach civilization with trying to eliminate strife and competition from human activity. These things are undoubtedly indispensable. But opposition is not necessarily enmity; it is merely misused and made an *occasion* for enmity.

.   .   .

It is clearly not easy for men to give up the satisfaction of this inclination to aggression. They do not feel comfortable without it. The advantage which a comparatively small cultural group offers of allowing this instinct an outlet in the form of hostility against intruders is not to be despised. It is always possible to bind together a considerable number of people in love, so long as there are other people left over to receive the manifestations of their aggressiveness.

. . .

If civilization imposes such great sacrifices not only on man's sexuality but on his aggressivity, we can understand better why it is hard for him to be happy in that civilization. In fact, primitive man was better off in knowing no restrictions of instinct. To counterbalance this, his prospects of enjoying this happiness for any length of time were very slender. Civilized man has exchanged a portion of his possibilities of happiness for a portion of security. We must not forget, however, that in the primal family only the head of it enjoyed this instinctual freedom; the rest lived in slavish suppression. In that primal period of civilization, the contrast between a minority who enjoyed the advantages of civilization and a majority who were robbed of those advantages was, therefore, carried to extremes. As regards the primitive peoples who exist to-day, careful researches have shown that their instinctual life is by no means to be envied for its freedom. It is subject to restrictions of a different kind but perhaps of greater severity than those attaching to modern civilized man.

When we justly find fault with the present state of our civilization for so inadequately fulfilling our demands for a plan of life that shall make us happy, and for allowing the existence of so much suffering which could probably be avoided—when, with unsparing criticism, we try to uncover the roots of its imperfection, we are undoubtedly exercising a proper right and are not showing ourselves enemies of civilization. We may expect gradually to carry through such alterations in our civilization as will better satisfy our needs and will escape our criticisms. But perhaps we may also familiarize ourselves with the idea that there are difficulties attaching to the nature of civilization which will not yield to any attempt at reform. Over and above the tasks of restricting the instincts, which we are prepared for, there forces itself on our notice the danger of a state of things which might be termed 'the psychological poverty of groups.' This danger is most threatening where the bonds of a society are chiefly constituted by the identification of its members with one another, while individuals of the leader type do not acquire the importance that should fall to them in the formation of a group. The present cultural state of America would give us a good opportunity for studying the damage to civilization which is thus to be feared. But I shall avoid the temptation of entering upon a critique of American civilization; I do not wish to give an impression of wanting myself to employ American methods.

       .   .   .

Starting from speculations on the beginning of life and from biological parallels, I drew the conclusion that, besides the instinct to preserve living substance and to join it into ever larger units, there must exist another, contrary instinct seeking to dissolve those units and to bring them back to their primaeval, inorganic state. That is to say, as well as Eros there was an instinct of death. The phenomena of life could be explained from the concurrent or mutually opposing action of these two instincts. It was not easy, however, to demonstrate the activities of this supposed death instinct. The manifestations of Eros were conspicuous and noisy enough. It might be assumed that the death instinct operated silently within the organism towards its dissolution, but that, of course, was no proof. A more fruitful idea was that a portion of the instinct is diverted towards the external world and comes to light as an instinct of aggressiveness and destructiveness. In this way the instinct itself could be pressed into the service of Eros, in that the organism was destroying some other thing, whether animate or inanimate, instead of destroying its own self. Conversely, any restriction of this aggressiveness directed outwards would be bound to increase the self-destruction, which is in any case proceeding. At the same time one can suspect from this example that the two kinds of instinct seldom—perhaps never—appear in isolation from each other, but are alloyed with each other in varying and very different proportions and so become unrecognizable to our judgment. In sadism, long since known to us as a component instinct of sexuality, we should have before us a particularly strong alloy of this kind between trends of love and the destructive instinct; while its counterpart, masochism, would be a union between destructiveness directed inwards and sexuality—a union which makes what is otherwise an imperceptible trend into a conspicuous and tangible one.

       .   .   .

In all that follows I adopt the standpoint, therefore, that the inclination to aggression is an original, self-subsisting instinctual disposition in man, and I return to my view that it constitutes the greatest impediment to civilization. At one point in the course of this enquiry I was led to the idea that civilization was a special process which mankind undergoes, and I am still under the influence of that idea. I may now add that civilization is a process in the service of Eros, whose purpose is to combine single human individuals, and after that families, then races, peoples and nations, into one great unity, the unity of mankind. Why this has to happen, we do not know; the work of Eros is precisely this. These collections of men are to be libidinally bound to one another. Necessity alone, the advantages of work in common, will not hold them together. But man's natural aggressive instinct, the hostility of each against all and of all against each, opposes this programme of civilization. This aggressive instinct is the derivative and the main representative of the death instinct which we have found alongside of Eros and which shares world-dominion with it. And now, I think, the meaning of the evolution of civilization is no longer obscure to us. It must present the struggle between Eros and Death, between the instinct of life and the instinct of destruction, as it works itself out in the human species. This struggle is what all life essentially consists of, and the evolution of civilization may therefore be simply described as the struggle for life of the human species. And it is this battle of the giants that our nurse-maids try to appease with their lullaby about Heaven.

⋅ ⋅ ⋅

Another question concerns us more nearly. What means does civilization employ in order to inhibit the aggressiveness which opposes it, to make it harmless, to get rid of it, perhaps? We have already become acquainted with a few of these methods, but not yet with the one that appears to be the most important. This we can study in the history of the development of the individual. What happens in him to render his desire for aggression innocuous? Something very remarkable, which we should never have guessed and which is nevertheless quite obvious. His aggressiveness is introjected, internalized; it is, in point of fact, sent back to where it came from—that is, it is directed towards his own ego. There it is taken over by a portion of the ego, which sets itself over against the rest of the ego as super-ego, and which now, in the form of 'conscience,' is ready to put into action against the ego the same harsh aggressiveness that the ego would have liked to satisfy upon other, extraneous individuals. The tension between the harsh super-ego and the ego that is subjected to it, is called by us the sense of guilt; it expresses itself as a need for punishment. Civilization, there-fore, obtains mastery over the individual's dangerous desire for aggression by weakening and disarming it and by setting up an agency within him to watch over it, like a garrison in a conquered city.

As to the origin of the sense of guilt, the analyst has different views from other psychologists; but even he does not find it easy to give an account of it. To begin with, if we ask how a person comes to have a sense of guilt, we arrive at an answer which cannot be dis-puted: a person feels guilty (devout people would say 'sinful') when he has done something which he knows to be 'bad.' But then we notice how little this answer tells us. Perhaps, after some hesitation, we shall add that even when a person has not actually *done* the bad thing but has only recognized in himself an *intention* to do it, he may regard himself as guilty; and the question then arises of why the intention is regarded as equal to the deed. Both cases, however, presuppose that one had already recognized that what is bad is reprehensible, is something that must not be carried out. How is this judgement arrived at? We may reject the existence of an origi-nal, as it were natural, capacity to distinguish good from bad. What is bad is often not at all what is injurious or dangerous to the ego; on the contrary, it may be something which is desirable and en-joyable to the ego. Here, therefore, there is an extraneous influence at work, and it is this that decides what is to be called good or bad. Since a person's own feelings would not have led him along this path, he must have had a motive for submitting to this extraneous influence. Such a motive is easily discovered in his helplessness and his dependence on other people, and it can best be designated as fear of loss of love. If he loses the love of another person upon whom he is dependent, he also ceases to be protected from a variety of dangers. Above all, he is exposed to the danger that this stronger person will show his superiority in the form of punishment. At the beginning, therefore, what is bad is whatever causes one to be threatened with loss of love. For fear of that loss, one must avoid it. This, too, is the reason why it makes little difference whether one has already done the bad thing or only intends to do it. In either case the danger only sets in if and when the authority dis-

r the influence of a task that is set it by Eros and instigated by
ke—by the exigencies of reality; and that this task is one of
ng separate individuals into a community bound together by
nal ties. When, however, we look at the relation between the
ss of human civilization and the developmental or educative
ss of individual human beings, we shall conclude without much
ation that the two are very similar in nature, if not the very
process applied to different kinds of object. The process of the
ation of the human species is, of course, an abstraction of a
r order than is the development of the individual and it is
fore harder to apprehend in concrete terms, nor should we
e analogies to an obsessional extreme; but in view of the simi-
between the aims of the two processes—in the one case the
ration of a separate individual into a human group, and in the
case the creation of a unified group out of many individuals—
nnot be surprised at the similarity between the means em-
d and the resultant phenomena.

view of its exceptional importance, we must not long post-
the mention of one feature which distinguishes between the
rocesses. In the developmental process of the individual, the
amme of the pleasure principle, which consists in finding the
ction of happiness, is retained as the main aim. Integration in,
ptation to, a human community appears as a scarcely avoid-
ondition which must be fulfilled before this aim of happiness
achieved. If it could be done without that condition, it would
ps be preferable. To put it in other words, the development of
dividual seems to us to be a product of the interaction be-
two urges, the urge towards happiness, which we usually call
ic,' and the urge towards union with others in the com-
y, which we call 'altruistic.' Neither of these descriptions goes
below the surface. In the process of individual development,
have said, the main accent falls mostly on the egoistic urge (or
ge towards happiness); while the other urge, which may be
ed as a 'cultural' one, is usually content with the role of im-
restrictions. But in the process of civilization things are dif-
Here by far the most important thing is the aim of creating
out of the individual human beings. It is true that the aim
piness is still there, but it is pushed into the background. It
seems as if the creation of a great human community would
t successful if no attention had to be paid to the happiness of

covers it, and in either case the authority would behave in the same way.

This state of mind is called a 'bad conscience'; but actually it does not deserve this name, for at this stage the sense of guilt is clearly only a fear of loss of love, 'social' anxiety. In small children it can never be anything else, but in many adults, too, it has only changed to the extent that the place of the father or the two parents is taken by the larger human community. Consequently, such people habitually allow themselves to do any bad thing which promises them enjoyment, so long as they are sure that the authority will not know anything about it or cannot blame them for it; they are afraid only of being found out. Present-day society has to reckon in general with this state of mind.

A great change takes place only when the authority is internalized through the establishment of a super-ego. The phenomena of conscience then reach a higher stage. Actually, it is not until now that we should should speak of conscience or a sense of guilt. At this point, too, the fear of being found out comes to an end; the distinction, moreover, between doing something bad and wishing to do it disappears entirely, since nothing can be hidden from the super-ego, not even thoughts. It is true that the seriousness of the situation from a real point of view has passed away, for the new authority, the super-ego, has no motive that we know of for ill-treating the ego, with which it is intimately bound up; but genetic influence, which leads to the survival of what is past and has been surmounted, makes itself felt in the fact that fundamentally things remain as they were at the beginning. The super-ego torments the sinful ego with the same feeling of anxiety and is on the watch for opportunities of getting it punished by the external world.

At this second stage of development, the conscience exhibits a peculiarity which was absent from the first stage and which is no longer easy to account for. For the more virtuous a man is, the more severe and distrustful is its behaviour, so that ultimately it is precisely those people who have carried saintliness furthest who reproach themselves with the worst sinfulness. This means that virtue forfeits some part of its promised reward; the docile and continent ego does not enjoy the trust of its mentor, and strives in vain, it would seem, to acquire it. The objection will at once be made that these difficulties are artificial ones, and it will be said that a stricter and more vigilant conscience is precisely the hallmark of a moral man. Moreover, when saints call themselves sinners, they are not so wrong, considering the temptations to instinctual satisfaction to which they are exposed in a specially high degree—since, as is well known, temptations are merely increased by constant frustration, whereas an occasional satisfaction of them causes them to diminish, at least for the time being. The field of ethics, which is so full of problems, presents us with another fact: namely that ill-luck—that is, external frustration—so greatly enhances the power of the conscience in the super-ego. As long as things go well with a man, his conscience is lenient and lets the ego do all sorts of things; but when misfortune befalls him, he searches his soul, acknowledges his sinfulness, heightens the demands of his conscience, imposes abstinences on himself and punishes himself with penances. Whole peoples have behaved in this way, and still do. This, however, is easily explained by the original infantile stage of conscience, which, as we see, is not given up after the introjection into the super-ego, but persists alongside of it and behind it. Fate is regarded as a substitute for the parental agency. If a man is unfortunate it means that he is no longer loved by this highest power; and, threatened by such a loss of love, he once more bows to the parental representative in his super-ego—a representative whom, in his days of good fortune, he was ready to neglect. This becomes especially clear where Fate is looked upon in the strictly religious sense of being nothing else than an expression of the Divine Will. The people of Israel had believed themselves to be the favourite child of God, and when the great Father caused misfortune after misfortune to rain down upon this people of his, they were never shaken in their belief in his relationship to them or questioned his power or righteousness. Instead, they produced the prophets, who held up their sinfulness before them; and out of their sense of guilt they created the over-strict commandments of their priestly religion. It is remarkable how differently a primitive man behaves. If he has met with a misfortune, he does not throw the blame on himself but on his fetish, which has obviously not done its duty, and he gives it a thrashing instead of punishing himself.

Thus we know of two origins of the sense of guilt: one arising from fear of an authority, and the other, later on, arising from fear of the super-ego. The first insists upon a renunciation of instinctual satisfactions; the second, as well as doing this, presses for punishment, since the continuance of the forbidden wishes cannot

be concealed from the super-ego. We have als[...] severity of the super-ego—the demands of conscie[...] stood. It is simply a continuation of the sever[...] authority, to which it has succeeded and which[...] placed. We now see in what relationship the[...] stinct stands to the sense of guilt. Originally, ren[...] was the result of fear of an external authority: [...] satisfactions in order not to lose its love. If one[...] renunciation, one is, as it were, quits with the au[...] of guilt should remain. But with fear of the s[...] different. Here, instinctual renunciation is not [...] persists and cannot be concealed from the supe[...] of the renunciation that has been made, a sense [...] This constitutes a great economic disadvantag[...] a super-ego, or, as we may put it, in the forma[...] Instinctual renunciation now no longer has a [...] effect; virtuous continence is no longer rewar[...] ance of love. A threatened external unhappin[...] punishment on the part of the external aut[...] changed for a permanent internal unhappiness, [...] sense of guilt.

.   .   .

Some readers of this work may further hav[...] they have heard the formula of the struggle b[...] death instinct too often. It was alleged to char[...] civilization which mankind undergoes but it [...] connection with the development of the indi[...] tion, it was said to have revealed the secret o[...] eral. We cannot, I think, avoid going into t[...] three processes to one another. The repetition[...] is justified by the consideration that both t[...] civilization and of the development of the inc[...] processes—which is to say that they must shar[...] characteristic of life. On the other hand, evi[...] of this general characteristic fails, for the very[...] nature, to help us to arrive at any differer[...] processes], so long as it is not narrowed dow[...] tions. We can only be satisfied, therefore, if we[...] of civilization is a modification which the vit[...]

the individual. The developmental process of the individual can thus be expected to have special features of its own which are not reproduced in the process of human civilization. It is only in so far as the first of these processes has union with the community as its aim that it need coincide with the second process.

Just as a planet revolves around a central body as well as rotating on its own axis, so the human individual takes part in the course of development of mankind at the same time as he pursues his own path in life. But to our dull eyes the play of forces in the heavens seems fixed in a never-changing order; in the field of organic life we can still see how the forces contend with one another, and how the effects of the conflict are continually changing. So, also, the two urges, the one towards personal happiness and the other towards union with other human beings must struggle with each other in every individual; and so, also, the two processes of individual and of cultural development must stand in hostile opposition to each other and mutually dispute the ground. But this struggle between the individual and society is not a derivative of the contradiction—probably an irreconcilable one—between the primal instincts of Eros and death. It is a dispute within the economics of the libido, comparable to the contest concerning the distribution of libido between ego and objects; and it does admit of an eventual accommodation in the individual, as, it may be hoped, it will also do in the future of civilization, however much that civilization may oppress the life of the individual to-day.

The analogy between the process of civilization and the path of individual development may be extended in an important respect. It can be asserted that the community, too, evolves a super-ego under whose influence cultural development proceeds. It would be a tempting task for anyone who has a knowledge of human civilizations to follow out this analogy in detail. I will confine myself to bringing forward a few striking points. The super-ego of an epoch of civilization has an origin similar to that of an individual. It is based on the impression left behind by the personalities of great leaders—men of overwhelming force of mind or men in whom one of the human impulsions has found its strongest and purest, and therefore often its most one-sided, expression. In many instances the analogy goes still further, in that during their lifetime these figures were—often enough, even if not always—mocked and maltreated by others and even despatched in a cruel fashion. In the same way, indeed, the primal father did not attain divinity until long after he had met his death by violence. The most arresting example of this fateful conjunction is to be seen in the figure of Jesus Christ—if, indeed, that figure is not a part of mythology, which called it into being from an obscure memory of that primal event. Another point of agreement between the cultural and the individual super-ego is that the former, just like the latter, sets up strict ideal demands, disobedience to which is visited with 'fear of conscience.' Here, indeed, we come across the remarkable circumstance that the mental processes concerned are actually more familiar to us and more accessible to consciousness as they are seen in the group than they can be in the individual man. In him, when tension arises, it is only the aggressiveness of the super-ego which, in the form of reproaches, makes itself noisily heard; its actual demands often remain unconscious in the background. If we bring them to conscious knowledge, we find that they coincide with the precepts of the prevailing cultural super-ego. At this point the two processes, that of the cultural development of the group and that of the cultural development of the individual, are, as it were, always interlocked. For that reason some of the manifestations and properties of the super-ego can be more easily detected in its behaviour in the cultural community than in the separate individual.

The cultural super-ego has developed its ideals and set up its demands. Among the latter, those which deal with the relations of human beings to one another are comprised under the heading of ethics. People have at all times set the greatest value on ethics, as though they expected that it in particular would produce especially important results. And it does in fact deal with a subject which can easily be recognized as the sorest spot in every civilization. Ethics is thus to be regarded as a therapeutic attempt—as an endeavour to achieve, by means of a command of the super-ego, something which has so far not been achieved by means of any other cultural activities. As we already know, the problem before us is how to get rid of the greatest hindrance to civilization—namely, the constitutional inclination of human beings to be aggressive towards one another; and for that very reason we are especially interested in what is probably the most recent of the cultural commands of the super-ego, the commandment to love one's neighbour as oneself. In our research into, and therapy of, a neurosis, we are led to make two reproaches against the super-ego of the individual. In the severity of its commands and prohibitions it troubles itself too little about the happiness of the ego, in that it takes insufficient account of the resistances against obeying them—of the instinctual strength of the id [in the first place], and of the difficulties presented by the real external environment [in the second]. Consequently we are very often obliged, for therapeutic purposes, to oppose the super-ego, and we endeavour to lower its demands. Exactly the same objections can be made against the ethical demands of the cultural super-ego. It, too, does not trouble itself enough about the facts of the mental constitution of human beings. It issues a command and does not ask whether it is possible for people to obey it. On the contrary, it assumes that a man's ego is psychologically capable of anything that is required of it, that his ego has unlimited mastery over his id. This is a mistake; and even in what are known as normal people the id cannot be controlled beyond certain limits. If more is demanded of a man, a revolt will be produced in him or a neurosis, or he will be made unhappy. The commandment, 'Love thy neighbour as thyself,' is the strongest defence against human aggressiveness and an excellent example of the unpsychological proceedings of the cultural super-ego. The commandment is impossible to fulfil; such an enormous inflation of love can only lower its value, not get rid of the difficulty. Civilization pays no attention to all this; it merely admonishes us that the harder it is to obey the precept the more meritorious it is to do so. But anyone who follows such a precept in present-day civilization only puts himself at a disadvantage *vis-à-vis* the person who disregards it. What a potent obstacle to civilization aggressiveness must be, if the defence against it can cause as much unhappiness as aggressiveness itself! 'Natural' ethics, as it is called, has nothing to offer here except the narcissistic satisfaction of being able to think oneself better than others. At this point the ethics based on religion introduces its promises of a better after-life. But so long as virtue is not rewarded here on earth, ethics will, I fancy, preach in vain. I too think it quite certain that a real change in the relations of human beings to possessions would be of more help in this direction than any ethical commands; but the recognition of this fact among socialists has been obscured and made useless for practical purposes by a fresh idealistic misconception of human nature.

I believe the line of thought which seeks to trace in the phenomena of cultural development the part played by a super-ego promises still further discoveries. I hasten to come to a close. But there is one question which I can hardly evade. If the development of civilization has such a far-reaching similarity to the development of the individual and if it employs the same methods, may we not be justified in reaching the diagnosis that, under the influence of cultural urges, some civilizations, or some epochs of civilization—possibly the whole of mankind—have become 'neurotic'? An analytic dissection of such neuroses might lead to therapeutic recommendations which could lay claim to great practical interest. I would not say that an attempt of this kind to carry psycho-analysis over to the cultural community was absurd or doomed to be fruitless. But we should have to be very cautious and not forget that, after all, we are only dealing with analogies and that it is dangerous, not only with men but also with concepts, to tear them from the sphere in which they have originated and been evolved. Moreover, the diagnosis of communal neuroses is faced with a special difficulty. In an individual neurosis we take as our starting-point the contrast that distinguishes the patient from his environment, which is assumed to be 'normal.' For a group all of whose members are affected by one and the same disorder no such background could exist; it would have to be found elsewhere. And as regards the therapeutic application of our knowledge, what would be the use of the most correct analysis of social neuroses, since no one possesses authority to impose such a therapy upon the group? But in spite of all these difficulties, we may expect that one day someone will venture to embark upon a pathology of cultural communities.

For a wide variety of reasons, it is very far from my intention to express an opinion upon the value of human civilization. I have endeavoured to guard myself against the enthusiastic prejudice which holds that our civilization is the most precious thing that we possess or could acquire and that its path will necessarily lead to heights of unimagined perfection. I can at least listen without indignation to the critic who is of the opinion that when one surveys the aims of cultural endeavour and the means it employs, one is bound to come to the conclusion that the whole effort is not worth the trouble, and that the outcome of it can only be a state of affairs which the individual will be unable to tolerate. My impartiality is made all the easier to me by my knowing very little about all these things. One thing only do I know for certain and that is that man's judgments of value follow directly his wishes for happiness—that, accordingly, they are an attempt to support his illusions with arguments. I should find it very understandable if someone were to point out the obligatory nature of the course of human civilization and were to say, for instance, that the tendencies to a restriction of sexual life or to the institution of a humanitarian ideal at the expense of natural selection were developmental trends which cannot be averted or turned aside and to which it is best for us to yield as though they were necessities of nature. I know, too, the objection that can be made against this, to the effect that in the history of mankind, trends such as these, which were considered unsurmountable, have often been thrown aside and replaced by other trends. Thus I have not the courage to rise up before my fellow-men as a prophet, and I bow to their reproach that I can offer them no consolation: for at bottom that is what they are all demanding— the wildest revolutionaries no less passionately than the most virtuous believers.

The fateful question for the human species seems to me to be whether and to what extent their cultural development will succeed in mastering the disturbance of their communal life by the human instinct of aggression and self-destruction. It may be that in this respect precisely the present time deserves a special interest. Men have gained control over the forces of nature to such an extent that with their help they would have no difficulty in exterminating one another to the last man. They know this, and hence comes a large part of their current unrest, their unhappiness and their mood of anxiety. And now it is to be expected that the other of the two 'Heavenly Powers,' eternal Eros, will make an effort to assert himself in the struggle with his equally immortal adversary. But who can foresee with what success and with what result?

Bertrand Russell

25

My Philosophical Development

Contemporary Western philosophy has moved largely in the direction of realism and positivism, shunning metaphysical speculation that results in unified philosophical systems; indeed, the twentieth century has been preeminently "The Age of Analysis," the time of "The Decline and Fall of the Absolute." One of the most influential thinkers to advance the cause of analysis and epistemological realism is Bertrand Russell (1872–   ), the English philosopher, logician, and mathematician. A member of one of England's great families, he was awarded the Nobel Prize for literature in 1950 for his brilliant and influential work. Russell has also been a prolific publicist whose libertarian and humanitarian views have made him a kind of moral gadfly of the Western world.

Russell created no new system but worked rather to change the role of philosophy itself. He insisted that its function was critical, that is, to clarify human knowledge of the world, to analyze the certainty, consistency, and precision of scientific postulates. He was primarily interested in the relations between facts rather than in the substance or attributes of reality, and he relied chiefly on logical analysis of scientific statements, the language in which they were couched, and the process of perception. His greatest work, written in collaboration with Alfred North Whitehead, *Principia Mathematica* (1910–1913), was largely responsible for the rejection of Aristotelian logic and the acceptance of mathematical or symbolic logic. Russell never arrived at complete certainty, and his tentative conclusion was that one could accept as true only what could not be disproved, that is, the immediate perceptions of the qualities of matter. For him, there was no central unity in nature but only a collection of short and haphazard events. Over the years, as Russell's thought developed, his theory of knowledge has become increasingly subjective, and his theory of reality increasingly materialistic.

All of Russell's work has been characterized by a passion for clarity and economy. He is always clear but not simple; he is often highly abstract but never loses sight of human experience. He has also been very active in supporting moral and social causes; he has even suffered imprisonment and ridicule for his views, notably for his support of pacifism. He has been animated by a strong, moral individualism in the tradition of John Stuart Mill, but has insisted that his feelings were unrelated to his philosophical views.

In the selection from *My Philosophical Development* (1959), Russell gives a clear, nontechnical statement of his present philosophical position and how he arrived at it.

MY PRESENT VIEW OF THE WORLD

The view to which I have been gradually led is one which has been almost universally misunderstood and which, for this reason, I will try to state as simply and clearly as I possibly can. I am, for the present, only endeavouring to state the view, not to give the reasons which have led me to it. I will, however, say this much by way of preface: it is a view which results from a synthesis of four different sciences—namely, physics, physiology, psychology and mathematical logic. Mathematical logic is used in creating structures having assigned properties out of elements that have much less mathematical smoothness. I reverse the process which has been common in philosophy since Kant. It has been common among philosophers to begin with how we know and proceed afterwards to what we know. I think this a mistake, because knowing how we know is one small department of knowing what we know. I think it a mistake for another reason: it tends to give to knowing a cosmic importance which it by no means deserves, and thus prepares the philosophical student for the belief that mind has some kind of supremacy over the non-mental universe, or even that the non-mental universe is nothing but a nightmare dreamt by mind in its un-philosophical moments. This point of view is completely remote from my imaginative picture of the cosmos. I accept without qualification the view that results from astronomy and geology, from which it would appear that there is no evidence of anything mental except in a tiny fragment of space-time, and that the great processes of nebular and stellar evolution proceed according to laws in which mind plays no part.

If this initial bias is accepted, it is obviously to theoretical physics that we must first look for an understanding of the major processes in the history of the universe. Unfortunately, theoretical physics no longer speaks with that splendid dogmatic clarity that it enjoyed in the seventeenth century. Newton works with four fundamental concepts: space, time, matter and force. All four have been swept into limbo by modern physicists. Space and time, for Newton, were solid, independent things. They have been replaced by space-time, which is not substantial but only a system of relations. Matter has had to be replaced by series of events. Force, which was the first of the Newtonian concepts to be abandoned, has been replaced by energy; and energy turns out to be indistinguishable from the pale ghost which is all that remains of matter. Cause, which was the philosophical form of what physicists called force, has also become decrepit. I will not admit that it is dead, but it has nothing like the vigour of its earlier days.

For all these reasons, what modern physics has to say is somewhat confused. Nevertheless, we are bound to believe it on pain of death. If there were any community which rejected the doctrines of modern physics, physicists employed by a hostile government would have no difficulty in exterminating it. The modern physicist, therefore, enjoys powers far exceeding those of the Inquisition in its palmiest days, and it certainly behooves us to treat his pronouncements with due awe. For my part, I have no doubt that, although progressive changes are to be expected in physics, the present doctrines are likely to be nearer to the truth than any rival doctrines now before the world. Science is at no moment quite right, but it is seldom quite wrong, and has, as a rule, a better chance of being right than the theories of the unscientific. It is, therefore, rational to accept it hypothetically.

It is not always realized how exceedingly abstract is the information that theoretical physics has to give. It lays down certain fundamental equations which enable it to deal with the logical structure of events, while leaving it completely unknown what is the intrinsic character of the events that have the structure. We only know the intrinsic character of events when they happen to us. Nothing whatever in theoretical physics enables us to say anything about the intrinsic character of events elsewhere. They may be just like the events that happen to us, or they may be totally different in strictly unimaginable ways. All that physics gives us is certain equations giving abstract properties of their changes. But as to what it is that changes, and what it changes from and to—as to this, physics is silent.

The next step is an approximation to perception, but without passing beyond the realm of physics. A photographic plate exposed to a portion of the night sky takes photographs of separate stars. Given similar photographic plates and atmospheric conditions, different photographs of the same portion of the sky will be closely similar. There must, therefore, be some influence (I am using the vaguest word that I can think of) proceeding from the various stars to the various photographic plates. Physicists used to think that this influence consisted of waves, but now they think that it consists of little bundles of energy called photons. They know how fast a photon travels and in what manner it will, on occasion, deviate from a rectilinear path. When it hits a photographic plate, it is transformed into energy of a different kind. Since each separate star gets itself photographed, and since it can be photographed anywhere on a clear night where there is an unimpeded view of the sky, there must be something happening, at each place where it can be photographed, that is specially connected with it. It follows that the atmosphere at night contains everywhere as many separable events as there are stars that can be photographed there, and each of these separable events must have some kind of individual history connecting it with the star from which it has come. All this follows from the consideration of different photographic plates exposed to the same night sky.

Or let us take another illustration. Let us imagine a rich cynic, disgusted by the philistinism of theatregoers, deciding to have a play performed, not before live people, but before a collection of cine-cameras. The cine-cameras—supposing them all of equal excellence—will produce closely similar records, differing according to the laws of perspective and according to their distance from the stage. This again shows, like the photographic plate, that at each cine-camera a complex of events is occurring at each moment which is closely related to the complex of events occurring on the stage.

There is here the same need as before of separable influences proceeding from diverse sources. If, at a given moment, one actor shouts, 'Die, Varlet!' while another exclaims, 'Help! Murder!' both will be recorded, and therefore something connected with both must be happening at each cine-camera.

To take yet another illustration: suppose that a speech is recorded simultaneously by a number of gramophones, the gramophone records do not in any obvious way resemble the original speech, and yet, by a suitable mechanism, they can be made to reproduce something exceedingly like it. They must, therefore, have something in common with the speech. But what they have in common can only be expressed in rather abstract language concerning structure. Broadcasting affords an even better illustration of the same process. What intervenes between an orator and a man listening to him on the radio is not, on the face of it, at all similar either to what the orator says or to what the listener hears. Here, again, we have a causal chain in which the beginning resembles the end, but the intermediate terms, so far as intrinsic qualities are concerned, appear to be of quite a different kind. What is preserved throughout the causal chain, in this case as in that of the gramophone record, is a certain constancy of structure.

These various processes all belong purely to physics. We do not suppose that the cine-cameras have minds, and we should not suppose so even if, by a little ingenuity on the part of their maker, those in the stalls were made to sneer at the moments when those in the pit applauded. What these physical analogies to perception show is that in most places at most times, if not in all places at all times, a vast assemblage of overlapping events is taking place, and that many of these events, at a given place and time, are connected by causal chains with an original event which, by a sort of prolific heredity, has produced offspring more or less similar to itself in a vast number of different places.

What sort of picture of the universe do these considerations invite us to construct? I think the answer must proceed by stages differing as to the degree of analysis that has been effected. For present purposes I shall content myself by treating as fundamental the notion of 'event.' I conceive each event as occupying a finite amount of space-time and as overlapping with innumerable other events which occupy partially, but not wholly, the same region of space time. The mathematician who wishes to operate with point-instants can construct them by means of mathematical logic out of assemblages of overlapping events, but that is only for his technical purposes, which, for the moment, we may ignore. The events occurring in any given small region of space-time are not unconnected with events occurring elsewhere. On the contrary, if a photographic plate can photograph a certain star, that is because an event is happening at the photographic plate which is connected by what we may call heredity with the star in question. The photographic plate, in turn, if it is photographed, is the origin of a fresh progeny. In mathematical physics, which is only interested in exceedingly abstract aspects of the matters with which it deals, these various processes appear as paths by which energy travels. It is because mathematical physics is so abstract that its world seems so different from that of our daily life. But the difference is more apparent than real. Suppose you study population statistics, the people who make up the items are deprived of almost all the characteristics of real people before they are recorded in the census. But in this case, because the process of abstraction has not proceeded very far, we do not find it very difficult to undo it in imagination. But in the case of mathematical physics, the journey back from the abstract to the concrete is long and arduous, and, out of sheer weariness, we are tempted to rest by the way and endow some semiabstraction with a concrete reality which it cannot justly claim.

There is a possibility of a further stage of analysis in which events are no longer the ultimate raw material. But I will not consider this in the present discussion.

We have seen that, for purely physical reasons, events in many different places and times can often be collected into families proceeding from an original progenitor as the light from a star proceeds from it in all directions. The successive generations in a single branch of such a family have varying degrees of resemblance to each other according to circumstances. The events which constitute the journey of the light from a star to our atmosphere change slowly and little. That is why it is possible to regard them as the voyage of single entities called photons, which may be thought of as persisting. But when the light reaches our atmosphere, a series of continually odder and odder things begins to happen to it. It may be stopped or transformed by mist or cloud. It may hit a sheet of water and be reflected or refracted. It may hit a photographic plate and become a black dot of interest to an astronomer. Finally, it may happen to hit a human eye. When this occurs, the results are very complicated. There are a set of events between the eye and the brain which are studied by the physiologist and which have as little resemblance to the photons in the outer world as radio waves have to the orator's speech. At last the disturbance in the nerves, which has been traced by the physiologist, reaches the appropriate region in the brain; and then, at last, the man whose brain it is sees the star. People are puzzled because the seeing of the star seems so different from the processes that the physiologist discovered in the optic nerve, and yet it is clear that without these processes the man would not see the star. And so there is supposed to be a gulf between mind and matter, and a mystery which it is held in some degree impious to try to dissipate. I believe, for my part, that there is no greater mystery than there is in the transformation by the radio of electro-magnetic waves into sounds. I think the mystery is produced by a wrong conception of the physical world and by a Manichaean fear of degrading the mental world to the level of the supposedly inferior world of matter.

The world of which we have been speaking hitherto is entirely an inferred world. We do not perceive the sort of entities that physics talks of, and, if it is of such entities that the physical world is composed, then we do not see the eye or the optic nerve, for the eye and the optic nerve, equally, if the physicist is to be believed, consist of the odd hypothetical entities with which the theoretical physicist tries to make us familiar. These entities, however, since they owe their credibility to inference, are only defined to the degree that is necessary to make them fulfil their inferential purpose. It it not necessary to suppose that electrons, protons, neutrons, mesons, photons, and the rest have that sort of simple reality that belongs to immediate objects of experience. They have, at best, the sort of reality that belongs to 'London.' 'London' is a convenient word, but every *fact* which is stated by using this word could be stated, though more cumbrously, without using it. There is, however, a difference, and an important one, between London and the electrons: we can see the various parts of which London is composed, and, indeed, the parts are more immediately known to us than the whole. In the case of the electron, we do not perceive it and we do not perceive anything that we know to be a constituent of it. We know it only as a hypothetical entity fulfilling certain theoretical purposes. So far as theoretical physics is concerned, anything that fulfils these purposes can be taken to *be* the electron. It may be simple or complex; and, if complex, it may be built out of any components that allow the resultant structure to have the requisite properties. All this applies not only to the inanimate world but, equally, to the eyes and other sense organs, the nerves, and the brain.

But our world is not wholly a matter of inference. There are things that we know without asking the opinion of men of science. If you are too hot or too cold, you can be perfectly aware of this fact without asking the physicist what heat and cold consist of. When you see other people's faces, you have an experience which is completely indubitable, but which does not consist of seeing the things which theoretical physicists speak of. You see other people's eyes and you believe that they see yours. Your own eyes as visual objects belong to the inferred part of the world, though the inference is rendered fairly indubitable by mirrors, photographs and the testimony of your friends. The inference to your own eyes as visual objects is essentially of the same sort as the physicist's inference to electrons, etc.; and, if you are going to deny validity to the physicist's inferences, you ought also to deny that you know you have visible eyes—which is absurd, as Euclid would say.

We may give the name 'data' to all the things of which we are aware without inference. They include all our observed sensations—visual, auditory, tactile, etc. Common sense sees reason to attribute many of our sensations to causes outside our own bodies. It does not believe that the room in which it is sitting ceases to exist when it shuts its eyes or goes to sleep. It does not believe that its wife and children are mere figments of its imagination. In all this we may agree with common sense; but where it goes wrong is in supposing that inanimate objects resemble, in their intrinsic qualities, the perceptions which they cause. To believe this is as groundless as it would be to suppose that a gramophone record resembles the music that it causes. It is not, however, the *difference* between the physical world and the world of data that I chiefly wish to emphasize. On the contrary, it is the possibility of much closer resemblances than physics at first sight suggests that I consider it important to bring to light.

I think perhaps I can best make my own views clear by comparing them with those of Leibniz. Leibniz thought that the universe consisted of monads, each of which was a little mind and each of which mirrored the universe. They did this mirroring with varying degrees of inexactness. The best monads had the least confusion in their picture of the universe. Misled by the Aristotelian subject-predicate logic, Leibniz held that monads do not interact, and that the fact of their continuing to mirror the same universe is to be explained by a pre-established harmony. This part of his doctrine is totally unacceptable. It is only through the causal action of the outer world upon us that we reflect the world in so far as we do reflect it. But there are other aspects of his doctrine which are more in agreement with the theory that I wish to advocate. One of the most important of these is as to space. There are for Leibniz (though he was never quite clear on this point) two kinds of space. There is the space in the private world of each monad, which is the space that the monad can come to know by analysing and arranging data without assuming anything beyond data. But there is also another kind of space. The monads, Leibniz tells us, reflect the world each from its own point of view, the differences of points of view being analogous to differences of perspective. The arrangement of the whole assemblage of points of view gives us another kind of space, different from that in the private world of each monad. In this public space, each monad occupies a point or, at any rate, a very small region. Although in its private world there is a private space which from its private point of view is immense, the whole of this immensity shrinks into a tiny pin-point when the monad is placed among other monads. We may call the space in each monad's world of data 'private' space, and the space consisting of the diverse points of view of diverse monads 'physical' space. In so far as monads correctly mirror the world, the geometrical properties of private space will be analogous to those of physical space.

Most of this can be applied with little change to exemplify the theory that I wish to advocate. There is space in the world of my perceptions and there is space in physics. The whole of the space in my perceptions, for me as for Leibniz, occupies only a tiny region in physical space. There is, however, an important difference between my theory and that of Leibniz, which has to do with a different conception of causality and with consequences of the theory of relativity. I think that space-time order in the physical world is bound up with causation, and this, in turn, with the irreversibility of physical processes. In classical physics, everything was reversible. If you were to start every bit of matter moving backwards with the same velocity as before, the whole history of the universe would unroll itself backwards. Modern physics, starting from the Second Law of Thermodynamics, has abandoned this view not only in thermodynamics but also elsewhere. Radioactive atoms disintegrate and do not put themselves together again. Speaking generally, processes in the physical world all have a certain direction which makes a distinction between cause and effect that was absent in classical dynamics. I think that the space-time order of the physical world involves this directed causality. It is on this ground that I maintain an opinion which all other philosophers find shocking: namely, that people's thoughts are in their heads. The light from a star travels over intervening space and causes a disturbance in the optic nerve ending in an occurrence in the brain. What I maintain is that the occurrence in the brain *is* a visual sensation. I maintain, in fact, that the brain consists of thoughts—using 'thought' in its widest sense, as it is used by Descartes. To this people will reply 'Nonsense! I can see a brain through a microscope, and I can see that it does not consist of thoughts but of matter just as tables and chairs do.' This is a sheer mistake. What you see when you look at a brain through a microscope is part of your private world. It is the effect in you of a long causal process starting from the brain that you say you are looking at. The brain that you say you are looking at is, no doubt, part of the physical world; but this is not the brain which is a datum in your experience. *That* brain is a remote effect of the physical brain. And, if the location of events in physical space-time is to be effected, as I maintain, by causal relations, then your percept, which comes after events in the eye and optic nerve leading into the brain, must be located in your brain. I may illustrate how I differ from most philosophers by quoting the title of an article by Mr. H. Hudson in *Mind* of April 1956. His article is entitled, 'Why we cannot witness or observe what goes on "in our heads".' What I maintain is that we *can* witness or observe what goes on in our heads, and that we cannot witness or observe anything else at all.

We can approach the same result by another route. When we were considering the photographic plate which photographs a portion of the starry heavens, we saw that this involves a great multiplicity of occurrences at the photographic plate: namely, at the very least, one for each object that it can photograph. I infer that, in every small region of space-time, there is an immense multiplicity of overlapping events each connected by a causal line to an origin at some earlier time—though, usually, at a very slightly earlier time.

A sensitive instrument, such as a photographic plate, placed any-where, may be said in a sense to 'perceive' the various objects from which these causal lines emanate. We do not use the word 'perceive' unless the instrument in question is a living brain, but that is because those regions which are inhabited by living brains have certain peculiar relations among the events occurring there. The most important of these is memory. Wherever these peculiar rela-tions exist, we say that there is a percipient. We may define a 'mind' as a collection of events connected with each other by memory-chains backwards and forwards. We know about one such collection of events—namely, that constituting ourself—more intimately and di-rectly than we know about anything else in the world. In regard to what happens to ourself, we know not only abstract logical structure, but also qualities—by which I mean what characterizes sounds as opposed to colours, or red as opposed to green. This is the sort of thing that we cannot know where the physical world is concerned.

There are three key points in the above theory. The first is that the entities that occur in mathematical physics are not part of the stuff of the world, but are constructions composed of events and taken as units for the convenience of the mathematician. The second is that the whole of what we perceive without inference belongs to our private world. In this respect, I agree with Berkeley. The starry heaven that we know in visual sensation is inside us. The external starry heaven that we believe in is inferred. The third point is that the causal lines which enable us to be aware of a diversity of ob-jects, though there are some such lines everywhere, are apt to peter out like rivers in the sand. That is why we do not at all times per-ceive everything.

I do not pretend that the above theory can be proved. What I contend is that, like the theories of physics, it cannot be disproved, and gives an answer to many problems which older theorists have found puzzling. I do not think that any prudent person will claim more than this for any theory.

THE RETREAT FROM PYTHAGORAS

My philosophical development, since the early years of the present century, may be broadly described as a gradual retreat from Pythagoras. The Pythagoreans had a peculiar form of mysticism which was bound up with mathematics. This form of mysticism greatly affected Plato and had, I think, more influence upon him than is generally acknowledged. I had, for a time, a very similar outlook and found in the nature of mathematical logic, as I then supposed its nature to be, something profoundly satisfying in some important emotional respects.

· · ·

My interest in the applications of mathematics was gradually replaced by an interest in the principles upon which mathematics is based. This change came about through a wish to refute mathematical scepticism. A great deal of the argumentation that I had been told to accept was obviously fallacious, and I read whatever books I could find that seemed to offer a firmer foundation for mathematical beliefs. This kind of research led me gradually further and further from applied mathematics into more and more abstract regions, and finally into mathematical logic. I came to think of mathematics, not primarily as a tool for understanding and manipulating the sensible world, but as an abstract edifice subsisting in a Platonic heaven and only reaching the world of sense in an impure and degraded form. My general outlook, in the early years of this century, was profoundly ascetic. I disliked the real world and sought refuge in a timeless world, without change or decay or the will-o'-the-wisp of progress.

· · ·

One effect of [the First World] War was to make it impossible for me to go on living in a world of abstraction. I used to watch young men embarking in troop trains to be slaughtered on the Somme because generals were stupid. I felt an aching compassion for these young men, and found myself united to the actual world in a strange marriage of pain. All the high-flown thoughts that I had had about the abstract world of ideas seemed to me thin and rather trivial in view of the vast suffering that surrounded me. The non-human world remained as an occasional refuge, but not as a country in which to build one's permanent habitation.

In this change of mood, something was lost, though something also was gained. What was lost was the hope of finding perfection and finality and certainty. What was gained was a new submission to some truths which were to me repugnant. My abandonment of former beliefs was, however, never complete. Some things remained with me, and still remain: I still think that truth depends upon a relation to fact, and that facts in general are non-human; I still think that man is cosmically unimportant, and that a Being, if there were one, who could view the universe impartially, without the bias of *here* and *now*, would hardly mention man, except perhaps in a footnote near the end of the volume; but I no longer have the wish to thrust out human elements from regions where they belong; I have no longer the feeling that intellect is superior to sense, and that only Plato's world of ideas gives access to the 'real' world. I used to think of sense, and of thought which is built on sense, as a prison from which we can be freed by thought which is emancipated from sense. I now have no such feelings. I think of sense, and of thoughts built on sense, as windows, not as prison bars. I think that we can, however imperfectly, mirror the world, like Leibniz's monads; and I think it is the duty of the philosopher to make himself as undistorting a mirror as he can. But it is also his duty to recognize such distortions as are inevitable from our very nature. Of these, the most fundamental is that we view the world from the point of view of the *here* and *now*, not with that large impartiality which theists attribute to the Deity. To achieve such impartiality is impossible for us, but we can travel a certain distance towards it. To show the road to this end is the supreme duty of the philosopher.

Twentieth-Century Poetry

Twentieth-century literature cannot be understood apart from the intellectual crisis of contemporary culture. Our time has seen the alienation of man from his environment and from himself, as well as the progressive fragmentation of the concepts of man and society, with all the accompanying uncertainty, anxiety, and despair. In this situation, literature has tried to express the intractable material of a hostile civilization in the language of the imagination. While registering the futility and the anarchy of contemporary life, it has endeavored at the same time to transform and triumph over the realities of our age. More than most philosophy, which has tended to become technical and irrelevant, modern literature has sought to frame the fundamental problems and dilemmas of modern man and offer some solutions to them. Writers have sought a meaningful reality on the subjective level, in the depths of consciousness. Here they hoped to recapture the simple but enduring elements of human experience that might give form and direction to the shattered surface of life. To serve these new purposes, they have had to devise new forms of expression and a new vocabulary. The results have been complex, shocking, and often obscure, with a raw or dreamlike quality that has tended to alienate a large part of the audience.

Modern poets, in trying to cope with a hostile world and their own alienation from it, have written about it with relentless, analytic frankness, often tinged with mockery of man's tragic plight. They have discarded the conventional techniques and have experimented freely, while insisting on the need for a rigorous poetic discipline. They have used a new language that aimed at both precision and allusiveness; this quality has made their poems difficult, requiring all the reader's careful and informed attention.

Robert Frost (1874–1963), Thomas Stearns Eliot (1888–   ), and William Butler Yeats (1865–1939) are three of the greatest poets of the twentieth century writing in English. Frost's "After Apple-Picking" (1914) is a realistic account of a rural New England scene written in the ordinary rhythms of speech. The poem's surface simplicity, however, is deceiving. The poet skillfully suggests, through a series of contrasts, man's need to create ideals out of and beyond his ordinary work and experience.

T. S. Eliot, an American who settled in England, is one of the most influential poets and critics of our time. In the dramatic monologue, "The Love Song of J. Alfred Prufrock" (1917), he uses irregular meters, chance rhymes, strange metaphors, and obscure allusions to compel the reader's attention and stimulate his imagination. The poem pictures the frustrations and loneliness of a timid, neurotic, yet intelligent man, who has lost his faith and creative ability, but is still aware of a dignity he himself can never attain. Prufrock is the symbol of this tragedy of twentieth-century man.

"The Second Coming" (1921) by Yeats, the Irish poet and nationalist, expresses a grim view of the future in harsh, broken rhythms and astringent, symbolic language. Turning from the sentimental, Christian hope for a millennium as illusory, Yeats sees the advent of an iron age of harshness and brutality succeeding the chaos of the present.

ROBERT FROST: *After Apple-Picking*

My long two-pointed ladder's sticking through a tree
Toward heaven still,
And there's a barrel that I didn't fill
Beside it, and there may be two or three
Apples I didn't pick upon some bough.
But I am done with apple-picking now.
Essence of winter sleep is on the night,
The scent of apples: I am drowsing off.
I cannot rub the strangeness from my sight
I got from looking through a pane of glass
I skimmed this morning from the drinking trough
And held against the world of hoary grass.
It melted, and I let it fall and break.

But I was well
Upon my way to sleep before it fell,
And I could tell
What form my dreaming was about to take.
Magnified apples appear and disappear,
Stem end and blossom end,
And every fleck of russet showing clear.
My instep arch not only keeps the ache,
It keeps the pressure of a ladder-round.
I feel the ladder sway as the boughs bend.
And I keep hearing from the cellar bin
The rumbling sound
Of load on load of apples coming in.
For I have had too much
Of apple-picking: I am overtired
Of the great harvest I myself desired.
There were ten thousand thousand fruit to touch,
Cherish in hand, lift down, and not let fall.
For all
That struck the earth,
No matter if not bruised or spiked with stubble,
Went surely to the cider-apple heap
As of no worth.
One can see what will trouble
This sleep of mine, whatever sleep it is.
Were he not gone,
The woodchuck could say whether it's like his
Long sleep, as I describe its coming on,
Or just some human sleep.

T. S. ELIOT: *The Love Song of*
J. Alfred Prufrock

S'io credesse che mia risposta fosse
A persona che mai tornasse al mondo,
Questa fiamma staria senza più scosse.

Ma per ciò che giammai di questo fondo
Non tornò viva alcun, s'i'odo il vero,
Senza tema d'infamia ti rispondo.[1]

Let us go then, you and I,
When the evening is spread out against the sky
Like a patient etherised upon a table;
Let us go, through certain half-deserted streets,
The muttering retreats
Of restless nights in one-night cheap hotels
And sawdust restaurants with oyster-shells:
Streets that follow like a tedious argument
Of insidious intent
To lead you to an overwhelming question . . .
Oh, do not ask, 'What is it?'
Let us go and make our visit.

In the room the women come and go
Talking of Michelangelo.

The yellow fog that rubs its back upon the window-panes,
The yellow smoke that rubs its muzzle on the window-panes
Licked its tongue into the corners of the evening,
Lingered upon the pools that stand in drains,
Let fall upon its back the soot that falls from chimneys,
Slipped by the terrace, made a sudden leap,
And seeing that it was a soft October night,
Curled once about the house, and fell asleep.

And indeed there will be time
For the yellow smoke that slides along the street
Rubbing its back upon the window-panes;
There will be time, there will be time
To prepare a face to meet the faces that you meet;
There will be time to murder and create,
And time for all the works and days of hands
That lift and drop a question on your plate;

[1] This epigraph is quoted from Dante's *The Divine Comedy*. One of the damned in *The Inferno* speaks as follows: "If I believed that my answer were to someone who might ever go back to the world, this flame would shake no more. But since, if I hear truth, no one ever returned alive from this pit, I respond to you without fear of infamy."

Time for you and time for me,
And time yet for a hundred indecisions,
And for a hundred visions and revisions,
Before the taking of a toast and tea.

In the room the women come and go
Talking of Michelangelo.

And indeed there will be time
To wonder, 'Do I dare?' and, 'Do I dare?'
Time to turn back and descend the stair,
With a bald spot in the middle of my hair—
[They will say: 'How his hair is growing thin!']
My morning coat, my collar mounting firmly to the chin,
My necktie rich and modest, but asserted by a simple pin—
[They will say: 'But how his arms and legs are thin!']
Do I dare
Disturb the universe?
In a minute there is time
For decisions and revisions which a minute will reverse.

For I have known them all already, known them all—
Have known the evenings, mornings, afternoons,
I have measured out my life with coffee spoons;
I know the voices dying with a dying fall
Beneath the music from a farther room.
    So how should I presume?

And I have known the eyes already, known them all—
The eyes that fix you in a formulated phrase,
And when I am formulated, sprawling on a pin,
When I am pinned and wriggling on the wall,
Then how should I begin
To spit out all the butt-ends of my days and ways?
    And how should I presume?

And I have known the arms already, known them all—
Arms that are braceleted and white and bare
[But in the lamplight, downed with light brown hair!]
Is it perfume from a dress
That makes me so digress?

Arms that lie along a table, or wrap about a shawl.
　And should I then presume?
　And how should I begin?

　　　　　　　·　·　·　·　·

Shall I say, I have gone at dusk through narrow streets
And watched the smoke that rises from the pipes
Of lonely men in shirt-sleeves, leaning out of windows? . . .

　I should have been a pair of ragged claws
Scuttling across the floors of silent seas.

　　　　　　　　　·　·　·　·　·

And the afternoon, the evening, sleeps so peacefully!
Smoothed by long fingers,
Asleep . . . tired . . . or it malingers,
Stretched on the floor, here beside you and me.
Should I, after tea and cakes and ices,
Have the strength to force the moment to its crisis?
But though I have wept and fasted, wept and prayed,
Though I have seen my head [grown slightly bald] brought in upon
　　a platter,
I am no prophet—and here's no great matter;
I have seen the moment of my greatness flicker,
And I have seen the eternal Footman hold my coat, and snicker,
And in short, I was afraid.

　And would it have been worth it, after all,
After the cups, the marmalade, the tea,
Among the porcelain, among some talk of you and me,
Would it have been worth while,
To have bitten off the matter with a smile,
To have squeezed the universe into a ball
To roll it toward some overwhelming question,
To say: 'I am Lazarus, come from the dead,
Come back to tell you all, I shall tell you all'—
If one, settling a pillow by her head,
　　Should say: 'That is not what I meant at all.
　　That is not it, at all.'

And would it have been worth it, after all,
Would it have been worth while,
After the sunsets and the dooryards and the sprinkled streets,
After the novels, after the teacups, after the skirts that trail along
    the floor—
And this, and so much more?—
It is impossible to say just what I mean!
But as if a magic lantern threw the nerves in patterns on a screen:
Would it have been worth while
If one, settling a pillow or throwing off a shawl,
And turning toward the window, should say:
   'That is not it at all,
   That is not what I meant, at all.'

      . . . . .

No! I am not Prince Hamlet, nor was meant to be;
Am an attendant lord, one that will do
To swell a progress, start a scene or two,
Advise the prince; no doubt, an easy tool,
Deferential, glad to be of use,
Politic, cautious, and meticulous;
Full of high sentence, but a bit obtuse;
At times, indeed, almost ridiculous—
Almost, at times, the Fool.

   I grow old . . . I grow old . . .
I shall wear the bottoms of my trousers rolled.

   Shall I part my hair behind? Do I dare to eat a peach?
I shall wear white flannel trousers, and walk upon the beach.
I have heard the mermaids singing, each to each.

I do not think that they will sing to me.

   I have seen them riding seaward on the waves
Combing the white hair of the waves blown back
When the wind blows the water white and black.

   We have lingered in the chambers of the sea
By sea-girls wreathed with seaweed red and brown
Till human voices wake us, and we drown.

WILLIAM BUTLER YEATS: *The Second Coming*

Turning and turning in the widening gyre
The falcon cannot hear the falconer;
Things fall apart; the centre cannot hold;
Mere anarchy is loosed upon the world,
The blood-dimmed tide is loosed, and everywhere
The ceremony of innocence is drowned;
The best lack all conviction, while the worst
Are full of passionate intensity.

Surely some revelation is at hand;
Surely the Second Coming is at hand.
The Second Coming! Hardly are those words out
When a vast image out of Spiritus Mundi
Troubles my sight: somewhere in sands of the desert
A shape with lion body and the head of a man,
A gaze blank and pitiless as the sun,
Is moving its slow thighs, while all about it
Reel shadows of the indignant desert birds.
The darkness drops again; but now I know
That twenty centuries of stony sleep
Were vexed to nightmare by a rocking cradle,
And what rough beast, its hour come round at last,
Slouches towards Bethlehem to be born?